Rediscovering public services manageme

D0240885

Rediscovering public services management

Leslie Willcocks and Jenny Harrow

Editors

McGRAW-HILL BOOK COMPANY

London · New York · St Louis · San Francisco · Auckland
Bogotá · Caracas · Hamburg · Lisbon · Madrid · Mexico
Milan · Montreal · New Delhi · Panama · Paris · San Juan
São Paulo · Singapore · Sydney · Tokyo · Toronto

Published by
McGRAW-HILL Book Company Europe
Shoppenhangers Road, Maidenhead, Berkshire, SL6 2QL, England
Telephone 0628 23432
Fax 0628 770224

British Library Cataloguing in Publication Data
Rediscovering public services management.
 I. Willcocks, Leslie   II. Harrow, Jenny
 361.60941

 ISBN 0-07-707430-0

1234PB9432

Photoset by Rowland Phototypesetting Ltd
Bury St Edmunds, Suffolk
and printed and bound in
Great Britain by Page Bros, Norwich

Contents

Notes on contributors

LESLIE WILLCOCKS is Fellow in Information Management, Templeton College, Oxford. He was formerly Director of CUSIM at City University Business School. He is also Executive Editor of the *Journal of Information Technology*. Co-authored publications include *Computerising Work* (Blackwell Scientific, 1992), two books on *Systems Analysis and Design* and two forthcoming titles: *Of Capital Importance—Evaluation of Information Systems Investment*, and *Evaluation of Information Systems Investments*, both for Chapman and Hall.

DR JENNY HARROW is Principal Lecturer in Management Studies at South Bank Polytechnic's Centre for Management Studies. She is Course Director of the Centre's MSc Public Services Management programme for senior managers in public and voluntary services, and a major contributor to the Centre's MBA and MBA (Education) programmes. Her current research interests include managing risks in public and voluntary service organizations, and a comparative study of management issues in community care delivery in the UK and Sweden.

DR EVERTON DOCKERY is a Research Fellow at the City University Business School. He has researched on technological change and the strategic use of information systems in financial services, and on the implications of computer-based information systems for managerial work. He is currently researching aspects of the competitive use of information systems technology, mergers and managerial performance in the building society industry.

TERENCE GRANGE, MSc Superintendent, Avon and Somerset Constabulary has been a police officer for 20 years, serving in the Metropolitan Police in Wembley, Kilburn, Hampstead and other parts of Northwest London and New Scotland Yard for 16 years prior to leaving London for his present force.

He is presently Superintendent in command of Bristol Central Police Sub Division, having previously been deputy divisional commander to Traffic Division. He recently conducted preliminary research as foundation for Force reorganization. He holds a Masters Degree in Public Service Management.

PROFESSOR CLIVE HOLTHAM is Bull. HN Professor of Information Management, City University Business School. An accountant by background, he was a finance director immediately prior to joining the business school, with extensive experience in managing information technology, and in public services management. Co-authored publications include *Public Sector Accounting and Financial Control* (Van Nostrand Reinhold, 1989) and *Improving Financial Management* (CIPFA, 1988).

ANNABELLE MARK, MSc, FHSM, has ten years' experience as an administrator in the NHS, and, academically, has worked with London University, South Bank Polytechnic and the Open University. She is an educator with the City University Management MBA, and examiner for the Institute of Health Services Management. She is presently a senior lecturer at Middlesex Business School.

DR DAVID McKEVITT lectures in strategic management and public services management at the Open Business School. He has worked in the public services and the private sector and his research interests are in the field of public services control. A recent publication is *Health Care Policy in Ireland* (Hibernian University Press, 1990).

PETER O'HARA has ten years' experience working in local government, six of these as project manager in Camden Borough social services, developing information systems there. Currently he is product development manager for Online Systems. He is a visiting lecturer at Birmingham and City Universities. A forthcoming publication, with Gill Smith and Leslie Willcocks, is *Managing Public Services in an Information Era* (Routledge).

HILARY SCOTT, MSc, AHSM, is general manager at Enfield and Haringey Family Health Services Authority. She has worked in the NHS since 1978, in acute service management posts until her most recent appointment in 1989. She has worked with health service management students in a number of educational institutions.

DR GEORGES SELIM, B.Comm, M.Comm, FIIA, is Deputy Dean of City University Business School, and Director of the Centre for Internal Auditing. He is at present President of the Institute of Internal Auditors—UK, being the only academic to be elected to such a post. His research interests encompass internal auditing, the evaluation of management information and accounting theory.

GILL SMITH is a consultant with Oracle UK. She maintains an interest in the human aspects of computer-based systems and uses both analytical and creative approaches to explore what organizations want to achieve from their use of computers. Assignments have included systems for community care, and information systems requirements for hospitals.

MALINA SHAW runs courses for public services managers. She has extensive experience in higher education and an MSc in public policy from the London School of Economics. Her present research interests include accountability in quasi-governmental agencies, and the effects of decentralization on service delivery in public transport systems.

GERALD VINTEN is Professor of Business Policy at Luton College of Higher Education, visiting professor at the University of Buckingham and editor of the *Managerial Auditing Journal*. Until recently he was Course Director of the MSc in Internal Audit and Management, City University Business School. He has held senior posts in local government and the National Health Service. Publications include *Internal Auditing* (co-author) (Pitman, 1987). He has published widely on public services management.

SALLY WOODWARD, BA, MSc, C.Psych, AFBPsS, is a chartered occupational psychologist and has been a Research Fellow in the Centre for Personnel Research and Development at City University Business School for ten years. Her research interests span various aspects of personnel management, organizational behaviour and occupational psychology as applicable to both private sector and public services organizations. At present she is investigating future role and skill needs of two key groups: IT 'workers' and management consultants.

List of abbreviations

BMA	British Medical Association
C&AG	Comptroller and Auditor General
CBIS	Computer-based Information Systems
CHC	Community Health Council
CIPFA	Chartered Institute of Public Finance and Accountancy
CIS	Client Interface System
CPS	Crown Prosecution Service
CRE	Commission for Racial Equality
CSF	Critical Success Factor
DH	Department of Health
DHA	District Health Authority
DHSS	Department of Health and Social Security
DRG	Diagnostic Related Groupings
DSS	Department of Social Security
ECGD	Export Credit Guarantees Department
FHSA	Family Health Service Authority
FMI	Financial Management Initiative
FPC	Family Practitioner Committee
NHSTA	National Health Service Training Authority
GP	General Practitioner
HSO	Human Service Organization
IHSM	Institute of Health Services Management
IIA	Institute of Internal Auditors
IS	Information System
IT	Information Technology
KPI	Key Performance Indicator
LEA	Local Education Authority
LGTB	Local Government Training Board
LMS	Local Management in Schools
MAS	Management Accounting System
MBO	Management by Objectives
MH	Ministry of Health
MIS	Management Information System
NAHA	National Association of Health Authorities

NHS	National Health Service
OECD	Organization for Economic Cooperation and Development
OHE	Office of Health Economics
PACE Act	Police and Criminal Evidence Act
PBO	Policing by Objectives
PMS	Performance Measurement System
POA	Prison Officers Association
PPBS	Planning, Programming and Budgeting System
PROMIS	Problem-Oriented Medical Information System
RCN	Royal College of Nursing
RHA	Regional Health Authority
RMI	Resource Management Initiative
SBU	Strategic Business Unit
SSU	Strategic Service Unit
SWOT	Strengths, Weaknesses, Opportunities and Threats

Introduction

The book explores how public services have been, are and can be managed in the United Kingdom. The period of study is largely restricted to that of 1979 onwards, not least because it is generally accepted that some sort of distinctive revolution was attempted in public services management from the accession of a Conservative government to office in that year. Hood (1991) is correct in suggesting a longer time scale and an international dimension to the development of what he calls 'the new public management'. It is also clear that explanations for that development are not reducible merely to the characteristics of a political leader or even to the accession to power of a political party. A complex set of short- and long-run historical factors conjoin where explanations are sought (Armstrong *et al.*, 1984; Hood, 1990; Jessop *et al.*, 1988; Perkin, 1989; Pollard, 1982). These are considered at various points in the book, in overview chapters and those on particular service sectors. However, the main focus here is not on such factors and explanations, but rather on rediscovering from 1979 what managing in public services has been and can be about.

'Rediscovery' is a rich theme and the word is used in several senses here. The first sense is the most obvious—that is, looking again at the area and its accumulated overlay of interpretation and analysis. One suggestion here will be that narrow definitions of management have often led to a lot of managing that occurs in public services being discounted as not management at all. A second sense is of a rediscovery, but about future possibilities and alternatives, including guidelines for action deriving from the analysis of the period from 1979. In another sense rediscovery refers to self-reflection. A burgeoning literature is increasingly inclined to assign to the modern manager a 'thinking doer' epithet. In a period of rapid change and large, surprising, often novel challenges, reflection on how management is constituted and can be conducted would seem to be a particularly urgent requirement. In so far as this is carried out by practising managers in the public services, the rediscovery may well become a professional one. A further sense of rediscovery is that of looking in detail at what public services managers have actually been doing and the contexts in which they have been operating through means of their own sectoral and case analyses. Public services managers, as their own researchers, have too often been neglected in public sector studies, and part of the rediscovery in this book involves specific analyses and findings by such managers, particularly in the National Health

Service, police service, local government and social services in the period under review.

There is a further sense in which a rediscovery continually needs to be made. This is in the area of the relationship between government policy-making, whether at central or local levels, and its implementation. The management initiatives pursued by central governments from 1979 were based on at least three major assumptions. These were that public services management was inadequate, needed to be streamlined, and, so far as it continued to exist, could be sharpened into an instrument capable of delivering government policy. The solutions lay in what Pollitt (1991) has called the new managerialism. Hood (1991) has usefully described its main parameters: hands-on professional management; explicit standards and measures of performance; greater emphasis on output controls; shift to disaggregation of units; shift to greater competition; stress on private sector styles of management practice; and a stress on greater discipline and parsimony in resource use. There is little sense in all this of 'management' failure being possibly a policy failure, as perhaps in the most celebrated case of poll tax reform, or being related to inadequate allocation of resources, as often argued in the NHS case; or there being weaknesses in the management prescriptions and models being introduced, or how they were advanced, as will be explored in detail in this book.

Finally rather than a rediscovery, a belated discovery may still be waiting to be made. The metaphor of an athlete reaching peaks of achievement—or in terms of Metcalfe and Richards (1990), the 'health farm' analogy—is commonly deployed by those seeking to convince an audience that public service management structures, and, by implication, the managers in them, improve the quality of their work by cutting away excess fat. In 1980 Sir Ian Bancroft, then Head of the Home Civil Service, foresaw the civil service of the 1980s as 'a smaller, leaner and fitter organisation' (Bancroft, 1981). It is tempting to argue that the continued stress on this aspect of the environment in which public service managers operate—which has continued unabated in the public sector throughout the 1980s and early 1990s—can, at some point, turn from a solution into a sign of disease, in this case fitness addiction of the kind that we now learn afflicts the more purposive and single-minded marathon men and women; it is an addiction that, if taken to extremes, renders the body unfit to cope with unexpected assaults and problems.

The rediscovery theme begins in this introduction. Debate in Britain concerning the performance and effectiveness of public services management—its objectives, quality, quantity and output—has taken place against a background of uncertainty as to the terms employed as well as a now virtually ritualized criticism of that activity, when compared to its supposedly vigorous and delivery-minded private sector equivalent. What, however, are the boundaries of the public sector? Has the term 'service' to be seen in a value-laden context, signifying public servants' choice of their work and personal commitment to those they serve? What are to be understood as the tasks of public services 'management': advising manifesto-minded politicians, neutrally administering, regardless of policy content; acting as convenient buffers between pessimistic publics and optimistic elected members; or perhaps as voices and advocates for the publics they serve? Why do some writers now use the phrase 'public management'? Does the omitted term 'service' sit uncomfortably with the idea that 'managers must manage'? What do public services managers do? Is management work only performed by those called 'managers'? To assist with the answers to such questions, and to provide a context for later chapters, here we provide working definitions and a framework for understanding the complexities of management functions: how and why management work is distributed in the public services and differences between strategic, administrative and operational management across public services organizations.

0.1 Conceptualizing management: a contingency framework

Throughout the book, the public services are taken to be those services provided and managed by the public domain (that is, funded predominantly by government-raised income and subject to direct or indirect control of elected politicians) whose business is in some sense processing people rather than materials. These organizations include: personal and environmental health services; the personal social services; the probation and after-care services; the police services; the prison service; social security; employment and training services; and housing, recreation, transport and education authorities. As a working definition only, their multiple management involves making, implementing and monitoring plans to achieve organizational objectives. The term 'public services management' will be used to refer to those complex tasks which, though differentially distributed and present within such public organizations, have at their base the 'service' rationale, in the sense of conduct tending to the welfare or advantage of another. There are considerable difficulties in being more precise than this, but as we shall argue, and as a number of reviews of research on managerial work, jobs and behaviour show (Hales, 1986; Martinko and Gardner, 1985; Stewart, 1989), this has more to do with the state of management studies than with management in the public services.

The continuing return to the question 'What is management?' in practitioner and academic circles indicates widespread ambivalence and confusion as to the nature of management and managerial work. This has its origins in the relative youth of management as a field of study, characterized by Whitley as a 'fragmented adhocracy' marked by its ability to produce only 'diffuse, discursive knowledge of common-sense objects' (Whitley, 1984a, 1989). However, as Hales (1986) and Whitley (1984b) suggest, these problems also derive from the nature of the objects and activities studied. How this is the case will emerge if the nature of managerial work is considered more closely.

The most generalized and most widely accepted definitions are in functional terms—for example, that management is planning and achieving work through the activities of others (Rees, 1990; Stewart, 1961). At such a general level, it is not difficult to recognize a high degree of commonality between management functions in public services and private sector organizations. While it has become customary to deride 'classical' definitions of management, Hales (1988) and Carroll and Gillen (1987) have argued that Fayol in particular grasped the main parameters of the management function as a whole, as distinct from what individual managers are likely to be actually found doing, in a way that subsequent theorists have rarely surpassed. Thus from Hales' perspective, based on Fayol and Drucker, to manage work in general still means planning, allocating, motivating, coordinating and controlling (Hales, 1988). Interestingly all these writers focused their attention on the management of private sector organizations. So far as public services management is concerned, the tendency has been to extrapolate these schemas across, with little consideration as to their relevance, rather than to research and develop public sector schemas.

This has not been accomplished just at the level of theory. Thus, in the 1980s elements of this 'traditional' management model have been used as a branch with which to beat the public sector, and as an exemplar of what standard public services management practice should be (Metcalfe and Richards, 1987; Tomkins, 1987). However, the appropriateness of the 'traditional' model even to the private sector has been questioned by a range of studies. Thus Kotter (1982), Mintzberg (1973) and Stewart (1976), focusing on behaviour, reveal the manager not as a systematic, reflective planner deciding on the basis of 'hard' information and following through decisions, but as a responsive, intuitive decision maker, with complex tasks, and decisions based on informal contacts and 'soft' information, taken at a hectic pace, constrained rather than innovative. To complicate the picture, Smith (1985) found that managerial jobs change over time, and posited a number of stages or cycles that managerial jobs commonly pass through. As Mumford (1987) suggests, these studies seem to lie much closer to the reality of managerial experience both in the public and private sectors.

However, the lack of congruence between classical management functions and managerial behaviour may be the least of the problems in the management studies field. In a critical review of 29 studies of what managers do, including only two from the public sector (of necessity because of the relative paucity of such studies), Hales (1986) concluded that these revealed an immense diversity of behaviour, practice and job content, thus making for difficulty in identifying commonality. Moreover, such empirical studies rarely commented on whether their findings revealed good or bad managerial practice, and rarely shared a common conceptualization of management, or shared categories for analysis. Crucially they rarely examine the institutional contexts, market situations, internal and external social and political factors which help explain *why* managers do the jobs and behave as they do in the private sector. Nor do they examine the extent to which tasks done by those called 'managers' may not be considered 'managerial' in other organizations, or the degree to which 'managerial' tasks are assigned to and accomplished by non-managers. What emerges as significant here is the degree to which 'management' is a social construction in organizations. This may be particularly important in public services, where the lack of people with the title 'manager' has too often and too easily been taken for a corresponding dearth of relevant management activity. In truth, as Carroll and Gillen (1987), Hales (1986), Stewart (1989) and Willmott (1987) suggest in separate reviews of the evidence, the idea that the studies to date of management theory, models, behaviour, jobs and practices form the basis for erecting a theory of management and standardized prescriptions on managerial competencies and practices across private, let alone public, sector organizations must be countenanced with considerable caution.

One understandable response is to return to classical definitions in order to establish some theoretical consistency and clarity (Carroll and Gillen, 1987; Hales, 1988). The problem here is that such clarity rarely seems to inhabit actual organizational practices. This seems to have become increasingly the case, making organizations more complex places to manage, and causing faster role shifts and internal job change than ever before. Another response has been to reconstitute management. The widely recognized need to do so may help to explain the enormous popularity of books like that of Peters and Waterman (1982). Here 'classical' principles are explicitly denied in favour of a 'humanistic' management achieving productivity through people, decentralization, the ability to live with and manage change, innovate, be externally oriented, provide leadership and manage organizational meaning and culture. In the search for improved quality and speed of service to customers, a related approach has been to recast management as a service to front-line staff (Carlzon, 1989).

A further response, building on the work of Child (1974), Harrison (1979), Hales (1988) and Luthans and Stewart (1977) is to recognize that what constitutes appropriate management functions in a specific organization is dependent on a range of influences. As a result, these functions may approximate to the 'classical,' 'humanistic' or other definition of management. What then becomes important is how these management functions are translated into 'managerial' and 'non-managerial' jobs, activities and behaviours to produce an emergent organization-specific model of management more or less related to the achievement of organizational effectiveness. Such a model helps to explain why studies of general managers, like Kotter's work of (1982), find them not just specialized but sometimes narrowly so; permits the impacts of delegation, and the role of managerial discretion and choice, as researched by Stewart (1982); and builds on the empirical findings of Hirsh and Bevan (1988) and Barham *et al.* (1988) that register considerable doubt in the private sector about what core managerial activities and competencies are and provide evidence supporting the variety of managerial practice and the organizational specificity of relevant skills.

It is worth considering the issue of generalizable competencies and skills in a little more detail in a UK context. From the mid-1980s at least three influential reports pointed to the inadequacies of British private sector managerial practice. Interestingly, however, Constable and McCormick (1987), Handy (1987) and Mangham and Silver (1986) remained largely silent on the theme of what competencies British managers need to develop in order to match their international competitors. Can there be such core competencies? By 1988 a series of research projects had been launched to identify what these might be. The fact that satisfactory core managerial competencies had not been identified before such endeavours, despite the fact that management has been studied for over 80 years, would suggest the need for some scepticism on that score. Notwithstanding this, by 1988 a Chartered Management Initiative had been launched under the aegis of the British Institute of Management, The Confederation of British Industry and the Foundation for Management Education to devise a professional structure for managerial work in Britain, based on the gradual attainment of competence in core managerial skills. Dixon convincingly questions this approach. He posits a theatre where the curtain falls unexpectedly and someone comes to the front to ask 'Is there a doctor in the house?' He asks if the professional services of managers could be requested in the same way: 'If someone asked "Is there a manager in the house?", there would be only one sensible reply, to wit: "What *sort* of manager?"' (Dixon, 1988).

Management itself would seem to embrace a great variety of activities, and the skills and competencies necessary would seem to depend on the circumstances prevailing. Thus Hirsh and Bevan found that even where large companies used the same terms, such as leadership or communication, each assigned a different meaning to them: 'If we ask "Is there a shared language for management skills?" the answer seems to be yes at the level of expression, but no at the level of meaning' (Hirsh and Bevan, 1988).

A European-wide survey by the Ashridge Management Reseach Group attempts to identify management skills for the future. Many differ from the 'classical' management skills, and many of the skills identified would appear to be organization specific, or true mainly, even only, for the large companies surveyed (Barham *et al.*, 1988).

The argument so far points to the need for a contingency framework when studying management. One such framework, underpinning the book, is shown in Fig. 0.1. This has been developed from Harrison (1979). Environment refers to external political social, economic and technological factors, and 'task' environment factors such as suppliers, customers, labour market, competition. These, together with the dominant coalition, will have an influence upon what the necessary management functions will be (for Harrison they are, necessarily, setting objectives, formulating plans, organizing, staffing, directing and control-

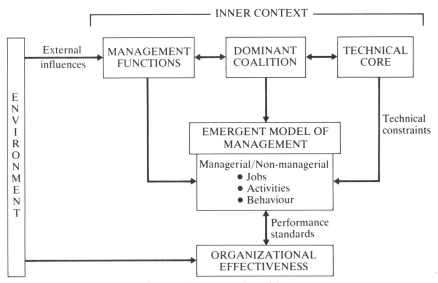

Figure 0.1   Management and managing a general model

ling). These generate constraints on the technical core—where the prevailing technology is applied to raw inputs in the process of transforming them into finished outputs. The technical core thus consists of equipment, techniques (methods, procedures, skills and routines) and people. In turn, technical factors, the dominant coalition, management functions and performance standards (largely set by managers) operate as constraints to produce an emergent model of management. The figure is necessarily simplified—many contextual factors are not shown in detail and the analytical constructs must be understood as dynamic and interactive—but highlights how differences in environmental influences, objectives, dominant coalition, technical core and performance standards can influence the management functions that will be appropriate and how these will be distributed throughout the organization. This becomes particularly important when considering differences in managing not only between private sector organizations but also, and more crucially for present purposes, contrasts between private sector and public services organizations.

In summary, there emerges no coherent, systematic, agreed view of management or what managers do, or what they should be doing in private sector organizations. There is some irony, then, that in a period when the nature of management has been questioned as never before, the UK public services have found themselves judged against 'traditional' management criteria, which are themselves suspect, and been found wanting. With this background of uncertainty, efforts to establish distinctions between the organizational settings in which public and private sector managers manage become the more critical, and are now considered.

0.2   Public services: distinctive contexts, pressures and managerial behaviour

It is neither necessary nor reasonable to argue that public services management possesses fully unique characteristics and contexts that require its managers to be shielded from private sector developments and modes of operation. This is particularly pertinent in a period when public services are experiencing changing contexts and pressures, which in turn, following the argument implicit in Fig. 0.1, may require a reassessment of how management is best accomplished. Furthermore, following Tomkins (1987), not all organizational forms fall easily into a two-fold classification of 'fully private' or 'public: without competition'. Rather a continuum between these extremes can be posited; for example, private with part state ownership, joint private/public ventures, private regulated, public infrastructure/private operating, contracted out, public with 'managed competition', with considerable implications for how they may need to be differently managed (Tomkins, 1987, p. 21). Furthermore, it is possible that case study-based research would demonstrate some close parallels in at least operational management functions and behaviour between, for example, some public services bodies and the community affairs departments of large firms, and between some private firms and the management services departments of large public organizations. Nevertheless, it is important to establish that, especially for public services (the vast majority being still located at the far 'public' end of Tomkin's continuum), there are important dissimilarities between the contexts, both inner and outer, and the pressures bearing upon public and private management. Thus, essentially different managerial divisions of labour and behaviours may be required for 'management' to take place, so limiting the value of the importation of private sector management approaches in a wholesale fashion.

Allison's question, 'Public and private management—are they fundamentally alike in all unimportant respects?', provides a familiar starting point for reviewing differences and similarities between public and private management activities (Allison, 1979). For analytical purposes the differences in contexts and pressures may be considered in terms of environment, dominant coalition and technical core (Fig. 0.1). Allison, in fact, finds essential dissimilarities emerging in three major areas: in environmental factors, in organizational and environmental transactions and in internal structures and procedures. In their work, public sector managers face less market exposure and more formal constraints than their private counterparts. They are subject to a greater diversity and intensity of external informal influences; greater public expectations of probity of actions and scrutiny of those actions; and greater vagueness and intangibility of objectives. Their behaviour tends to show greater cautiousness and rigidity, their workforce showing lower organizational commitment than their private sector counterparts. Smith Ring and Perry (1985), reviewing strategic management in United States' public and private organizations, go further.

The difficulty of public sector strategic management is such that, while likely to be found inadequate in private sector terms, when judged against standards grounded within the public sector, different conclusions may be drawn. For them, public services managers experience more ill-defined policy directions than their private sector equivalents; greater constraints on their action caused by greater openness in decision-making; more direct and sustained contact from interest groups seeking to influence them; and more artificial time constraints on their actions. These and other major differences in environmental and dominant coalition factors are summarized in Table 0.1.

Table 0.1 Major differences between management of public services and the private sector

Public services	*Private sector*
1 Statutory and parliamentary regulation; codes of conduct	Board of directors; company planning frameworks
2 Needs of national economic management	Marketplace signals, e.g. business lending rate
3 Relative openness of government and decision-making; stress on representatives	Relative secrecy; stress on business confidentiality
4 Attentive publics; wide stakeholder base; impact of subsidiary regulatory bodies	Primary focus on shareholders and management
5 Multiple values and goals: • Service • Public interest • Equity • Professionalism • Consumer participation • Complex trade-offs	Relatively restricted
6 Primary resource base from public taxes	Primary resource base from operational returns and borrowing
7 Extensive accountability	Accountability restricted
8 Responsiveness to political masters and short political time-horizons	No real national/local politician overlay; less artificial time constraints
9 Primary social goals, e.g. safe streets, health, no user charge	Primary profit goals
10 Complex and debated performance indicators	Mainly quantitative financial measures
11 More ill-defined policy directives; complexity of policy implementation	Relatively less ambiguous policy

The 'technical core' also needs consideration. Public services tend to be distinguished by both high labour intensity and high professionalization—with specific implications for what management is and how it is to be accomplished. Furthermore, the core 'service' output renders management models and prescriptions applied in 'product' organizations—for example, vehicle and chemical manufacturers—less apposite. Indeed, one might argue that, in order to compete and differentiate their market offerings, such firms have much to learn from 'service' organizations. It may well be that public services have more to learn from private 'service' organizations, for example, on establishing service quality, market research and marketing, but the learning might not be all one way. For example, labour and skills shortages have increasingly pushed private sector firms into equal opportunities programmes, the management of which has a respectable history in the public sector.

The application of Information Technology (IT) has considerable implications for both private sector and public services organizations and their emergent models of management. As Willcocks (1991) argues, 'managing in' IT, and indeed its subsequent management may throw up common problems for public and private sector organizations. IT systems have the potential to alter relationships between managers—for example, in the civil service, making middle managers more autonomous and important by increasing local control over resources (Hyde, 1988), or, in other instances, reducing the role of middle managers and supervisors, and even giving employees skills and tasks formerly seen as the preserve of management (Zuboff, 1988). However, distinctive contexts and pressures raise specific issues in the design and application of IT systems for public services. In particular, information systems in areas like social, health and police services straddle the need for data protection, client confidentiality, public access/openness, government and management information in ways rarely required in the private sector. A further point is that the determining nature of technology can often be overstressed, especially with a technology as flexible as IT. More frequently the dominant coalition is the major influence upon the uses to which IT is put and whose interests it serves, and thus the factors that distinguish dominant coalitions (Table 0.1) will help to explain the differing impacts of IT in the public services and the private sector, what management is and how it is accomplished (Willcocks and Mark, 1988; Willcocks and Mason, 1992).

So far this section has argued for distinguishing public services from private sector management through their differing contexts and pressures. However, this distinctiveness needs to be demonstrated further in terms of the consequences for management function and managerial behaviour. One case for illustrative examination using specific examples and for testing through research is provided by Ranson and Stewart (1989). They argue for distinguishing the private services management function as 'uniquely' complex by virtue of its 'duality of publicness', suggesting that managers need to enable both citizens' involvement *and* government's collective action (Ranson and Stewart, 1989, p. 19). They thus focus on a critical aspect: in public services settings, far from the manager managing, the manager may never be the principal actor. Task distinctiveness lies in supporting the many (citizens) and the few (elected representatives), with the role of such managers being the role of counterpoise. While it is not necessary to accept their accompanying view—that private sector management tasks are unilinear—two illustrative cases support a distinctiveness that is predicated on seeking a balance between a variety of competing and legitimate public needs and demands, and on the need to respond to types of policy inexplicitness inherent in the public services.

Managerial responses to violence faced by staff provides a critical illustration of an area where no real private sector practice model exists for public services managers to follow. For example, there are few 'good practice' prescriptions available for deciding where to locate panic buttons for decentralized social services or library staff. Furthermore, some public services staff may represent physical targets when their service is of a different kind from that which the potential recipient desires, or when their regulatory work intervenes in people's lives to an extent that is not found in much private sector employment. Many inner city commercial establishments have responded to violence towards staff and property, but usually in the form of managerial decisions to increase spending on security. Costs may be passed on to customers, an option not fully available to public services managers. More importantly, in some public services, their objectives and rationale are such that 'preparing for violence' could be seen to represent a denial of their very purpose. Thus, the type of private sector response of full behind-screens security may not be feasible, when the service in question exists to work towards improvement of an already disadvantaged clientele.

The area of managerial response towards violence to staff also illustrates the likelihood of the lack of explicit policy directives often faced by public services managers. Studies of the impact of violence on public services staffs have tended to emphasize the ensuing interpersonal aspects, to the detriment of identifying appropriate and specific managerial responses relating to staff insurance cover, the organization's policy on prosecutions, its relationship with the police, and whether and, if so, how to train staff for 'violence awareness'. Moreover, no private sector prescriptions are available; for example in a Health and Safety Executive report only one of ten case studies on preventing violence to staff was located in the private sector (Poyner and Warne, 1988). As a result in public services *ad hoc* policy development occurs, with internal management practice varying from organization to organization, and to an extent from job to job.

A second illustration concerns decisions within police services to charge bodies organizing major sports events for police attendance. Legislation empowers such charges for special police services to be made, but seems to provide no precise guide as to the circumstances. Thus Weatherill notes that charging decisions are based on *ad hoc* arrangements and informal compromises (Weatherill, 1989, p. 127). Some police authorities, for example, decline to charge for all police officers attending inside sports grounds, and thus far have generally 'refrained from charging for services outside the grounds' (Weatherill, 1989, p. 125). While some private firms may operate 'no charge' policies in certain circumstances—for example, as a 'loss leader'—these are unlikely to carry the major cost implications of, for example, the external policing of football grounds.

The important point is that the managerial behaviour here relates to context —such decisions being based on senior police officer perceptions of public as well as private benefits accruing from their presence. These private events had implications for a wider public that needs policing, thus justifying a less than complete approach to charging.

Weatherill's concern is to argue the case for legislative clarity in identifying appropriate charging situations and to enable parliamentary debate upon the issue. He emphasizes how such public services managers are required to 'know the politicians' minds' until such time as the latter spell out their policies. It is also possible, given the loss of life during a major football match in Sheffield in April 1989, that this example will yield an illustration that much policy is only made explicit after public scandal or tragedy, in atmospheres not necessarily conducive to quality policy-making. This again would support Ranson and Stewart's view of the public services manager as facing inherent tensions as they seek to achieve a balance in their managerial tasks which reflects the current values of both the many and the few. In terms of Fig. 0.1, the external influences for the public services manager are such that managing the degree of impact of those influences is itself a managerial task with the resulting emergent model of management one in which involvement in the political process is central, not marginal, to the manager's role.

This section has sought to establish that the differing organizational contexts in which managers manage have such a central bearing on management functions and the emergent models of management that efforts to bring public and private sector managements closer in line can be misplaced. A critical example emerges from the apparent extent of intra-organizational friction and disagreement in public services, promoting uncertainty, alternative agendas, and preventing managers from managing. One private sector prescription has been to truncate such discord by subordinating some groups, allegedly not managers, to those so described—as evidenced by the introduction of general management into the NHS. That public services managers' roles *include* those of engaging in, even encouraging, debate as to organizational goals and purposes, has not often been acknowledged. Taking the health service example, Klein argues forcibly that 'management everywhere in health care is political, in the fundamental sense of involving decisions about who gets what, and a continuing debate about the values that ought to shape its activities' (Klein, 1985, p. 587), but ensuring that managers manage, as seen from a private sector viewpoint, appears to be regarded as requiring at least a limitation of such debate. This prescription fails to take into account not only the extent but the value of intra-organizational groupings in the public services. A useful way of modelling these in order to consider the implications for managerial jobs and behaviour is to be found in the influential work on domain theory by Kouzes and Mico (1979). Several chapters of the book apply this work to specific service organizations and all are sympathetic to its main parameters, therefore the opportunity is taken here for providing a detailed consideration of the general theory.

0.3   Applying domain theory in public services organizations

Kouzes and Mico emphasize the importance of familiarization with the internal characteristics of public sector organizations and the 'worlds' they constitute. Their work helps to explain the internal conflicts that may occur in such organizations between managers and others working in service or policy-making capacities, and may mistakenly be perceived as mismanagement, needing to be unlearned. Their theoretical framework is applied to Human Service Organizations (HSOs), whose primary function is to define or alter the person's behaviour, attributes or social status, and to maintain or enhance her or his well-being. For Kouzes and Mico each HSO tends to comprise multiple systems, divisible into three domains, each with its own set of governing principles, success measures, structural arrangements and work modes that are incongruent with the others. Briefly, these are the policy domain, where governing policies for action are formulated by appointed or elected members; the management domain, where cost-effectiveness and efficiency issues dominate and attempts are made to mirror industrial management approaches; and the service domain, comprising professionals seeing themselves as self-governing, with the necessary expertise.

Domain theory can be operationalized fairly comfortably within British public services organizations. As one example, Kakabadse (1982) studied twelve social services departments and produced a three-fold classification of power, role and task 'cultures' operating largely as delineated by Kouzes and Mico. Again, Brazell (1987), in research on doctors as managers, found similar patterns in public health service organizations, as did Willcocks and Mark (1989) researching the difficulties of introducing IT for managerial purposes into the National Health Service. Accepting domain theory as a powerful explanatory schema, there are a number of outcomes that further our understanding of public services management.

Firstly, the presence of at least three domains in the same public service organization will create discordance, disjunction and conflicts as perennial features at their boundaries. This engenders struggles for power, control and internal stability that in themselves have to be managed. Thus, additional managerial tasks result from the conditions of uncertainty that multiple domains promote. However, these tasks are compounded by the fact that managers in HSOs will lack, by definition, the degree of control enjoyed by their business counterparts, with such tools to hand as the discretionary use of authority, rewards systems, or structural arrangements designed to integrate their systems. If such a framework is applied to other HSOs—education, policing, etc.—then internal organizational inter-domain discord is an expected phenomenon in the public services, and public services managers' tasks involve a working through of these tensions, not, as in the private sector, making efforts to eliminate them.

Secondly, domain theory assists in explaining the difficulties encountered in implementing management initiatives into public services—for example, the introduction of management budgeting into the NHS from 1983. Thus Rippington (1988) describes how pilot schemes were unable to take the medical profession along with them; how agreement was reached in 1986 between the NHS management board and the joint consultative committee of the medical profession jointly to sponsor new schemes in which medical staff could be fully involved; but how 'some disappointment has been registered at the limited progress made' (Rippington, 1988, p. 64). Management learning has been taking place; but it seems to have been of the internal variety, which has been forced to recognize the practical effects of inter-domain disagreement.

Thirdly, domain theory underpins the model delineated in Fig. 0.1 in a number of ways. Thus it becomes clear that in public services different parts of the management functions (defined, albeit loosely, as making, implementing and monitoring plans) are carried out in different domains within the same public service body. Furthermore, given the legitimacy and appropriateness of these different domains in public services, one would expect differences in the way that the work of management in each is organized, assigned and accomplished. Following Hales (1986), management functions can be, and indeed in the public services have been, fractionalized in an immense variety of ways, and responsibilities allocated to a wide range of organizational members. There thus emerges the need to take a task perspective of managerial activity—emphasizing what those who manage in the public services do as opposed to searching for core public services managerial skills, attributes and knowledge, finding them wanting and substituting private sector prescriptions. Underpinning this approach is Hales' argument that 'managers are rarely, if ever, merely managers, but are defined by what they manage' (Hales, 1986, p. 110).

In bringing together the theoretical work of Kouzes and Mico and Hales there further emerges the likelihood that 'management' occurs in all domains, whether or not it is recognized as such. 'To varying degrees, non-managers have been and remain part of the management function' (Hales, 1988, p. 6). Thus doctors, even while rejecting the label, have always been managers (Brazell, 1987). Social service department receptionists, junior adjuncts to the service domain, are invariably, perforce, the most important managers of violent clients. Home help organizers have not been defined as managers, but as part of the service domain, although their activities are managerial. The retitling of their qualification, in the late 1980s, as the Diploma of Domiciliary Care Management may have helped to redress this situation; although its very speciality might serve still to confine them to the service domain.

Domain theory provides a major basis for assessing the degree and importance of the plurality of managerial activity within and between public services, so diminishing the appropriateness of reference to a unified public sector. One inherent danger with utilizing domain theory is that it can become a managerial alibi for things never going right, for accepting domain walls and the presence of conflict as reasons for non-achievement, and for refusing to learn from possibly applicable management practices originating outside a specific domain. This type of parochial defensiveness would not be supported by the contributors to this book. However, even within public services fields with apparent clear unity —for example, health—internal domains may act to separate off management styles. This would bear examination in relation, for example, to Klein's distinction between managers of health care systems and managers of health care institutions, where differing criteria for judging good management practice may be required (Klein, 1985 p. 58). It also enables inter- and intra-organizational conflict to be seen as an inherent element of the environment in which management takes place rather than aberrant behaviour which detracts from managing. This assists in identifying the dominant coalitions in Fig. 0.1 which lead to the development of a particular model of management.

0.4   This book

These considerations underpin and inform the contributions that follow. The book is organized into two main parts. The first four chapters form a general overview of management initiatives in public services from 1979. They suggest that these have represented a partial revolution in two senses, namely (1) the revolution was incomplete, and (2) was driven from a specific set of assumptions that shaped a certain view on both the content of the management initiatives set in train, and how they were to be managed in. Part 1 also seeks to suggest ways forward for public services management, and these are derived from analyses of the learning experience for public services that the period from 1979 represents.

The main overview chapter (Chapter 1) is provided by Gerald Vinten who gives a historical perspective to management in central and local government and the National Health Service, before reviewing critically the events and possibilities since 1979. David McKevitt (Chapter 2) then seeks to provide a framework for understanding and reviewing strategic management in public services. He evaluates the usefulness in the public services environment of a range of strategic models, thus building on the framework put forward earlier in this Introduction. He then reports on recent comparative research in a number of European countries where a general strategy model assisted in appraising health care policy. This is then used to assess the relevance of private sector models in the public services environment of the 1990s. In Chapter 3, Jenny Harrow and Leslie Willcocks then consider in detail the main dimensions and limitations of the major UK management initiatives from 1979. They use innovation theory to evaluate the feasibility of these initiatives and discover a range of problems in attempting to introduce into public services environments notions of risk, consumerism, entrepreneurialism, and managerial and organizational learning derived from assumed 'best' private sector practice. They then suggest ways forward on how public services and their managers may accomplish useful learning into the mid-1990s. In Chapter 4, Clive Holtham complements these approaches and concludes the first part of the book by addressing, from a practitioner viewpoint, the major challenges facing public services in the 1990s and advancing an analysis of how these can be managed.

The second part of the book deals, firstly, with three major issues informing the post-1979 management initiatives: improved service to the public as customers; performance measurement; and the utilization and management of Information Technology in public services settings. Such concerns would seem to be at the heart of management in the 1990s, not least as an inheritance from the initiatives of the 1980s. In all three cases Jenny Harrow and Malina Shaw (Chapter 5), Georges Selim and Sally Woodward (Chapter 6) and Leslie Willcocks (Chapter 7) examine in detail the proposals, how they have impacted on public services, the difficulties experienced, how far they have been managed and with what degree of success. In all three chapters the authors make detailed suggestions for future action on these areas. The book then has four final chapters which represent detailed case studies prepared by practising managers in public services to illustrate from their experience, and from analyses of specific services, the complexities, difficulties and challenges faced in the period under review. Annabelle Mark and Hilary Scott (Chapter 8) utilize domain theory in detail in their analysis of past and future initiatives and their impacts in the NHS. In discussing their work in social services, Gill Smith and Peter O'Hara (Chapter 9) link up with the earlier chapters by Davis McKevitt and Leslie Willcocks. They point out the need to develop strategic approaches to large-scale policy initiatives and unpredictable environments for public services. They also discuss how public services organizations can be developed through the way in which information systems are designed and implemented. In Chapter 10, Everton Dockery focuses less on technology and more on the information needs of managers, in this case in local government, during periods of considerable change in public services environments and management structures. He compares and contrasts these needs with his research findings on information needs of private sector managers, thus continuing the analysis of private/public services managerial work threading through earlier chapters. The final chapter, by Terence Grange, provides a detailed description and assessment of the major management initiatives in the police service since 1979. He also demonstrates the applicability of domain theory to this service, considers the impacts of decentralization and flexible rostering, and how the police service may continue to develop a more responsive relationship with a demanding and often critical consumer. It is a fitting chapter with which to conclude a book about rediscovering much of the distinctiveness of public services work and its management.

LESLIE WILLCOCKS
JENNY HARROW

References

Allison, G. T. Jr (1979) 'Public and private management: are they fundamentally alike in all unimportant respects?', Public Management Research Conference Paper, Brookings Institution, Washington, DC. (Reprinted in Perry, J. L. and Kraemer, K. L. (eds) (1983) *Public Management: Private and Public Perspectives*. Mayfield Press, California.)

Armstrong, P., Glyn, A. and Harrison, J. (1984) *Capitalism Since World War 2*. Fontana, London.

Bancroft, I. (1981) Address to RIPA annual meeting, 9 December 1980, in *Public Administration*, **59**, Summer.

Barham, K., Frazer, J. and Heath, L. (1988) *Management for the Future*. Ashridge Management College and Foundation for Management Education.

Brazell, H. (1987) 'Doctors as managers', *Management Education and Development*, **18** (2), 95–102.

Carlzon, J. (1989) *Moments of Truth*. Harper & Row, New York.

Carroll, S. and Gillen, D. (1987) 'Are the classical management functions useful in describing managerial work?', *Academy of Management Review*, **12** (1), 38–51.

Child, J. (1974) 'What determines organization performance? The universals v. the it-all-depends', *Organizational Dynamics*, Summer, 2–18.

Constable, J. and McCormick, R. (1987) *The Making of British Managers*. A report for the British Institute of Management and the Confederation of British Industries into Management Training, Education and Development, BIM/CBI, London.

Dixon, M. (1988) 'How best to find out what managers need', *Financial Times*, 6 April.

Hales, C. (1986) 'What do managers do? A critical review of the evidence', *Journal of Management Studies*, **23** (1), 88–113.

Hales, C. (1988) 'Management processes, management divisions of labour and managerial work: towards a synthesis', Paper presented at the Labour Process Conference, University of Aston, Birmingham.

Handy, C. (1987) *The Making of Managers*. MSC/NEDO/BIM, London.

Harrison, F. (1979) 'Towards a general model of management', *Journal of General Management*, **5** (2), 33–41.

Hirsh, W. and Bevan, S. (1988) *What Makes a Manager?* Institute of Manpower Studies Report No. 144, Institute of Manpower Studies, Brighton.

Hood, C. (1990) 'Beyond the public bureaucracy state? Public administration in the 1990s', Inaugural lecture, London School of Economics, 16 January.

Hood, C. (1991) 'A public management for all seasons?', *Public Administration*, **69** (Spring), 3–19.

Hyde, P. (1988) 'The consequences of IT in the UK civil service', *International Journal of Public Sector Management*, 1 (2), 21–30.

Jessop, B., Bonnett, K., Bromley, S. and Ling, T. (1988) *Thatcherism*. Polity Press, Cambridge.

Kakabadse, A. (1982) *Culture of the Social Services*. Gower, London.

Klein, R. (1985) 'Management in health care: the politics of innovation', *International Journal of Health Planning and Management*, 1, 57–63.

Kotter, J. (1982) *The General Managers*. Free Press, New York.

Kouzes, J. M. and Mico, P. R. (1979) 'Domain theory—an introduction to organisational behaviour in human service organisations', *Journal of Applied Behavioural Science*, 15 (4), 449–69.

Luthans, F. and Stewart, T. (1977) 'A general contingency theory of management', *Academy of Management Review*, 2 (2), 181–95.

Mangham, I. and Silver, M. (1986) *Management Training—Context and Practice*. School of Management, University of Bath.

Martinko, M. and Gardner, W. (1985) 'Beyond structured observation: methodological issues and new directions', *Academy of Management Review*, 10 (4), 676–95.

Metcalfe, L. and Richards, S. (1987) 'The efficiency strategy in government: an impoverished concept of management', *Public Money*, 7 (1), 29–35.

Metcalfe, L. and Richards, S. (1990) *Improving Public Management*. Sage, London.

Mintzberg, H. (1973) *The Nature of Managerial Work*. Harper & Row, New York.

Mumford, A. (1987) 'Using reality in management development', *Management Education and Development*, 18, (3), 223–43.

Perkin, H. (1989) *The Rise of Professional Society*. Routledge, London.

Peters, T. and Waterman, R. (1982) *In Search of Excellence: Lessons from America's Best-Run Companies*. Harper & Row, New York.

Pollard, S. (1982) *The Wasting of the British Economy*. Croom Helm, London.

Pollitt, C. (1991) *Managerialism and the Public Services: the Anglo-American Experience*. Blackwell, Oxford.

Poyner, B. and Warne, C. (1988) *Preventing Violence to Staff*. Tavistock Institute of Human Relations and the Health and Safety Executive, HMSO, London.

Ranson, S. and Stewart, J. (1989) 'Citizenship and government: the challenge for management in the public domain', *Political Studies*, 37 (1), 5–24.

Rees, W. (1990) *The Skills of Management*. Croom Helm, London.

Rippington, T. (1988) 'The National Health Service: an annual report', in Jackson, P. and Terry, F. (eds), *Public Domain, a yearbook for the public services*. Public Finance Foundation/Peat, Marwick, McLintock, London, pp. 55–76.

Smith, P. (1985) 'The stages in a manager's job', in Hammond, V. (ed.), *Current Research in Management*. Pinter, London.

Smith Ring, P. and Perry, J. L. (1985) 'Strategic management in public and private organisations: implications of distinctive contexts and constraints', *Academy of Management Review*, 10 (2), 276–86.

Stewart, J. and Ranson, S. (1988) 'Management in the public domain', *Public Money and Management*, 8 (1/2), 13–19.

Stewart, R. (1961) *The Reality of Management*. Pan Management, London.

Stewart, R. (1976) *Contrasts in Management: a study of different types of managers' jobs, their demands and choices*. McGraw-Hill, Maidenhead.

Stewart, R. (1982) *Choices for the Manager*. Prentice Hall, Englewood Cliffs, New Jersey.

Stewart, R. (1989) 'Studies of managerial jobs and behaviour: the ways forward', *Journal of Management Studies*, 26 (1), 1–10.

Tomkins, C. R. (1987) *Achieving Economy, Efficiency and Effectiveness in the Public*

Sector. Kogan Page and Institute of Chartered Accountants of Scotland, London.

Weatherill, S. (1989) 'Buying special police services', *Public Law*, Spring, 106–27.

Whitley, R. (1984a) *The Intellectual and Social Organisation of the Sciences*. Clarendon Press, Oxford.

Whitley, R. (1984b) 'The development of management studies as a fragmented adhocracy', *Social Science Information*, **23** (4/5), 775–818.

Whitley, R. (1989) 'On the nature of managerial tasks: their distinguishing characteristics and organisation', *Journal of Management Studies*, **26** (3), 209–24.

Willcocks, L. (1991) 'Information systems and human resources in the 1990s—integration through culture', Paper at the Fifth Annual British Academy of Management Conference, Bath University, 22–24 September.

Willcocks, L. and Mark, A. (1988) 'Information technology in the NHS: from strategy to implementation', *Public Money and Management*, **8** (3), 41–3.

Willcocks, L. and Mark, A. (1989) 'IT systems implementation: research findings from the public sector', *Journal of Information Technology*, **4** (2), 92–103.

Willcocks, L. and Mason, D. (1992) *Computerising Work: People, Systems Design and Workplace Relations* (2nd edn). Blackwell Scientific, Oxford.

Willmott, H. (1987) 'Studying managerial work: a critique and a proposal', *Journal of Management Studies*, **24** (3), 249–70.

Zuboff, S. (1988) *In the Age of The Smart Machine*. Basic Books, New York.

PART 1

The public services since 1979: a partial revolution

1

Reviewing the current managerial ethos

Gerald Vinten

1.1 Introduction

The public sector in the United Kingdom has lived in partnership with private and voluntary sectors ever since it was sensible to make such distinctions. There was little idea of conflict as the need for public sector involvement became increasingly apparent from the mid-nineteenth century onwards. Initial involvement tended to be occasional and spasmodic, and was achieved by government grants being given to existing non-public sector organizations. Thus grants to schools were provided through the two denominational societies in the 1830s. As the century progressed this piecemeal approach was viewed as inadequate as the mass urban migration and population growth reached new levels. Municipalities involved themselves increasingly in school and hospital provision, although central government continued to pay grants to the denominational schools. Sanitation became another significant area of public sector involvement. All this was seen as contributing to the overall public good, just as later nationalization, perhaps somewhat more controversial, was nevertheless easy to justify in terms of the strategic needs of post-Second World War Britain. This consensus view changed with the advent of the Thatcher era in 1979, the ideology of the minimalist State, and a wish to bring about radical reform of the public sector. Competition, market forces and their price mechanisms reflected badly on the traditional public sector ethos and the welfare state, and public services were to be imbued with the operating style of the private sector, if not to be privatized, and in the privatization case be removed completely from the public sector. This chapter provides some historical perspective on public services in central and local government, and the National Health Service, before discussing the new managerial ethos.

In section 1.9 we suggest six factors that may differentiate public and private sectors, but also argue that there is a growing convergence between the two. However, as argued throughout the book, this does not mean that the public sector must sit at the feet of the private sector and learn from it. Both must be in a reciprocated learning attitude, and can mutually benefit.

3

We consider what secondments and the Aston Group can contribute to the debate, and conclude that the differences between sectors are more of degree than of kind, and are no different from the variations one may equally find within sectors.

1.2   The private/public sector debate

There has never been an absolute distinction between public sector and private sector, nor has a 'pure' public or 'pure' private sector ever existed. With the passage of history the distinction takes on increasing significance in capitalistic countries. The socialist countries retain for the longest period the mythology, but not always the reality, that there is no private sector, nor should there be one. The whole Marxist revolution in the USSR and China was a conscious attempt to move away from the tradition of a profit-making private sector. With this aspect of Marxism being dismantled during the late 1980s and early 1990s, one of the last bastions of merging public and private sector, although not officially recognizing the private sector, is rapidly crumbling.

In the past era the mixed economy predominates, and in this each sector relies symbiotically very much on the other. With government controls and influence over the private sector, and moves to cross-fertilize the public services with best commercial practice, it is sensible to regard the two as a continuum thus: Pure Public Sector←⋯→Pure Private Sector. The typology of Tomkins (1987) was delineated in the Introduction (see page xvi).

Neither of its extremes is likely to be found in practice, but both convey a certain meaning, and are an aid to discussion and thought. We are dealing with a Weberian ideal type, the aim of which is not to produce a carbon copy of reality, but rather to produce an explanatory model that is of more assistance than it is a nuisance. 'Bureaucracy' may be regarded as another example of an ideal type. It is interesting to note that in some countries the distinction is not meaningful when it comes to public nationalized industries, for these are simply regarded as industries irrespective of whether State or shareholders, or a combination, are the owners. The immense variety within the public sector make easy generalizations difficult, with a range of intermediary categories from the utility companies of gas, electricity and water, to the coal and steel industries, the health service, the peculiar bedfellows of industrial and commercial concerns that came under the former National Enterprise Board (now the British Technology Group), to the more traditional institutions of central and local government. Indeed, it is often more a matter of political ideology or convenience as to whether an industry or service is part of the public or private sector; the situation is fluid over time, and some can be both at the same time (such as health or education).

There was also a time, not too many decades distant, when the distinction of public and private sector seemed to be far less obtrusive than now. There was an economy that contributed to the general welfare—some making this contribution through the public sector, some through the private sector, and some through the voluntary sector (Vinten, 1989). There was an interdependence and a mutual recognition. Peter Hennessy refers to how discussion in this country has been off-beam:

> Equally powerful in me is the belief that we have wasted, in this country uniquely, masses of nervous energy and time over that fruitless debate about the boundary between the public and private sector. What the Curzon Line is or was for the Poles, the boundary between the public and private has become to us. It has dominated the political debate in all our lifetimes.
>
> (Cave *et al.*, 1990, p. 16)

Even at the beginning of the decade being analysed here (1980s) there is a report that considered the trading interdependence between the public sector and firms in the private sector, particularly with regard to the impact of public investment expenditure on the flow of orders and output in the private sector. The report also gave attention to the extent to which public expenditure and private investment were linked through competing demands for resources in the economy (Brech, 1981). The publisher of the report, the National Economic Development Office, is a tripartite organization representing government, management and unions, and there is no indication to contradict the idea that all economic sectors are mutually beneficial. Dick Taverne of the Public Policy Centre, commenting on the Thatcher era, considers that a major flaw has been the devaluation of the public sector. Referring to the crucial public needs that the market economy cannot begin to satisfy, he argues:

> Now if the minimisation of the public sector were in fact essential to the enterprise culture, it would make many of us less enthusiastic seekers after the cultural change. The quality of life depends to a considerable extent on the quality of public services which people would still need even if they were all the most thoroughly independent individualists.
>
> (Taverne, 1987)

Conservative education secretary John MacGregor, announcing that the Department of Education and Science was providing money for scholarships at the Royal Ballet School for 1990–92, also commented that a private charitable foundation was providing a substantial sum to strengthen teaching quality and for a new studio and performing area. Addressing the school in January 1990, he stated that: 'These two initiatives illustrate just how much can be achieved when public and private sector funding are brought together in partnership in pursuit of excellence.'

Although opponents of Mrs Thatcher will claim that she was anti-public sector, it is clear that although she represented a significant shift along the public–private sector continuum, we are not dealing with polar opposites, and the managerial consequences are likely to require a sideways shift or adjustment rather than a quantum leap. Lord Rayner has drawn attention to the practical problems of implementation that Mrs Thatcher failed to face:

> Here are these proposals for major change, involving a million people. We are going to do it all on D-day next year. What are the allowances for start-up costs. None. The whole thing to me was a total nightmare. There is no way Marks and Spencer could turn itself upside down overnight—it took five years to make the changes we wanted. There is no way we would do it without making the necessary resources available to manage the change. There is no way we would do it without proper experiment and evaluation.
>
> (Geoffrey Owen interview with Lord Rayner, *Financial Times*, 4 February 1991, p. 34)

Lord Rayner summarized the achievement obtained:

> There is a greater awareness of the need for accountability and a desire in some parts of Whitehall to do things better. It had been worthwhile, but I would not claim the change had been significant.

He concluded by commenting on Mrs Thatcher's inability to harness the talent of the civil servants around her:

> There is enormous quality in the Civil Service. It is a pity Mrs Thatcher took too much advice from theoretical people and too little from the talent that existed in the service.

It is instructive that the Treaty of Rome forbids discrimination between the public and the private sector. In some European countries the public sector has such a privileged position that it positively discriminates against the private sector through hidden subsidies, 'soft' equity injection or cancelling losses, whether directly by the State or through nationalized banks as holding companies. Public ownership can create monopoly rights, creating distortions of competition. Also, publicly owned companies cannot be taken over even though they themselves may be active predators. What would be equally intriguing to consider is the extent to which the private sector discriminates against the public sector. The public sector is in a weaker position if it is regarded as simply ancillary to the private sector rather than being a co-equal partner.

1.3   Historical perspective: central government

It would be historically inaccurate to regard the events of the 1980s as being in any sense *sui generis*. Those who have lived a lifetime in the public sector may temper current events with the thought that *plus ça change, mais c'est la même chose*. There have always been peaks and troughs, and these have quite often been irrespective of dominant party. Industrial relations has an interesting story to tell. A pertinent example was the Joint Statement by the National Whitley Council and the Final Report by the Wider Issues Review Team entitled *Civil Servants and Change* (Civil Service Department, 1975). The front cover depicted an hour glass. In the top part appeared a traditional stereotypical bowler-hatted civil servant. In the lower part, about to gain ascendancy, was a younger male-model-looking individual. The report drew attention to the fact that the civil service would soon be in the hands of the post-war generation with different values, assumptions and attitudes. The service had a disturbing time in the preceding ten years. There had been frequent changes in policies, reorganization, staff shortages and the pursuit by successive governments of economic and social objectives that ran counter to the service's managerial needs. Departments were created, merged and abolished, and these changes undermined valuable traditions and old loyalties. The consequent need to institute new working procedures and to assimilate new staff frustrated ongoing efforts to improve departmental performance, and distracted central and line management from what they regarded as their proper work. This was compounded by staff shortages, high turnover and manpower ceilings which then made it difficult to achieve up to standard. It was in 1973 that the civil service first experienced industrial action on a national scale, and the reason was undermanning. Public expenditure cuts had their toll, with poor quality accommodation and maintenance. Relocation out of London occurred at the expense of efficiency and staff wishes, and was more to do with the needs of the importing areas. The report concluded that civil servants 'have been mucked about a lot' and that 'there is an atmosphere of sourness'. Management was seen as being crucial to a solution:

> Better management of staff and their work is going to require increased attention by departments; in particular how the job itself can be made worthwhile and how the staff collectively and as individuals are managed so that one and all they can give their best.

(ibid., p. 31)

As we enter the Thatcher period, there emerge two approaches to the public services in general and the civil service in particular. The first is that they are too big, and the second that they are badly managed. The first led to the commitment to cut civil service numbers by 14 per cent over five years. The second led to the so-called 'efficiency strategy' (Plowden, 1985, p. 398). Initially the approach was piecemeal but significant, particularly with techniques such as the Rayner scrutinies, which, although they would continue to have a role, would yield diminishing returns, and two commentators correctly predicted in 1984 that there would be a wish to make progress on a broader scale and to move away from the impoverished concept of management which overemphasizes routine control and understates other dimensions, such as managing change and relationships within organizations (Metcalfe and Richards, 1984).

The Financial Management Initiative, launched in May 1982, did much to provide a coherent framework. At the beginning of the decade principal finance officers, with direct responsibility for financial control, and the permanent secretaries, as accounting officers for their departments, were not expected to have any training or expertise in accounting or financial management. By the end of the decade this cavalier attitude had been well and truly put to rest (Metcalfe and Richards, 1990). Greater sophistication in the cash limits system (Bevan *et al.*, 1981), better management information support in systems such as MINIS (Management Information for Ministers, developed by Michael Heseltine (Taylor and Popham, 1989, pp. 120–1) revamped and more professional internal and external audit, and developments in performance indicators (see Chapter 6) all assisted in promoting the change culture.

A cursory examination through the Public Expenditure White Papers shows about 1200 output and performance measures in 1986, rising to around 2300 by 1989. At the beginning of the 1980s such indicators were crude.

> The Eskimos are supposed to have 17 different terms for snow: the British politician or senior official has tended to have very few for the performance of the organizations under their scrutiny or control.
>
> (RIPA, 1986, 59)

Despite their prolific growth, there is still some considerable way to go, and they have neither universally taken root in the evolving managerial culture nor been wisely or judiciously used. Evaluation theorists talk of two strategies commonly adopted in the face of theoretical uncertainty and diversity of organizational objectives and methodologies. One is to avoid comprehensive evaluation and to concentrate on precise and limited objectives and audiences; the second is to try to synthesize multiple evaluation methods and approaches.

> The British Government felt no necessity to heed these complications, and, in fact, largely by-passed the debates about the modes and perils of different forms of evaluation. Those in authority determined to set clear objectives based on limited evaluative criteria. Where the market could not render judgements through prices and quantities bought and sold, other techniques such as inspection and audit could be applied.
>
> (Cave *et al.*, 1990, pp. 180–1)

The performance indicators, apart from becoming more numerous, have borne testimony to the new value system in the public sector as being resource-driven rather than needs-led. The work of the National Audit Office, and of the Audit Commission for local government and the NHS, have also witnessed the move to the world of the market and consumerism rather than that of the public bureaucrat. They were both reconstituted in 1983 to achieve this end.

1.4   Historical perspective: local government

Matters were not further advanced in local government on the eve of the Thatcher decade. It is perhaps comforting that Professor Robson has been writing on the crisis in local government since 1931:

> ... the failure of successive Governments, parliaments and the public to recognise the nature or even the existence of these problems had produced a situation of the utmost gravity to the local government system.
>
> (Robson, 1966)

He describes those matters afflicting the system of local government as a profound malaise. It was certainly not for want of a whole series of official reports

(Mallaby, 1967; Maud, 1967; and Redcliffe-Maud, 1969), which directly led into the Local Government Act 1972 and which gave considerable attention to questions of structure and management. The next major report returns to the language of crisis, by entitling one of three parts 'The nature of the crisis' (Layfield, 1976). Although the report is chiefly concerned with changes to financial arrangements, there are sections on overstaffing, complaints by the public, value for money, and performance review. On the eve of the 1980s the then government was putting forward far-reaching proposals for so-called organic change. This meant that the structure of local government could and should vary between different parts of the county according to local circumstances. The main management problem would have been that there would no longer be a common county area for the exercise of county services (Stewart *et al.*, 1978). Ill-considered reorganization after reorganization is not peculiar to the public sector. Mergers, acquisitions and divestments mania can create a similar effect in the private sector, and not all of these are in the public interest or in the interest of any other than the corporate predators. Others may regard it as a natural part of a dynamic economy (Chiplin and Wright, 1987; Roberts, 1987). As in the public sector, the human and internal managerial aspects are generally neglected (Hunt *et al.*, 1987). What is distinctive in the public services is the large impact one piece of legislation can make. It is not piecemeal, as in acquisitions, mergers and divestments, but has a significant across-the-board effect, given the numbers of staff and geographical areas involved covering the whole country, and in some areas being the major employer, although the multinational company could have a similar impact in some areas.

Spending cuts had been demanded since 1976, but Mrs Thatcher's election in 1979 intensified this demand. This was coupled with the government's decision first to encourage, then to compel, many of their services to be open to competitive tendering, producing changes in working practices and industrial relations. The Code of Practice for Compulsory Competition was first issued in March 1981 following the passing of the Local Government, Planning and Land Act 1980, which also legislated for various intermediate output measures that were to be made available to the local authority electorate. Five subsequent amendments were made to the Code, the last in 1989 following the extension of compulsory competition by the Local Government Act 1988. The Act applies to

- Refuse collection
- Catering
- Ground maintenance
- Internal cleaning of buildings
- Street cleansing
- Vehicle repairs and maintenance.

An immense amount of time over the decade went into specifying the contract (CIPFA, 1987, 1988, 1989), and lucrative consultancies sprang up simply to do this. Much had previously been taken for granted, but now to do so meant the service was no longer provided under a private contract. The pros and cons of competitive tendering spawned a huge literature (Hulme, 1990; Kemp, 1990; Parker and Hartley, 1990). The arguments are summarized in Table 1.1.

As a contribution to exploring the managerial issues involved the example of pest control is provided. Each case of contracting out needs to be carefully examined on its merits, and there is no foregone conclusion that advantages of contracting out services will outweigh the disadvantages.

The Environmental Health Department provides a generalized public service over a wide area. The contractor provides a narrower, more specific service and can thus avoid most of the overhead cost the local authority has to bear. Part of this overhead would be the need to monitor the work of the contractor and to supplement it where it is necessarily deficient. Pests are no respectors of the neat geographical areas of individual local authorities and the following are some of the additional overheads the local authority must incur in order to fulfil its statutory duty to provide a comprehensive service:

1 Monitor demographically the relation between infestations and areas.

Table 1.1   The pros and cons of contracting out

For contracting out	Against contracting out
1 Private firms are in a competitive, market-led situation, and so need to be lean in structure and fully responsive to consumer demand	There may be less competition, particularly in near monopoly situations
2 Private firms have a cost discipline, and the ever present possibility of bankruptcy	Private firms can be lackadaisical, and company failure is not unknown in this sector
3 Efficiency increases	Poor quality has sometimes resulted, with the resultant penalty sums exceeding the income
4 Cost reduction results	Cost reduction could be at the expense of consumer satisfaction
5 Periodic re-contracting introduces flexibility as service levels and standards may be reviewed	The authority has the hidden overheads of contracting to bear, such as evaluation and monitoring
6 Accounting is done on a similar basis, and so the best decision may be made	Conditions of service may deteriorate for the labour force
7 Experience gained elsewhere may benefit the authority	Management buy-outs may benefit the management rather than the electors

2 Liaise with other departments and divisions of the local authority, with contiguous authorities and with related public sector bodies, such as central government, health and water authorities.
3 Develop a comprehensive database of which pest control is only one element.
4 Develop and improve management information and monitoring.
5 Educate the public and when necessary conduct intensive publicity campaigns on specific pests.

The cost comparisons are always hazardous. The central government regularly claims to make large savings on, say, health service reorganization or charging those from overseas for medical treatment. Yet it rarely provides the basis on which the calculations are made. The savings claimed often turn out to be illusory. Like is not compared with like, and savings are at the margin rather than absolute. Such savings may disappear when it is considered that only the lucrative work has been creamed off, and the public service aspects neglected. In other areas of the public services, contracts have specified that the private concern must provide a comprehensive service. Since this is not possible with pest control, because of statutory responsibilities, the role of the contractor will be limited and at the margin of provision. On theoretical grounds it is difficult to see how a private contractor with the profit motive, operating an identical service to a local authority, could do so more cheaply. If the message is the need for greater productivity from the public sector, then there should be more means to achieve this.

This issue shows the limitations to the scope of contracting out. Nevertheless this initiative did force a cost discipline on authorities' direct labour organizations, and forced the compilation of accounts that were comparable to those of the private sector. Most direct labour organizations were able to survive under market conditions, though inevitably some went under. Local authority managers had the additional responsibility to liaise with the private sector contractors and to monitor quality and compliance with the conditions of the contract.

Another cultural change was introduced into primary and secondary schools (CIPFA, 1989a, b, c):

> The Local Management in Schools (LMS) introduced by The Education Reform Act 1988 brought about fundamental changes to the management of the education service. The introduction of needs-based formula funding and increasing delegation of financial and managerial responsibilities to governing bodies significantly enhanced the role of governors. It also moved the Local Education Authority (LEA) away from its traditional day-to-day management of schools towards concentrating upon standard setting and monitoring of the quality of service being provided.
>
> It is important to appreciate that LMS was not simply concerned with financial decisions, but was designed to put virtually the whole management of schools, including decisions of numbers and grades of staff, most building maintenance and budgetary control firmly in the hands of governors and head teachers.
>
> The Act required each LEA to prepare a scheme for local management of schools. The scheme had to be approved by the Secretary of State and be submitted to him by

the 30th September 1989, and had to include two main elements:

- details of a formula by which the LEA would allocate the bulk of its funds to each of its schools apart from nursery and special schools; and
- details of the arrangements it would make to delegate the responsibility for the spending of these funds to the governing bodies of all secondary schools, and primary schools with 200 pupils or more.

It is informative to close this section with the official rhetoric of the government in its response to the Widdiscombe Committee of Inquiry into the Conduct of Local Authority Business:

Local Government has a very important role in the democratic life of this country. Local authorities provide or promote a wide range of public services that are best administered locally, under democratic control. They are able to do so in a way that is responsive to local needs.

(HMSO, 1988)

Certainly this view was not always seen by those in local government as being an accurate portrayal of the reality of government intervention in local government.

1.5   Dominant organizational principles of local authorities

Three dominant organizational principles in traditional local authorities have been identified by Stewart (1989):

1 Functionalism—the division of the organization around particular tasks and responsibilities.
2 Uniformity—the provision of services to a common standard and a common pattern.
3 Hierarchy—organization through a large number of tiers with accountability running from the field workers to the chief officers and eventually the committee.

Stoker (1989) argues that these dimensions are attributable to local authorities being influenced by Fordism in the private sector. The concept of Fordism relates to the development of mass-produced standardized goods (or services) in tune with the philosophy of Henry Ford. Fordism entailed economies of scale, the use of automation and reorganization of skilled/unskilled labour. A universal wages bargaining and conditions of employment were adopted for each industry.

Similarities can be drawn between the above brief description and the present local authorities' *National Conditions of Service* (Purple Book) where uniformity is rife. Many of the products of local authorities are 'standard' insofar as they are derived from Acts of Parliament or national guidelines.

It can therefore be argued that the beliefs of the Fordist private sector were adopted by local government together with the necessary management styles. Stoker (1989) cites references which explain how the techniques of programme budgeting, systems analysis and corporate management, developed in the private sector, were transferred into the public sector in the 1960s and 1970s, stating: 'That local Authorities should look to the private sector for management lessons should not surprise us. It reflects the economic and cultural domination of Private capital.'

The government actively encouraged, or rather demanded by way of legislation, competition with the private sector. To be able to compete, the culture of the public sector must change and adopt a more commercial approach where 'risk' is accepted and managed. Hitherto risk was not a concept readily adopted within the public sector, whereas in the private sector it is a fact of life. The issue of 'risk' in public services is discussed in more detail in Chapter 3.

A shift is therefore still taking place from the public sector culture to that of the private sector. But in order to change one must understand not only where one wants to go but more essentially where one is.

> Talking about Corporate Culture is much easier than creating or sustaining it. From hard experience, I know that 'making it happen' requires example, emphasis and evangelism from all managers every day of the week.
>
> (Dr Anthony J. F. O'Reilly,
> President and Chief Executive Officer, H. J. Heinz Co. Inc.)

1.6 Dominant features of local authority management

The dominant features of traditional local authority management (see below) have been called 'facts of life' rather than assumptions (Stewart, 1986).

1 The committee setting

Committees define the work of local authority departments to achieve the political policies of elected members thereby carrying forward the principle of democracy. The formal committee system tends to define a councillor's role as 'merely getting through the agenda', which is invariably based on the department's operational functions rather than politics. Stewart (1986) argues that:

> The Committee system influences the working of departments, the role played by Councillors and the relationship between them. As the chair speeds from one item to another on the agenda, the opportunity for Local Government is lost.

2 The bureaucratic mode

The dominant organizational principles of functionalism, uniformity and hierarchy cited earlier encapsulate the bureaucratic mode. As Stewart (1986) explains, they have become written into the thought processes of those who work within the local authorities. They have become not principles, the application of which can be discussed, but assumptions that are rarely challenged.

3 *A professional culture*
The professional culture dominates local government so much that professions have been 'created' to serve it, i.e. Institution of Municipal Engineers (now part of the Institution of Civil Engineers) and Chartered Institute of Public Finance and Accountancy, among others. Professionalism greatly influences local government as commitment, specialist skills and knowledge are required to provide satisfactory services to the public. The public have a view that professionals can be trusted to provide the services for which they are trained:

> Professionalism is a strength in the provision of established services, but that very strength can restrict the exercise of local choice that is the role of local Authorities as local Government.
>
> (Stewart, 1986)

The values required of local government in the past were based, it is argued, on those values prominent in the private sector at that time. The private sector has changed with the times in an attempt to survive in the real competitive world. The public sector has, until recently, changed little since adopting pseudo-Fordist values. This has resulted in public sector bodies needing rapidly to acquire relevant values and cultures from the private sector in order to agree with the enforced changes from central government. It has been said that:

> ... this drive for great economy, efficiency and effectiveness is indicative of the strong desire within the Government to change the culture within local Government from one of mass public providers towards a kind of publicly run holding company for local services.
>
> (Stewart, 1986)

1.7 Historical perspective: National Health Service

It will by now not surprise us to discover no relief to the situation found in central and local government when we turn to the National Health Service (NHS). From its inception in 1948 the NHS has been plagued with reorganization, mini-reorganization and restructuring, barely adjusting at each transition. The Department of Health and Social Security (DHSS-cum-NHS) planning system was not always of the greatest help either, and tended to produce an overload for managers (Vinten, 1983). The 1974 reorganization, of which this planning system was part, also spawned the tripartite organization, with the DHSS on top, as shown in Fig. 1.1. This was generated by McKinsey and others, based on the rational planning model, and relies upon frequent iterations of management information flows in all directions. In practice there were too many tiers, and the area level was abolished on 1 April 1982, a not inappropriate date. Nurses represent the largest group of staff in the NHS, and their managerial hierarchy had been determined in 1966 under a committee chaired by

---

DEPARTMENT OF HEALTH AND SOCIAL SECURITY
|
Regional Health Authority
|
Area Health Authority
|
District Health Authority

Figure 1.1 Health service organization 1974–1982

Brian Salmon (HMSO, 1966). Grades were allocated on a scale ascending to ten, although in practice only the numbers at the top end of the range were referred to and, not surprisingly, nurses preferred to use descriptive titles such as senior nursing officer. Rather like the overall organization structure with its area level, many considered that the hierarchical pyramid was too long, and motivation and quality of management suffered in this key group of staff. There were perhaps fewer moans from nurses in the earlier years of the NHS when the sabre-toothed matron reigned supreme. Since those halcyon days nurses have been uninterruptedly dissatisfied with their lot, and nothing before or in our decade does much to dispel this feeling. The Royal Commission on the NHS had been appointed in May 1976 'to consider the interests both of the patients and of those who work in the NHS' (Royal Commission, 1979). A feeder research paper, based on a sample of regions, areas, districts and hospitals, spoke of prolonged disturbances.

The report relates to a period of prolonged disturbances in the NHS:

- the 1974 reorganisation itself (especially the creation of many authorities from scratch, the switch from management by hospital to functional management, and the change in the government of teaching hospitals);
- the 'cuts' in expenditure (more properly, reductions in the rate of growth), and the allocation of extra sums from time to time; also the specific restriction of management costs;
- the continuing reallocation of resources between regions in the interests of equity and need;
- the introduction of cash limits;
- the introduction (in England) of an ambitious system of strategic and operation planning;
- the growth of sectional militancy in some parts of the service, and of opposition by the public to changes of use and to closures.

(Royal Commission, 1978)

The NHS, prior to the 1987 General Election, was described by Mrs Thatcher as being 'safe in our hands'. It does appear that the claim of a breakdown of the post-war consensus, which some place at the door of Mrs Thatcher, does not apply to the NHS (Flynn, 1990, p. 61). Even an author who believes that the Conservative Government 'threw most institutions in the public sector into turmoil and created deep demoralisation and a permanent atmosphere of financial crisis and retrenchment' (Gamble, 1988, p. 123) finds no significant evidence of cuts in health care spending. The same cannot be said of structure, process and management, and as the decade progressed the measures became more and more radical. Not even the sacred cow of the medical profession was left unaffected, with clinical and medical audit becoming part of normal organizational life, and doctors being required to manage. In 1980 it was a problem to find even a small handful of volunteer clinicians to participate in a clinical budgeting experiment. By the end of the decade, with the Resource Management Initiative and grants to clinicians for management education and training, this had become a fact of life.

The changes in health care provision suggested by the Government White Paper *Working for Patients* (HMSO, 1989) necessitated a radical new approach to management philosophy. The most important change in the White Paper was the separation for buying and delivering health care from 1991. Purchasers, generally a district health authority, evaluated and met the needs of a defined population. They could buy, from a number of providers, the hospitals and general practitioners. This division of roles as between purchaser and provider allowed the classic dynamics of the marketplace to operate, including business plans, strategic planning, resource management and enhanced use of information technology. Option appraisals then became the order of the day, and capital costs had to be included. More stringent analysis was required to decide the need for services, and to determine referral patterns, trends in medical technology and other factors impacting on future provision. The managerial shift in the White Paper was so radical that only a comprehensive re-evaluation would then suffice. Districts needed to divorce their role in directing unit-managed services from their new overall role to assess health care needs in the communities in which they were situated. They needed to form clear contracts to meet those needs from the resources available. The White Paper required authorities to adopt major emphases on value for money audits, cost improvement programmes, financial management, and project appraisals in addition to the factors previously mentioned. The new expertise demanded was a mastery of the arcane Customs and Excise regulations that permit VAT refunds.

Equally radical were the new contracts negotiated with general practitioners. Larger practices of at least 8000 patients would have their own practice budgets to cover prescribing, most out-patient treatments and diagnostic tests, and a limited range of mainly elective in-patient treatments (Crafts, 1989). The National Health Service (Fund-holding Practices) (Applications and Recognition) Regulations made under the 1990 National Health Service and Community Care Act aimed to put practices on a more business-like footing, as well as taking pressure off the more expensive hospital prevention. They also intended to integrate general practitioners more into the workings of the NHS, and were part of the wider initiative for doctors to take more of a role in managing staff and resources in addition to just patients (see Chapter 8).

1.8   Management in the Thatcher era

It was plain as we entered the Thatcher period of 1979 onwards that structural and managerial problems in the public sector were nothing new. It might almost appear to be a chronic public sector disease, except that there is no great managerial skill called for in managing in conditions of complete predictability and stability, any more than there is in marketing to a captive audience which urgently needs the good or service and has no immediate alternative source of supply. The term for public sector management used to be administration, and this is still reflected in the premier research organization for the public services, the Royal Institute of Public Administration. The professional body for health services managers was formerly the Institute of Health Service Administrators, but changed its title to Management. This has been the trend over the decade in reaction to the environment in which the public sector is now operating. As a political commentator put it:

> The eighties is the decade when Britain's post-war consensus flew apart. Its fissiparous tendencies had long been evident, but what caused the eventual breach was the emergence, on both flanks of politics, of powerful personalities who decided the times were ripe for radical change. This pattern of revolution was confused, however, by other equally powerful personalities in the Centre, who wanted to break the mould and create a new political consensus.
> The decisive event in this political revolution took place before the decade began. This was the seizure, first of the leadership, and then of control, of the Conservative Party by Margaret Thatcher, at the head of a faction in the grip of an economic doctrine they originally called monetarism but quickly transformed into a political creed called Thatcherism.
>
> (Cole, 1987, p. 1)

In the wish to portray the Labour and Conservative parties as polar opposites, it is often forgotten that the Labour Party had also espoused monetarism. In the mid-1970s it was Her Majesty's Treasury that was doggedly Keynesian, whereas the Bank of England, under its governor, Gordon Richardson, managed to win Chancellor Denis Healey over to the virtues of monetarism:

> In retrospect, Richardson's most significant victory in 1976 was to persuade the Chancellor of the virtues of practical monetarism . . . the government was beginning to take money seriously again, for the first time since the Second World War.
>
> (Fay, 1988, p. 78)

Although the Thatcher decade shared with previous eras continuing crisis talk about public sector management, Mrs Thatcher had a reforming year which placed the public sector right at the centre of her change programme. Her reforms were unidirectonal, with the single purpose of reducing the rise and influence of the public sector, and permitting market forces to be the main governing principle. We now had naked, untrammelled monetarism, rather than use being made of monetarist principles as under the Labour administration.

> In the area of economic policy making it is, therefore, unambiguously the case that the policy initiatives of the Conservative governments were a significant and clearly signalled departure from that which had gone before. The policy initiatives did not represent the simple continuation of prior policies nor were they a marginal adjustment to the existing regime. Instead, a revolution had taken place with the ordering of the instruments of macro-economic policy being turned on its head.
>
> (Jackson, 1981, p. 1)

As the decade progressed, and with an electoral majority appearing to confirm a wish for more of the same, the emphasis on the desirability of private sector management techniques for the public sector was enhanced. There may well be some confusion here between economics and management. Adopting the premise that monetarism is desirable, and that monetarism works in and through the global financial marketplace, and that so-called 'market forces' are the determining factor is one thing. To assert that some idealized management approach which is seen to accompany this should be generated across the whole economy is another. As argued in the Introduction, it is certainly idealized, since the private sector is not homogenous, and possesses infinite variety. The 'cook-book' approach to management rarely works, and those, such as Tom Peters, who attempt to adopt it in any form, find they need to revise their books frequently as their prime private sector managed companies end up failing or being surpassed (Peters, 1988; Peters and Waterman, 1982). Similarly, Ronnie Lessem puts his faith in the Bank of Credit and Commerce International as the supreme example of the 'metaphysical management' which he sees as the superior managerial appproach (Lessem, 1989). The indictment of this bank for fraud and the laundering of drug monies on a large scale, plus the handling of large staff lay-offs in the United Kingdom, and a less than responsive attitude to dealing with the customer complaint, make this bank an unlikely candidate for the honour it was accorded. As an editorial in *The Banker* puts the matter, '. . . its staff, like others worldwide, can only look at its commitment to its employees with deep cynicism' (Blanden *et al.*, 1991). Yesterday's successes can quickly become tomorrow's has beens, and several companies such as Coloroll, Laker and the Sock Shop, praised by Mrs Thatcher in the 1980s, are failing rapidly in the 1990s. One can only be thankful that these particular companies were not accepted as public sector role models.

1.9   Convergence of public and private sectors?

With the various strategies adopted over the decade to infiltrate the public sector with best private sector management approaches, it is not surprising that some convergence should be taking place. This will never amount to total identity, since we have already briefly considered some of the hallmarks of the public sector prior to the Thatcher revolution, and we then consider how far convergence has taken place in the 1980s to 1990s. The following six items are suggested as a suitable schemata for pursuing the discussion started in the Introduction to this book, and we shall take each one in turn.

1 Scale, complexity, society-wide basis
2 Consistency and conformity more significant
3 The political element
4 The immeasurability of certain public sector work
5 The concept of accountability
6 Hierarchical, bureaucratic, life-time career, with inflexible pay and promotion.

1.9.1 SCALE, COMPLEXITY, SOCIETY-WIDE BASIS

The public sector is big business. It is a major employer of labour. In some local government areas the local authority is the largest employer, and the local labour market therefore depends heavily on this source of employment. It can certainly be compared with the largest of companies, and indeed with the multinationals. It is also highly complex. The average company is small, with owner-managers, little working or share capital, and a single product or very small product range. Even large companies find advantage in sometimes divesting themselves of some of their products or subsidiaries in the interests of simplicity, market concentration and increased profitability. The public sector can afford no such luxury. It tends to take on a growing range of responsibilities which not even the multinationals can match. The interrelations of these responsibilities are highly complex. This is particularly so since entry into the European Community, and with the need to adopt a world perspective. The public sector covers the whole of society. It cannot choose to opt out, as can a company opt out of operating in a particular type of market. The range of issues are vast, from housing the homeless, waste collection, inner-city policy, fire-fighting, to running diplomatic missions abroad, encouraging free trade, providing education and social services and safeguarding the consumer interest. It is possible to avoid the products of an individual company, except in the few monopoly cases; it is not possible to avoid the output of the public sector, which touches everyone's life.

A number of departments end up as repositories of a rag-bag of functions simply because they have to find a home there. In central government the Home Office looks after such divergent functions as immigration, law and order, children and young people, and broadcasting. The local government equivalent is the environmental health department, which has accumulated functions piecemeal through various isolated Acts of Parliament.

A parallel to the divestment strategy of the private sector has been the 'hiving off' of part of the responsibility of departments. There is nothing new in this, and the Fulton Report of 1968 contained this as a recommendation (Fulton,

1968). Gone are the days of the mega-departments of central government, although the mergers that led to them were not always sustained for long. The process has worked in both directions, leading to fission and fusion alternating. The fissions of the Department of Economic Affairs under a Labour administration and the Civil Service Department subsequently become fused. The one-time fusion of the Department of Health then becomes fissioned into the Department of Health and the Department of Social Security. A related extension of this has been the creation of the Executive Agency which may be regarded as a form of task and role amplification through divestment.

The average public sector manager, who does not, of course, have to cope with all this complexity personally, will have a discrete and manageable segment of it to cope with, and this also obtains with managers in the private sector. The complexity of the public sector is spread wide, and so one is not exactly comparing like with like. This in turn suggests a contingency approach to management, and that applies both within the two sectors and across them.

1.9.2   CONSISTENCY AND CONFORMITY MORE SIGNIFICANT

Consistency and conformity are more significant. There is less scope for individual creativity and initiative. Risk-taking in a commercial sense is often outlawed. This was plain from the Fay Committee on the Crown Agents (report by the Committee of Inquiry appointed by the Minister of Overseas Development into the circumstances that led to the Crown Agents requesting financial assistance from the Government in 1974.) The Crown Agents had indulged in some speculative investments that then went bad. This was due to incompetence rather than to misconduct. It was considered unwise for the Crown Agents to have attempted to operate as financiers on their own account. The public sector is more likely to be governed by the rule-book and procedural manuals, with a standard means of communication being the memorandum and the report, successively altered by the many layers of higher management, sometimes on purely stylistic grounds rather than for reasons of content.

An example of a government department where risk-taking is of the essence is the Export Credit Guarantees Department (ECGD). It assists exporters both of goods and services in the following ways. Firstly, it insures them against the risk of not being paid—whether through the default of the buyer or through other causes, such as restrictions on the transfer of currency, cancellation of valid import licences on the transfer of currency, or cancellation of valid import licences. Secondly, it furnishes guarantees of 100 per cent repayment of banks. On this security banks provide finance for the support of export contracts at favourable interest rates. The ECGD insures new investment overseas against the risk of war, expropriation and the restriction of remittances. The ECGD also provides protection against part of the increases in UK costs for large capital goods contracts with long manufacturing periods, supports the issue of performance bonds, and guarantees contracts expressed in acceptable international currencies as well as sterling, including cover against fluctuations in exchange rates adversely affecting an exporter's tender price in a foreign currency.

In providing these facilities, the ECGD offers two main benefits to exporters. In insuring them against the risks of non-payment it enables them to pursue a bolder marketing policy, taking on new buyers and breaking into new markets without fear of crippling losses. And ECGD support for export finance can help exporters offer competitive terms and win contracts they might otherwise lose.

Although the ECGD is a government department its credit insurance operations involve no expense to the taxpayer. It operates as a business, balancing income and outgoings over the years. Applying normal insurance principles it offers a full export credit insurance service at a reasonable price.

This department has very close private sector analogues, and the part that is most close can always be susceptible to being hived off and privatized.

A newly created agency, the Civil Service College, still largely practises its old civil service ways of consistency and conformity, although it shows some degree of innovation and creativity in its top management courses, which latterly have been attracting the top of the office, as well as those outside the civil service. In the bulk of its courses it is trying hard to shed its past of delivering courses that are recognizable as originating in the civil service mould. *The Times Higher Education Supplement* has contained several critical articles. The emphasis has tended to be on classroom delivery, while the range and depth of work included in research as yet could not be compared to a university, whether privately or publicly funded. The College is making sustained efforts to improve both image and culture. This may not be assisted by the practice of short-term secondments of lecturers from mainstream departments, whereby they return home just as they have found their feet as lecturers. British Telecom is a privatized organization which still betrays vestiges of its civil service origins, and it has had much longer to readjust than have the executive agencies. Similarly the Post Office, as a half-way stage between public and private, still betrays its origins as a civil service department in its ethos and operating procedures.

1.9.3   THE POLITICAL ELEMENT

It is certainly true that there are board politics in companies, and in the multinational company there may be many similarities to what goes on in Parliament, Whitehall and the Town Hall. Nevertheless the operating situation is different, with a distinction between members (MPs and councillors) and officers (civil servants and local government professional officers). This can lead to a fudging of responsibility and a resistance to action on both sides. Many or most company board members will be executive directors, and thereby top managers in their own right, able to directly compel adherence to their directives, and not needing to overcome resistance from a civil servant or local government officer who will likely be more knowledgeable and better briefed than they are.

1.9.4   THE IMMEASURABILITY OF CERTAIN PUBLIC SECTOR WORK

It is much easier to measure the output of a car factory than that of a social services department or the police service. Ultimately output generally, whether of public or private sector, needs to be measured in terms of consumer satisfaction, and this probably presents equal problems to both. Professor Cyril Tomkins draws attention to the problems of defining effectiveness in the public sector. Many of the claims that effectiveness has been defined, measured, and assessed turn out to be false, or only the easy-to-measure options have been looked at (Tomkins, 1987). Additionally, one respect in which the public sector is quite different from the private sector is that it is extraordinarily difficult to keep campaigns for efficiency away from politics, and this introduces an additional element to the production of sensible evaluations. At the same time models and methods of evaluation multiplied, and conflict developed among evaluation theorists. Some considered they were value free social scientists in the Weberian tradition, applying rigorous methods of analysis within the framework established by policy makers. Others said no particular claim to truth or authority could be made. The assumptions of the British Government in the 1980s gave no heed to these complexities (Henkel, 1991).

1.9.5   THE CONCEPT OF ACCOUNTABILITY

Accountability involves the fulfilment of a formal obligation to disclose periodically, in adequate detail and in consistent form, all directly and indirectly responsible or properly interested in the

- purposes
- principles
- procedures
- relationships
- results
- income and expenditure

of any activity so that evaluations and decisions can be made. Briefly, it is an obligation to reveal, explain and justify what one does or how one discharges one's responsibilities. For a further view on accountability see Chapter 6.

Since tax, rate or poll tax payers are captive subscribers, there is a need to be more fully accountable to them. This does involve a higher cost, as does the political process, but it is seen as being vital to the nature of the public sector. The National Audit Office, the external auditor for central government, owes accountability to Parliament, and this leads to only an indirect relationship with the taxpayers, and a style of public report which may be less than fully informative to the taxpayer, especially since heads of government or related departments may forbid the printing of certain detail. By way of contrast, the Audit Commission, as the external auditor for local government and the National Health

Service, has a direct relationship with the local government electorate, which can raise detailed questions and objections to items of expenditure. This leads to detailed reports 'in the public interest' as well as guides to good managerial practice and global value-for-money reports, a handful being researched each year.

The difference in public and private sector accountability may be seen in how far it is possible to push a consumer complaint. Civil servants, local government officers and other public sector workers, whose work brings them into contact with the public, will recall huge files relating to one or two of their 'customers', the size of whose complaint is only exceeded by their ability to enter into incessant correspondence with everyone from the Pope to the Prime Minister. The private sector would not be so resilient in dealing with such interminable matters, however justified in themselves. A story recounted by former MP Robert E. Bean illustrates the lengths to which the public sector may go on rare occasions. An elderly woman, living alone, had a phobia that there was a conspiracy to electrocute her through lightning. The cost to the local authority, electricity board, Department of Energy, the MP and no doubt others in answering her letters was astronomical. Bob Bean asked if the local authority would erect a steel structure outside her home that would look like an electrical conductor? They agreed. It worked, and the woman returned to a slightly more normal life—certainly one that was not a burden on others. Although the expenditure of a few hundred pounds could not be considered 'material', one wonders about the Audit Commission reaction. It seems a suitable item of expenditure under the 'Care in the community' philosophy, and a way to work with someone's mental illness, rather than against it.

Accountability is seen at its highest in the right of the local government poll tax payer to question expenditure through the Audit Commission auditors, and even to see invoices substantiating expenditure, and to raise issues of value for money. Outside pressure groups, such as those representing the commercial tax payers, can put local authorities to a lot of time and pressure with lengthy investigations, and results reported back to relevant committees before a final report can be compiled (Henney, 1984). In central government, welfare-benefits-paying departments or tax-collecting departments have quasi-judicial tribunals of appeal, and there is always the report to the MP, Minister or Ombudsman. Nationalized industries, a half-way stage between public and private, were automatically provided with a consumer consultative committee on the grounds that they were monopolies or near monopolies, and control by market forces could not be presumed. After privatization this arrangement has been continued, for example, with gas and telecommunications, since the number of market entrants remains extremely low.

Although, in the final analysis, accountabilities in the public sector are bound to be higher, it has been argued, in the most thorough analysis of accountability in the public sector, that the emphasis of public policy has been to respond to complexity mainly by setting up new institutions of accountability. This may then lead to excessive complexity and create dead-ends (Day and Klein, 1987). In addition, the private sector does have its own institutions of accountability, such as a statutory ombudsman for building societies, and a voluntary scheme for banking and insurance. In the mainstream financial institutions consumer complaints can be pushed as far as in the public sector, and there are also the various Self-Regulatory Organizations under the Securities and Investment Board. Elsewhere there are voluntary Codes of Practice in a number of consumer areas, and these are encouraged by the Office of Fair Trading. Just like the aggrieved public sector consumer who wishes to challenge lack of ministerial implementaiton of statutory duty through a judicial review, so the private sector consumer ultimately has redress to the law courts.

1.9.6   HIERARCHICAL, BUREAUCRATIC, LIFE-TIME CAREER, WITH INFLEXIBLE PAY AND PROMOTION

Most parts of the public sector may be considered as hierarchic and bureaucratic, but then so is most of the private sector, unless we consider worker cooperatives, and even these display some bureaucratic tendencies. Bureaucracy, as defined by Max Weber, has ten major features:

1 Staff are personally free, observing only the impersonal duties of their offices.
2 There is a clear hierarchy of offices.
3 The functions of the offices are clearly specified.
4 Officials are appointed on the basis of a contract.
5 They are selected on the basis of a professional qualification, ideally substantiated by a diploma gained through examination.
6 They have a money salary, and usually pension rights. The salary is graded according to position in the hierarchy. The official can always leave the post, and in certain circumstances it may also be terminated.
7 The official's post is the sole or major occupation.
8 There is a career structure, and promotion is possible either by seniority or merit, and according to the judgement of superiors.
9 The official may appropriate neither the post nor the resources that go with it.
10 The official is subject to a unified control and disciplinary system.

Despite criticism that this 'classical' view of management is incomplete as a synoptic view of management, it is nevertheless true that it has a number of abiding principles. Even Weber did not make absolutist claims for his theory:

> Thus, contrary to many interpretations, Weber did not maintain that bureaucratic organizations operate as efficiently as 'slot machines'. He said rather that such organizations operate more efficiently than alternative systems of administration and that

they increase their efficiency to the extent that they 'depersonalize' the execution of official tasks.

(Bendix, 1966, p. 427)

Weber did recognize the inefficiencies that could accompany bureaucracy, what we call red tape, but he coined no word for it, and has been frequently criticized for choosing to de-emphasize it (Albrow, 1970, pp. 45–6). He did perceive that bureaucracy could separate staff from the means of production and lead to a growth of formalism in organizations, and he seemed to view this prospect with resigned pessimism.

The public sector has, then, in common with the private sector a bureaucratic strand, and bureaucracy will be more or less present according to the needs of the situation. However, the public sector may be considered to have a leaning towards the bureaucratic as compared with the private sector. This is in consequence of the factors that have already been discussed. One of the leading texts on management consultancy puts it thus:

Managerial attitudes and behaviour in public sector organizations constitute a key issue which consultants have to deal with in most assignments. It is very much a systems problem, as managers tend to act in accordance with the written and unwritten behavioural rules proper to the public enterprise system. Thus, if risk taking is not encouraged, most of them will avoid it. If conformity is valued more than drive and originality, most managers will be conformists. Therefore, if there are flaws in the system, these flaws inevitably affect managerial behaviour and efficiency at all levels.

(Kubr, 1988, p. 311)

Matters have been far from static during the Thatcher era. At one time the inflexibility could be almost total. For example, the civil service and National Health Service found it difficult to recruit staff anywhere other than at the lowest incremental point on the salary range. The NHS actually needed approval from the Department of Health and Social Security, and it was let known that this would not be granted. The result was that unsuspecting short-listed victims would arrive at interview, at the end of which starting salary was discussed, and since their existing salary might well be above the new salary minimum, they then discovered they needed to take a cut. This wasted their time and led to inefficient recruitment. This climate belongs to a past era, although one does still find isolated pockets of it.

The civil service was forced into less restricted recruitment criteria by being found guilty of sex discrimination by specifying upper age limits of 32 for certain executive officer and related posts, which was held to be unfair to women applicants. As is so often the case, this legal finding was of immense benefit to men also. There is a greater openness about recruitment, although some of this has resulted from the push to bring in private sector talent into the civil service, with increasing numbers of jobs being nationally advertised. Again, residual attitudes and values linger on. The Civil Service Commission discriminate against candidates they consider to be overqualified, and personnel management is still underdeveloped in the civil service.

Recent job advertisements show just how much the culture has changed in the public sector. A chief executive position at Westminster City Council is advertised as 'managing director'. The Head of Education Management Services at the London Borough of Southwark, not noted for support of Mrs Thatcher, has 'to provide Business Management expertise to enable the Department to operate efficiently, economically and effectively and to provide professional advice on Business Management matters to the Director'. Internal management consultants are increasingly being sought. Leased cars and other perquisites may be offered as an inducement for senior posts, and performance-related pay is very much the order of the day. In August 1990 the revolutionary step was taken to extend this to senior nursing staff.

It is also considered perfectly appropriate to talk of entrepreneurs in government, as discussed in more detail in Chapter 3. A biographical exploration of this theme suggests that public sector bosses do matter, although so do structures, missions and settings, since these alter over time. The following facets of the entrepreneurial executive were all found to be present in the public sector (see Doig and Hargrove, 1987):

1 Identify new missions and programmes for their organizations.
2 Develop and nourish external constituencies to support the new goals and programmes, and to support the organization generally, while neutralizing existing and potential oppositions.
3 Create internal constituencies that supported the new goals (while eliminating opposition), through changes in organizational structures, in recruitment systems and key appointments, and in reward and penalty systems.
4 Enhance the organization's technical expertise (through recruitment of skilled personnel and addition of new equipment) in order to improve its capacity to identify and develop interesting programme options, and to implement new goals and programmes.
5 Motivate and provide training for members of the organization so that they would have the skills to work efficiently in old and new programme areas and the desire to extend their efforts beyond standard or accepted levels of performance.
6 Systematically scan organizational routines, and points of internal and external pressure, in order to identify areas of vulnerability (to mismanagement and corruption and to loss of the leaders' own power and position), followed by remedial action.

1.10 Secondments—*vive la différence*

Secondments between government and business are not new. The first formal scheme followed in the wake of the Fulton Report in 1968. The next watershed was in 1977 when the government decided to seek a 'sharp and substantial increase' in the number of civil servants seconded to business organizations. The latest thrust forward was initiated in March 1989 by Lord Young and Richard Luce, and entitled the Bridge Programme 'to build more bridges between government and industry'. A survey on such secondments, sampling between 1986 and 1989, found that they were mutually beneficial both to the secondees, who received benefit in terms of personal and career development, and the host organizations, which found benefit in the skills and knowledge that secondees brought with them. The seconding organizations were also blessed with more developed employees. Host organizations considered that secondees brought new skills and helped in areas of skill shortage (Gosling and Nutley, 1990).

Certainly the benefits were not just from the private to the public sector. To show how the secondments were of mutual benefit we quote from a civil servant secondee to IBM in 1984, reported by Richard Marriott, IBM's Director of Communications and External Programmes:

'The whole of IBM is characterized by a singleness of purpose and direction. Few Civil Servants on the other hand enjoy the same unanimity of purpose and consensus for the policies they are progressing. Everyone in IBM knows what he is doing and why, and even where objectives do conflict, they do so in the context of shared interests and guidelines so that colliding interests still manage to produce forward motion. On the other hand, in a complex democracy there are no over-riding national objectives to which all disparate interests will subscribe.'

Despite this, he felt that it would be possible to set Civil Servants clearer job objectives and to introduce remuneration for performance to improve the motivation of civil servants and to force improvements in the line management of staff.

About IBM people, he had this to say.

'To a man and woman, Very Nice People, but too introspective and insular. It was disconcerting to find such a passive view of a dramatically changing world among such intelligent and closely involved people and I believe it should worry you.'

Our Chairman, Sir Edwin Nixon took up these words of warning and wrote in IBM's management journal that

'it was no longer enough for IBMers to demonstrate a lively mind. We must remain alert to signals coming from outside and be sensitive to the changes taking place, many of which will affect how we do business. Keeping wide horizons is a matter of basic professionalism.'

(Marriott, 1984)

It is clear that accommodation would help on both sides, and it is particularly interesting to observe how Sir Edwin Nixon took immediate action on the observations of the civil service secondee.

1.11   Conclusion

In reviewing developments in the public sector over the past decade we have seen that there has been a steady shifting of the boundaries of the State. This has, however, not necessarily been quite so radical as many commentators have suggested, and we have traced antecedents in earlier periods. We have also traced a growing convergence between the three sectors of the economy: public, private and voluntary. None of these sectors is in itself uniform, homogeneous or monochrome, and this means that it is possible to find aspects in each that are similar to those in the others. We have seen that the experience of secondments suggests that there are mutual benefits to be gained, and that the rough-and-ready political shorthand—that private sector managerial analogues are desirable, and public sector analogues are undesirable—is not therefore supported. There may be greater differences within than between sectors. This suggests more modesty and openness of approach in the debate than is sometimes found in the political rhetoric.

We have reviewed six 'ideal type' differences between public and private sectors, but we have also seen how the severity of these differences has been gradually eroded, although the remaining differences do suggest the need to modify the managerial approach to fit. This is, however, a facet of moving between any two organizations, which will inevitably not possess identical cultures.

Although one would never read too much from any one piece of management research, the findings emanating from the Aston Group suggest that the form of 'ownership' (public, private or voluntary) made little difference to the structuring of activities and the concentration of authority (Hickson and McMillan, 1981). The same applied to technology, which was reflected in only a few aspects of structure. The initial research had studied 46 highly diverse public and private sector organizations, ranging from chocolate and car manufacturers, to local government, public services and retail outlets. What was found to matter much more for the form taken by an organization was its size, and its degree of dependence upon other organizations.

The larger the organization, the more likely employees will work in very specialized units, with formal documentation and standardized procedures, and this will give rise to bureaucratic characteristics. Where there is dependence upon just a few owning, supplying or customer units, the less autonomy there will be in decision-making, and even those that remain will probably be centralized within the organization itself, rather than decentralized. The research of the Aston Group leads to a 'culture-free hypothesis' that these basic relationships would apply irrespective of differences between societies or economic sectors.

The four main types of resulting organization are presented in Fig. 1.2.

The public services organizations of central and local government, according to the Aston Group, will often be based on hiring, promoting and firing. Smaller units within large public or private sector organizations are said to be full bureaucracies, with a combination of the high structuring of the workflow variety, and highly concentrated authority of the personnel type. One could

		Structuring of workflow	
		LOW	HIGH
	HIGH	Personnel bureaucracies	Full bureaucracies
Concentration of authority			
	LOW	Non-bureaucracies	Workflow bureaucracies

Figure 1.2   Structuring of activities

argue about these positionings, and with the shifts of the 1980s and before it may be necessary to qualify or alter some of the positionings. As the executive agencies mature and become a significant norm within central government, it will be interesting to discuss where they should fit in. The important point, though, is the support this management theory provides to the convergence hypothesis.

So, to conclude, although there are differences between the sectors, it is a matter of degree rather than of kind, and it supports our earlier positioning of the two sectors on a continuum. The difference of degree is, however, quite sufficient to suggest a difference of managerial approach as we travel along the continuum.

It is instructive to observe companies and organizations that were at one time within the civil service or public sector, but now operate outside it, with profit and performance being all important. One of these, displaying its commercial orientation, now appoints marketing project managers to see through, from start to finish, various marketing endeavours, such as the marketing of special services or convincing the customer of the quality of the product or service provided. The trouble is that the underlying organizational culture is overly bureaucratic and restrictive with tight budgetary restraints, none of which encourages the creativity demanded in the marketing function. Complicated and out-of-date systems, resistance to change, budgetary and staffing restrictions, ingrained operational viewpoints, and a constant time battle between maintaining existing systems and generating and implementing new marketing projects, jeopardize the effectiveness of the contribution that marketing can make. One could say that there has been an inability of this organization to throw off the shackles of its civil service or public sector background. This would betray the viewpoint of public sector management = bad, private sector management = good. This organization has now had a clear generation to adjust to its changed positioning, and so it is more accurate to regard the problems as being general organizational problems, rather than the legacy of the public sector past.

As we face the challenges of the future—which are likely to be even greater than in the past, with not only convergence of public, private and voluntary sectors, but also between the communist and non-communist worlds—the productive response would seem to be to take advantage of managerial experience wherever it can be found, and to focus on what can be learned that is useful, rather than on where it emanated from.

References and further reading

Albrow, M. (1970) *Bureaucracy*. Macmillan, London.

Bendix, R. (1966) *Max Weber. An Intellectual Portrait*. Methuen, London.

Bevan, G., Sisson, K. and Way, P. (1981) 'Cash limits and public sector pay', *Public Administration*, 59 (Winter).

Blanden, M., Timewell, S. and Laurie, S. (1991) 'BCCI blues', *The Banker*, 141 (779), 15 January.

Brech, M. (1981) *The Interdependence of the Public and Private Sectors*. National Economic Development Office, London.

Cave, M., Kogan, M. and Smith, R. (1990) *Output and Performance Measurement in Government*. Kingsley, London.

Chiplin, B. and Wright, M. (1987) *The Logic of Mergers*. Institute of Economic Affairs, CIPFA, London.

CIPFA (1987, 1988, 1989) *The Extension of Compulsory Competition. Meeting the Challenge*. Chartered Institute of Public Finance and Accountancy, London.

CIPFA (1989a) *The Audit Implications of Local Management in Schools*. Chartered Institute of Public Finance and Accountancy, London.

CIPFA (1989b) *Managing Education in the 1990s*. Chartered Institute of Public Finance and Accountancy, London.

CIPFA (1989c) *Managing Education in the 1990s—Local Management in Practice*. Chartered Institute of Public Finance and Accountancy, London.

Civil Service Department (1975) *Civil Servants and Change*. Civil Service Department, London.

Cole, J. (1987) *The Thatcher Years. A Decade of Revolution in British Politics*. BBC Books, London.

Crafts, R. (1989) *Commissioning Health Services: Contract Funding in the NHS*. Public Finance Foundation, London.

Day, P. and Klein, R. (1987) *Accountabilities. Five Public Services*. Tavistock, London.

Doig, J. W. and Hargrove, E. C. (eds) (1987) *Leadership and Innovation. A Biographical Perspective on Entrepreneurs in Government*. Johns Hopkins, Baltimore.

Eichrodt, W. (1966) *Man in the Old Testament*. SCM Press, London.

Fay, S. (1988) *Portrait of an Old Lady. Turmoil at the Bank of England*. Penguin, London.

Flynn, N. (1990) *Public Sector Management*. Harvester Wheasheaf, London.

Fulton, Lord (1968) *Report of the Committee on the Civil Service*, Cmnd 3538, HMSO, London.

Gamble, A. (1988) *The Free Economy and the Strong State: The Politics of Thatcherism*. Macmillan, London.

Gretton, J. and Harrison, A. (eds) (1987) *Reshaping Central Government, 1979–1987*. Policy Journals, Newbury.

Gosling, R. and Nutley, S. (1990) *Bridging the Gap. Secondments between Government and Business*. Royal Institute of Public Administration, London.

Henkel, M. (1991) *Government, Evaluation and Change*. Kingsley, London.

Henney, A. (1984) *Inside Local Government. A Case for Radical Reform.* Sinclair Browne, London.

Hickson, D. J. and McMillan, C. J. (eds) (1981) *Organization and Nation: The Aston Programme IV.* Gower, Aldershot.

HMSO (1966) *Committee on Senior Nursing Staff Structures (Chair, Brian Salmon).* HMSO, London.

HMSO (1988) *The Government's Response to the Widdicombe Committee Report on the Conduct of Local Authority Business.* HMSO, London.

HMSO (1989) *Working for Patients.* Cmnd 555, HMSO, London.

Hulme, G. (1990) 'Contract funding and management in the National Health Service', *Public Money and Management*, **10** (3), 17–23.

Hunt, J. W., Lees, S., Grumbar, J. J. and Vivian, P. D. (1987) *Acquisitions—The Human Factor.* London Business School, London.

Jackson, P. M. (ed) (1981) *Government Policy Initiatives 1979–80: Some Case Studies in Public Administration.* Royal Institute of Public Administration, London.

Kemp, P. (1990) 'Can the Civil Service adapt to managing by contract?', *Public Money and Management*, **10** (3), 25–31.

Kubr, M. (1988) *Management Consulting. A Guide to the Profession.* International Labour Office, Geneva.

LAMSAC (1986) *Managing to Compete. Conference Proceedings, Eastbourne, 21–24 April 1986.* LAMSAC, Geneva.

Layfield, F. (1976) *Local Government Finance.* HMSO, London.

Lessem, R. (1989) *Global Management Principles.* Prentice Hall, Hemel Hempstead.

Mallaby, G. (1967) *The Staffing of Local Government.* HMSO, London.

Marriott, R. (1984) 'Secondments: A triple success', Paper presented at the Royal Institute of Public Administration Conference *The Shifting State: Rules, Roles and Boundaries in the 1980's* held at the University of Aston, 14–15 September 1984.

Maud, J. (1967) *The Management of Local Government.* HMSO, London.

Maxwell, R. (ed) (1988) *Reshaping the National Health Service 1979–1987.* Policy Journals, Newbury.

Metcalfe, L. and Richards, S. (1984) 'The impact of the efficiency strategy: political clout or cultural change?', *Public Administration*, **62** (4, Winter).

Metcalfe, L. and Richards, S. (1990) *Improving Public Management* (2nd edn). Sage, London.

Parker, D. and Hartley, K. (1990) 'Competitive tendering: Issues and evidence', *Public Money and Management*, **10** (3), 9–16.

Parkinson, M. (1987) *Reshaping Local Government.* Policy Journals, Newbury.

Peters, T. J. (1988) *Thriving on Chaos: A Handbook for Management Revolution.* Macmillan, Basingstoke.

Peters, T. J. and Waterman, R. H. (1982) *In Search of Excellence: Lessons from America's Best-Run Companies.* Harper & Row, London.

Plowden, W. (1985) 'What prospects for the Civil Service?', *Public Administration*, **63** (4, Winter).

Redcliffe-Maud, J. (1969) *Royal Commission on Local Government in England.* HMSO, London.

RIPA (1986) *Policy Management and Policy Assessment.* Royal Institute of Public Administration, London.

Roberts, J. (1987) *Megalomania, Managers and Mergers.* Pitman, London.

Robson, W. A. (1966) *Local Government in Crisis.* Allen and Unwin, London.

Royal Commission (1978) *National Health Service. Management of Financial Resources in the NHS.* Research Paper No. 2, HMSO, London.

Royal Commission (1979) *National Health Service, Report*. Cmnd 7615, HMSO, London.

Savage, S. P. and Robins, L. (1990) *Public Policy under Thatcher*. Macmillan, Basingstoke.

Stewart, J. (1986) *The New Management of Local Government*. Allen and Unwin, London.

Stewart, J. (1989) 'The changing organisation and management of local authorities', in Stewart, J. and Stoker, G. (eds), *The Future of Local Government*. Macmillan, Basingstoke.

Stewart, J. D., Leach, S. and Skelcher, C. K. (1978) *Organic Change*. A report on constitutional, management and financial problems. Institute of Local Government Studies, University of Birmingham.

Stoker, G. (1989) 'Local government for a post Fordist society', in Stewart, J. and Stoker, G. (eds), *The Future of Local Government*. Macmillan, Basingstoke.

Taverne, D. (1987) 'Sir Robert Birley Memorial Lecture', Department of Social Sciences, City University, London.

Taylor, I. and Popham, G. (eds) (1989) *An Introduction to Public Sector Management*. Unwin Hyman, London.

Tomkins, C. R. (1987) *Achieving Economy, Efficiency and Effectiveness in the Public Sector*. Kogan Page, London.

Vinten, G. (1983) 'Managing the Health Service. Planning—are promises ever fulfilled?', *Health Visitor*, April, 122–5.

Vinten, G. (1989) 'Charities: regulation, accountability and audit', *Working Paper No. 95*. City University Business School, London.

2

Strategic management in public services
David McKevitt

2.1 Introduction

The 1980s heralded quite dramatic changes in the structure and framework of the United Kingdom's public services. These changes were driven by a number of features, not least the doctrinaire assumptions of government that the State should reduce its public sector expenditure, that the private sector has much to teach the public sector, that efficiency and effectiveness campaigns would reduce the 'waste' in public services provision and that a cultural change was required in the management of the public sector. These assumptions, in many cases unsupported by empirical evidence, constitute part of the environment within which public services managers have had to operate and the new programmes and initiatives in public services delivery pose a significant challenge to the practitioner and researcher. When one disposes of the rhetorical injunctions, how representative is the UK's experience among its European counterparts and does the UK have anything to learn from the experience of other European countries?

A comparative perspective is important as the recent developments in the structure and delivery of public services in the UK have been based on a number of assumptions that may not be valid when tested against the experience of other countries. Similarly, the UK model of legislative change, agency restructuring and performance measurement is as yet unexamined from a strategic perspective that would embrace *both* policy objectives and subsequent programmes of service provision. A number of the chapters in this book critically examine the recent experience in specific service areas, for example, the NHS, the social services and the police. The purpose of this chapter is to evaluate the usefulness of strategic models in the public services environment, to discuss recent research in a number of European countries where a general strategy model has been used to appraise health care service policy and to assess the relevance of private sector models in the public services environment of the 1990s.

The use of strategy models and the search for appropriate strategic frameworks to explore the public sector is an important intellectual and practical exercise. Intellectually, the use of models can have a number of important consequences; they can assist in the *description* of the organization and its environment and help in the formulation of better practice in the management task. The emergent models of strategy, discussed later in this chapter, are based on this premise of organizational learning. *Prescriptive* models, which are represented by the corporate planning models, are intended to be descriptions of the 'rules' of the management tasks and are expressions of the rational, analytic, school of decision-making. The advocates of the application of private sector techniques in public sector management largely base their prescriptions on the classical, rational, strategy models. The research model described in this chapter (Scott, 1963, Open System Model of the Firm) is a general corporate strategy model that does not rely on a prescriptive stance; it attempts to describe the relationship between the policy centre of the organization and its dealings with subunits through the use of a strategic control framework that acknowledges diversity, and the conflicting interests of the coalitions that occur in any large complex organization.

The model is, therefore, applicable to a public sector environment that is itself complex, decentralized and subject to the influence of powerful professional interest groups. The model does not, however, yield prescriptive, 'how-to' results; it is concerned with the description of the general management task in complex organizations.

The research propositions derived from the use of the model may, therefore, assist in the generation of better practice in public sector management *without* inappropriate reliance on private sector techniques. The model mirrors the complexity of the policy-making process and does not attempt to 'explain away' implementation failures as the result of inefficient control systems. It is, therefore, appropriate to the inter-organizational world of the public sector which has to rely on a complex web of relationships that seek to accommodate diversity and uncertainty.

The argument presented in this chapter does not concentrate on the disputed territory that the public sector is different *nor* on the perspective that the public sector has much to learn from the private sector. The central premise of the present argument is that the provision of public services, such as health care or education, give rise to a complex mix of financial, social and administrative arrangements that present particular challenges for government and the public services managers. Such challenges pose important organizational and human questions and a management approach grounded in an accepted and documented corporate strategy model provides a perspective that allows for a serious exploration of the issues involved. The question relates to the organizational and human factors in the provision of a public service, as distinct from the target or ostensible purpose of that service. In relation to control systems, the provision of a public service can be treated by much the same analytical techniques as the activities of a business enterprise, allowing that one is 'not for profit' and the other is 'for profit'. At the back of these analytical techniques is the view of the individual in a social context most appropriately expressed by Rabbi Hillel: 'If I am not for myself, then who is for me? And if I am not for others, then who am I? And if not now, then when?' Management is about people in organizations and about ways of resolving the conflicting claims of individual self-interest and of social conscience. The reductionist approach of the New Right or the grandiose designers of democratic socialism ignore this real managerial challenge. Their vocabulary of efficiency or equality substitute for serious exploration of the management challenge in the provision of public services.

2.2   Strategy and the search for significance

To date, as Willcocks and Harrow observe in the Introduction, the importation of private sector techniques into the public sector have not yielded much in the way of improved performance. The search for emergent models of management may well be more appropriate in the public services environment. This may be sufficient for the academic but how well does it address the needs of the public services manager? Much of the 'classical' literature on strategy and business policy in the 1960s and 1970s was based on the idea of the general manager as implementor, and it was more a product of the machine bureaucracy of the 1950s in the US than a reflection of the organizational reality of the 1990s. A distinctive literature has grown up in the decision process school of strategy (Mintzberg and Waters, 1982) which sees strategy as the result of a myriad of decisions and not the logical outcome of economic and technical rationality. The research was based on the premise that investigation of what managers *actually did* in the strategic direction of their enterprise was more relevant than the search for prescriptive models. The research, which was in part a reaction to the older corporate planning models, led to the description of strategy as plan, perspective, pattern and position, and to Quinn's (1978) description of logical incrementalism to characterize the role of the chief executive in the direction of strategy. The central proposition of this research was that strategy was contingent on *both* the nature of the organization (its size, its value system, its degree of specialization) *and* its external environment (stable, unstable). Thus, strategy could be seen as a continuum with deliberate, planned, strategy as one end and the idea of emergent strategy at the other end. Planned strategy emphasizes direction and control of the organization and it is thus more suited to a predictable external environment. Emergent strategy, including logical incrementalism, puts the emphasis on organizational learning whereby corrective action can be taken to alter strategic direction and to experiment, adapt, and revise the original decision in the context of changing circumstances. The importance of organizational learning in public services settings is further discussed in Chapter 3.

Here, strategy and decision-making are as much influenced by the organization's external environment as they are a reflection of the internal consistency of the organization. That is, strategy is contingent; it is not a 'once-for-all' deterministic plan and the 'classical' assumption of environmental stability (and economic growth) no longer hold. You will, no doubt, see reflections of this uncertainty in the ongoing debate on the utility of private sector 'techniques' in the public services environment. In many ways, as Keynes remarked in the context of political leaders, managers (and academics) may be in thrall to the models and ideas of long defunct theorists!

The decision process school is concerned with the way in which organizations come to formulate strategies and its importance lies in the emphasis it places on the internal characteristics of the enterprise. In the public services context, an emergent strategy would be characterized by experimentation, pilot sites, a focus on organizational learning, all of which is in contrast to the more *dirigiste* model of legislation and 'model contracts' that emphasize stability, predictability and the formulation of universal provisions for the calculation of efficiency in service provision. While the decision process school does, therefore, assist in the search for appropriate intra-organizational structures, it does not help in the sphere of policy formulation in the public sector context where the political process determines the 'rules of the game' on policy formulation. Because of its weakness in looking at the external environment, the decision process school does not help to clarify the nature of strategy formulation in a public services context albeit that it can certainly contribute to our understanding of strategy implementation in such an environment. The Open Systems Model of the Firm described later in this chapter seeks to account for *both* the organizational decision-making process *and* the effect of the environment on this process.

Let us pause to consider one of the primary characteristics of public services provision, especially in the social area such as health and education. A central difficulty in assessing investment in social provision is the uncertainty as to its likely outcome as there are no clear means–ends relationship in such an environment. Do you provide additional kidney dialysis machines or spend more money on pre-natal care? Invest in upgrading pre-school facilities while holding steady on the training budget for 17 year olds? Which investment strategy will yield greater returns? An additional challenge in public provision is the issue of professional compliance whereby producer interests have a dominant voice in the formulation of policy and in the delivery of services.

The influence of professional groups within an organization, especially public services organizations, can have a profound effect on the policy formulation process. The development of welfare state policies, predicated on distributive allocation of social goods, also gave rise to the emergence of powerful professional interest groups, representative of producer interests, such as doctors, teachers and civil servants. In a sense as Klein (1983) remarked 'The Welfare State . . . creates the constituency for its own perpetuation'. The growth of State regulation of the professions was intended to act as a countervailing power on the strength of producer interests and hence to control individual self-interest. The influence of professionals and their regulation by systems of performance measurement was a growth activity in the United Kingdom in the 1980s. Thus, for example, the emergence of the National Curriculum could be viewed as an attempt to control the teachers' influence as much as it was a programme for curriculum development. The creation of a 'market' in the National Health Service seeks to distance the physician in the hospital from the referral pattern of the general practitioner and, hence, to introduce a price signal that would determine consumption of services rather than rely on the traditional referral patterns.

The distrust of professional interests, their regulation and control, led to the emergence of State control based on the simulation of the market model in a public services context. Privatization, contracting out, the competitive tendering for services aim to introduce the desired efficiency into the provision of public services. The reliance on private sector-like incentives and measurement displayed a touching belief in the efficacy of the 'market' mechanism that Adam Smith would not have shared. The drive for micro-efficiency at the level of service delivery presupposed the existence of an environment that mirrored the competitive conditions of the private sector. We shall review later in this chapter the particular distinctiveness of the public policy environment that determines the 'rules of the game' for service provisions and it will be seen that ambiguity, uncertainty and the absence of a clear means–ends relationship characterize investment decisions in social provision. Given such an environment, the reliance on a planned, deliberate, strategy to achieve change was both inappropriate and inadequate to the desired policy objectives sought by government.

The lack of a clear means–ends relationship in public investment decisions requires a strategy that incorporates such uncertainty. The dilemma of the central civil servants in such allocation decisions is a very real one. How to operate appropriate control while preserving appropriate autonomy and judgement at the point of delivery of the service? Eckstein (1964), in his study of the National Health Service, neatly captured this dilemma:

> In a situation which practically precludes fully rational behaviour, planners tried to create a set of conditions in which a high degree of calculated decision-making is possible, even if those conditions are irrelevant to, or impede, the achievement of their goals. They try to maximise the conditions of the formally rational at the expense of substantively rational behaviour; in short, they tend to re-create in the planned system the very faults of the spontaneous system.

A programme of control and regulation that is predicated on such a model will increase the tendency towards centralization of decision-making; such a development was apparent in the United Kingdom throughout the 1980s. The inappropriate use of strategic models can have quite interesting and unintended consequences.

2.2.1   STRATEGY AND THE PUBLIC SERVICES ENVIRONMENT

Just as the classical strategy models underestimate (or ignore) the influence of an unpredictable environment on the organization's capacity to plan its future, so too do the traditional policy implementation models of public sector decision-making fail to capture the ambiguity and uncertainty in the policy-making process. Indeed, the criticism of the bureaucratic model that it is unresponsive, untimely or inefficient heralded much of the private sector 'imports' into the public sector. As March and Olsen (1975) observed: 'Rationality in policy-making is typified by planning, analysis, forecasting and the paraphernalia of decision-making and management science; it is the logic of most recent efforts to improve the quality of decision-making in public policy.'

Such initiatives rested on the assumption that implementation was the key critical component that required improvement. The policy process was seen as unambiguous and certain; the growth of conviction politics in the UK throughout the 1980s was predicated on the belief that policy was clear; it was simply a matter of improving the delivery, i.e. implementation. Much of the Rayner scrutinies and their successors, up to the Next Steps initiatives, were part of the Manichean world view that saw bureaucratic failure as the prime reason for an unresponsive public service. The new theology, therefore, sought salvation in the imputed efficiency of the private sector model; as we have seen, this model is itself an expression of machine bureaucracy where the production function is given, where the task is simple and where the 'means–ends' relationship is clear. The public sector, as Vinten argues in Chapter 1, does not possess such certainty.

The literature on strategic management is strongest in the area of analysis and calculation; it is much less developed in the area of decision-making and implementation. The model of process research, advocated by Pettigrew, seeks to redress this imbalance. The Pettigrew model seeks to link three important components of strategic research—the content, process and context of strategy formulation and implementation in the enterprise and its environment. The research model examines both the rational/objective and the political/subjective aspects of strategy through a longitudinal study of the organization.

The context refers to the 'why' of strategy formulation, the process is the 'how' of the organization's response and the content refers to the 'what' of actual strategy implementation. In a preliminary application of the model (Pettigrew et al., 1988) to changes in the National Health Service, Pettigrew refers to 'closing' the gap between strategic intent and operational implementation as the 'jugular management problem'. In a pilot study of three NHS regions, the authors contend that the model had relevance for the explanation of continuity and change in the management of the regions.

The emphasis on the decision-making process within the organization, coupled in its environment relationship, is echoed in the work of researchers concerned with the duality (and lack of predictability) of the classical policy-implementation model. This model, building on the traditional view of the public services as the instrument of implementation of government policy and unconcerned with its actual content, has been shown to be inadequate, partial and unrepresentative of the reality of public services organizations. March is a leading proponent of the 'non-rational' school of policy-making, and his observations on the process of policy-making are worth repeating:

> Policies are frequently ambiguous; but their ambiguities are less a result of the deficiencies in policy makers than a natural consequence of gaining necessary support for the policies, and of changing preferences over time. Conflict of interest is not just a property of the relations between policy makers on the one hand and administrators on the other; it is a general feature of policy negotiation and bureaucratic life.
>
> (Baier *et al.*, 1986)

The focus on implementation of policy- and decision-making in an uncertain environment requires a strategy of control that will take account of this uncertainty. The term 'judgemental strategy' has been used by Thompson to define decisions where cause–effect relationships are uncertain but where outcome preferences are clear. Thompson (1967) goes on to assert that 'the more numerous the areas in which the organization must rely on the judgemental decision strategy, the larger the dominant coalition'. Thompson's work was concerned with large complex organizations and their decision processes; the organization was conceptualized as 'an open system, indeterminate and faced with uncertainty, but subject to criteria of rationality and hence needing certainty'. Daft (1983) extended Thompson's decision matrix to show how a decision depends upon goal consensus (the ends) and technical knowledge (the means); his contingency framework is shown as Fig. 2.1. It will be apparent that Cell 1 is synonymous with the rational command–control activity of the corporate planning model while Cell 2 looks to the more problematic policy-implementation school represented by March. Cells 3 and 4 are representative of the decision process school and can be linked to the incremental, emergent, model of strategy formulation.

If uncertainty and ambiguity characterize both the ends *and* means of public services provision, then how do we describe the strategic management task in such an environment?

The next section outlines the application of a corporate strategy model to the control of publicly funded health care in a number of European countries. The research addresses the uncertainty of public provision and the challenge of control that issues from such uncertainty. It advocates that the management of public services provision be seen as part of a wider policy-implementation agenda that is consistent with the complexity of public services organizations.

2.3 Control of national health care strategies

The post-1989 reforms in the NHS demonstrate the continuing search for political solutions to economic and managerial problems. The setting up of quasi-

GOAL CONSENSUS

	High	Low
High	1 Individual: 　Rational approach, 　computation Organization: 　Management science	2 Individual: 　Bargaining, 　coalition formation Organization: 　Carnegie model
Low	3 Individual: 　Judgement, trial and error Organization: 　Incremental decision process model	4 Individual: 　Bargaining and judgement, 　inspiration and imitation Organization: 　Carnegie and incremental decision 　process models, evolving to 　garbage can models

Figure 2.1   A contingency framework
(Based on Daft, 1983.)

markets with general practitioners and hospital trusts, as independent decision makers, is predicated on removing the decision to purchase medical care from the providers of such care and, it is argued, thereby create competition between providers and improve the overall efficiency of the system. The fact that the 'contracts' between general practitioners and hospital trusts will not be actionable in the courts makes one wonder whether the quasi-market model will actually produce the intended results. The working out of the recent NHS reforms echoes quite clearly March's comments on ambiguities in the policy process. To what end are the NHS 'reforms' being pursued? The search for efficiency and value-for-money is a valid one in any area of public spending; yet if policy on health care provision extends no further than technical solutions, how likely is it that the overall system will meet its objectives and, indeed, how clear are these objectives?

Control of health costs is high on the agenda for debate in every modern country. The specific characteristics of the debate vary from country to country and are related to the economic circumstances of the time, the organizational framework for the delivery of health services, the relative contribution of public and private revenues for health service provision and the role of the State in the organization of the service. Solutions advanced range from the strategic—a reduction in the health care system—to structural change, greater private provision of health services, through to operational improvements such as greater efficiency in the delivery of health services. At the core of health expenditures and the State's attempt to control their growth is the assumption that the money is being properly managed and that it is effective in achieving its objectives. Underlying this assumption is the concern that 'proper control' is difficult to achieve and that, in some manner, the money spent is not being used to best effect. The evaluation of effectiveness can take a number of forms. First, that there is effective financial control so that the money is spent and accounted for in accordance with legislative or regulatory policy. Second, that the money is used in a manner supportive of the policy of the legislature or control department to achieve specific objectives; for example, that hospital expenditures are properly managed so as to contain overall costs and allow for some re-allocation to other areas of the health care system such as primary and community care. Third, and most intractable, that the money is not being diverted or captured by health care workers (through wage increases or increasing sophistication of equipment) to the detriment of patient care expenditure.

Recent research in the control of European systems of health care strategies examined the management model utilized in three countries (Sweden, the Netherlands and Ireland) for evidence of convergence in management practice (McKevitt, 1990). The research used the corporate strategy model—An Open Systems Model of the Firm—developed by Bruce Scott in the Harvard Business School. The model asserts that:

1 any organization relates to its environment via a strategy for advancing its interests as it perceives these interests;
2 the interests of the various subunits of an organization often differ from those of the organization as a whole; and
3 thus the central or general headquarters of the organization must bring continuous influence to bear on the subunits in order to motivate them to act in conformity with the general or shared interests of the organization.

Scott went on to note that the most important means of influence are the ability to allocate resources, to establish and alter organizational structures, to measure and reward performance and to formulate policy limits or 'rules of the game'.

The Open Systems Model has been applied by McArthur and Scott (1969) to a study of post-war planning in France whose economic performance attracted critical attention from the United States in the 1950s and 1960s. In their assessment of French economic planning, McArthur and Scott paid particular attention to the role of central government in their use of the 'means of influence' available for national economic planning. While they concluded that the beneficial role of government was overestimated (because of post-war demand) the use of the model demonstrated the validity of assessing national policies using a corporate strategy model. Its use in the assessment of national health care systems derived from the observation that in studies of comparative health care 'there is usually no clear model for analysis, even in those studies that in other respects could be classified as analytical . . . Models and theories are seldom dealt with' (van Atteveld *et al.*, 1987). In the United Kingdom, the study of health care is primarily economic in its orientation or is prompted by the social policy analysis developed by Abel-Smith (1984). The appraisal of health care systems using a corporate policy model allows one to examine *both* the national policy process *and* its implementation from a perspective that acknowledges organizational diversity and the conflicting values of the main professional groupings within the system. That is, the model accepts the validity of different strategies that are themselves dependent on economic, social or political contexts.

The use of a corporate strategy model to examine public management issues allowed the formulation of research propositions that derived from general management and were not predicated on the traditional view of the public service as a different environment. Thus, the model and propositions did not deal with the implied uniqueness of the public sector enterprise but sought, instead, to assess the relevance of a general strategy model to the concerns of public sector managers. These concerns are rooted in the practical issue of how can one assess the investment decision in health care and ensure compliance between overall policy and its implementation in practice.

The research (McKevitt, 1990) examined the national health care policies of Sweden, the Netherlands and Ireland from a strategic perspective to determine whether the management of their acute hospital systems formed part of a coherent and integrated national health case strategy. Historically, and world-wide, hospitals are the most cost intensive part of the health care delivery system and most countries have failed in their attempts to curtail expenditures in this area. Using the Open System Model of the Firm, hospitals were seen as a subunit of the overall national health care system and government policies (the 'general headquarters') were assessed for coherence and consistency between the hospital system and other parts of the national health care structure. Thus, the 'mission' or strategy was assessed at national level *prior* to a detailed examination at the hospital level. Given that health care control is a European-wide challenge for government, the different national strategies were evaluated for evidence of convergence in management practice. The research framework assumed that successful European economies were likely to adopt broadly similar strategic frameworks, even if their operational management systems differed.

Control in health care yields similar challenges to politicians, civil servants and health care professionals under different financing systems for service delivery. Control, *per se*, is rectificatory and not restorative; that is, it is about the maintenance of norms, the following of patterns and the rules once these have been laid down. Ireland, unlike Sweden and the Netherlands, did not adapt to the challenge of control largely because its legislative framework did not contain any explicit strategy, nor were the performance of health service professionals subject to any sustained scrutiny. The Swedish and Dutch systems, in contrast, which differ quite markedly in their financial support for health care, share common features in their concern for explicitness in legislation, their attendance to the sovereign importance of measurement and information systems and in their willingness to adapt and modify their control systems to refocus their investment decision. It is clear that legislation provides the basic control framework for investment decisions in health care provision ('the rules of the game') and that such frameworks need to be adapted and modified in the context of changing environmental conditions.

The theme of adaptation of legislative control frameworks to suit emergent environmental conditions is quite central to the development of appropriate strategic control at the national level. Thus, for example, the 'greying' of the population and the objective of care-in-the-community impose quite specific policy objectives for both hospital usage and the framework for service delivery. Both Sweden and the Netherlands, in their planning for health care in the year 2000, have looked to divert resources from the hospital sector to other parts of the health care system. Their legislative frameworks are quite explicit in this regard and hence operational control and the measurement system are predicated on the implementation of such policy. There is in the public policy process in these countries an attempt to adapt strategy in the light of changing circumstances. The process is emergent and dependent on collective expression of policy through legislative change. It seeks to adapt to the decision environment of the public sector (macro level) rather than to impose additional pressure on the organization to achieve change at the micro level.

Thus, for example, both Sweden and the Netherlands have developed and modified their legislative frameworks to incorporate strategic policy at the heart of the control framework. In this regard, they have sought to address the ambiguity identified by March in the policy-formulation process. While their legislative frameworks differs greatly—Sweden has a prescriptive legislation outlining its health care strategy, while the Netherlands has evolved a complex series of very detailed regulatory provisions—both countries have made quite explicit strategic choices.

A central proposition of the research was that control of health care required a clearly specified 'mission' or strategy whereby operational management could align investment decisions to clearly articulated programme objectives. Mission is an important concept in the analysis of social expenditure programmes and it can be viewed as similar to corporate strategy which is a set of objectives against which progress in the desired direction may be measured and a timed series of conditional moves for deploying skills and resources with a view of obtaining one's objectives. The term 'mission' embraces the legislative basis for health care policy, government decisions on service provision and the response of the civil service in the implementation of the policies.

The most important outcome of the research was that investment in health care should be regarded as a decision which requires a clear strategic focus, supported through consistent action on the part of the administrative 'centre' and accompanied by consistent use of the means of influence available to the state. The political decision to invest in the Irish health care services, without clear legislative objectives, severely restricted the State's capacity to control its investment decision. A producer-orientated system resulted and there was no impetus to clarify health care objectives. In the UK the situation is reversed; lacking any updating or revision of its 1946 strategic framework, the emphasis has been on administrative and managerial reform, while environmental and economic conditions have rendered the original framework inappropriate. Similarly, the UK 'policy' process was based on conviction politics, in contrast to the quite lengthy process of research, debate and review of strategic change in other European countries. A central feature of successful strategy is consistency of objectives *over time*; the persistent alterations and change to UK administrative structures in the health care area signal an organization that has no clear consistent policy.

2.4   The United Kingdom: a comparative analysis

The most striking difference in assessing the UK experience in health care strategy (and indeed in much of the education initiatives) with other European countries is that management reforms in the UK have concentrated on what, in the strategic literature, are business level or operational changes. That is, the emphasis has been on the production function rather than on the strategic level. Figure 2.2 depicts the generally accepted division of strategy in the private

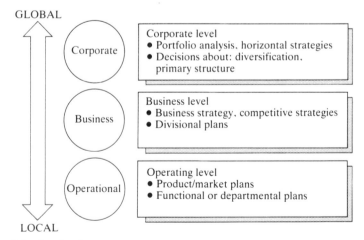

Figure 2.2   Levels of strategy
(Adapted from Unit 1, *Strategic Management*, Open University, 1989.)

sector. European countries such as Sweden, the Netherlands and Finland, in assessing the challenge of health care management and control, have revisited and revised the basic strategic questions that underlie health care provision. Who is to benefit, at what cost, and with what safeguards for the disadvantaged in society? The UK strategy proposals for the health service are contained in the 1946 Health Act which outline the basic framework of the welfare state provision in health care. All subsequent legislation, from a strategic perspective, is concerned with operational improvements in management or the administrative machinery for delivery of care. It is hardly surprising that the 'debate' in the United Kingdom has been restricted to the efficiency arena when the policy process has been replaced by the re-assertion of conviction politics.

In terms of the research model described in this chapter, the State (as 'general headquarters') has been selective in its application and use of the means of influence open to it. Thus, there have been many initiatives in the use of organizational structures, the measurement function, and, to some degree, the use of resource allocation models (RAWP). What distinguishes the United Kingdom from most other European countries is the absence of any use of the means of influence central to strategic direction and control—'the formulation of policy limits or "rules of the game"'. The concentration on budgets, operational improvements and information technology are important initiatives, yet they do not, in strategic terms, constitute a clear mission or strategy. Indeed, in a real sense such initiatives do not address the second question posed by Rabbi Hillel: 'If I am not for others, then who am I?' Undue emphasis on the 'cost' of a service and the form of the accounting procedures can lead to what Hopwood and Tomkins (1984) have described as the 'routinisation of concern' with plans becoming more important than planning, budgets more than the process of budgeting and costing more than the ascertainment of costs.

We have already seen that uncertainty and ambiguity characterize much of the public service investment decision, especially in the area of social provision where there are few 'means–ends' relationships. Another common feature of the public service is professional dominance of the policy process, whereby the dominant coalition tend to 'capture' the basic premises of the policy-formulation phase. While the 1980s in the UK witnessed quite a degree of government-led intervention in the self-regulation of professions, the policy process itself was still largely predicated on professional assumptions. Thus, for example, hospital-based medicine still dominates the health care model despite its expense and, in many cases, the lack of evidence that a hospital-based system actually results in better health care (Blaney, 1983).

The Galbrathian idea of the State as a 'countervailing' influence on dominant coalitions (economic or professional) has little effect if the State does not clarify the 'rules of the game', i.e. revise its strategy. Weatherill's (1989) concept of legislative clarity is relevant here, as the evidence of the present research supports the argument that clarity in the policy process is achieved by clear legislative expression of aims, i.e. strategy.

In the United States, which has a largely private insurance-based health care system, there is an interesting example of State regulation transferring to the private sector. The development of cost containment programmes found a coalition of parties, including business, federal and State government, that were concerned with the escalation of health spending. The Diagnostic Related Groupings (DRG) model for reimbursement of hospital costs was originally designed to control State Medicare patients and it is now utilized by private insurers to control their hospital costs. While the DRG model has not yielded as much benefit as its proponents hoped, it is an example of the transfer of regulation that can occur between the public and private health care markets. It is also an example of the use of appropriate techniques for control that are soundly based on the actual role of the State rather than on some ideal prescriptions of efficiency. The use of the cost containment programmes derived from a more general perception of the State's rising health bill rather than from a conviction that efficiency *per se* was desirable.

The need for legislative expression of policy objectives (strategy) is the same whether or not the State adopts a majority or minority stake in the provision of a public service such as health care. The *manner* in which the State formulates its legislative statement of strategy may be compared to the distinction in the strategic literature between deliberate or emergent strategy. The former is more akin to the notion of strategic planning and is predicated on clear intention/aims within a predictable environment. An emergent strategy, in contrast, is the result of decisions that seek to align the organization with the demands and challenges of its external environment. Such a strategy emphasizes learning and organizational design, and finds expression in legislative change that is based on the bargaining model of policy formulation.

An important additional feature of strategic control is the structuring of the organization so that it is best positioned to carry out its objectives. The delivery of health care is, by its nature, a decentralized activity requiring decisions as to allocation of resources and modes of treatment at the point of service. While recent UK initiatives emphasize the delegation of responsibility to self-governing hospital trusts, the UK management model, in a European perspective, is a highly centralized one. Centralization of decision making in commercial enterprises is found where either the organization is entrepreneurial, or where the production task is a simple one and the environment is stable. None of these structural or service characteristics obtains in the health care system, yet the management model applied in the NHS presupposes the presence of these conditions.

The research model incorporates the imperative of decentralization within agreed policy limits or 'rules of the game'. In a European context, the UK model of high centralization of decision making runs counter to the strategic initiatives of other European countries and to the structural characteristics of the health care system. In policy terms, the activities of an enterprise cannot be appraised without a clear statement of its strategy. The UK lacks such an expression of its legislative strategy in health care that takes account of the complexity of public services management, the observed phenomenon of disparity in resource usage between different socio-economic groups (Le Grand, 1982) and the requirements for external scrutiny of the performance of professional groups within the delivery system. In strategic terms there is a 'lack of fit' between the challenge of the environment and the capacity of the organization to respond to changing environmental conditions.

2.5   Conclusion

The emergence of 'public' management as a distinct area of research is still in its early stages. The debate on the 'difference' between the public and private sector obscures quite a degree of common ground. The management of financial, human and technical resources draws quite heavily on a common core of skills, regardless of which sector of the economy the enterprise resides. Indeed, the claims for public services distinctiveness can sometimes appear to be rationaliz-ation or special pleading, predicated on an outdated policy-implementation dichotomy that fails to take account of the complexity of modern social econo-mies and inter-organizational networks. In large measure, the distinctiveness argument can also rest on an outdated view of the strategic literature where classical command—control models and rational decision-making purported to describe organizational reality.

The difference between public and private models may themselves be lessening as new evidence and research is accumulated. We are aware that models and theories are appoximations of real life and embedded in them are the values and choices of their designers. Quite often, however, such values and choices are not made explicit. Argyris puts the case succinctly:

> the criteria (for effectiveness) are a matter of personal choice, and personal choice, in turn, is related to governing values of the actors or of the organization. Theories of control must therefore make explicit the governing values which the actions are intended to satisfy.
>
> (Argyris, 1987)

Without the clear statement of governing values, the models themselves may mislead the practitioner as, for example, command—control strategy models mislead the public services manager into believing that implementation is the primary determinant of effectiveness. Such a view ignores the policy level where ambiguity and trade-offs may render the policy itself ineffectual, however efficient its implementation. The idea of public good as the end of organizational activity in the public sector is itself a conception open to much debate and conflict as it is dependent for its expression on the interplay of social, political and economic forces that can vary from country to country. Brunsson (1989), in a review of politics within and between public organizations, puts the case as follows:

> Every organization (then) has to reflect in itself the inconsistencies in the conception of the public good, becoming more self-sufficient and possessing greater autonomous legitimacy . . . According to this hypothesis, politics at the organizational level could be expected to be particularly strong in countries such as Scandinavia and West Germany, where state ownership, national planning and capitalistic theory are particularly weak.

A further test of strategy is whether it is 'appropriate, feasible and suitable'. In respect of recent UK initiatives we have seen that their primary impact is at the operational or business unit level, with their central objective the improvement of implementation and delivery. In this respect, such initiatives can hardly be described as strategic. Even allowing for the difficulty in comparing public and private sector environments, it is evident that the uncertain decision environment of public policy and implementation requires a strategy that is appropriate to its domain. The command-control framework of recent UK legislation, the increasing centralization of authority, the neglect of the experience of other European countries combine to question the feasibility and suitability of the UK model. The policy process, predicated in the strategic literature as one of 'search, screening and decision', has been co-opted to one of conviction politics where the end is given, and search is restricted to the operational and implementation domain. Such a process is neither strategic nor representative of recent European experience. It places the practitioner at a disadvantage as the core of strategy is the continuous, iterative, process of evaluation and review of policy objectives. When the policy objectives are not subject to such scrutiny, the manager (at whatever level in the organization) is confined to tactical, day-to-day concerns. The vocabulary of efficiency has substituted for the search for effectiveness.

References

Abel-Smith, B. (1984) *Cost-Containment in Health Care: A Study of Twelve European Countries*. Bedford Square Press, London.

Argyris, C. (1987) 'Review essay: first-and-second-order errors in managing strategic change: the role of organisational defensive routines', in Pettigrew, A. (ed.), *The Management of Strategic Change*. Blackwell, Oxford, pp. 342–51.

Baier, V., March, J. G. and Saetern, H. (1986) 'Implementation and ambiguity', *Scandinavian Journal of Management Studies*, May, 197–212.

Blaney, R. (1983) 'Applications of evaluations in acute hospital care', in Holland, W. (ed.), *Evaluation of Health Care*. Oxford University Press, Oxford, pp. 93–107.

Brunsson, N. (1989) *The Organization of Hypocrisy*. Wiley, Chichester.

Daft, R. (1983) *Organisational Theory and Design*. West Publishing, St. Paul.

Eckstein, H. (1964) *The English Health Service*. Harvard University Press, Boston.

Hopwood, A. and Tomkins, C. (1984) *Issues in Public Sector Accounting*. Allan, London.

Klein, R. (1983) *The Politics of the National Health Service*. Longman, London.

Le Grand, R. (1982) *The Strategy of Equality*. Allen Unwin, London.

McArthur, J. H. and Scott, B. R. (1969) *Industrial Planning in France*. Harvard University Press, Boston.

McKevitt, D. (1990) *Health Care Policy in Ireland*. Hibernian University Press, Cork.

March, J. G. and Olsen, J. P. (1975) 'The uncertainty of the past: organisational learning under ambiguity', *European Journal of Political Research*, 3, 147–71.

Mintzberg, H. and Waters, J. A. (1982) 'Tracking strategy in an entrepreneurial firm', *Academy of Management Journal*, 465–99.

Pettigrew, A., McKee, L. and Ferlie, E. (1988) 'Understanding change in the NHS', *Public Administration*, 66, 297–317.

Quinn, J. B. (1978) 'Strategic change: logical incrementalism', *Sloan Management Review*, Fall, 7–21.

Scott, B. R. (1963) *An Open System Model of the Firm*. Unpublished DBA, Harvard University.

Thompson, J. D. (1967) *Organisations in Action*. McGraw-Hill, New York.

Van Atteveld, L., Broeders, C. and Lupre, R. (1987) 'International comparative research in health care', *Health Policy*, 18, 105–36.

Weatherill, S. (1989) 'Buying special police services', *Public Law*, Spring, 106–27.

3

Management, innovation and organizational learning

Jenny Harrow and Leslie Willcocks

3.1 Introduction

The debate on the extent to which public services managers can and should learn from private sector managers' principles and practices gathered pace in the 1980s. Major sources of its stimulation included central government sponsorship of private sector advice; for example, the Rayner Scrutinies into the civil service, the Griffiths Report on the National Health Service, and the widespread use of externally based management consultants across public services organizations. Haigh and Morris (1990a,b) describe a pattern of public services transformation in this period, when freedom from profit-based motives in public organizations was seen as an inherent problem, and the solution was a replacement of an administrative culture by a managerial culture derived from private sector decision-making frameworks. This has seen in public services the pursuance, particularly by central government, of what Gunn (1988) has called the 'Five E's' of economy, efficiency, effectiveness, excellence and enterprise, new forms of 'managerialism', structure, performance indicators and financial management. The literature has sought to variously build upon these developments (e.g. Audit Commission, 1988; Exley, 1989; Flynn, 1988; Jackson, 1988) or oppose or qualify them (e.g. Faulkner, 1990; Flynn, 1990a; Gunn, 1988; Metcalfe and Richards, 1987; Minogue, 1983; Painter, 1991; Stewart and Ranson, 1988).

Strongly placed support for the view that private sector managerial practice deserves replication in public services remains widespread. The 1990 study of Management and Leadership in NHS Trusts, by Coopers and Lybrand Deloitte for the Department of Health:

> . . . looked for private sector models capable of wider application . . . (since) . . . the changes involved are so major and so new that there is no model within the health sector that can be used as a basis to define the skills required to create and manage the change.

While recognizing that the Trusts 'must be able to match the best practice criteria identified in all sectors', interestingly this study draws its examples

50

only from private sector-style applications. Among academic commentators and advisers, however, there is growing unease regarding the assumptions that unidirectional learning, predicated on the superiority of private sector behaviour and practice, is appropriate for public services managers working in periods of major uncertainty (e.g. Barrett and McMahon, 1990; Kingdom, 1990; Pollitt, 1990). A series of concerns therefore arise in relation to the limits to learning from private sector management models by public services managers and organizations. At one level, this relates to the possibility, minimally discussed, that poor management practices in some areas might be imported during this one-way learning transference. This is despite the widespread acceptance of the research findings of Handy (1987) and Constable and McCormick (1987) concerning the neglect by the UK private sector of management development and training; and growing criticism of, and dissatisfaction with what has been referred to as 'rational' or 'traditional' management models dominating private sector practice (Barham et al., 1988; Kanter, 1983; Peters and Waterman, 1982).

A related concern is extent of transferability of managerial practices across and between organizations, given the potential for organizational variation both within and between public services organizations (see Introduction). Thus, some private 'solutions' may be inappropriate in some public services. More generously, they may not provide these solutions within the expected—and demanded—time scales; and where private sector prescriptions have worked in one public services organization they may not in another, or even in another section of a large organization.

Most importantly, at a more general level, the possibility must be considered that in modelling themselves—whether forced or by personal preference—on believed private sector managerial styles, some public services managers have '. . . over-identified with what may be seen as a primitive form of management —aggressive, domineering, short term delivery oriented' (Willcocks and Harrow, 1991). The 'can do' model of management might, for example, be seen as stemming from a misunderstanding about best practice in private sector managerial behaviour. Further, where public services managers have emulated private sector practice, this has tended to result in identification with traditional forms of management, borrowed from manufacturing rather than service organizations; ironically, increasingly regarded as inappropriate for managing in some private sector environments (see, for example, Carlzon, 1989; Kanter, 1989; Kilmann, 1989; Lessem, 1990).

This chapter, in pursuance of the 'rediscovery' theme, therefore challenges the notion of the continuing validity and utility of unqualified transfer of private sector management practices into public services management settings. Four aspects in public services management which particularly exemplify the trend to pattern managerial behaviour on private sector experience are examined— those of managing innovation, consumerism, entrepreneurialism and managing risk. Central notions concerning organizational learning specifically derived from public services experience and know-how are then assessed, as against the continual borrowing of organizational learning models derived also from private sector organization experience. In support of the learning theme the chapter utilizes findings from research work with public service managers carried out by the authors during 1990 and 1991. Finally, ways forward on learning in public services management are then detailed. As a prelude to this, however, and to begin the argument, the nature of innovation, and management initiatives in selected UK public services, are examined.

3.2   Applying innovation theory to public services management initiatives

The range of public services management initiatives undertaken during the 1980s and 1990s have been predominantly private sector experience driven. They reflect a borrowing of a private sector ethos, with particular emphasis on an increasing organizational focus on objectives and the application of output-based performance measures; the speedy harnessing of new technologies; the reorientation of professionals as managers; and the achievement of cost-effectiveness, mainly through restricting resources consumed rather than maximizing outputs (Harrow and Willcocks, 1990a; Hood, 1991). One small, but illustrative, example of the continued received wisdom that 'private is preferred' may be seen in the awards for the RIPA/Hay Prizes for Managerial Innovation in the Public Sector, in 1990, on the theme of 'Overcoming skills shortages in the public sector'. Here, Brighton Health Authority's commended entry—a creation of a staff benefits package (including priority outpatient appointments and treatment, free eye tests, discounts on spectacles and free chiropody)—was described by the judges as '. . . an inexpensive, popular and good example of something the private sector does often but that is rarely seen in the public sector and certainly not in the NHS' (RIPA Report, 1990).

Innovation from within the public services, and particularly that based on professionally developed practices, may exist and be sought but gives the innovators a far lower managerial profile. In fact the tendency among practising managers, not surprisingly, has been to follow the lead established in the larger scale initiatives. In survey work carried out on innovation practice in public service organizations, the authors investigated the question: 'What would count as innovation in your organization and why?' (see Willcocks and Harrow, 1991). The large majority of respondents cited measures of believed cost saving or those which simply contrasted with current working practices, as by implication, these would be preferred:

   . . . anything that challenges conventional modes of working (NHS);

   . . . more decisions per dollar . . . (District Council);

... providing the same—if not higher—levels of service with less financial resources ... (The authority) believes in Value for Money which many of us interpret as Something For Nothing ... (County Council);

A flexible approach to a formerly rigid cultural problem ... or income generation of any sort (NHS).

The general approach is observable in the most celebrated case, the Financial Management Initiative (FMI) at central government level. What began in some cases as an initiative—the action of taking the first steps, or the lead—however, tended to become recognized as something grander—an 'innovation', with legislation ensuring that what was experimental became mandatory management practice. In local government, two examples of this shift are the moves on compulsory tendering by local authorities and the delegation of financial management to schools. A further example has been the growth of the concept of the internal markets within public services organizations, as differing sections become buyers and sellers or purchasers and providers, in the health service, and civil service. Where the term initiative has been retained, this seems to be related to those less publicized managerial efforts, without private sector comparisons, such as those relating to health service and local authority joint working in community services (McNaught, 1991).

More recent developments within the civil service, the 'Next Steps' project, had the aim of increasing the number of freestanding executive agencies within government departmental frameworks—clearly a businessization practice, with the assumption that such developments enable the creation (and achievement) of firm objectives for these organizations, leading to improved performance. In such settings it is axiomatic to some that the resulting freeing up and innovation opportunity will be enjoyable. Kemp (1990), as project manager for 'Next Steps', considered that 'in terms of fun, the place to be is the agency. There people have the opportunity to develop new services, be innovative, and give an expert service to the public.'

It is noticeable that the term 'initiative' carries with it connotations of acceptable, even exemplary practice; as does the wider concept of innovation, with its conceptual links with societal and organizational progress. The alternative but not equivalent term 'experiment', also applicable to the importation of some private sector management approaches into public service settings yet carrying the connotation that things may go wrong as well as right, seems not to have been used. Given the linkage of the concepts of innovation (an idea, practice or object, perceived as new by individuals or organizations) and initiative (a one-off 'try-out' of that idea, in full or part), it is helpful to review innovation theory as the basis for considering some current public services initiatives which derive from private sector management practice. Rogers and Kim (1985) are helpful in identifying five attributes of innovations which affect adoption rates, namely their:

- relative advantage (over preceding practices)
- compatibility (with potential adopters' needs and values)
- complexity
- trialability (testing possible on a limited basis)
- observability (results visible to others).

They argue that innovations with the greater utility—that is, having greater advantage, compatibility, trialability and observability, as well as less complexity—are more readily and rapidly adoptable than others. In the context of public services innovation based on private sector practice, however, the recognition of these important attributes has not been critical in explaining adoption. In the particular case of 'compatibility', adoption of innovation has often been encouraged if it calls into question those very existing values of the organization and would-be adopters. This is the reason for the view that innovatory practice in public services is more likely to reflect what has hitherto not been done than to represent a building in past practice. One outcome of this might be a less than successful innovation; for example, and interestingly, the FMI has been accompanied by considerable internal departmental efforts to impose its own agendas on its development and impacts (Richards, 1988). Similar stakeholder responses were observable in the case of the NHS White Paper of April 1989.

Some key innovations such as competitive tendering for local authority services or health services have not been subject to extensive trialability over time, in the sense of testing, but have been held to be successful in the sense of money saving. However, those savings have related to the direct costs of providing services; yet, as Flynn (1990b) stresses, such competition 'also introduces new indirect costs . . . with the "buyer" side of the organization employing people to specify, supervise, monitor and police the contracts'. In this area, however, the choices over innovation are curtailed by, for example, legislation requiring local authorities to achieve a phased introduction of competitive tendering for defined services, and government circulars setting out contracting requirements in health services work. Parker and Hartley (1990) note that the Local Government Act 1988 requires that nearly 2000 local government service contracts, with a value of approximately £2.7 billion, are subjected to compulsory competitive tendering. The speed with which such initiatives have reached the status of innovations, to be compulsorily introduced, ironically raises questions about the ability of the private sector to make adequate response. Parker and Hartley, for example, emphasizing issues of both speed and scale, ask '. . . is there sufficient capacity amongst private cleansing firms to compete effectively for all contracts?' Comparable problems in the personal social services are highlighted by Flynn (1990b): 'when Griffiths is implemented, if community care organisations are supposed to provide alternatives . . . someone will have to set them up, which may imply a "business development" role . . . for social services departments'. Thus, the imposition of one type of innovation externally requires the mastering of yet another; although as Flynn also implies the relevant public services may have within them the internal expertise to cope: '. . . this activity . . . (business development) . . . used to be known as "community development"'.

In relation to observability, the progress of the FMI has been called into question, with increasing tension identified between the introduction of new management systems and the overriding concern to control public spending. Beeton and Collins (1988, p. 43) are specific:

> There is a reluctance to decentralise, if giving departments more authority might threaten tight control of the 'nominal' economy and an unwillingness to invest strategically in better management approaches—so the financial management initiative has been done on the cheap.

The attributes of complexity, trialability and observability come strikingly together in the example of the rush to implement IT designed to provide management information crucially supporting the NHS general managers appointed following the Griffiths proposals. Willcocks and Mark (1988a,b) identify major implementation problems as in part arising from the IT programmmes being treated as 'initiatives' rather than as evolutionary processes growing with the organization. Pressures have been placed on managers to meet short-term targets, producing inappropriate time scales for implementation, and leaving dissatisfied and sceptical clienteles. None of this supports successful innovation. Furthermore the implementation of information systems for managerial purposes is highly dependent on data collection by interest groups spread throughout policy, management and service domains (see Introduction and Chapter 7).

The issue of 'compatibility' also arises. People who collect data of little use to themselves, but which might serve managerial purposes in assessing their performances, are unlikely to have a high degree of commitment to IT implementation. A more politically aligned approach to IT design might be needed. Anderson and Sims (1990), establishing public spending on IT as substantial— some £2 billion by central government and £650 million by local government —provide reinforcement for this view, describing 'unhappy experiences' as stemming not from technology inadequacy but 'the imposition of unrealistic time scales, inadequate planning and lack of clear objectives'. Furthermore, Willcocks and Mark's call for a consolidation period here highlights the importance of observability of innovation as a precursor to further widespread innovation adoption.

Generally, public service innovations that follow from private sector practice in emphasizing money saving, and thus overall efficiency, are those that look to the first attribute—the 'relative advantage' for widespread adoption. Such innovations have value for those public services managers designated as such, because association with them shows evidence of their willingness to get to grips with value-for-money issues. In some cases, their adoption may have consequences that outweigh the visible resulting savings, giving rise to situations with which private businesses would not have to reckon. For example, savings obtained through improvement of central government purchasing arrangements in 1986/87 were £286 million, with the progress report on government purchasing identifying targets of £388 million for 1987/88 and £447 million for 1988/89 (Central Purchasing Unit, 1987). However, Beeton and Collins speculate that competitive purchasing policies, having worsened home unemployment (with contract awards to foreign firms), have led to increased social security spending by a margin large enough to outweigh equipment cost savings (Beeton and Collins, 1988, p. 41).

The 'relative advantage' and 'compatibility' criteria can be applied also to the devolution of management to school levels. It is arguable whether all head teachers (as with other professionals, like doctors) wish to, can and will manage their establishments in the ways required. In some areas, the re-emergence of posts that are in essence, if not in title, those of school bursars may suggest that some head teachers seek to exit from their new managerialist guise. Furthermore, the type of training offered them—mainly on running budgets and keeping down costs—reveals that the 'impoverished concept of management' flowing from the efficiency strategy in central government, and its concomitant weaknesses as identified by Metcalfe and Richards (1990), also have further parallels at local government level (Burns, 1987). As will be discussed below, on these two innovation criteria doubts can also be raised on the importation into public services management of concepts of consumerism, entrepreneurialism and risk.

Yet the language of innovation theory is near-universally one which praises the early adopter of innovation, as against the sceptics who wait and see. Danhof (1949), focusing on the firm, identifies four types of potential behaviour: innovators (first to achieve); initiators (following soon after); fabians (adopting innovations only after widespread recognition of their utility); and drones (last to adopt innovations). This tone is repeated by Rogers (1962), whose final category of innovation adopter is designated a 'laggard'. This pro-innovation stance is the norm rather than the exception in the major literature on innovation diffusion. There the warning of Rogers and Kim (1985) in relation to the public sector, that it should not be assumed that the diffusion and adoption of all innovations are necessarily desirable, seems singularly disregarded.

It is with the instability of results of innovation that those public services managers seeking sanction for their wariness of management initiatives *per se* may find support. Briefly, what occurs in one situation does not occur in another; and attempts to transfer an innovation from one context to another may founder. This may occur within as well across organizations, as discussed by Holtham (1986) in examining managerial practices introduced in the London Borough of Hammersmith and Fulham during the 1980s, and considering that many such practices 'would not survive transplantation across departments'. Circumspection may yet become recognized as a positive public services management attribute.

Calling for experimentation rather than across-the-board innovation based on fast and limited judgements, may of course be seen as classic public services management stalling in the face of the inevitable. Yet, ironically, it may have been in part the readiness of those managers to respond positively to externally directed innovation that has caused public services difficulties. Easterby-Smith (1987), for example, reviewing the role of corporate strategy in pursuing innovation in higher education, notes that, with the emphasis on inter-institutional competition, 'despite some ritual complaints, institutions have willingly buckled down to the challenge'. In practice he argues for wariness among those encouraged to accept 'the copying of management structures and systems that are believed to be commonplace in industry'. Many such systems, he argues, are actually fraught with difficulty when used in industry, and may be subject to regular rethinking, as evidence of system failure arises.

In higher education, but most importantly in the health service, the development of the concept of the internal market seems to have caught the imagination of many managers. Here, however, the argument for caution has been made. Bowden (1989), for example, commenting on media disclosure of forthcoming health service review proposals on NHS internal markets, was reported as stating 'we do need experiments. There is no real evidence that they are going to work and we need to work that through.' This practitioner view may now be seen as reinforced by the assessment of Burke and Goddard (1990) that in health service contexts the imposition of internal markets may represent 'the road to inefficiency'. Their assessment focuses on the increased opportunity for managerial and clinical opportunistic behaviour, itself incurring costs; the changing and expensive managerial burdens, requiring intensive and closely monitored procedures (for example, in billing each other); and on the destruction of goal congruence among staff.

Such an assessment is not presented as an argument for rejecting innovation; rather for experimentation and, by implication, 'triability', where greater consideration of the organizational costs in the widest sense can be allowed for. This casting of doubt upon the implicit efficiencies and effectiveness to be derived via internal market mechanisms may be seen to give support to the view, discussed above, that some understandings of private sector practice have in fact been flawed in the race to 'businessize'. Burke and Goddard, suggesting that internal market mechanisms will contribute significantly to an erosion of NHS culture—which they see as holding patient welfare above personal aims —comment on the irony of the NHS appearing ready to dismantle its culture 'in the name of business efficiency', just at a time when many private sector bodies are seeking to strengthen their organizational cultures for improving effectiveness.

Finally, following from this caution, there remains the issue of the extent to which work upon innovations should be controlled as well as both encouraged and demonstrated by public services managers. Klein's emphasis, for health service managers, on the need to find an appropriate balance between encouragement and control, given that in this area 'even effective innovations may not necessarily be affordable' (Klein, 1985, p. 59), again highlights indirectly the distinctiveness of public services management as an activity of counterpoise, and supports the case discussed in the Introduction to the book, and made by Ranson and Stewart (1989).

To this point, the application of innovation theory to the impact of innovation derived from private sector practice, or believed practice, has emphasized the extent to which cross sector learning may be limited in its long-term value for public services work. Both the process and content of recent initiatives have been questioned. At the very least, a uniform expectation of benefits arising must be queried, given the differing organizational contexts found in public services work. It remains to demonstrate more fully that there will be limits to learning in the public services from initiatives introducing private sector managerial methods. Before looking at the central issue of organizational learning, we shall focus on the concepts for which such limits are particularly the case, namely consumerism, risk and entrepreneurship.

3.2.1 CONSUMERISM AS A PUBLIC SERVICES MANAGEMENT INITIATIVE

In many ways, stress on consumerist aspects in public services provides an acceptable and attractive blend of the language of the marketplace with that of caring public service professionals. Zemke (1989), in discussing the approaches of United States' government agencies 'taking clues' from the private sector on improvement in customer service, sees as a primary reason for such government agency overhaul the renewal of pride in government employees. Our own research on public service managers found a positive response to the impact of the concept on their work (Willcocks and Harrow, 1991). The predominant perception is represented by the following comments:

> It makes managerial roles more global. (NHS)

> Useful as our customer is also our paymaster. (Local government)

However, this view was frequently qualified by another emphasizing that in some areas where the organization's work, legislatively determined, was often interventionist (such as that relating to child protection), the notions of 'service' and 'product' had to be handled with caution.

The interchangeability of terms such as consumer, client, customer and user creates a perennial uncertainty. The very disparate nature of services consumers leads to continuing problems of definition—problems that also exist for private sector organizations but are less well aired. Devanney (1988), for example, in relation to local authority services, defines a consumer-led service as one with the user group having ability to 'influence, change, direct or control the policy development of service delivery practices in order to reflect and meet their changing needs more effectively'. As a councillor, he has clearly linked his definition with a structural response—in this case, the authority's extensive decentralization policy—as a means of enhancing consumer contact. Such an open-ended definition, however, might be held virtually to exclude much of the discretion which arguably is still important to the performance of the managerial task. Further, it raises questions as to the relative influence of non-service users and would-be users in service delivery; perhaps eliminating a managerial input that emphasizes also the intangible but critical wider public interest.

Even comparisons among public services managers have limited value. Joseph (1990), as Governor of HM Prison, Liverpool, was forthright in explaining to treasury officials his rejection by treasury of managerial task comparisons between hospital and prison management. In the latter case, in contrast to the behaviour of hospital customers: '. . . our numerically highest group don't want to be with us, don't like us, and take great delight out of upsetting our plans'.

It is against this background of conceptual uncertainty that public services managers are nevertheless encouraged to emulate private sector customer emphasis, on the assumption in any event that the latter has generally got it right. That resistance to putting the consumer at the centre of organizational affairs exists widely in private sector settings tends not to be well-publicized by those advocating the transformation of public services. Myers (1989, p. 168), for example, in advocating a company policy of 'customer management', recognizes that companies may be resistant to the idea: 'You may have to sell your organization on the concept of customer management.' His four basic principles of customer management are:

> . . . defining when certain customer deviations are acceptable; creating a menu of options; pricing all services; and designing the price structure as an array of incentives to be implemented over several years.

These not only raise implicitly the existence of much private sector customer neglect but indicate where public and private managers must part company, in relation to the issue of customer incentives, to service pricing, and in relation to relative stability of policy over a period of years. In examining the language of consumerism, as understood in private and public sectors, it is also important to recognize where generally descriptive terms have in practice different meanings and thus different managerial implications. For example, Walton (1989, p. 124), in reviewing the study, 'Getting New Clients', notes that by 'client-centred approach' the authors 'were talking about targeting clients, not working with and from the needs of clients'.

The range of consumer-led initiatives appears to be growing in public services in Europe, with accompanying interest in dissemination of experience (OECD, 1987). However, the degree of usefulness of many of the initiatives may be questioned – for example, 'complaints hotlines' to senior managers. It is also possible that such an openness to customer perspectives is in fact a misreading of much private sector practice, where frequently it is only the largest and the latest customers who are held to be significant.

Initiatives that open up public organizations to consumer opinions, and most likely, consumer complaints, are those that may place public services managers in positions where they cannot deliver the customer satisfaction demanded by a consumerist stance. Tomkins (1987) notes that public service efforts to improve the client/staff interface follow obvious private sector parallels, such as the advertising of American Express or Barclays Bank, emphasizing their friendly approach. However, while this may encourage improved communication and consumer feedback, it cannot contribute much towards solving serious supply and resource problems, or staff shortages that may lie behind the non-delivery or poor quality of service. As Tomkins observes tellingly, a smiling doctor or nurse is not contributing much to effectiveness in telling a patient that he or she has to wait months for an operation. In such situations, public services managers will need particular qualities of resolution; whether refusing services, absolutely or temporarily. They will be likely to be found edging customers away from the service if they seem to need them less than others— an activity described by Stewart (1989, p. 172) as 'de-marketing', an area where private sector experience (except perhaps its mistakes) will tend not to be so relevant.

Moreover, the nature of the relationship with the customer—presumed in the private sector and innovatory public services literature to be a positive one—must be taken into account. Government publications frequently urge a customer-oriented approach. The Audit Commission, for example, characterizes a well-managed council as one which, among other factors, 'understands its customers' (Audit Commission, 1988, p. 1). Thus public services managers will be seeking to respond to such ideas with the implications that the customer may go elsewhere. Camfield (1990), in his account of the programmes of Braintree District Council for 'Putting customers first', reflects this view:

> We no longer consider ourselves a monopoly provider of services which we think the public needs—we have to examine very carefully what the customers want, what competition we have, and how a service can be provided within an environment that is, at best, often hostile to local government.

However, managers will also recognize that some customers form a captive clientele for whom withdrawal of custom, or service, is not an option, no matter how reluctant in some cases the customer might be—for example, people on probation, elderly people in residential homes, homeless single parents. Furthermore, where tasks include managing constrained budgets and the consequences of political decisions to cut or to limit supplies or alter rules and conditions on which services can be gained, the managerial need will not be to satisfy the customer because this will not be possible, but in fact to disappoint those customers and do so in ways seen by that customer, the public and elected representatives as acceptable. The innovatory programmes for coping with the long-term housing waiting list applicant, or the well-qualified would-be student for the course that is oversubscribed, while maintaining a consumerist stance towards the non-consumer, based on private sector know-how, are awaited.

This is not to argue that consumerist concepts have little to offer public services management, or that the myriad consumer-oriented initiatives that make public organizations approachable—attractive signposting, comprehensible forms, speedy complaints responses—have little value. Rather it is to suggest that initiatives which merely reflect private sector practice will have little staying power or long-term impact on the organizations concerned. As public and private contexts of consumer activity will differ, so consumer behaviour is likely to differ also. It might be necessary to move away from what Pollitt (1988) calls the narrow private sector 'supermarket' model and its treatment as a 'bolt-on extra' in public services. The narrowness of private sector practices may be revealed when measured against the consumerist criteria raised by Potter (1988), namely: access (to goods/services), choice, information, redress and representation. As Pollitt suggests, efficiency, the dominant value in private sector consumerism, may be important but by itself is inadequate for a public service model, where the concept of the citizen-consumer suggests also that equity, equal opportunities, representation and participation must be integral to public services management practice.

The tensions that public services managers experience in balancing these alternative elements in consumerism, the consumerist rationales they employ, the key managerial levels having close consumer contact and the issue of identifying good practice in consumer-oriented initiatives are discussed more fully in Chapter 5. Consumerist initiatives, like any other, are accompanied by risk; in this case of raising expectations further, being unable to satisfy already unmet demand, of creating (and, on limited resources, having to respond to) new demand where hitherto none was expressed. The issue of risk in a public services managerial context is therefore now reviewed.

3.3.2 RISK AND ENTREPRENEURSHIP IN PUBLIC SERVICES MANAGEMENT

Risk is inherent in all the initiatives considered so far. It is reviewed here in terms of its relevance to the management of public services; the internal contradictions in some management initiatives; the questions which risk-taking raises for the consumers of public services, notably the basis of 'acceptable risk'; and the possibility that the increasing encouragement of entrepreneurship in public services contexts represents in its own right a risky management strategy.

How applicable are risk-taking and the practice of entrepreneurship in public service settings? Many of the 1980s management initiatives in the public sector have been partly predicated on criticism of politicians unwilling to give their public servants their heads, and of public servants themselves, seen as unnecessarily protected from both the strains as well as rewards of managerial risk-taking. As a result, one observable element in these management initiatives has been the development of a more risk-taking, entrepreneurial culture. Typical means to this end have included the appointment of general managers—some drawn from the private sector, devolution of decision-making, budget-holding and discretion to local managerial levels, the growing use of private sector advisers and management consultants, the encouragement of market forces through internal and private/public sector competition, and the substitution of privately manned though publicly funded services for those provided directly by public service employees.

Among our survey of public services managers' concerns, cited above, it appeared that internal competition engendered, for example in the NHS, now demanded a risk-taking managerial orientation. As one respondent remarked: 'You could possibly be denying the consumer better treatment by not taking risks with your resources.' While this response reflects an entrepreneurial approach, arguably it may also result in the type of (potentially expensive) opportunism, as examined by Burke and Goddard (1990) and discussed above.

The major stumbling block to the success and acceptability of some of the management initiatives in the public services is the question mark against the extent of risk-taking that may be borne in an organization that has the public common weal at the centre of its purpose. From such a perspective it is not entrepreneurialism, but risk avoidance in the form of the provision of security, health and/or safety that is central to the role of the public services manager. This debate was well illustrated by the widely reported expressions of concern regarding the efficacy and appropriateness of a private security company patrolling Ministry of Defence premises, following a terrorist attack on military property, in September 1989 (*Financial Times*, 1989). A demanding public— 'consumers' of services in the widest sense—were then portrayed by the media as requiring all major risks in such a policy to have been identified, and weighed, and action taken to all but eliminate disaster.

It emerges that public services managers can face major contradictions when making key judgements—with their being required to deliver services effectively, efficiently, speedily, cheaply and with entrepreneurial flair; yet against a background of the near-elimination of risks to public lives and property. To extend this point, many of the central assumptions and activities of entrepreneurialism fit uneasily with notions of public service. Thus, for Kirzner: 'Entrepreneurs are attracted into the market by the pure profit opportunities reflected in . . . price discrepancies: they tend to buy where the price is low, and sell where the price is high' (Kirzner, 1979, p. 175).

In practice the public services manager will experience tensions and clashes between, on the one hand, taking opportunities to exploit price differences in the economy provided by the ignorance of others, and, on the other, fulfilling the roles of public representative and public servant—offering equity of treatment, keeping the consumer informed, and, generally, proffering conduct tending to the welfare and advantage of the other. Furthermore, the greater restrictions operating on public services managers due to their wide accountability, and the regulatory frameworks in which they operate, cut across the opportunism and risk at the heart of entrepreneurial activity. Issues of similarities and dissimilarities of private and public services managers' contexts, pressures and basic tasks come again to the fore. It is possible that in the latter area, the asking of too many 'what if' questions may be thought to represent a poor career move, identifying a manager as unwilling to grasp the entrepreneurial nettle, rather than as taking seriously the managerial role in risk analysis (Harrow and Willcocks, 1990b). The difficulty, culturally, for public services managers, is that an overemphasis on risk analysis, in the face of entrepreneurial proposals, may be taken inaccurately for managerial passivity; or rejection of innovating opportunity.

Moreover, it is not certain that risk-taking, entrepreneurial managers are effective or appropriate even in all private sector settings. Dixon (1989) reports recent research showing business success linked with employing managers with an innovative disposition at the growth and decline stages, but efficiency-inclined managers at the maturity stage of a company's main product. Again, a range of commentators (for example, Handy, 1985; Lawrence and Lorsch, 1967) have argued for different managerial cultures and structures for different types of operation, even within the same organization. Covin and Slevin's research on 80 firms suggests that organic structures promote entrepreneurial activity, while mechanistic structures promote certainty and order (Covin and Slevin, 1988). Thus entrepreneurial activity alone does not constitute a panacea for improving organizational performance, and can be warranted only when organizational frameworks are supportive. Yet, even allowing for the floating of proposals in the late 1980s for 'opting out' for such institutions as schools and hospitals, there will be limits to the degree of organic structure that can prevail in public services, given the overriding need for accountability of the equity in provision. It follows from such research that one less recognized learning point from the private sector might be that 'entrepreneurialism' needs to be applied at least as selectively in public services settings.

One major irony, pinpointed by Parsons (1988), is that in substance the major management initiatives, for example the FMI and those guided by the Griffiths Report and the Rayner Scrutinies, themselves directly contradict the development of public services risk-taking and entrepreneurship:

> Entrepreneurial activity cannot occur within a framework emphasising such 'value for money' goals as objective costs, comparative certainty regarding outcomes, beliefs in

discovering an unproblematic 'social good', etc. . . . Nor can individuals be singled out and decreed to be (or to have to act as) entrepreneurs.

(Parsons, 1988, p. 38)

Moreover, such clashes within the management model being applied to public services are exacerbated by how change is managed, and then become translated into managerial practice. The point is underlined by the comment of one NHS district manager:

On the one hand we are exhorted to import into the health service commercial behaviour and commercial principles—and then on the other we have outdated rules and regulations thrown at us. The politicians can't have it both ways . . . there is a lack of leadership and a tendency to interfere in details as well as management by flavour of the month. Within the last twelve months . . . we have had thirty separate initiatives, sometimes on quite small issues where the (Management) Board has seen fit to give authoritative advice. They should be there for leadership not for regulatory purposes.

(Minty, 1987, p. 23)

A further major difficulty with risk-taking and entrepreneurship, particularly in public services, is that it becomes praiseworthy only if the risk comes off. Public services managers, taking their lead from private service style cultures where writers such as Peters (1987) enjoin organizations, for the sake of business, 'to support fast failures' (p. 262), will find little comfort in the public sphere, where public accountability models will not accept the likelihood of first getting it wrong. Public outcries over a variety of decisions or non-decisions regarding children's welfare over the years appear to have helped to catalogue the unacceptable risks to be taken by managers; but have not produced guidelines for managers on what *are* acceptable risks in such circumstances.

Even praise for some successful risk-taking may be dampened by possible contravention of regulatory frameworks—for example, in 1989 when several local authorities were found to have raised capital and dealt in sophisticated instruments in financial markets. Critics of such developments may describe them as examples of managerial gambling, but the line between risk-taking and gambling is very fine. As March and Shapira (1988, p. 90) argue: 'What is meant by gambling is risk taking that turns out badly.'

The literature on managers' attitudes towards risk-taking and managerial risk-taking behaviour suggests a high degree of uncertainty as to the nature of the links between innovation and risk-taking; and between risk-taking and entrepreneurialism. Brockhaus (1980), for example, in examining the risk-taking propensity of entrepreneurs, is reported by March and Shapira as having found no difference in risk propensity as between 'regular managers' and those leaving their managerial posts to take up business ventures. Although risk-taking might conventionally be seen as the hallmark of the well-established organization, with a cushion of reputation and resources, March and Shapira (1988 p. 84) cite managerial opinion surveys suggesting that fewer risks would and should be taken when things are going well; and that riskier choices are likely to be made when the organization is failing. Applying this to public services management, the latter perspective may well accord with some public services managers' views of current behaviour within their own organizations; and if so, may well put some valuable initiatives in doubt. For other public services managers, whether or not inclined by personality to take and live with risk in decision-making, there may be seen to be the need to develop a pro-active if ultimately defensive managerial strategy in educating the public into a greater acceptance of risk, as an inherent part of public services provision.

Among the key issues that need to be addressed particularly are what types of risk are centrally important in moving public services forward; and, further, what types of innovations and schemes constitute acceptable risks for public services managers to take. It is useful here to call upon Fischhoff's framework for assessing the acceptability of risk in decision-making (Fischhoff et al., 1981, p. 54). A scheme should be considered as acceptable risk where it is:

- comprehensive
- legally sound
- practical
- open to evaluation
- politically acceptable
- compatible with the institution
- conducive to learning.

The application of such a framework to a number of risk-associated decisions by public services managers seems likely to produce disagreement as to the acceptability of those decisions, with the consumerist perspective frequently at odds with the entrepreneurialist vision. While Bryson's argument—that public service strategic planners should recognize the value of 'small wins' as well as 'big wins' (making projects do-able, quickly making change 'real'), both as a means of ensuring major success eventually and of keeping the risks within bounds—offers hope, it remains the case that conventionally it is only the 'big wins' of managers that receive applause (Bryson, 1988). For many managers, therefore, going for 'big wins' will inevitably be an acceptable risk. What seems most at issue in applying Fischhoff's framework is the question of whether the risks associated with a particular scheme would be conducive to learning. In most public service contexts—for example, health and policing—the price of learning may be seen to be very high, both politically and personally.

Whatever the progress of re-examining more precisely the nature of risks properly taken by public services managers, it seems likely that as the inherent value of risk-taking continues to be accepted as evidence (however flawed) of an entrepreneurial spirit, then some who are public services managers, whether or not by title, will be increasingly less likely to remain as career public servants. The likely fading of the career public service represents risk-taking itself on a whole new scale. While private sector-based initiatives dominate the public sector, the risk also remains that existing public services managers will be less likely to own—or feel they own—the managerial prescriptions with which they are charged. Consequent mistrust of such managers by politicians, pointing to 'low calibre staff' and 'poor institutional response', may then be compounded; with public service management failure becoming a self-fulfilling prophecy.

The discussion thus far, linking the concepts of risk and entrepreneurialism, as reflected in private services-based literature, has implied the inherent drama associated with managing risks—big decisions are implied throughout. In many public services contexts, however, as Whiston (1991) demonstrates, much managerial risk-taking relates to small decisions that are nevertheless critical for service recipients and the public. She cites, for example, cases in community services where clients with learning difficulties developing the daily living skills of coping with public transport have become temporarily lost and thus at risk; or where clients with challenging behaviour, now living in community settings, suddenly cause damage to neighbouring property, to the ultimate public cost. Service managers in such situations must assess client needs in the light of client capabilities and development gains if the risks are taken, but also will need to take into account wider issues of public risk that may then be created. It follows, therefore, that the notions of risk in public services management need to be those that go well beyond the perspective of those associating risk and entrepreneurialism, where risk has been seen to be taken on large scales for large rewards, and where issues of public education as to the risks the public may expect from public services are to the fore. A rather more bleak model may be one that looks to public services managers purchasing individual indemnity insurance as at least one form of protection against 'getting it wrong'.

Whatever the type and degree of risk management required in running public services, it is clear from the discussion so far that central to the notions of initiative, innovation and risk-taking are those of managerial and organizational learning. The remainder of this chapter examines in more detail the types of learning engendered by the major public services initiatives under study, and the extent to which public services managers are again being enjoined to take guidance from the organizational learning occurring in private sector settings.

3.3 Organizational learning in public and private sectors

From innovation and experimentation, risk-taking, entrepreneurial behaviour and consumer responsiveness, managerial learning occurs. The literature shows that all these activities feature centrally in what has become known as 'organizational learning' (Bennis and Nanus, 1985; Fiol and Lyles, 1985; Meyers, 1990; Stata, 1989). In examining the limitations of a unidirectional learning on managerial practice from private to public services, it is logical to examine notions of organizational learning; and in particular in public services contexts.

Organizational learning is defined by Meyers (1990) as 'the ability of an enterprise to observe, assess and act upon stimuli which are either internal or external to the organisation in cumulative, inter-active and purposeful ways'. The goals of organizational learning—organization survival, development and expansion—are apposite for public services as for private. However, the literature is predominantly derived from private sector experience; and especially from large firms, with manufacturing and 'high tech' industrial bases. A selection from that literature is shown in Table 3.1. Such extracts represent a guide only to what may have value for comparative purposes.

The concepts in two sources are worth discussing in more detail for what follows. Thus Cohen and Levinthal (1990) examine companies' 'absorptive capacity' (their ability to recognize the value of new external information, assimilate and apply it to commercial ends) and identify the behaviour of companies where resistance to external innovative ideas occur—the 'Not Invented Here' syndrome. As discussed above, it is arguable that the reverse of this syndrome has been occurring in public services organizations, where ideas are valued precisely because they have not emanated from within the organization. The other source is Argote et al. (1990). In the context of experience in the aircraft and shipbuilding industries, they examine the persistence of organizational learning, showing a rapid depreciation of knowledge arising from a variety of organizational factors. They highlight the need to pay attention to those factors affecting 'organizational forgetting'. It may be argued that the very shift in public services managers becoming purchasers rather than direct providers of services will lead to critical 'forgetting' of this kind; with accompanying barriers to competent service monitoring, and means of ensuring the continued full accountability of those new service providers.

While the extensive organizational learning literature provides a starting point

Table 3.1   Extracts from the organizational learning literature derived from private sector practice and example

Fiol and Lyles (1985)	Four contextual factors 'affect the probability that organizational learning will occur': corporate culture, conducive to learning; strategy that allows for flexibility; organizational structure that allows innovativeness and new insights; and the environment.
Stata (1989)	The drive to innovate is explicit and is a means of 'learning as survival': '. . . the rate at which organizations and individuals learn may be the only sustainable competitive advantage, especially in the knowledge-based industries'; '. . . organizations can learn only as fast as the slowest link learns . . . change is blocked unless all the major decision makers learn together . . .'.

Bedeian (1986)	identifies organizational learning in terms of the processes that occur, with organizations '(appearing) to learn by borrowing from other organizations . . . by introducing incremental changes in existing practices based on feedback in their environment, through original innovation and through blind variations'.
Meyers (1990)	identifies types of organizational learning, in an ascending order of complexity and degree of innovation: <ul><li>maintenance learning—comparably stable procedures made more efficient, less costly;</li><li>adaptive learning—change tolerated but room for experiment constricting;</li><li>transitional learning—major changes in emphases, crisis altering dominant learning mode;</li><li>creative learning—intense period of redefining activity, constructive conflict, restructuring, inventing and temporary coalitions/partnerships initiated.</li></ul>
Cohen and Levinthal (1990)	claim a 'new perspective on learning and innovation', based on firms' R&D investment behaviour. A firm's ability to recognize the value of new external information, assimilate and apply it to commercial ends is its 'absorptive capacity'. Firms not investing in absorptive capacity in quickly moving fields may never exploit new information—the organizational condition of 'Lockout'. A parallel condition occurs where firms resist innovative ideas from the environment—the Not-Invented-Here syndrome.
Lyles (1988)	Learning transference occurs successfully in firms operating joint ventures in international contexts, 'taking place through people'. Mechanisms for achieving this include 'training and socialisation'; and 'top management overseeing the process'.
Klein (1989)	quotes Greiner (1987), dividing the 'unlearning model' for organizations into three: <ul><li>the extinction model (removing undesirable knowledge from individuals);</li><li>the replacement model (disseminating new information); and</li><li>the exorcism model (removing inappropriately behaving individuals).</li></ul>Klein adds a fourth model of organizational 'unlearning', the salvation model, with the arrival of the 'mythical manager-saviour who will lead the organization to prosperity'.
Argote *et al.* (1990)	examine organizational learning persistence, showing that 'knowledge acquired in production depreciates rapidly'. Depreciation may occur through individuals leaving or forgetting task knowledge, records inadequacy or obsolescent technology. Thus, attention should be paid to 'factors leading to organizational forgetting'.

from which public services managers may review their own organizational and individual learning capacities and approaches, the direct applicability of much of that literature must be borne in mind. Much of the literature, for example, deals directly or indirectly with issues of inter-organizational competition—certainly now encouraged in public services, but, as discussed above, with potential for dysfunctional effects on public services overall. The shared value base and objectives of many areas of public services, for example, have hitherto encouraged openness in exchanging ideas and organizational practices. In any event, it might be argued that such organizational knowledge in one sense should generally be publicly available. Yet Handy (1990) characterizes the 'learning organization' as not only clear about its role, goals and future, but 'properly selfish'; hardly an appropriate ethos for public services. If organizational learning is to be directed towards such inter-organizational competition, then, as argued by Mark and Willcocks (1989) for post-April 1991 NHS arrangements, public services will increasingly adopt the tactics of commercial secrecy and the wider public interest is unlikely to be served.

There is a small literature deriving from public services experiences, and much of it echoes private sector norms and needs. The major sources are given in Table 3.2. Edmonstone (1990), for example, emphasizes that public sector bodies have more inhibitors to organizational learning than organizations in

Table 3.2 The public services as learning organizations—the special complexity of public services

Edmonstone (1990)	'What price the learning organization in the public sector?' reviews the inhibitors to learning common to all organizations (e.g. managers wishing to oversimplify interpretations of events, fragmented structures of thought imposed on staffs . . .). For the public sector however, '. . . the problem is . . . exacerbated because most (public) . . . organizations are both bureaucracies and contain many professionals. The scope for fragmentation, goal displacement, etc., is very great indeed.' The particular problems, using NHS examples, include 'ambiguity over core purpose', 'task obsession' and 'no rewards for risk-taking'. What is required includes '. . . changes in the meaning of "professions" and "professionalism", which is unlikely to come about without a significant degree of political support'. Political will is thus at the heart of ensuring that organizational learning occurs.
Attwood and Beer (1988)	in examining development work in Mid Essex Health Authority, note '. . . the struggle to become a "learning organization" . . .'; and state '. . . the goal for those who seek to develop "learning organizations" in which planned organizational and personal change is highly integrated'. To move to this position, required activities include refining the organizational strategy for planned change.

Hopkins
(1988)

WHO's successful smallpox eradication campaign offers organizational lessons:
- ensure clear problem definition, assemble an organization retaining the capacity to interpret experience and weigh evidence with minimum
- degree of prejudice;
- develop a flexible mode of management;
- promote adaptation to task environment;
- provide incentives for accurate reporting and performance;
- seek affected population participation;
- establish unambiguous and correct measures of task achievement.

Individual managerial responsibility for ensuring organizational learning—public services managers 'speaking out'

Barth
(1987)

In US contexts, from an organizational learning viewpoint, a limited role for the career civil service is dysfunctional and detrimental to double-loop learning, which involves a critique of the administration's assumptions and ideologies. 'Careerists' are confined to single-loop learning, with a failure to serve the public interest optimally, and should have a mandate to question policy constructively.

Ventriss and
Luke
(1988)

review contemporary concepts of organizational learning, noting that 'their predominant focus is the immediate moment'. Public services need an 'enlarged' conception of learning, and they propose a 'substantive learning' approach. This 'involves the process of improving publication through knowledge that critically examines the domain assumptions and normative implications of public policies in an interconnected political environment'.

Public servants are thus required to 'critically reflect (and act) upon the intended and unintended substantive outcomes of enacted organizational policies in an inter-governmental and intersectoral environment'.

Critical here is the particular—inter-connected—nature of public organizations, where unilateral action has impact elsewhere. In managerial terms, this requires a learning framework where policy issues are 'problem-posing' not 'problem-solving' exercises.

Argyris
(1990)

based on the working of the US Cabinet under Reagan, the NASA Challenger disaster and consultancy experiences, identifies two sorts of error in organizations—first order, arising from ignorance, and second order, designed error, 'skilled incompetence'. In the latter case, workers learn to cover up to aid organizational survival, and display 'fancy footwork', to avoid accusations of defensiveness. Such routines may be seen as needing to be by-passed rather than confronted.

general, because of their bureaucratization and professionalization. That these two factors might also be promoters of learning (for example, through the development of peer review), is not acknowledged. Attwood and Beer (1988), examining developmental work in Mid Essex Health Authority, note 'the struggle to become a "learning organization"'.

From the perspective of this chapter, which queries the overt adoption of private sector style managerial prescriptions as providing inevitably for more effective and efficient services, the most valuable theoretical development comes from the work of Ventriss and Luke (1988). In an echo of concerns over the 'can do' mentality, Ventriss and Luke review contemporary concepts of organizational learning, and note their predominant focus on the immediate moment. Drawing on American experiences, they argue that public services require an 'enlarged concept of learning', and advocate the development of a substantive learning approach. This would require public servants to reflect and act upon the intended and unintended outcomes of organizational policies, by implication to challenge and think through policy implications, particularly where public organization interconnectedness is involved. In managerial terms this requires a learning framework where policy issues for managerial action need to be seen as problem-posing and not simply problem-solving exercises. Does this exist in UK public services? What sort of learning is being undergone? To provide insight into managerial attitudes and perceptions and types of managerial and organizational learning occurring in UK public services, detailed research was undertaken, and preliminary findings appear in Harrow (1990) and Willcocks and Harrow (1991). The section that follows details selective and subsequent findings from the research.

3.4   Public services managers' perspectives—survey evidence

The gathering from practising managers of empirical data on organizational learning issues was undertaken during September and October 1990. This was seen as an appropriate means of redressing the balance in the literature, hitherto heavily emphasizing trainers' and chief executives' perceptions of organizational learning—perceptions prone to reflect views of what ought to be, or what was intended, rather than what is. A total of 30 public services managers, at middle managerial levels with predominantly operational responsibilities, participated. Of these, approximately 50 per cent were from local government, 33 per cent from the health service, and the remainder from the protective services (fire and police services) and public agencies. The average period of time spent in their current managerial post was three years, and their average period of time working in public services was 12.5 years. The selection of these 30 managers related to their having already sought a route for extending their personal managerial learning. All were participating in formal management education programmes. To this extent, therefore, they were a homogenous grouping, who could be expected to have some insights into their employing organizations' learning capacity and potential, having already given thought to, and acted upon, their own learning needs.

Two parallel pilot studies were undertaken. The first was with the smaller group of 12 managers. Here group work was undertaken to introduce and promote discussion about organizational learning concepts, and to familiarize respondents with the relevant language. This was followed by the completion of a questionnaire by each of the 12 managers. The questionnaire had a predominantly unstructured format, and focused on aspects of organizational learning that they were currently experiencing in their managerial roles. The second study, with the larger group of 18 managers, commenced with promotion of group discussions, on focus group lines, on managing organizational change. Participants then completed questionnaires, again in a predominantly unstructured format, which sought data on the known areas of organizational life which figure largely in the learning literature, including the impact of the political dimension on managing, the risk-taking climate, the means of disseminating innovatory ideas, and the impact of manager/professional relationships on encouraging or inhibiting organizational change. Both questionnaires were completed, respectively, in September and October 1990. This section records selective findings from this work, and from subsequent in-depth interviews carried out through 1991, with particular reference to the learning that occurs in managing risk.

Predominantly, responsibility for encouraging organizational learning was seen to rest with senior managers, for example: 'inasmuch as the concept is embraced, it is considered to be the prerogative of senior managers . . .'. A minority of respondents differentiated between the more mundane, if important 'adaptive' learning focused on service-delivery managers, and 'creative learning' which remained a senior officer responsibility (see Table 3.1). Generally, preferences for organizational learning styles were related to respondents' position on the managerial ladder. Interestingly, those in more senior positions professed some degree of exhaustion with the rate and content of learning being experienced. This view was typified by the respondent who sought 'a period of maintenance learning, for the quiet consolidation of radical change'. Those managers at less exalted levels were more likely to evince disappointment at their lack of involvement in developing strategies for creative learning, with one respondent wanting 'more *levels* to engage in . . . blue sky processes . . . at present the prerogative of senior groups in a labour intensive organization'.

In a consideration of the types of organizational learning actually occurring in respondents' organizations, only a minority of respondents recorded congruence between senior managers' expectations and organizational reality. One respondent noted the existence of 'no organizational learning, only change'. Crisis-based learning was seen as not necessarily producing the transitional learning state that Meyers (1990) identifies. One respondent, for example, described how 'people (tend) to put "tin hats" on and sit tight till the storm blows over, even if overtly everyone is actively seeking value for money ideas'.

A major organizational learning mode, held to characterize much of recent public services change, was that of 'organizational adaptation'—to be distinguished from the more specific 'adaptive learning' category of Meyers, where experimentation is the means of encouraging change. The majority of respondents recognized public services managers as having organizational adaptation 'skills', whereby organizational shifts of various kinds were made in the direction of externally imposed policies. Examples included improving 'Right to Buy' programmes, police–community consultation, and the involvement of parents in child protection decisions. Of these respondents there was roughly equal division between those who regarded the adaptation skills as inhibitors, and those who saw them as enhancers of learning.

From the group of managers considering specifc issues relating to organizational learning, content analysis of responses has shown that the major concerns included the following:

1 the need for adequate, appropriate, and known communications structures for disseminating learning;
2 expectations that senior management should take responsibility for organizational learning; but reservations that their perceptions of the learning in fact occurring would be over-positive;
3 a minimal role offered for elected members as organizational learning agents (and, by implication, participants in learning processes);
4 recognition of the limitations on learning imposed by crisis approaches to policy-making and management;
5 uncertainty and some disappointment as to the likely organizational effort to link individual learning to the organization's present and future needs;
6 problematic experiences of creative (innovation based) learning; the issue of maintaining the learning momentum was raised often.

From the group of managers examining aspects of managerial activity that might contribute to creating learning levers for organizations, less united responses were revealed. The following issues, however, were among those central to these managers' concerns:

1 'good' managerial practice linked overwhelmingly to budgetary saving in the context of maintaining certain service levels;
2 models for learning on managerial practice coming less from senior managers and more from colleagues in middle management positions;
3 differing experiences on organizational dissemination of learning, but a predominance of 'top down' systems, leaving middle managers to interpret the learning to staff and service users;
4 a minority undertaking risk-taking in managerial roles, often without models

to follow and isolated from less enthusiastic colleagues; only a small minority able to participate in formal reflection on that risk-taking;

5 innovation seen predominantly as activities or systems in contrast with those in use, that is, valued because the innovation source was external to the organization.

Particularly varying responses occurred on the issue of the validity of making comparisons between public and private sector management. A similar variation occurred on the related issue of the extent to which public services can learn from private sector practice. The respondents could be categorized into four groups:

1 the 'resisters'—basing their responses on the failure of the private sector to give leads in their areas and on the special nature of public services, being electorally driven;
2 the 'doubters', uncertain of the value of comparison, given the eclectic nature of their work and the multiple objectives of their organizations;
3 the 'inevitable accepters', wanting more data on the methodology of comparison and recognizing certain areas where private sector practice might compare well with public sector work, e.g. in trades union liaison;
4 the 'welcomers', who saw comparison as a means of helping focus thinking on job content and performance, as well as potentially improving remuneration or conditions.

Such varied responses from some of the middle managers responsible for operationalizing the 1980–90s change initiatives in public services would suggest that implementation could face something less than unequivocal support. This would argue for some caution being necessary at the level of practice in pursuing private sector style management initiatives, and in assuming the feasibility of unidirectional learning from private sector management practice.

3.5   Learning in public services: ways forward

From the discussion so far it is clear that the shaping of public services management, while influenced by a range of factors, not least legislative mandate, is also intimately related to how organizational learning is conceptualized, by whom, and how learning proceeds within public services organizations. In this final section, the learning models that have been implied and emergent from recent public services management initiatives are questioned, and further models are developed and evaluated.

Detailed content analysis was undertaken of the survey and interview data discussed selectively in the previous section. Implicit in the range of responses referring to policy change, the need to maintain service quality and facing financial restraints were a variety of models of public service management. This suggested a way forward, by identifying such models and correlating these to relevant organizational learning modes.

A general grouping of the nature and content of the responses in particular provided a close parallel with the three-fold public services management model proposed by Ackroyd *et al.* (1989). They designate the predominant public services management model as that of 'custodial management'; 'because the primary aim is to preserve and perpetuate customary standards of service provision'.

Two variants from this main type are 'policy management', where strategic shifts in thinking are attempted, and 'budgetary management', where resource allocation is the primary means of controlling–managing work. This typology, notwithstanding the intimidatory tone of the predominant management mode, suggests an opportunity to review custodial, policy and budgetary management practices in action; and the types of learning organization that derives from or is inhibited by them. At a superficial level, for example, the management modes and related learning occurring might be expected to be as shown in Table 3.3.

Further work in this area might be useful, where, for example, models of management and recognized types of formalized organizational learning were not synchronized. Such a basic typology could be extended and enhanced by relating it to the area of domain theory as discussed in the Introduction, where the three major domains of activity in human services organizations—service, policy and managerial—would appear to conform to the three interrelated models of management action discussed. Thus a potential pattern emerges, as shown in Table 3.4

Researching the existence of such interlinked models and their related organizational learning modes would have particular value in public services settings where inter-service and inter-agency cooperation, formal or informal, legislatively based or development arising from local need, is taking place or is sought. At the same time, the impact and experiences of the player/managers, predomi-

Table 3.3 Management modes and related learning

Management mode	Organizational learning occurring
Custodial	incremental, professionally based, based on consensus about 'good practice'; some experimentation;
Policy	'thinking unthinkable'; widespread innovation; personal and organizational survival skills; some failures;
Budgetary	priority setting by wide range of actors; hard choices and their implications; quantifying and living with risk-taking.

Table 3.4   Models of management action

Domain of activity	Management mode	Organizational learning occurring
Service domain	Custodial model	Professionally based with consensus about good practice
Policy domain	Policy model	Innovation widespread; personal and survival skills
Management domain	Budgetary model	Priority setting and hard choices; risk-taking

nant in public services management because of that very emphasis on 'service', raises questions about the ability of individuals and groups of managers to move their domains of work; and to take their learning with them, as typified by that domain and its managerial mode.

The marked references to crisis-induced learning from respondents suggests a further area for exploration; particularly if it is held that 'budgetary manage-ment' is not a variant of another model but the predominant managerial approach in public services. This would be to take as the basis for organizational behaviour in public services those theories relating to organizational crises; and examine learning strategies in relation to those crisis responses. To some extent, this approach has been begun by Gill and Frame (1990), in three case studies of 'managing financial stringency' (the polytechnic sector, a psychiatric hospital, a social services department). Here they utilize the hypothesis of Fink et al. (1971) that organizational crisis can be modelled on patterns of personal crisis —through shock and defensive retreat to acknowledgement and adaptation/ change. Their work has not focused on organizational learning as such. How-ever, it has implications for those wishing to begin or to sustain organizational learning activities in fraught organizational climates, particularly where such crises may have been deliberately induced as a learning exercise (for example, budgetary cuts). It would further seem to interrelate with Argyris' notions of 'skilled incompetence' and resulting 'fancy footwork' in public organizations (see Table 3.2). At the same time, however, equating organizational crisis theory and organizational learning may have important limitations, not least of which is that the theory as earlier outlined does contain assumptions about crisis resolution and eventual crisis diminution; and such a view of progression through crisis may not be seen as fully appropriate for some parts of public services.

From our own research it appears that in public services organizations where organizational learning concepts are promoted or at least not ruled out, a 'scatter gun' effect is hoped for—that is, that learning will occur sporadically throughout the organization, and potentially encompass all the organization's concerns. This may in part be an inevitable consequence of the multiple objectives of public services bodies. It can be argued, however, that it would be helpful to break down the focus and direction of organizational learning in a manner that recognizes the contributions of organization members at the operational service-delivery end of the work; and which recognizes also the operational-level public services manager as representing a buffer or a mediator between external demands and needs and internal demands and needs.

It would seem more helpful, therefore, to examine organizational learning from two distinct perspectives:

1 The INWARD LEARNING of the organization: relating to collective and individual memory and experience, understandings of alternative practice possibilities, sharing ideas; storing and utilizing individual and group knowledge about successful and unsuccessful policy and practice.
2 The OUTWARD LEARNING of the organization: concerning the acceptance and adoption of ideas and techniques from outside the organization; finding new ways to complete tasks; and importing external advisers and practitioners.

For those who see public services' salvation in adopting private sector mechanisms and modes of delivery, 'outward learning' has the greater organizational value, and is certainly being exemplified in organizations such as the NHS. Here, for example, the documentation of successful applicants for Trust status seems to show that those bodies have learned ways of projecting themselves and their capabilities from external models. However, what seems critical also is the type of outward learning that takes place. In the ways in which it has been applied in the public services, 'outward learning' has more frequently followed the 'single loop' error-correction learning model of Argyris and Schon (1978) since much of it is immediate-solutions based. Furthermore, the model has often had the effect, intentional or otherwise, of undermining, restricting, even replacing the potential for 'inward learning' of both the single-loop and double-loop (reassessment-of-norms) types.

Whether the public service concerned is 'protective' (an alternative to 'custodial'), 'market oriented' or moving towards a competitive stance, it seems currently the case that inward learning is likely to be the more neglected. Our own research data contain implicit and explicit evidence of this. They also imply a potential explanation of that neglect. This is that senior managers may be themselves so burdened with the tasks of implementing and delivering externally imposed strategies that they find it not only convenient but essential to set aside ideas coming from within the organization. However regrettable, this might also be a practice to ensure personal survival. A reverse of the Not-Invented-Here syndrome could thus be seen to be in operation.

Furthermore, it seems likely that the neglect of inward-learning structures and routines, and the failure to develop 'soft structures' for inward-learning purposes may be contributing to 'organizational forgetting'. It is possible to argue that some such forgetting is positively beneficial, but equally some may be dangerous—as in the case of lack of any direct managerial experience in relation to service provision when contracts are being set and standards inspected. An increased emphasis on inward learning—recording, storing, utilizing and thus above all valuing the accumulated knowledge and experience of organization members—is a practical means of integrating the individual and organizational learning tracks. Such an emphasis may provide a more appropriate way forward than a stress on outward learning, encouraging organizations to compare themselves, often unfavourably, with organizations which they do not, and perhaps should not, resemble. It may increase internal organizational members' self-confidence to the point where a substantive learning model is seen as being a welcome, realistic and career-progressive—rather than a career-threatening and defeatist—learning mode for public services managers. Finally, a renewed emphasis on inward learning may well represent a more appropriate borrowing from private sector managerial practice, at least in the form that that practice is represented in the more recent literature on developing learning organizations (Easterby-Smith, 1990; Holden, 1990; Lessem, 1990; Stata, 1989).

3.6   Conclusions

Public services management is a rich and complex area of management activity, where important and justified variations occur in managerial behaviour in differing areas of provision. Some of the warnings implicit in innovation theory have been disregarded by what appears an unseemly rush to innovate from private sector practice. This has necessitated often hard organizational learning, which is, in the longer term, an inefficient use of organizational resources. Even the increased brushes with forms of consumerism—embraced by some public services managers as a respectable borrowing from the private sector—must have limited utility, particularly when related to the need for equity of treatment of public services clients, and accountability of such managers to the public generally.

A selective attitude towards those sectors that provide valuable learning models and give the private sector pre-eminence, may retard public services management practice; which might more usefully look within its own borders for practice possibilities and initiatives or experiments. Such an approach, stressing the need to reorientate public services organizational learning towards an 'inward' perspective, has been advocated by Willcocks and Harrow (1991). Ironically the much smaller organizational learning literature relating to joint venture operations points to the possibility of joint public services working, and joint public services/voluntary service working as both strong fields for gathering organizational learning data.

An overemphasis on the risk-taking, entrepreneurial manager, borrowed from a perhaps too-briefly sketched private sector model, should be recognized as in itself constituting risk, especially when so many of the public services are concerned with the delivery of security, assistance and, in one form or another, safety. As McMahon (1990, p. 16) argues, managers in the public sector are 'managing for social result', with a value base that includes but extends well beyond those rooted in concerns about efficiency and effectiveness. To subject the public services manager, for learning purposes, to invidious comparison with a purportedly dynamic private sector counterpart, and to leave the boundaries of that learning unchallenged and its pace over-fast, represents a high risk 'big win' strategy for those seeking to make lasting improvement in the quality and quantity of public services. It is the low risk 'small win' strategy that better fits the evolutionary nature and ethos of the public services. This latter approach merits attention for success in the long run, if the goals remain what they are commonly held to be: namely, greater efficiency, better management and better service.

References and further reading

Ackroyd, S., Hughes, J. A., and Soothill, K. (1989) 'Public sector services and their management', *Journal of Management Studies* **26** (6), 603–19.

Anderson, A. and Sims, R. (1990) 'Managing for quality: getting the right frameworks for information technology', *Public Money and Management*, **10** (3), 33–8.

Argote, L., Beckman, S. L. and Epple, D. (1990) 'The persistence and transfer of learning in industrial settings', *Management Science*, **36** (2), 140–54.

Argyris, C. (1990) *Overcoming Organizational Defenses—Facilitating Organizational Learning*. Allyn & Bacon, Boston.

Argyris, C. and Schon, D. (1978) *A Theory of Action Perspective*. Addison Wesley, New York.

Ascher, K. and Nare, B. (1990) 'Strategic planning in the public sector', *International Review of Strategic Management*, **1** (1), 297–315.

Attwood, M. E. and Beer, N. (1988) 'Development of a learning organisation; reflections on a personal and organisational workshop in a district health authority', *Management Education and Development*, **19** (3), 201–14.

Attwood, M. E. and Beer, N. F. (1990) 'Towards the definition of a learning organization', in Pedler, M. *et al.* (eds), *Self-Development in Organizations*, McGraw-Hill, London.

Audit Commission (1988) *The Competitive Council*. Management Papers No. 1, March, HMSO, London.

Barham, K., Frazer, J. and Heath, L. (1988) *Management For the Future*. Ashridge Management College and Foundation for Management Education.

Barrett, S. and McMahon, (1990) 'Public management in uncertainty: a micro-political perspective on the health service in the United Kingdom', *Policy and Politics*, **18** (4), 257–68.

Barth, T. J. (1987) 'Should careerists question public policy?', *Bureaucrat*, **16** (4), 55–8.

Bedeian, A. (1986) 'Contemporary challenges in the study of organisations', in

Hunt, J. G. and Blair, J. D. (eds), *1986 Yearly Review of Management of the Journal of Management*, **12** (2), 185–201.

Beeton, D. and Collins, B. (1988) 'Public spending', in Jackson, P. and Terry, F. (eds), *Public Domain, the Public Services Yearbook, 1988*. Public Finance Foundation and Peat, Marwick McLintock, London, pp. 33–53.

Bennis, W. and Nanus, B. (1985) 'Organisational Learning: the management of the collective self,' *New Management*, **3** (1), 6–13.

Bowden, D. (1989) Comment by the President of the Institute of Health Services Management. Reported in *The Independent*, 5 January.

Brockhaus, R. H. Sr (1980) 'Risk-taking propensity of entrepreneurs', *Academy of Management Journal*, No. 23, 509–20.

Bryson, J. (1988) 'Strategic planning: big wins and small wins', *Public Money and Management*, **8** (3), 11–15.

Burke, C. and Goddard, A. (1990) 'Internal markets; the road to inefficiency?', *Public Administration*, **68** (3), 389–95.

Burns, D. (1987) 'Heads control school budgets. Going local', *Newsletter of the Decentralisation Research and Information Centre*, 8 (July). Polytechnic of Central London, School of Planning, London, pp. 21–2.

Camfield, B. (1990) 'Putting customers first', *Management, Education and Development*, **21** (5), 389–93.

Carlzon, J. (1989) *Moments of Truth*. Harper & Row, New York.

Central Purchasing Unit (1987) *Government Purchasing: Progress Report to the Prime Minister*. HMSO, London.

Cohen, W. M. and Levinthal, D. A. (1990) 'Absorptive capacity: a new perspective on learning and innovation', *Administrative Science Quarterly*, 35, 128–52.

Constable, J. and McCormick, R. (1987) *The Making of British Managers*. A Report for the British Institute of Management and the Confederation of British Industries into Management Training, Education and Development. BIM/CBI, London.

Covin, J. G. and Slevin, D. P. (1988) 'The influence of organization structure on the utility of an entrepreneurial top management style', *Journal of Management Studies*, **25** (3), 217–34.

Danhof, C. (1949) *Change and the Entrepreneur*. Harvard University Press, Boston.

Devanney, M. (1988) 'Consumer-led services: Fashionable dogma or practical necessity', in Allen, I. (ed.), *Hearing the Voice of the Consumer*. Policy Studies Institute, London.

Dixon, M. (1989) 'The very model of a mythical manager', *Financial Times*, 10 May, p. 24.

Easterby-Smith, M. (1987) 'Change and innovation in higher education: a role for corporate strategy', *Higher Education*, **16**, 37–52.

Easterby-Smith, M. (1990) 'Creating a learning organization', *Personnel Review*, **15**, 24–8.

Edmonstone, J. (1990) 'What price the learning organization in the public sector?' in Pedler, M. *et al.* (eds), *Self-Development in Organizations*. McGraw-Hill, London.

Exley, M. (1989) 'Accelerating change in the public sector: some practical lessons', Paper presented at the Managing People in the Public Sector Conference, London Business School. March.

Faulkner, H. (1990) 'Looking to public management', *Canadian Public Administration*, Autumn, 383–8.

Financial Times (1989) 24 September.

Fink, S. L., Beak, J. and Taddeo, K. (1971) 'Organisational crisis and change', *Journal of Applied Behavioural Science*, **7** (1), 15–41.

Fiol, M. and Lyles, M. A. (1985) 'Organisation learning', *Academy of Management Review*, 10 (4), 803–13.

Fischhoff, B., Lichtenstein, S., Slovic, P. *et al.* (1981) *Acceptable Risk*. Cambridge University Press, New York.

Flynn, N. (1988) 'A consumer-oriented culture', *Public Money and Mangement*, 8 (2), 27–31.

Flynn, N. (1990a) *Public Sector Management*, Harvester Wheatsheaf, Brighton.

Flynn, N. (1990b) 'The impact of compulsory competition on public sector management: competition within the field', *Public Policy and Administration*, 5 (1), 33–43.

Gill, J. and Frame, T. (1990) 'Managing financial stringency in the public sector', *Public Administration*, 68 (Winter), 517–37.

Gunn, L. (1988) 'Public management: a third approach?', *Public Money and Management*, 8 (2), 21–5.

Haigh, B. and Morris, D. (1990a) 'Implementing public policies in an era of change', *Public Policy and Administration*, 5 (2), 3–4.

Haigh, R. H. and Morris, D. S. (1990b) 'The National Health Service, the management/administration interface—a test to destruction?', *Teaching Public Administration*, 10 (1), 47–53.

Handy, C. (1985) *Understanding Organizations*. Penguin, Harmondsworth.

Handy, C. (1987) *The Making of Managers*. MSC/NEDO/BIM, London.

Handy, C. (1990) *The Age of Unreason*. Arrow Books, London.

Harrow, J. (1990) 'Public services managers—experiences of and perspectives on organisational learning, a pilot survey', unpublished paper. Centre for Management Studies, South Bank Polytechnic, London.

Harrow, J. and Willcocks, L. (1990a) 'Public services management: activities, initiatives and limits to learning', *Journal of Management Studies*, 27 (3), 281–304.

Harrow, J. and Willcocks, L. (1990b) 'Risk and the public service manager', *Public Money and Management*, 10 (3), 61–4.

Holden, N. (1990) 'Preparing the ground for organisational learning', *Management Education and Development*, 21 (3), 241–61.

Holtham, C. (1986) 'Management in British Local Government in the 1980s: theory and practice,' *Nagarlok*, 18 (3), 84–95.

Hood, C. (1991) 'A public management for all seasons?', *Public Administration*, 69 (1), 3–19.

Hopkins, J. W. (1988) 'The eradication of smallpox: organisational learning and innovation in international health administration', *Journal of Developing Areas*, 22 (3), 321–32.

Hyde, P. (1988) 'The consequences of IT for the UK Civil Service', *International Journal of Public Sector Management*, 1 (2), 21–30.

Jackson, P. (1988) 'The management of performance in the public sector', *Public Money and Management*, 8 (4), 11–16.

Joseph, A. N. (1990) 'Management, leadership and effectiveness', *Prison Service Journal*, 77 (Winter), 2–7.

Kanter, R. M. (1983) *The Change Masters: Corporate Entrepreneurs at Work*. Allen and Unwin, London.

Kanter, R. M. (1989) *When Giants Learn to Dance: Mastering the Challenges of Strategy, Management and Careers in the 1990s*. Simon and Schuster, New York.

Kemp, P. (1990) 'Can the Civil Service adapt to managing by contract?', *Public Money and Management*, 10 (3), 25–32.

Kilmann, R. (1989) *Managing Beyond the Quick Fix*. Jossey Bass, San Francisco.

Kingdom, J. (1990) 'Public administration or public management: a discipline in crisis', *Public Policy and Administration*, **5** (2), 5–29.

Kirzner, I. (1979) *Perception, Opportunity and Profit: Studies in the theory of entrepreneurship.* University of Chicago Press, Chicago.

Klein, R. (1985) 'Management in health care: the politics of innovation', *International Journal of Health Planning and Management*, **1**, 57–63.

Klein, J. I. (1989) 'Parenthetic learning in organisations: towards the unlearning of the unlearning model', *Journal of Management Studies*, **26** (3), 291–308.

Lawrence, P. and Lorsch, J. (1967) *Organization and Environment: Managing Differentiation and Integration.* Harvard University Press, Boston.

Lessem, R. (1990) *Developmental Management.* Blackwell, London.

Lyles, M. A. (1988) 'Learning among joint venture sophisticated firms', *Management International Review*, **28**, 85–98.

McMahon, L. (1990) 'Private thoughts on public values', *Health Manpower Management*, **15** (3), 15–16.

March, J. G. and Shapira, Z. (1988) 'Managerial perspectives on risk and risk-taking', in March, J. G. (ed.), *Decisions and Organisations.* Blackwell, Oxford.

Mark, A. and Willcocks, L. (1989) 'The secret of success', *Health Services Management*, December.

McNaught, A. (1991) 'Whither community health services? Harnessing the new public health and the new managerialism', in McNaught, A. (ed.), *Managing Community Health Services.* Chapman and Hall, London.

Metcalfe, L. and Richards, S. (1987) 'The efficiency strategy in government: an impoverished concept of management,' *Public Money*, **7** (1), 29–35.

Metcalfe, L. and Richards, S. (1990) *Improving Public Management.* Sage, London.

Meyers, P W. (1990) 'Non-linear learning in large technological firms: period four implies chaos', *Research Policy (Netherlands)*, **19** (2), 97–115.

Minogue, M. (1983) 'Theory and practice in public policy and administration', *Policy and Politics*, **11** (1), 63–85.

Minty, C. (1987) 'Exchanging ideas on management', *Public Finance and Accountancy*, 18 December, 14–23.

Myers, R. (1989) 'Suppliers—manage your customers', *Harvard Business Review*, November/December (6), 160–8.

OECD (1987) *A Survey of Initiatives for Improving Relationships between the Citizen and the Administration.* Organisation for Economic Cooperation and Development, Paris.

Painter, C. (1991) 'The public sector and current orthodoxies', *Political Quarterly*, **62** (1), 75–89.

Parker, D. and Hartley, K. (1990) 'Competitive tendering: issues and evidence', *Public Money and Management*, **10** (3), 9–16.

Parsons, S. (1988) 'Economic principles in the public and private sectors', *Policy and Politics*, **16** (1), 29–39.

Peters, T. (1987) *Thriving on Chaos: Handbook for a Management Revolution.* Pan Books/Macmillan, London.

Peters, T. and Waterman, R. (1982) *In Search of Excellence: Lessons from America's Best-Run Companies.* Harper & Row, New York.

Pollitt, C. (1988) 'Consumerism and beyond,' *Public Administration*, **66** (2), 121–4.

Pollitt, C. (1990) 'Doing business in the temple? Managers and quality assurance in the public services', *Public Administration*, **68** (Winter), 435–52.

Pollitt, C. (1991) *Managerialism and the Public Services: The Anglo-American Experience.* Blackwell, Oxford.

Potter, J. (1988) 'Consumerism and the public sector: how well does the coat fit?', *Public Administration*, **66** (2), 149–64.

Ranson, S. and Stewart, J. (1989) 'Citizenship and government: the challenge for management in the public domain', *Political Studies*, **37** (1), 5–24.

Richards, S. (1988) 'Management in government: the next steps', *Public Money and Management*, **8** (1/2), 87–90.

Rogers, E. M. (1962) *Diffusion of Innovations*. Free Press, New York.

Rogers, E. M. and Kim, J.- I. (1985) 'Diffusion of innovations in public organisations', in Merritt, R. L. and Merritt, A. J. (eds), *Innovation in the Public Sector*. Sage, Beverly Hills, 85–108.

Royal Institute of Public Administration (1990) 'RIPA Report', **11** (3), 1.

Stata, R. (1989) 'Organizational learning: the key to management innovation', *Sloan Management Review*, **30** (3), 63–74.

Stewart, J. (1989) 'In search of a curriculum for management for the public sector', *Management Education and Development*, **20** (Part 3), 168–75.

Stewart, J. and Ranson, S. (1988) 'Management in the public domain,' *Public Money and Management*, **8** (1/2), 13–19.

Tomkins, C. R. (1987) *Achieving Economy, Efficiency and Effectiveness in the Public Sector*. Kogan Page and Institute of Chartered Accountants of Scotland, London.

Ventriss, C. and Luke, J. (1988) 'Organizational learning and public policy: towards a substantive perspective', *American Review of Public Administration*, **18** (4), 337–57.

Walton, M. (1989) 'Book Review: "Getting New Clients", R. A. Connor and J. P. Davidson', *Management Education and Development*, **20** (Part 1), 124.

Warren, G. and Harrow, J. (1991) 'Working with local authorities', in McNaught, A. (ed.), *Managing Community Health Services*. Chapman and Hall, London.

Whiston, J. (1991) 'Managing risks in community services', MSc Public Services Management, South Bank Polytechnic (unpublished paper).

Willcocks, L. and Harrow, J. (1991) 'Developing the learning organisation: its applicability in the management of public services', Paper, Association for Management Education and Development and Ashridge Management College Conference, *Individual and Organisation Development—Conflict and Synergy*, January.

Willcocks, L. and Mark, A. (1988a) 'Information for management? A review of progress on IT and general management in the UK National Health Service', *Working Paper No. 92*, April. City University Business School.

Willcocks, L. and Mark, A. (1988b) 'Information technology in the NHS: from strategy to implementation', *Public Money and Management*, **8** (3), 41–3.

Williams, D. (1988) 'Have we achieved better management, better health?', *Health Service Manpower Review*, **14** (1), 11–14.

Zemke, R. (1989) 'Putting the service back into public service', *Training: The Magazine of Human Resources Development*, **26** (November), 42–50.

4

Key challenges for public services delivery
Clive Holtham

4.1 Introduction

This chapter outlines steps needed to revitalize and strengthen public services management. Its core argument is that public services management of the 1990s needs to develop a 'new professionalism'. This can be contrasted with 'traditional professionalism'. But traditional professionalism contains much that is still of relevance. Developing public services management in the 1990s should explicitly seek to retain and build on the strengths of traditional professionalism, rather than reject them completely.

It will be noted that the phrases 'public services' and 'public services management' are used throughout this chapter, in preference to the phrase 'public sector'. This is deliberate. The phrase 'public sector' creates a definition based solely on ownership. It defines what is in the 'public' domain by reference to its legal status. There are two disadvantages to this approach.

Firstly, there can be organizations within the public services by dint of public ownership, but which have little in common with what many would define as public services. The corollary may also apply—services within the private sector but which, in many societies, could and should be regarded as 'public services'.

The second reason is not a semantic one. It relates to the adage 'What's in a name?' Names can carry great significance, particularly the names we give ourselves or like to be called. The word 'bureaucrat' is, technically, a perfectly respectable neutral definition of a functionary, but it is so often used as a derogatory term that it is not highly valued by those working in the public services.

There is nothing inspirational or particularly interesting about being called a 'public sector manager'. The phrase 'public services manager' is evocative of a deep motivator for many in the public services—the desire to serve the public.

British public services management has left the 1980s in a position of weakness, of low morale, of self-doubt and of concern even for its basic survival. It should be noted that similar problems are not wholly absent in the private sector (Banham, 1989). Yet there could not be a greater contrast between

84

negative images of the public services and the enormous commitment and belief of those actually working in the public services. No visitor to an average school or hospital or prison can fail to be impressed with the loyalty and dedication to serving the public that still exists. Though often the voice of the public servant is one of resigned despair, the actions show that they are driven not by purely professional or financial concerns, but with a belief in their jobs and the people they are working for.

Though this chapter is in many ways critical of the conventional public services approach to management, or indeed the lack of such an approach, it is rooted in the belief that there is an important role for the public services in the 1990s and beyond. It believes that the loyalty and dedication just referred to are among the key strengths of public services professionals that can and must be built on to revitalize the public services. Alone they cannot achieve it, however. They must be complemented by a managerial style.

Part of the job as managers is to take a personal responsibility for the future (and indeed survival) of their organizations and services. The aim here is to suggest practical ways in which managers can personally do something. It is essential in this to understand and then build on the distinctive nature of the public services.

4.2   Features of the public services

Before going on to deal with meeting the challenges facing the public services, it is essential to examine their nature. Public organizations not only *are* different from private organizations but they *ought to be* different from private organizations. Particularly, they have a different structure of accountability. They involve different public and consumer expectations.

This is not to say that there is a hard and fast boundary between the public services and the private sector. It can be seen with the former nationalized industries how undertakings can be transferred from the public services to the private sector. Once an organization is actually part of the public services, like it or not it runs to a different approach than if it ran in the private sector. Deciding what is and what is not part of the public services is a political question.

Once an organization is part of the public services, working out how to run it most effectively is still partly a political question but also involves managerial issues. It is not the job of officials to solve political problems as such. But it is not only the job of officials to solve managerial problems, it is their duty to do so.

Among the more clear-cut features of the public services are the following:

- Generally cannot choose customers
- Roles limited by legislation

- Politics institutionalizes conflict
- Complex accountability
- Very open to scrutiny
- Actions must be justified
- Objectives—outputs difficult to state/measure.

Characteristics of the public services have been discussed in detail in the Introduction and Chapter 1. However, a few additional points are worth making. One of the noticeable features of the British public services in particular is the extent to which its managers have typically little experience of managing in other types of institutions, whether in public services or in the private sector. There is, for example, very little interchange between the civil service and local government. There have also been too few examples of people moving from the private sector to managerial positions in the public services.

This has a number of disadvantages. Firstly, it has stunted the development of a distinctive generic public services approach to management. There may (or may not) have been a civil service or a health service or a local government approach to management, but there has certainly not been a public services approach. As a consequence, there has been far too little learning across the different parts of the public services. It has been frustrating to see the managerial innovations of one area repeated, often with exactly the same mistakes, in another area several years later.

There are unfortunately very few bodies who have both an interest across the public services and an ability to build on that interest to catalyse what has become known as 'read across'. Indeed, it is interesting that some of the most active initiatives have come from management consultancies who have a broad public sector remit.

The lack of experience across the public services also means that boundary problems, requiring a deep understanding of, say, both a health and local government perspective, are more difficult to resolve. This is perhaps most noticeable at central government level, where those responsible for developing legislation and regulations have almost never physically worked in the services over which they have some degree of control.

Various vehicles for improving across-public services experience and understanding have been attempted. In the key social services/health service interface a joint planning system was set up in the 1970s, with joint finance available so that at least part of the health budget would be allocated to social services on a jointly agreed basis. There are some areas of central government that have recruited from the ranks of managers in other relevant parts of the public services. The most noticeable examples are the Inspectorates—in social services, education and police for example.

There have also been small-scale efforts at secondments as discussed in Chapter 1, but not at such a regular and sustained level that would materially improve understanding.

The second major problem area from the relatively narrow career profiles of many public services managers is that they have typically no direct experience of the private sector. Such experience is not a necessity for the public services manager, given that there are fundamental differences between the two areas. And there is always the possibility of reading about private sector experience and talking to colleagues in the private sector.

However, two specific problems do arise from the lack of direct experience. The first is that many public services managers have in the past tended to be unaware of what are regarded as key areas of private sector operations such as marketing and strategic planning. The second problem is that public services managers are vulnerable to innovations that were originally developed in the private sector, for reasons that may well have had validity in that context, but which may well be of considerably less relevance in the public services.

A recent example is the area of performance-related pay. This, even now, is by no means as universal or significant in the private sector as is believed by public services managers. It is one thing to apply performance-related pay to private sector employees who have a quantitatively based short-term target, e.g. sales during the calendar year, but it is quite another to apply it to public services employees who may have a multiplicity of objectives, few of which are quantifiable and some of which may be in conflict with each other.

This is not to say that there is no place for performance-related pay. It is to argue a more general point that public services managers lack sufficient practical knowledge of the reality of private sector practices to know whether the theory of these practices (often promoted as panaceas) can be applied to the public services.

In local government, one of the effects of compulsory competitive tendering legislation has been to promote the introduction of relevant commercial and general managerial competencies. An illustrative list of appropriate competencies is given below in the following section.

4.2.1   COMPETENCIES FOR DIRECT SERVICE MANAGERS

The main areas where management development has been needed for DSO managers are:

1 Legal framework. A clear understanding of precisely what the legislation does and does not involve.
2 Individual council policy. Where this has been clarified it needs to be communicated; where it has not or is ambiguous the limitations arising need to be explored.
3 The financial regime. The basic concepts of a trading account and the computation of rates of return must be clear.

4 The tendering regime. The process of tendering and the pricing and other strategies that this will involve.
5 Business planning and strategy. Identifying the alternative ways of operating, costing them and gaining acceptance of the preferred option.
6 Setting up the contractor function and implementing the operational/business strategy either before being subject to tender or after winning the tender. This involves the management of internal change, and also the negotiation of new relationships with the client function and central services.
7 Management accounting and management information systems. Traditional systems are likely to be ill suited to the needs of a DSO, being stewardship and historically orientated.
8 Quality. This has to be monitored in a much more systematic way, but more fundamentally the whole organization needs to be conceived and operated in a way that promotes the achievement of quality.

4.3   Future challenges—meeting them now

The public services currently face many challenges. They are no strangers to challenges. There is much controversy and even disagreement about how far the public services have successfully met the challenges of the last few decades. That is now history. Much can be learned from history, and arguably not enough has been learned from both the failures and successes of recent years.

The task facing those in the public services now, and who are likely to be in the public services for years to come, is facing future challenges. Dealing with these future challenges is not a matter for long-term planners and strategists. It is a task for each and every person working in the public services in their day-to-day activities here and now. All managers in the public services should share some responsibility for dealing with the challenges.

4.4   Challenges

Looking at scenarios serves as a useful reminder that the future will not be the same as the past or the present. It prompts us to consider the action that we should be taking *now* to cope with the future. But scenarios are broad-brushed: something more specific is needed relating to practical issues. These can be called 'challenges'. In the discussion below five topics are highlighted as challenges:

- Mission
- Public services delivery
- Efficiency and effectiveness
- Equal opportunities
- Managing for survival.

4.4.1   MISSION

The legislative roots of the public services typically mask the purpose of individual functions of the public services. Administrative and bureaucratic machinery thinks more typically in terms of what has to be done than why it has to be done. One of the key leadership tasks of a public services manager is to identify and promulgate the mission of the organization. The advantage of using a relatively new term such as 'mission' is that it distances itself conceptually from well-worn phrases as 'goals and objectives'. Mission relates to fundamental purpose. It is almost certainly value-laden. It is a symbol as much as a mechanistic, managerial tool. It carries risks and dangers. It serves as a rallying call.

A mission statement is potentially an immensely powerful symbol. It encapsulates precisely the reason why most people work in the public services. It really can represent an overriding shared value of the organization. However, very great care is needed when using such powerful symbols. They can easily become mere slogans; repeated recitation serving as a substitute for action. Both consumers and employees can quickly become disillusioned when the actual level or nature of services delivered falls short of their perception of what is really needed to serve the community. Where the mission statement or logo promotes the idea of more consumer-orientated public services, then it is essential that there are visible changes in the style of the organizations that meet that objective.

There are an increasing number of meaningful mission statements. Here is an example from North Lincolnshire Health Authority:

Mission statement—finance function
Our mission is to provide, and to be seen to provide, a comprehensive, cost effective and efficient financial service and advisory function to support the health authority in achieving and furthering its health care aims.

We will achieve this objective with enthusiasm, competence and integrity, responding to the changing needs of our customers.

We will apply our talents in an innovative and informative fashion and manage our resources so as to meet the demands required in a courteous and timely manner.

(Stockmarr, 1991)

4.4.2   PUBLIC SERVICES DELIVERY

There is a tremendous bonus to the public services in being able to call on the motivation inherent in service to the public. It can be a far more potent motivator than pecuniary considerations alone. However, the strength of commitment in many public services employees can be a mixed blessing. Their commitment can be so high that they can become demotivated if they feel that those at the top of their organization are not as committed as they are to the effective delivery of services to the public. There are few private sector organizations where the employees enter into industrial action because of their dissatisfaction at the level of service to the customers.

4.4.2.1 *Services delivery—to the consumer or public?*

There is a growing body of literature on how to improve service to the customer in the private sector, e.g. Normann (1984). Although this literature also touches on public services applications of strategies for emphasizing consumer service, it does not take account of any specific characteristics of the public services as opposed to the private sector. They tend to see the public services as simply another type of industry. In many ways there is some logic to this approach; but, as argued also in Chapter 5, its limitations must be appreciated.

There is a growing realization in the public services that techniques that were originally developed for private sector market organizations are, with amendments, applicable to non-market organizations. Marketing is a particular case in point, where the historic tendency in the public sector has been to treat consumers as given or fixed, and to treat them as people for whom services are provided, not consumers whose views actually need to be taken into account when deciding on what services are to be provided (for example, see Bryson, 1988 and Kotler and Andreasen, 1987).

There can be no doubt that the idea of public services needs to encompass many elements of consumer service. However, it is a fact that many people working in the public services derive very strong motivation from the notion that they are working not for themselves or for an impersonal organization, but in the service of the public. It is therefore possible to argue that there is an intrinsic quality in servicing the public which is additional to the basic notions of consumer service.

It is paradoxical, despite the strong philosophical and motivational force concerning public services, that the actual delivery of services to the public is in some respects much less efficiently organized than is perceived to be the case in the private sector. In reality, of course, large bureaucratic private sector organizations often have as many problems organizing service delivery as the public services. Often public services organizations with complex services, relationships and stakeholdings are compared with private sector organizations where performance is actually quantifiable and the products can be physically seen. A hamburger chain provides an extremely limited range of services in a way that can be replicated, not only nationally but also internationally. There are very few public services where this would be possible.

4.4.2.2 *Customer service to generate income*

There are a variety of ways in which marketing concepts can be applied in the public services (Call, 1989; Lovelock and Weinberg, 1984; Walsh, 1989). Taking local government as an example, it should be almost essential for Economic Development Units to engage in high-quality marketing effort, not only in relation to promotional material, but also to the ways they use market research techniques to identify the needs of business and community.

The leisure and recreation service can draw on marketing skills, particularly in relation to the income-generating services.

A council's computer department can develop a range of software or management facilities, and some have appointed marketing managers to carry out a full range of marketing functions for these products.

The word 'marketing' can be somewhat misleading, since many local government services are not sold. However, it remains the case that techniques and ideas from conventional marketing can be applied to a wide range of local authority services.

Much of the traditional style of public services management involves policy-making bodies setting policies, procedures, rules and guidelines under which departments, divisions and establishments operate. This approach will be complemented by professional training and cultures. Neither traditional management nor traditional professionalism is rooted in the consumer-orientated approach. This is not to say that politicians or managers, individually or collectively, have wilfully ignored consumers. Of course, there has always been good practice, which has been sensitive to the consumer. But it has to be admitted that much of public services management practice looks both inward to its own functions and upwards to the policies of the organization, rather than outwards to the consumers being served.

To make explicit attempts to discover 'what the consumers want' before reaching decisions that affect these consumers is not necessarily a welcome prospect for either politicians or managers.

Those who have been involved in a number of forms of public participation and consultation may not be attracted immediately to the idea that these traditional forms are appropriate to more effective decision-making. It is clearly essential to experiment with new methods of consultation, including a much greater use of surveys along the lines that authorities such as Cleveland County Council have been doing for some time.

However, these various techniques must be seen in perspective. They are means, not ends. What is really important to concentrate on is the creation of a culture where service is seen not as a frill or a public relations exercise but as the *raison d'être* of the organization. How often is the question of consumer service discussed explicitly in management teams and committee reports? How far are good examples of customer service by staff praised and rewarded (or even known about)? How far are staff and managerial promotion opportunities related to attitudes to customer service? All too often, the immediate pressures of managing a complex organization in a climate of uncertainty have diverted attention from consumer service.

The notion of a service orientation, although it presents few theoretical problems to implement, in practice represents a fundamental and radical challenge to the traditional ways that public services organizations have operated and to the implicit priorities for political and managerial attention.

To change a culture towards a service-orientated approach is a long and difficult process. It requires constant self-questioning. It requires an orientation not only of policies but also of the day-to-day actions of the entire organization. It requires the commitment not only of politicians and senior managers, but of everyone directly providing services.

In this context, the role of training is of prime significance. Training and development are two of the few available tools by which to catalyse change on the scale necessary (Stewart and Clarke, 1987). A training and development section needs to carry out a thorough review of its own role in the light of the question of consumer service.

If the pyramid of public services is to be inverted, with the broad base of service to the consumer being placed at the top, and the narrow requirements of management (in the broadest sense) being placed beneath it, then almost the first issue that is highlighted is the role of those delivering at the 'front line'. Also of significance is the relationship between the front line and the 'back office' functions. The back office is not only most of the central departments of an authority but also the central parts of the front line service departments. In a service-orientated organization, the back office must be seen to serve the front line (Baddeley and Dawes, 1987).

Ways must be found of breaking down the distance, both geographical and psychological, between the front line and the back office. Although the phrase 'close to the customer' (Peters and Waterman, 1982) has suffered from over-use, it remains a valid concept. The McDonalds hamburger chain are proud of the way that all employees, including directors, must spend at least part of the year physically working in individual shops. Even if this is only of symbolic value, in our view it would be worth while if all senior managers considered how they could spend more time physically at the front line. It is also essential that the fundamental central services upon which service delivery depend, such as mail, telephones, computers, etc., are operated efficiently.

4.4.2.3 Quality and cost

Those who have studied micro-economics will probably recall the significance of the 'production function'. This shows the volume of goods produced compared to cost of producing those goods. For local government and the public services generally, our primary concern is not with volume but with the quality of service delivered. I believe there is value in trying to use a 'production function' for local authority services. Figure 4.1 is an example of such a production function, with changes in costs being shown along the horizontal axis and the corresponding changes in quality along the vertical axis.

In real life actually measuring the quality of service, and thus drawing up such a production function, is likely to pose serious practical difficulties. The point behind using a production function is not mathematical. It is not to try to suggest there can be precise decision-making on the effects of marginal

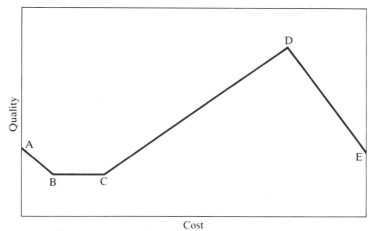

Figure 4.1 Quality–cost relationship

changes in costs. It is, in fact, intended to provoke discussion and debate about the quality–cost relationship. It is also intended to identify some possible (though not necessarily measurable) relationships between service quality and cost. It can also be used to illustrate the potential conflicts between efficiency and effectiveness.

The production function in Fig. 4.1 is just one of many possible functions. However, what is significant about it is the shape of the function, particularly its slope. In the middle section of the function (CD), the function is moving upwards: as costs increase, the quality of service rises. In real life, different services are likely to have different slopes: some may have a proportionately faster increase in quality than others as costs rise.

It is interesting to examine the lower cost part of the curve, which, as set out, highlights two particular issues. The first is a situation in which the function is flat (BC). In this situation spending more money does not lead to an increase in quality, probably because the nature of the service provided is discontinuous. An example would be a situation in which there is a very large volume of work to be done, and only one member of staff to do it. At least two members are required, but if a 5 per cent increase (i.e. 1.5 hours per week) in staffing is recommended, it is likely that the existing member of staff might have to spend as much time as that on additional management and supervisory duties, largely negating the benefits of the increased volume of hours.

The third situation is one in which the quality increases as costs reduce (BA). It must be stressed that this is not an issue related to efficiency. It is related to the quality of service delivery. The type of situation in which this could occur is where the present level of service is extraordinarily low in quality; for example, a cashier's facility that was only open for two hours a day in each of six physically separate offices. This is such a completely inconvenient service that little may be lost by reducing it or even withdrawing it altogether. In terms of public perceptions (which is a key element in the quality of service) it may be better in some cases to provide no service at all than to provide an extraordinarily low quality of service. The final position occurs at higher levels of costs and quality (DE). Where a very high quality of service is currently being provided a point can be reached at which further increases in the cost and volume of that service actually reduce the overall quality of service delivery. For example, suppose there is a consumer requiring advice. If there are too many advisers, they may be literally falling over themselves to give that advice, and perhaps, confusing and probably irritating the consumer.

The situations at the top and bottom end of the production function are important, and managers and policy makers need to be aware of their possible existence. However, it is possible to assert that for much of any public authority service's production function, as cost increases then so typically does the quality of service.

4.4.2.4 Strategies

Potentially one of the most potent uses of the production function is to encourage a discussion of strategy. A strategic options diagram, such as that shown in Fig. 4.2, is commonplace in private sector strategic management thinking. The idea is to conceive of the organization in radically different positions on the production function than it is at present. One of the valid criticisms of much of public services strategic thinking is that it is essentially incremental in nature. This involves only minor moves up and down the production function. Partly, this inevitably derives from the legal basis of much of the public services and also the practical and political problems underlying radical changes in service delivery.

The first conclusion that can be drawn from Fig. 4.3 (and this does relate to

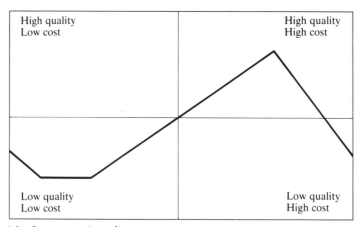

High quality
Low cost

High quality
High cost

Low quality
Low cost

Low quality
High cost

Figure 4.2 Strategy options diagram

the way in which the initial production function was drawn) is that it casts doubt on the ability to have a service delivery strategy that is both low cost and high quality. The only way in which that would be possible under the production function in Fig. 4.2 would be to use efficiency to move the whole line upwards and to the left. It is an extremely common view held by politicians that low-cost/ high-quality services are possible, and indeed that their own organization has many of them. What in fact more generally happens is that certain elements of the services are of high quality, but there are defects in the total service delivery system that go some way towards negating the high-quality elements.

It is much more likely that a high-cost strategy will also lead to a high-quality strategy, but the danger here is that the organization may in fact be on the downward slope of the line (DE) in Fig. 4.1. Again some politicians may argue that a high-cost service must be of high quality. The use of a production function in the way illustrated here could begin—in conceptual terms—to examine and question whether this actually is the case for a given service.

4.4.3   EFFICIENCY AND EFFECTIVENESS

The argument above appears to conflict with the commonly held belief that it is possible simultaneously to reduce costs and increase the quality of public services. This is certainly possible, but the situation in which it happens is exemplified in Fig. 4.3, which shows how efficiency relates to the production function. What in fact happens is that efficiency improvements move the whole of the production function upwards and to the left. As Fig. 4.1 summarizes a production function without efficiency improvements, Fig. 4.3 emphasizes the nature of efficiency improvements. Efficiency improvements can be used either to hold a given service quality level and reduce costs, or to hold costs level and increase the quality of service—or a combination of the two.

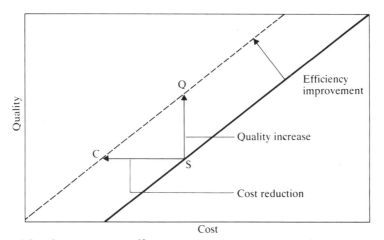

Figure 4.3   Improvement in efficiency moving the production gradient

Presented in diagrammatic form, efficiency appears to be achievable by changing working practices. However, the use of this production function method to illustrate efficiency does begin to address the managerial 'costs' of making efficiency savings. Many types of efficiency savings require considerable managerial effort. This is particularly true in organizations that have long since taken the 'easy' efficiency savings. So, even though the organization could theoretically achieve a more efficient position, it may lack the managerial resource needed to do so. It is then easier, in a budget restrained environment, simply to move down the production function to make savings. That is, it is easier to reduce quality and cost than to invest the effort to become more efficient. There appears to be an increasing body of evidence to suggest that this has been happening in places throughout the public services.

It should also be noted that even moving up and down the existing production function consumes managerial effort and capacity, but this is likely to be less problematic than the thinking and reworking of practices and procedures often necessary to achieve greater efficiency.

4.4.3.1 *Efficiency versus effectiveness*
The years since the Second World War saw a remarkable growth in both the size and the roles of the public services, combined with organizational changes to emphasize the provision of public services through the specialist rather than the generalist. When the pace of growth slowed in the wake of the oil crisis of the 1970s, it coincided with some of the long-term effects of the rapidly planned and implemented growth that were coming to light. The subsequent decade under successive central governments saw an increasing emphasis on the efficiency, and indeed the economy, of public services. This can be interpreted as an inevitable cyclical reaction to the period of growth, or as representing part of both a national and international trend away from collectivism and towards individualism. Although very few people will explicitly oppose the principle of efficient service provision, the reality is that achieving efficiency is a challenge to the status quo, and many can suffer in the short term through such challenges.

There is, however, a problem with efficiency: it is usually reduced to the common language of money, or at least to measurable factors. Effectiveness in the public services is only rarely reducible to monetary terms, and is still difficult to measure in non-monetary terms. As a consequence, when organizational performance is under consideration, it is relatively easier to discuss public services efficiency in measurable terms, than public services effectiveness.

It is but a short move beyond that to equate, either deliberately or accidentally, performance with efficiency. This is a major mistake. It is a mistake made by politicians of all parties. One set of politicians measures performance in terms of the monetary calculus of efficiency. Another set of politicians measures performance in terms of the monetary calculus of size and expenditure. Though both profess concern with effectiveness, there are relatively few examples of significant effort devoted either to the measurement of effectiveness or to the use of effectiveness measures in management decision-making (Hayes, 1977).

The glib quotation 'economy, efficiency and effectiveness' almost totally masks the fact that these three factors, far from reading along some continuous spectrum, in fact reflect three different dimensions that can and do conflict. What is needed in developing new thinking about the delivery of public services is an approach that can handle this conflict; one that can see that it is necessary to tackle simultaneously, but in different ways, issues of both efficiency and effectiveness and the relation (or otherwise) between them. These issues are explored in more detail in Chapter 6.

4.4.4   EQUAL OPPORTUNITIES

One of the foundations and strengths of the bureaucratic approach described in Chapter 1 has been an emphasis on equity. Bureaucracy should be a mechanism for dealing impartially with the public. There is now, however, an increasing body of research and other data to show that public authorities, despite traditional approaches to equity, have not actually delivered equal opportunities to the public they serve. This has happened both for conscious reasons and, more commonly, for unconscious ones.

It is not uncommon for equal opportunities to be identified as a 'political' issue. It certainly is true that much of the pioneering and experimental work on equal opportunities in the UK has latterly been carried out by politically motivated local authorities. But it has also been carried out in private sector firms who could not be accused of political motivation.

In reality, the vast majority of effort required to provide equal opportunities reflects and promotes good management practice. It is poor management practice not to be able to understand and respond to the needs of all consumers. It is bad management practice not to appoint and promote staff on objective as opposed to subjective criteria. A number of organizations are also using their purchasing power to promote equal opportunity practices among contractors and suppliers. This is not an experimental approach, as there has been considerable experience of this through all levels of government in the USA and the UK, specifically in Northern Ireland. It is also a challenge to professional bodies to be equally self-critical and review their working practices so that they, too, promote the equity that was once such an essential ingredient of public services.

It seems almost inevitable that the good practice now developing in some places will percolate far and wide over the next few years, regardless of politics locally or nationally (although politics will affect the pace of development).

There are essentially three approaches open to an organization considering its equal opportunity policies:

1 Equality of opportunity
2 Equality of starting point

3 Positive action.

The first approach was the commonplace assumption behind much of the legislative approach to equal opportunities in the 1960s and 1970s—for example, as embodied in the way the Race Relations Commission and the Equal Opportunities Commission were set up.

It was also very striking in the 1980s to see local authorities in particular going to great efforts to include in their recruitment advertising 'X County Council is an equal opportunities employer', almost as if that statement and its inclusion alone were sufficient to bring about the required policy. The truth is that many organizations never went beyond that type of statement, and that situation is still being found today in the public services and in the private sector.

One of the most striking features of recruitment by the late 1980s was the apparent conversion of a wide range of employers to equal opportunities. For example, banks had begun to take an interest in women returners, making arrangements for women who had left work to be involved in child care to be kept up to date with banking and encouraged to return to the bank when they wanted to do so.

The accountancy profession began to adopt equal opportunity recruitment practices after a period of not doing so. And government ministers began to quote equal opportunities as a reason for various policies, including, for example, more flexible employment practices to assist in the recruitment of nurses. In fact, for a number of reasons in particular the structured almost bureaucratic nature of civil service recruitment has actually embedded some good practice in terms of equal opportunity recruitment.

There are two interpretations of these moves towards espousal of equality of opportunity. One is that a fundamental change in attitude had taken place among employers, who now recognized the discriminatory nature of their past practices. The other interpretation was that there was some other reason, perhaps most typically recruitment difficulties, meaning that 'equal opportunities' was being espoused for pragmatic reasons or economic necessity rather than out of any underlying belief in the principles involved.

There is some evidence that the latter may occasionally be the case. For example, the major firms in the accountancy profession were subject to a comprehensive review by the Race Relations Commission (CRE, 1987). This led to an indictment of the profession and a series of detailed recommendations for improvement. At the same time, the profession was recruiting an increasing number of women, but one of the reasons popularly put forward to explain this was that the professional accountancy firms were in fact finding it increasingly difficult to recruit the type of men they had traditionally recruited, the latter being attracted by the relatively higher salaries on offer in the City and wider financial services industry.

Moving towards genuine equal opportunities is a difficult challenge to management and one that can be difficult to accept and follow through. It is, however, of particular significance to effective public services delivery.

4.4.5   MANAGING FOR SURVIVAL

Public services organizations are usually created by legislation, and legislation often dominates their routine concerns. Some public services functions may well have a long history through, perhaps, a variety of organizational forms. Customs and Excise, local tax collectors and the prison service can all point to several centuries of history.

Although in the last two decades there has been a ferment of proposed and actual structural change, and more recently a great increase in perceived insecurity, by and large the public services still retain traditions and beliefs of continuity. Some contrast with private sector companies is possible. Private corporations are unlikely to have a history of more than a century. Ownership of even fairly substantial corporations can change relatively quickly either through merger, take-over or insolvency.

In the UK one cannot but help notice how a sophisticated system of financial markets contributes towards a climate where the management of companies appear at times to spend almost as much effort on the lookout for predators as on actually running the business.

There was a time when the public services unequivocally offered a job for life, and removal from that job could only be through extreme forms of misconduct. Such a system is still commonplace, for example in other European countries. It is still formally the case in much of the British public services, but the last decade has led to four significant changes:

1 Some changes in the legal status of public services employees whether overtly, as with university lecturers beginning to lose tenure, or covertly through organizational changes that begin to loosen the traditional constraints on public services employment practice—for example, the creation of central government agencies and local management of schools.
2 There has been the explicit adoption of contract-based employment typically tied to performance appraisal. This clearly is a complete break from the 'job for life' tradition of the public services and is found not only at the very senior levels of organizations but also lower down.
3 A climate has been created, or has simply developed, whereby the public services and their employees have come under a degree of public criticism not only from the media, perhaps as part of a historic tradition of campaigning against bureaucratic incompetence, but also even from their own political employers. This creates a degree of insecurity in public services employees, regardless of their legal position.
4 The progression of privatization and enforced competition for the physical

provision of public services creates a climate whereby the security of the public services employees is subject to direct challenge, either as to whether a job will continue to exist or whether it will exist under public services terms and conditions of service.

In some parts of the public services the main issue is not managing for continuity, or even managing for change, but it is managing for survival. It should be noted that much of this issue relates to individuals' perceptions of their own situations, rather than necessarily the factual or legalistic situation. In a study of the management style of over 200 local authority chief executives, Greenwood (1987) found that 50 per cent could be categorized as 'reactive'; not necessarily the most appropriate style for the scale of challenge now faced.

If people brought up on a tradition of job security perceive their situation as insecure, then that is bound to affect their behaviour and attitudes. But there are also areas where the effects of compulsory competition, and radical internal reviews of the nature and method of delivery of services, have produced substantial challenges to traditional ways of delivering services.

There are potentially a whole host of methods of addressing such challenges. The following discussion concentrates on four approaches that are likely, between them, to have widespread relevance.

4.4.5.1 Accountability and delegation

The traditional structure of a public services organization is a hierarchical pyramid. Though this may be a necessary mechanism for setting out the physical structure of an organization, its accommodation and pay levels, it represents neither the reality of organizational functioning nor a prescriptive model. The historic approach to large bureaucracies, rooted in military and church thinking, was unashamedly 'top-down' in nature. In a modern democratic State, top-down thinking is not only undesirable, but also potentially dangerous. An organization needs to be structured along lines that respect the contributions of all the individuals working within it. It must be structured along lines that promote fertile and rich communications sideways, across structural divisions, and horizontally and vertically, without reference to traditional 'command' structures. Of course, there need to be leaders and managers, but there is no imperative that leaders have to treat their staff as followers or sheep. Many aspects of decision-making and creativity should be encouraged throughout the organization, and perhaps least of all at the top of it.

In many ways it would be desirable to create smaller public organizations overall, but in the meantime the large organizations that do exist must devote effort to creating smaller operating units.

There are risks and complexities in this approach, and it involves the evolution of a management style which, in many ways, differs from that traditionally found in public services bureaucracies.

4.4.5.2   *Managing change*

The job of management, both in the private sector and the public services, is increasingly seen not as managing a steady state, but as managing change. Much of conventional management theory and training emphasizes managing for the steady state. The management of change is, if included at all, only done as an afterthought.

Ultimately what is being sought is changed behaviour, both organizationally and individually. To do that, individuals in the organization will almost certainly need changed skills. They may additionally need changed attitudes. It is not enough to address individuals in managing change. It is also necessary to examine the organization as a whole, and in particular its style and culture (Callender and Leighton, 1989). The job of the leaders within an organization is increasingly seen as a role that involves managing culture and style.

4.4.5.3   *Tools of change*

Probably the single most important thing required to manage change is time and space. Managers will only very rarely be given such time and space. It is their job to find it.

Far too little attention is paid to the importance of symbolism in management. Employees often look much more carefully at the symbolic actions of senior managers than they do at what is professed in words and writing. For example, it is no use professing the significance of consumer service and then failing to allocate resources of time or money to major areas of deficiency in consumer service. It is no use professing a corporate approach while making active use of the memo as a weapon and the inter-departmental meeting as a battleground. Symbols can be both negative and positive, and the task of the manager of change is to make the positive symbols work.

Change is an unsettling process: it can undermine self-confidence; it can erode certainties of daily life; it can alter the pattern of relationships. Change requires face-to-face management of a high order. In particular, management needs to ensure that it is getting constant feedback from employees and is able to enter into open discussions with them. There is a reticence in the 'British character' that seems to make the whole process of counselling and individual appraisal difficult. There are many examples of appraisal schemes that are set up and fall into partial or comprehensive disuse for this reason.

Where appraisal and counselling identify shortcomings, the management needs to take positive action to assist employees to overcome these shortcomings. It is no use writing off the individual as beyond assistance. Often perceived individual shortcomings reflect the perhaps cumulative failures of management to assist and support the employee. In general, coaching and training must be planned for and integrated into the total process of the management of change.

Change does not take place overnight. It may take many years, and one of the tools that management has to develop is the ability to repeat constantly the message that is to be communicated. There is a considerable skill in the process of constant repetition. It does not mean saying exactly the same thing over and over again. It means saying more or less the same thing in slightly different ways in as many different places as possible over a lengthy period of time. It means the use of example as well as more overt forms of preaching. Not everyone receives messages in the same way, and it cannot therefore be regarded as an adequate managerial act simply to communicate important information in a single way on a single occasion.

An important approach to repetition is to design processes of involvement and consultation so that ideas do not suddenly appear *ex cathedra*, but are evolved as part of a genuine process of interaction, preferably on a non-hierarchical basis, if at all possible. It is clearly the case that the process through which the change gains commitment and understanding is as important as the actual substantive change itself.

4.4.5.4 *Action plan*

Although culture and values are enormously important, they do not of themselves produce and define action. It is therefore important to develop action plans. These need not be voluminous, or even necessarily published in the conventional sense. There must be some sort of explicit understanding—almost in the form of a contract—so that all those who have committed themselves to a particular course of action understand the nature of that commitment. In a situation where there is an enormously high degree of shared values, the action plans may be minimalist.

In most conventional organizations, and particularly those of any size, a written action plan is desirable, although once the writing of the action plan becomes an end in itself its value can quickly become lost. Once again, the significance lies in the process through which the action is produced, and the way in which commitment to action is coordinated and engendered. Action plans should be clear and should concentrate on action, not vague objectives. They should, wherever possible, indicate those people whose input is required to secure success, and they should be set out in such a way that it is possible to monitor, either quantitatively or qualitatively, the achievement of the action. There also needs to be an adequate process both for the ongoing monitoring of the plan and also, for example, annually, for the more comprehensive review of progress.

Many parts of the public services suffer from a fear of risk-taking. This engenders an attitude whereby it is better to set achievable objectives and achieve them, than to set ambitious ones and fail to achieve them. Management needs to give leadership to ensure that 'failure' is dealt with in a much more sophisticated fashion. The reward system needs to be adjusted so that as much credit is given for commendable effort on ambitious programmes as moderate effort on more straightforward programmes.

4.5   Case study: local authority finance department

During the mid-1980s the author in his position of finance director, together with his senior management colleagues, implemented many of the proposals set out in this chapter, so these experiences can provide a brief case study of developing the new professionalism in practice in a local authority department.

In mid-1983, the department produced its first Management Document. This document set out explicitly the role of managers at various levels and also outlined the management process that would be adopted by the department. Drafts of the document were discussed through the newly constituted management groups in the department, and the management philosophy and processes outlined there remained largely unchanged in subsequent years.

There had been relatively little formal management training and development made available, and this was particularly significant in view of the new skills that were required of managers to meet the more explicit management philosophy. The department was fortunate to be able to put a group of middle managers through a new programme developed by the Local Government Training Board for 'Rising Professionals'. This course proved an extremely valuable method, not only of improving the skills of the participants on the programme, but also of heightening awareness more generally about management development.

The Local Government Training Board published the experiences of the course members as a case study (LGTB, 1984).

These developments were essentially consolidated in 1984, and an updated management document was produced. In addition to this, each section of the department set out its explicit goals and targets for 1984/85 in a way that would facilitate subsequent monitoring of those goals and targets. This document was described as the Action Plan 1984/85, and its table of contents is shown in Table 4.1.

The emphasis on management development continued, using both in-house and external courses. But, additionally, the department, in conjunction with the personnel department's training and development section, set up its own senior management training programme. This typically consisted of one-day seminars on particular topics, such as appraisal, interviewing, industrial relations, etc. Latterly, the department set a target of at least seven days' full-time training per year for managers, to equip them with the range of skills needed to carry out the managerial role in a complex and ever-changing environment.

During 1985, there were further restructures of divisions of the department, including one division that had been restructured in 1983, but where the expected results from that first restructuring had not fully materialized. These

Table 4.1 Action plan contents

A   Introduction
B   The main issues
    (i) Greater devolution
    (ii) A questioning approach
        • Promoting the bottom-up approach
        • Economy, efficiency and effectiveness
        • Monitoring and review
    (iii) Relationships
        • with other departments
        • within the directorate
C   Meetings, tasks and roles
    (i) Meetings
    (ii) Managerial tasks
    (iii) Managerial roles
D   Practical action plan
APPENDICES
1   Management philosophy and action plan
2   Corporate management timetable
3   Departmental management meeting timetable
4   New departmental structure
5   Senior and middle management group
6   Guide to documentation
7   Corporate groups
8   Debrief forms
9   Management development programme

changes within the finance department were taking place against a background of change within the authority as a whole.

The chief officers of the council, led by the chief executive, decided in 1983 that it was necessary to appraise their own roles and the roles of the senior managers in the organization in the light of external changes.

They decided that the management of the authority had to develop new skills in the area of managing change, and set out a number of managerial issues that required priority, if the council's objectives, including expenditure restraint, were to be achieved with a minimum level of service reduction.

As part of the re-assessment of his own role, the chief executive decided to institute a system of 'chief executive's management and system reviews'.

This very innovative review process involved, firstly, the chief executive's staff visiting a department for several days to get a feel for the current issues within that department and to discuss with middle and senior managers their management plans, and most particularly matters arising from them. The chief executive then visited the department, and talked in particular to middle managers about how far departmental and authority-wide targets were being achieved, and the constraints working upon managers preventing such achievement.

The chief executive would then report orally to the management team of the department and follow that with a brief written evaluation of his visit. This review process was met with varying degrees of enthusiasm, not least because it was an extremely novel idea, and because it undoubtedly contained elements of monitoring the achievement and effectiveness of chief and senior officers. It was, however, a major step towards demonstrating visibly the need for a more analytical and questioning approach.

4.5.1 STATEMENT OF MANAGEMENT PHILOSOPHY

The departmental management team felt strongly that, for recruitment purposes, the department should make no effort to hide its distinctive management philosophy: it was not only necessary to attract staff who were interested in that philosophy, but also to indicate openly to staff who were less committed to that philosophy what they might expect. The outcome was a philosophy, which is contained in full below.

The important thing is less the precise headings and words used in the statement of philosophy, but more the fact that the management of the department was prepared to set out so clearly its managerial aims. This statement has attracted considerable interest, and was included in the Local Government's Training Board's report (LGTB, 1985) on good management practice in local government.

This philosophy remained totally unchanged for three years. The statement was undoubtedly a positive factor in improving recruitment to the department —its original objective—and it also formed the backbone of the successive management documents within the department. It was particularly emphasized during the staff induction programme.

However, it also has to be admitted that there can be problems arising from being so very explicit about managerial aims. In particular, it is very likely that expectations will be raised among both staff and managers, and when actions take place that are incompatible with the philosophy, this can lead to criticism and discontent.

4.5.1.1 *Departmental philosophy—finance department*

In recent years we in finance have been changing our attitude and style along with other departments within the authority. We realize that management in the 1980s is a totally different affair from the management of the 1970s. The way we want to move forward is outlined below and will help you decide whether or not your future is with us.

Local government is a hierarchy. Typically, decisions have to go upwards through the system and it is the task of senior management to set a policy framework. But given the hierarchical system we actively encourage the flow of ideas to come upwards and decisions to be taken at all levels.

We want staff to take initiatives rather than simply wait for instructions. There are risks involved in this style of management but we are committed to taking those risks in order to achieve economic and efficient operations.

You Matter   In finance we realize that people are our main asset. We want all members of staff to achieve their full potential. We know that the people are actually doing a job so we want to encourage:

- *A questioning approach to the way we all do things*
  The basic flow of ideas to be upwards rather than downwards. Management may not always be in a position to implement these ideas but a good idea is worth talking about.

- *Good communications—have you heard?*
  In a large directorate good communications are necessary upwards, downwards and sideways. We need staff to be committed to promoting and carrying out this responsibility both formally and informally.

- *A job well done*
  Personal accountability is the first step in achievement. When individuals in the directorate know exactly what their own responsibilities are, they can work effectively in a team. As well as this they are able to set their own targets in their field and develop not only their job but also the general efficiency in their section.

- *Working for the community*
  We are ultimately working directly for the residents of a borough that has many unresolved problems. They expect—and so do we—a high level of service and a degree of personal commitment. That commitment will vary between jobs and level within the directorate, but a higher level will be sought here than in local authorities with fewer problems or organizations not involved in public services.

- *Within the authority—a corporate approach*
  Finance is one of thirteen council departments all working together for the benefit of the community. With the responsibility for the financial dealings of the council, we have an important part to play in achieving monetary targets and helping councillors and officers to respond to the borough's needs.

- *Working efficiently*
  In all areas our goal is to achieve good working practices. We give a greater priority to doing an adequate job economically and efficiently than an excellent job at great expense. However, in all sections there are specific tasks or functions that have to meet high minimum standards.

4.5.2   RHETORIC VERSUS REALITY

One of the problems faced by practising managers is that often there can be a gap between rhetoric and reality. An outstanding text on the problems of managers in British local government (LGTB, 1983) all too accurately portrays the real world of the senior manager:

> Most management training would have us believe that if only we learn the lessons and techniques and try hard we shall end up with a well planned, well run department where decision making is thoughtful and systematic, where days are planned logically and orderly, where planning systems exist which are rationally based, where objectives are clear and consistent, where we steadily monitor progress against plans, where the budget is controlled and spent as planned . . . and so it goes on. The rhetoric consists of exhortations to reach for this organisational heaven. The reality is quite different. Many days seem like a shambles, at the end of which there seems so little to show for so much expended energy. A typical day in the life of a chief officer consists mostly

of interactions with other people, seeking, giving information, negotiating, pushing, pulling, cajoling. Many of the contacts are impromptu and unexpected which in turn set off chains of events as unpredictable as they are trivial or important. Decision making is a tangled web woven through bargaining and negotiation. Objectives are something chief officers often feel guilty about not having and which they resolve one day to get around to. In truth, they are relieved they never have to because they know instinctively they are unrealistic and part only of the rhetoric. For every problem solved and victory achieved there are several new problems to solve and defeats to endure. Each costs hours of careful preparation, persuasion, listening, talking, and compromising.

The above text highlights the problems that arise from the pressure and chaos of reality. Even though senior managers can take explicit steps to break out of the vicious circles of pressures, considerable effort is needed to do so, including support from all levels within the department.

4.6 Conclusion

Reviewing the experiences of the last 25 years, it is clear that there are no panaceas to improving management of the public services. It is very difficult to improve effectiveness just by changing structures or adopting new budgeting or planning systems or by putting more effort into market research or training. That is not to say that none of these has ever improved performance, because they clearly have. It is more to say that none of them in isolation can achieve the kind of major breakthrough that their protagonists have often claimed. Problems of this type are not limited to the UK, although it should be noted that other countries have adopted quite different types of innovation, for example in Sweden (Gustafsson, 1987).

Taken together, there is more chance that even then something over and above changing systems and processes is necessary to sustain developments and improvements over the relatively long time period needed to implement them successfully in the public services. This is the real significance of the need to develop an appropriate managerial culture. Creating a culture is extremely difficult; sustaining it is even more so. It is not a job that can be carried out in one or two years. It needs the consistent application of much hard work by many people over a long period of time. A well-established managerial culture will not wither away overnight, but it can be vulnerable to steady attrition from changes in external factors and personalities.

From the experience of recent years in the British public services, it would seem that organizational improvements are undoubtedly subject to entropy: the natural tendency is for organizations to revert to the lowest common denominator.

It is important to analyse why this is. Clearly of major significance are the professional and administrative cultures that abound throughout local and central government and the health service. These, historically, have never had any particular managerial orientation. They are not necessarily quickly picking up such an orientation now. For the last hundred years the public services in the UK have also worked along organizational systems that are of a classic Weberian bureaucratic form at a time when bureaucracy is under considerable challenge because of its acknowledged unresponsiveness and 'top-down' overloading. It is also necessary to remember that elements of bureaucracy are concerned with public services values that are still regarded as fundamental. These include:

- equity
- impersonality
- the organized achievement of political goals.

It is essential to create a 'new professional', who does not wholly reject the many strengths of traditional professionalism and bureaucracy, but who is at the same time able to meet both present and future challenges. The manager of today and the future is having to cope with an increasingly turbulent and uncertain environment and hence needs to develop and enhance the skills involved in managing change. It can certainly be suggested that, increasingly, the most fundamental role of the public services manager is managing change.

References

Audit Commission (1985) *Improving Economy, Efficiency and Effectiveness in Local Government in England and Wales*, Vol. III. Audit Commission, London.

Baddeley, S. and Dawes, N. (1987) *Information Technology Support for Devolution. Local Government Studies*, July/August, 1–16.

Banham, J. (1989) 'On professionalism and professions: the management charter initiative', *Journal of the Operational Research Society*, 20 (4), 315–21.

Bryson, J. M. (1988) *Strategic Planning for Public and Non-profit Organisations*. Jossey-Bass, San Francisco.

Call, M. (1989) 'Public servants', *Public Money and Management*, 9 (3, Autumn), 9–10.

Callender, C. and Leighton, P. (1989) *Changes and Trends affecting Employment*. Report by IMS on the skills required by Local Government in the 1990s. Local Government Training Board, Luton.

CRE (1987) *Chartered Accounting Training Contracts*. Report of a Formal Investigation into ethnic minority recruitment. Commission for Racial Equality, London.

Greenwood, R. (1987) 'Managerial strategies in local government', *Public Administration*, 65 (Autumn), 295–312.

Gustafsson, L. (1987) 'Renewal of the public sector in Sweden', *Public Administration*, 65 (Summer), 179–91.

Hayes, F. (1977) *Productivity in Local Government*. Lexington Books, Farnborough.

Kotler, P. and Andreasen, A. R. (1987) *Strategic Marketing for Non-profit Organizations* (3rd edn). Prentice Hall, Englewood, Cliffs, New Jersey.

LGTB (1983) *Guidelines for Departmental Development in Housing*. School for Advanced Urban Studies, Local Government Training Board, Luton.

LGTB (1984) *First Line Managers in Local Government—A Self Help Management Development Programme*. School for Advanced Urban Studies, Local Government Training Board, Luton.

LGTB (1985) *Good Management in Local Government: Successful practice and action*. Local Government Training Board (in conjunction with Audit Commission and INLOGOV), Luton.

Lovelock, C. H. and Weinberg, C. B. (1984) *Marketing for Public and Nonprofit Making Organizations*. Wiley, New York.

Normann, R. (1984) *Service Management: Strategy and Leadership in Service Businesses*. Wiley, Chichester.

Peters, J. and Waterman, R. H. (1982) *In Search of Excellence: Lessons from America's Best-Run Companies*. Harper & Row, New York.

Stewart, J. and Clarke, M. (1987) 'The public service orientation: issues and dilemmas', *Public Administration*, 65 (Summer), 161–77.

Stockmarr, A. (1991) 'Stating the mission for North Lincolnshire HA', *Public Finance and Accountancy*, 1 March, p. 25.

Walsh, K. (1989) *Marketing in Local Government*. Longman, Harlow.

PART 2

Issues and cases in modern public services
management

5

The manager faces the consumer

Jenny Harrow and Malina Shaw

5.1 Introduction

As discussed in earlier chapters, the language of consumerism now permeates
most major policy documents that public services managers interpret and operationalize. Although the terms 'customer' and 'consumer' are often undefined,
and used interchangeably, their deployment has encouraged a rediscovery of
the service element in public provision. As such, consumerism can be seen as an
acceptable import from the conventions of private sector business. Management
trainers have speedily offered private-style customer care programmes to public
services clients, and the academic support for what is known as the Public
Service Orientation has given the consumerist message much increased validity
(Stewart and Clarke, 1987). Of all the themes now dominating public services
with private sector provenance, it is unlikely that this would be questioned by
public services managers; indeed, it is becoming a further yardstick of achievement. Its philosophy allows value-for-money questions to be stated from the
perspective of service users rather than service financiers. Its assumptions about
enhancing consumers' welfare enable the retention of notions of responsive
and motivated public workforces, whose managerial and professional concerns
coincide.

While many public services managers are consumer-aware, using consumerist
stances as levers for change, more limited numbers may actually be facing
the consumer, personally and regularly, with all the implications for service
effectiveness and equality that that implies. It is possible that some public services managers' personal goals include being shielded from extensive overt consumerist demands which, in many cases, can conveniently be classified as the
operational rather than the strategic part of the business. If the current trend
towards public management by contract, rather than by direct service provision,
continues then the opportunities to stand even further away from direct consumer contact will increase, and consumerism may either become more important, or fade. Complaints to contractors may be encouraged by specific contract
terms, and consumerism itself may become a criterion for awarding contracts.
Alternatively, consumerism may fade as complainants are inhibited by service
deliverers from reaching public services managers.

Public services managers' rationales for using consumerism as a managerial device—for controlling, for motivating, for planning—are bound to be more complex than the desire to sell, to sell more, have customers return, and have customers commend the product to others. In custodial public services, customer return may be seen as service failure. Over-commendation of other services may lead to lower quality services for the increased number of users. As Flynn (1990) emphasizes, 'in the public sector the service relationship is varied and complex', with service users varying in their willingness to use the service and uncertainty as to the identification of all of the customers of a particular service. Thus an adoption of consumerist stances provides practical and professional challenges for public services managers.

This chapter, examining consumer/manager closeness, considers the opportunities offered and limitations imposed when consumerist perspectives are at the forefront of decision-making. Not least of those limitations will be the costs imposed upon those managers accepting exposure to consumers on the latter's terms, arising from heightened workloads, and recognition of the need to acquire and deploy particular areas of management skill. For many such managers may be added the cost of acceptance that the public service managerial role is that of reconciling demand and resources, and that consumer wishes cannot therefore be paramount. Further, those demands may not stem from consumers only, but from politicians exercising political control and speaking for service users as they see them. Flynn (1990, p. 136) goes so far as to suggest that where politicians' and public services managers' ideas on service running do not coincide, 'this may lead managers into a position where they have a split managerial personality, facing the users with one set of behaviours and the politicians with another'. Thus, managers who embark on increasing customer contact—for example, through routine user surveys—are certainly taking service and often professional risks. Despite an inherent pleasantness in many of the terms, manager–consumer relations is not an easy or safe area within which managers can succeed.

The chapter reviews the differing interpretations of the term 'consumer' in a variety of public services management contexts, and examines the rationales for managers using consumerist perspectives as a basis for reviewing organizational and individual managerial practice. It considers levels of managers having key consumer contacts and the degree of vulnerability or power that this provides. Also discussed is the critical collision of concepts facing public services managers, which is central to the consumerist debate; the concepts of dynamism on the one hand, and responsiveness on the other.

Presently, public services managers are sought who can be personally and organizationally dynamic, changing service content, style, and even provider; yet much responsiveness to consumers may mean blocking major change, or reversing change, as shown by complaints on hospital closures, or benefits reorganization. In this sense, therefore, it can be argued that public services managers cannot embrace consumerism wholeheartedly. In the light of this concept collision, the chapter then examines what may be seen as managerial good practice, and concludes by examining ways in which consumerist perspectives can be maintained within the complexity of public services management.

5.2   The consumer in the variety of public services management contexts

The nature of consumerism has been extensively debated, both in terms of consumer identification and in establishing the ideology that flows from a consumer-based perspective. Rhetoric may be more apparent than reality. Flynn's definitive discussion of the factors inhibiting public organizations from adopting a wholly private sector framework for relating to their customers emphasizes how the use of the word customer 'stretches the definition of that word' (Flynn, 1988). Stewart and Ransom (1988) point to the multiplicity of public services users—'. . . customers, clients, users, and . . . citizens'. If public services consumerism is seen as essentially a cultural stance involving an organization's willingness to be open to receiving and acting on customer views, then this may in any event be a 'misreading of much private sector practice, where frequently it is only the largest and the latest customers who are held significant' (Harrow and Willcocks, 1990)

In managerial terms, it is significant that Fenwick's local government-based definition of consumerism is action-oriented, and presented as a continuum of activity:

> . . . the term 'consumerism' will be taken to denote the varied initiatives currently underway within local government which seek a closer relationship between the public and their local authority . . . a variety of public sector innovations, ranging from fundamental . . . decentralisation programmes to more mundane adjustments to administrative style.
>
> (Fenwick, 1989)

Examples range from establishing telephone helplines and consulting disabled people on access issues to setting up One Stop Shop enquiry points and redesigning application forms. The possibly overworked but widely understood term 'user-friendly' is important here, with an apparent acceptance that where users receive more, even marginally, than that which they expected from a service, a degree of friendliness has been established.

Customer closeness phraseology reflects this 'doing' approach. For example, the Local Government Training Board's study, *Getting Closer to the Public*, (LGTB, 1987b), identifies ways of opening up services, from 'replying to all complaints within three days' and 'setting up customer panel meetings for regular discussions with staff' to 'giving all clients of a service, a statement of the service aimed at'. Consumerism here indicates a pro-active stance to, at least, the gathering of user views, which will generate action.

5.3   Categorizing public services consumers

That public services consumers require some categorization before reflection on the degree and nature of openness of service that they seek and need, is clear. Consumers' status may denote something about them—the most obvious example, a 'patient', who so described is generally held to be 'ill'—which, in turn, will affect a manager's rating of the quality and quantity of that consumer's demands and requests. Consumers may be patients, clients, customers, claimants, users, participants, residents, community charge payers, taxpayers; and even public services mangers from another or the same service. Most of these descriptive terms have different cultural connotations—'clients' and 'claimants' being dependants; customers, direct payers; participants, public spirited volunteers, and so on. An alternative categorization might be, cynically, in terms of the political damage they may do—the unstoppable, the buy-offable, and the neglectable. Membership of such categorizations will shift over time, with changing public interest and the impact of external factors, including public scandal over aspects of service provision; for example, in long-stay hospitals or with children at risk.

Categorization, however basic, may be seen to relate to manager/user responsiveness and provide background as to the relative rationales for managerial behaviour in relation to members of those categories. Figure. 5.1 provides such an indication, with managerial responsiveness to users being seen as a continuum of behaviour.

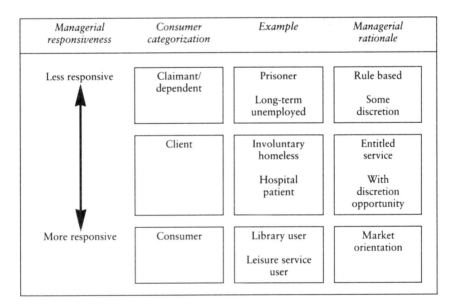

Managerial responsiveness	Consumer categorization	Example	Managerial rationale
Less responsive	Claimant/ dependent	Prisoner Long-term unemployed	Rule based Some discretion
	Client	Involuntary homeless Hospital patient	Entitled service With discretion opportunity
More responsive	Consumer	Library user Leisure service user	Market orientation

Figure 5.1   Managerial response—public services consumer categories

Such an explanation provides only an outline framework and starting point for an understanding of the variety of manager–user relationships in public services settings. Further dimensions, notably the external contextual factors and the personal traits of both the managers and users, come into play. Not only may membership of categories overlap—with users at different times potentially members of all three, yet finding their expectations geared to their treatment under one particular categorization—but users' treatment may differ according to the interaction of these contextual and personal factors. Figure. 5.2 gives an indication of the range of these factors.

The clearly service-oriented public provision, where recipients are more positive about receiving attention—education, personal and environmental health —would seem to have the easiest task in persuading service staffs to become more user-friendly. Even here, managers will find the consumerist perspectives providing for internal conflicts: who is the key customer in the case of school refusal, the pupil or the parent? When consumer involvement becomes statutory, how should managers respond when consumer numbers subsequently involved,

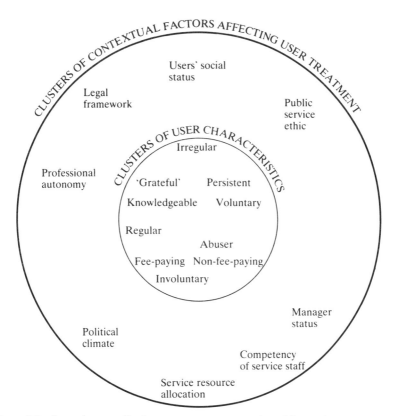

Figure 5.2   Some factors affecting consumer treatment in public services

declines, as evidenced by a lack of volunteers for school governorships? Applying the concept becomes increasingly problematic as the nature of the public service becomes more a matter of the decisions and expectations of others—particularly so in custodial services. In the prison service, for example, there will be continuing direct 'service users', but of two types and with intendedly differing status: convicted and remanded prisoners—and the irregular and indirect service users, such as prisoners' families, friends and other visitors, buttressed by members of boards of prison visitors, as representing both the direct user and the wider (i.e. all society) user interest.

Even here, the potential customers are in some direct contact with the service. In police services, for example, the 'public', as local communities and individuals, are seen as the ultimate users, being beneficiaries, whereas the focus of the service, the 'clients', are usually an unwilling focus of attention. In this field, a further category of important service user—the victim of crime—is another area of concern for police managers. To further complicate matters, the public services also contain managers whose customer contact experience is indirect, and often only instituted in cases of complaint. The staff of the former Family Practitioner Committees faced their organization's transition, under the White Paper *Working for Patients* (DH, 1989) from 'passive paying agency' to 'active manager of customer interests' (Jefferson and Carr-Hill, 1989), although the *direct* service supplier remains the family doctor. Further, there are those whose purpose includes that of 'consumer guardian', such as the range of government inspectorates; and most recently the Office of Water Services, under the aegis of the Department of the Environment.

A patrician view of consumerism, in the sense of senior managers' (or politicians') certainty that they best understand the longer term needs of their service users, thus may still be possible. It may also be practised *within* organizations, as the notion of the internal market as between 'servicing' work, such as training and direct provision increases. In large public services organizations managers may be learning to respond more towards their internal customers—who at least are more likely perhaps to appreciate the pressures facing them and to talk some of the same language—than to their external customers, with possibly inflated ideas of service delivery. This may be especially the case where external users are sources of major stress, such as violent or potentially violent clients, in which case the 'internal market' concept is a welcome relief inasmuch as some recipients of their work may appear satisfied. Even internal consumerism may, however, be problematic. A major example may be drawn from the health service where the introduction of Information Technology has in places been accompanied by a mismatching relationship between the IT professionals installing the systems and the operational and strategic managers needing to use those systems—a situation that may have arisen in part because the latter were or became unwilling customers (see Willcocks, 1990).

5.4   Openness and consumerism in public services

Much public services consumerism may best be characterized as relating to the degree of openness within the service—that is, in terms of extending the users' knowledge and providing opportunities for users to represent their experiences at a managerial level, and also in terms of the adequacy of opportunity for public scrutiny to focus on the service's achievements as well as its deficiencies. Thus, consumerism is seen as an openness continuum, with various public sector services located at various points in that continuum in terms of their relationships with their primary and secondary users, as depicted in Fig. 5.3.

Such an analysis must be partial and open to individual interpretation or rejection. The location of some services on the continuum outlined in Fig. 5.3 may further relate not so much to any desire by their managers to restrict openness as such but because the provision itself (for example, the community nursing services) takes place out of public sight. It seems likely that public services managers within particular services would not necessarily agree about where their service was, or should be. Some public services managers may well feel that their primary users' interests are best served by actively limiting openness at early stages of planning; for example, in discussing locations of community housing for former mental hospital patients.

Further, the complex nature of some public services limits the applicability of the openness continuum to an extent. The examples selected in Fig. 5.3 are all taken from direct and relatively tangible services, whether with voluntary or involuntary users. However, Flynn (1990, p. 135) has drawn attention to those

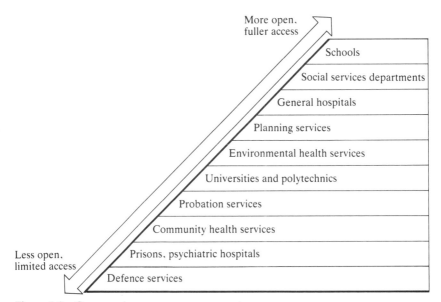

Figure 5.3   Consumerism as an openness continuum

public services with no end-users in the public sense of the term—those revolving around the development and provision of policy advice to ruling politicians. Here, openness of the kind implied above would be inappropriate; and such openness as there was would be within the relatively enclosed and internal policy advice world.

Nevertheless, the linkage between developing consumerist perspectives and encouraging service openness does exist. In practical terms, for many managers, it may well be seen as essentially a matter of 'getting a few small and public things right' and of 'being seen to try'. The extent to which the initiative-type of definition is sufficient will be discussed below in reviewing managerial beliefs and practices.

5.5   Public services managers' refusing consumer demands

A further major factor for public services impinging upon consumer-oriented responses, is the extent to which, unlike many private companies vying for consumer loyalty, customers of one service will also be customers of another; and that, especially for stretched services, far from seeking to *retain* customers, they may wish—and plan—to pass them on. Potentially disruptive clients may be one example; but so may very grateful customers. In the latter case, for the competent ward sister, managing a short-stay ward for elderly people, where rehabilitation and return to the community are the goals, particular professional and managerial tact will be needed to be responsive to the customers who wish to stay in their hospital beds. It is in the interlinking of public services and in the very under-researched area of saying no to consumers that the concept of consumerism, as applied to public sector settings, must be seen as involving far more than managers taking incremental steps to open up their services. A relevant example is that of the locality housing estate manager, refusing small-scale service requests (tightening of window catches, replacement of bath plugs) in the interests of resource allocation, in the knowledge that the tenant is fully able to undertake the minor repairs demanded vociferously. Here, the tenant has been translated, albeit unwillingly, from the 'consumer' to the 'prosumer', as designated by Toffler (1987)—a creature arising where the distinctions between producer and consumer are broken down. Flynn (1990, p. 141) prefers the term 'pro-user', combining producer and consumer into one. Yet even with such apparently trivial demands, where the manager's stance will be backed generally by commonsense notions, a degree of risk is being entertained by the manager involved; and the managerial rationales for the consumer stances chosen need consideration.

5.6   Rationales for managers adopting consumerist perspectives

Two major strands of thinking about consumerism in public services contexts join to provide the essential pro-user argument. Firstly, that consumer experiences are major keys to the effectiveness of rating services and, ultimately, quality (in Martin's terms, 'consumers . . . as a source of essential data'); and, secondly, that consumers have rights to express preferences and concerns, and to affect service delivery and planning (Martin, 1986). In both aspects of consumerism, the issue of 'proxy consumers' may need debating—carers speaking for disabled relatives, parents for pupils—but it seems clear that it is towards direct users that much public services management effort is engaged. It is 'the consumer as data—source and problem solver', that is, the private sector consumerist model, linked in particular to a variety of approaches for services marketing (Beltramini, 1981). In the second area, there are implicit and explicit challenges to be made to professional decision-making; and certainly to managers' opportunities to manage.

What rationales have and should public services managers employ for bringing the consumer voice at least into earshot? Such a question relates not only to those managers' subsequent own handling of consumer-based issues, but also to the presentation of the organization's consumer stance to their own staff. George's account of Trent Regional Health Authority's programme, 'Personalizing the service' emphasizes the need for an obvious commitment to action from managers as the basis for ensuring that staff do not regard personal service as a gimmick (George, 1988).

Rationale varies with context; and may include:

- gathering information on the current and future needs of existing services users, for planning, including issues of efficiency, and cost saving, and the wider issues of effectiveness and equity
- identifying alternative customers, 'unmet needs', and assessing the nature and balance of provision (including diversifying or contracting 'product' range)
- addressing issues of service access and image, for professionals and public users; expanding use of existing services
- testing out new products/services
- reviewing levels of satisfaction with services, developing quality measures, and qualitative performance indicators.

All of these have clear private sector equivalents, and may be reflected in the increasing application of marketing techniques to areas of public services such as library services (Day, 1989; Durcan, 1984). Ironically, the limitations of entrepreneurial activity within the public services, despite its blanket encouragement at one level, may be uncovered, with resulting frustration for the managers involved. Stone and Thomson (1987), for example, examining the use of marketing practices in the Scottish Further Education Sector, note that while these vary, there are external obstacles to overcome, notably those central and local government regulations imposing constraints on the types of courses that can be developed.

Beyond these, other rationales will come into play, which differ from private sector practice and reflect various managerial and political agendas. While they may not be described in this way, these may include:

- improving morale of staff, through customer perspectives which encourage or renew pride in their work
- service-defensive strategies to prove 'a good job well done', i.e. a survival rationale, based on customer popularity, and using consumers as a shield; making friends among consumers
- the empowerment of disadvantaged users in decision-making and the likely resulting limitations in professional influence.

Some managers, resource-pressed, may decide to encourage consumers to complain directly to politicians, in ways that managers themselves cannot do. Housing departments in some inner city authorities have been prime areas for such managerial strategies. Rather than managers becoming advocates for clients' needs, clients' demands might get the managers the resources they otherwise do not have. Urging users to put even greater pressure on already extended services might be cited as managerial irresponsibility; or as managerial responsibility by refusing to 'paper over the cracks' of inadequate service provision. In such situations, traditional advocacy roles are reversed.

Experience and anecdotal accounts of managing suggest that managers' consumerist rationales begin from the premise of the need for closeness to the public. Clearly, however, to actively seek consumer inputs into aspects of public services organization and delivery is to begin a process that is not then fully amenable to managerial, or political, control. Nevertheless, the strength of support for the inherent value of incorporating consumerist views when providing any area of public service, whether rooted in awareness of consumers' knowledge or in recognition of services' ultimate accountability to consumers, is so great that a rationale, unspoken but crucial for some managers, is that of the 'bandwagon'. To use the language of consumerism, and to be seen to nod in its direction—installing a suggestion box, creating senior managers' telephone 'hotlines'—will be a commonsense managerial activity.

The almost ritualistic use of satisfaction surveys among hospital patients, or completing students on courses, may flow partly from this approach, which is not always a cynical and self-protective one, but is one that recognizes a need to be seen to be pro-consumer. Andrew and Thompson (1988) contend that demand for participation in the NHS does not stop at the point of answering survey questions, but for some it may well do. Consequences of regular surveying may be a minimal number of outcomes in consumers' favour, because of the lack of room for manoeuvre in the services concerned.

Such rationales may lead managers to be afraid—quite realistically—of creating increasing consumer expectations that cannot be met and may overwhelm an already stretched workforce. Managerial rationales must therefore include consideration of the effects of consumerism of the workforces being managed.

The difficulties of coping at an inter-personal level with organized, vocal and hypercritical service users for public services workers should not be dismissed by those rarely responsible for face-to-face contact—an aspect of the consumerist debate highlighted implicitly by Flynn when he refers to those public services workers facing difficult contact with users as 'emotional labourers', (Flynn, 1990, p. 144).

One aspect of rationale remains: that of consumerist involvement as resource-focused—whether as money-savers, by identifying the service overlaps and time-wasting, or as money-spenders, by spurring on consumer demand for more and 'better' services. For managers, the pursuance of consumer views as part of a service review policy (for example, through the work of 'user panels') will not be accomplished cheaply, with the advent of the all-expenses-paid consumer, who may otherwise be unable or unwilling to provide an input. Much budgeting for consumerism seems, however, to be more associated with public relations campaigns than with the payment of taxi fares for disabled advisers to social services committees, or 'sitter' costs for the carer.

Senior managers' expressions of leadership for pro-active consumerism is a complex matter, with the difficulty that much action here can be seen as token association—the occasional dropping-in to day centres or clinic waiting rooms. The fact that middle managers have leadership opportunities here must also be recognized. Many of these will have the most—and the most important— consumer contacts, and will be responsible for implementing 'handed down' consumerist policies when their own staff may resist them. In particular, it is possible that first-line managers (those who, with their staff, interact with the public routinely, concerning practical service issues) are among the most skilled in customer relations and the practicalities of preventing demands completely swamping service availability. Housing and domiciliary care services managers are prime examples.

5.6.1   MANAGERS FACING THE CONSUMER—THE ACROSS THE COUNTER EXPERIENCE

Consumers in some public services, where shortages occur through high demand, face lack of choice and are relatively uninfluential. Low status users tend to have the attention of low status managers; hence regular meeting between consumer and provider is at lowly organizational levels. George (1988, p. 13) asks rhetorically: 'Why is it that those who make the first contact with the public in many service organizations are the most junior staff and are treated as such?'

With the exception of senior managers' telephone availability for complainants—by its nature likely to be time limited and to result in delegation of work —it will be operational rather than strategic managers who are coping with consumer demands and criticism. What are appropriate behaviours towards consumers by these managers, among whom defensive strategies may predominate because they themselves lack knowledge of departmental policy or resource levels? Is increasing public contact at these levels encouraging new managerial skills—particularly those emphasizing mediation between the user, the face-to-face manager, and senior managers high above the user encounter?

Given the importance of first appearances in consumer interaction, should first-line managers be like users in dress, style, even age? This is an approach, known anecdotally to the authors, to be used in some services such as housing. As operational managers face varying pressures to maintain or alter service direction ('programme bending'), it is important to consider what is known about their approach to consumerism and the extent to which they have adopted all or any of the rationales discussed above. Such questions become the more important if senior managerial public services post-holders are becoming more transient than hitherto.

This in turn raises the issue of defining who are the 'junior', 'less senior' or, the overworked term, 'middle' managers in the public services? Aucoin (1987), writing from a Canadian public service perspective, identifies the middle manager as occupying positions below senior management and above those who perform the operations; distinguishing in turn between those middle managers who have further managers below them and those who are within the 'operating core', supervising staff at front lines. A consumerist perspective will focus on the latter, whose functions are then identified as priority setting, establishing support from the organizational environment, managing resources and operations. This rather indeterminate group is the 'critical link' between governments and publics, since 'they constitute the level of management which must possess the greatest knowledge of the business of the organization and its clientele' (Aucoin, p. 192).

5.6.2   MIDDLE MANAGERS AND CONSUMERISM—SOME CASE EXAMPLES

What is known of the views of such core service managers on consumerism? Small-scale research by the authors during 1989 focused on this, through contact with the first two cohorts from a Domiciliary Care Management Diploma Programme (Harrow and Shaw, 1989). The key importance of this field had been highlighted by the Social Services Inspectorate's report on first-line managers in domiciliary and day care services, showing under 5000 first-line managers (FLMs) providing a home help service for half a million people, with '. . . few of them professionally qualified or . . . (having) received training for the management tasks they undertake' (SSI, 1988).

Respondents, only a minority of whom were still denoted by their employers as Home Help Organizers, were drawn from urban and rural areas, working for authorities demonstrating a range of social services departmental structures, decentralized, centralized and divisionalized. The research was based on the premise that a new range of managerial skills would be needed as 'facing the consumer' became essential. Responses, gained through questionnaires rather than interviews to ensure confidentiality, showed on the whole a cautious welcome to consumerist philosophies; but anxieties about its impact upon their own staffs, not on their abilities to develop and adapt.

For one respondent in a divisionalized structure, where a consumerist emphasis was just beginning, the 'efforts to involve staff at all levels . . . in discussions about the service being provided', as an important preliminary, was recognized as leaving that manager with an ongoing problem. Staff expectations about their work and the service provided had been raised, but realistically 'there is no indication that these expectations can be met' (Harrow and Shaw, 1989, p. 31). This approach leaves the manager to cope with disappointed users and would-be users plus disappointed and frustrated staff—the latter de-motivated by a re-emphasis on the service element in their work, and realizing how little could be changed.

Motivating staff in such situations became more complex when the service was physically organized to be so close to the public that the public were able to watch and comment adversely on staff moves. In one extensively decentralized London department, the local population seemed to have begun an informal Value For Money Watch by 'monitoring' staff attendance, requiring the manager to urge her staff to ignore this type of very public criticism:

> Local people have become obsessed with staff sickness. This has heightened many workers' awareness of the customer. They feel they are being watched. So, constant reinforcement of their (staff) value is my main role.
>
> (Harrow and Shaw, 1989, p. 33)

Such managing in a goldfish bowl, with hostile onlookers, does not seem to have been an expected feature of managerial work among those propounding an academic view of the Public Service Orientation. Not surprisingly, it was this manager who also highlighted the need for training for her staff with regard to aggression from the public as well as reporting a lack of training in any area prior to the decentralization move.

No particular organizational arrangements reported by respondents could claim a particular monopoly of consumerist concern, although a centralist structure did seem to give the strongest basis for what might be described as the only 'resister' in the survey to consumerism. Here, the respondent reported that despite her authority's acceptance of consumerist principles, this had 'not at all' impinged on her managerial tasks, and that she 'preferred to use the term client and will continue to use it for the time being' (Harrow and Shaw, 1989, p. 36).

Leadership—or lack of it—at this delivery level is thus critical, although the impact of this apparently quasi-professional reluctance to change style and language could not be assessed. Despite the clear user identification for home care services, and reasonable parallels with private sector equivalents, it may be that this approach reflected the felt need in this particular service to increasingly professionalize it (by managers gaining diplomas), and so create at least some distance between client and provider.

It is relevant to note that 'Managing to care', barely using the term 'consumer' and emphasizing the need for 'client-related skills' (including client advocacy), does not give the impression of encouraging user closeness. It also seems a slight and unintentional irony that while 'Managing to care', using task analyses, describes first-line managers as having an 'intuitive approach to management, which . . . in the main seemed to work in a haphazard and homely sort of way', a more vociferous consumerist stance might just be seeking exactly that 'homely' approach to the management of the service, as being acceptable, and above all comprehensible, to direct service users (SSI, 1988, p. 23).

The consumerist literature focuses on the end-user, but the survey responses raised a further issue as to where the primary loyalty of managers lay—to users, to political masters, or to the organization's own staff, including internal consumers of their work. One respondent was very clear that 'managers are answerable firstly to councillors, then to service users . . .' (Harrow and Shaw, 1989, p. 31). This highlights a potential area of tension for middle managers in local government who, while working to close the gap with the public, may be an increased focus of councillor contact, and face heightened expectations of performance from councillors. A further area of managerial skills, those political and communication skills hitherto seen as senior officer concerns, is therefore suggested. Again the mediation or brokerage management roles come into play; hampered if the middle managers lack the full picture of their organization's resources.

5.6.3   CONSUMERISM LINKED TO ORGANIZATIONAL STRUCTURES

In a parallel study of consumerism in a variety of organization structures— taking the structural base as the focus rather than specific social services work —three case studies of contrasting London boroughs (decentralized, divisionalized and centralized) were completed (Harrow and Shaw, 1989). Interviews with relevant managers were used. In the decentralized authority, with a series of neighbourhood offices with public inquiry counters, initial staff excitement of change had been dissipated by the anxiety generated when user inquiries required an in-depth knowledge and appreciation across the range of authority services. While mutual support seemed strong in one neighbourhood visited, the very public conscious policy of always staffing the counter during office hours meant that any internal staff briefings or training could never be accomplished with all staff together.

For middle managers, this seemed to characterize the dominant public relations orientation in their decentralization scheme—itself presented as more user-based and responsive—and relative neglect of associated staff needs. Even the rueful comment that their local CAB closed routinely for staff training and was not poorly regarded locally had not shifted this policy. As the steady but uncertain impact of consumerism was being felt on most middle managers, the authors' findings hinted that some consumer interests might be better served by a fairly centralized organizational structure, where equity, rather than local experimentation and difference, could be more relied upon.

5.6.4   MIDDLE MANAGERS' RESPONSES TO CONSUMERISM

From these acknowledged small-scale studies of middle managers' responses to consumerist imperatives, whether from above or below, a number of common experiences, all of them impinging on the performance of the middle management tasks, can be identified. These particularly included:

- new effort for motivating and re-motivating staff, themselves perhaps disappointed that a user orientation 'did not mean more' or was unreasonably criticized by a vigilant public; and
- the cultivation of self-protecting skills, in relation to aggressive users or would-be users, and in negotiations and mediation with them and with elected members.

On this basis, 'facing the consumer' in a middle management capacity is unlikely always to be a heart-warming event, confirming the choice of a public services career. Such managers are in an operational squeeze, between growing user requests and senior managerial imperatives for a customer emphasis, portraying the particular service in a responsive light. Although no direct questions were asked of the domiciliary care managers, or of the interviewees in the variety of organizational structures, about their own feelings of their job performance and personal levels of strain, the personal and professional effort required to maintain public fronts seems to have been considerable.

This aspect of facing the public—the need for self-esteem and the ability to 'keep cheerful'—may be an equally important factor in those areas of public services where more junior staffs have the first user encounters and, with the FLMs, perform a vital gatekeeper role for the organization and for the managers above. The receptionist role—*par excellence* in the private sector, a decorative public relations activity—is particularly important here, where issues of violence may particularly come to the fore (Childs, 1988).

Part of the difficulty for middle managers in the consumerist squeeze is that they may not be in a position finally to say 'yes' to particular consumer demands; or, conversely and perhaps more importantly, able finally to refuse. In this sense, middle managers may be in as weak a position as their user counterparts—not having full information and not having resources to hand. None of the respondents in the above research broached the issue of partnership between user and provider, but the impression was gained that these middle managers and their users had a common cause that was unlikely to be satisfied fully.

Facing the consumer may result in receiving thanks and in job satisfaction when personal problems can be resolved, but consumer encounters in a period when the public sector is under pressure are increasingly likely to be more rather than less stressful. From the research cited above, it was apparent that, certainly in decentralized settings where middle managers have no choice but to face consumers directly as an integral part of their work, the degree of self-reliance demanded from them and the self-confidence that they had gradually acquired was creating a new breed of junior/middle level decision makers with strong power bases (because of their intimate knowledge of the business) who would have a clear picture of what they wanted from their work and from their career. Confronting as well as siding with consumers seems to have helped some middle managers to see their own careers in perspective. It may have also made them —by virtue of knowledge, first-hand information and understanding of what is needed on the ground—very valuable indeed to their organizations and potentially hard to manage by their seniors.

5.7   The indifferent and the unwilling manager

While theorists and practitioners suggest models of managerial attitudes and subsequent behaviour, emphasizing caring and commitment, alternatives are developing in response to public services management becoming more overtly consumer-led. Among these is 'the indifferent manager', encompassing at least two distinct variables. One type of indifferent manager may be the genuinely detached manager, performing appropriately but not imbued with the public services ethic, formerly a strong characteristic of public administration. This form of indifference may, however, conceal a hostility to the public that is unexpressed in user encounters. This may not necessarily affect standards of service delivery; but it may be expressed among colleagues. The second type of indifference reflects the individual manager's personal coping strategy, whereby he or she is highly committed to public services but uses indifference as a protection against emotional involvement.

While most public service managers remain recruited from the services' professionals, so that management itself is strongly influenced by professionalism, 'indifferent' managers may be the exception. Even if this career structure persists, however, the increasing impact of rolling and fixed-term managerial contracts and managerial selection from outside public services may radically alter managerial attitudes and styles, in which indifference becomes an important component.

A second alternative is the 'unwilling manager'; in this case rejecting some key managerial tasks as not being the primary purpose of their employment. Such personnel—including some teachers, nurses, lecturers, police, social workers, and others, who avoid or evade managerial tasks, especially where these have been delegated—have exited from their jobs, in full or in part, while formally remaining in post. Though such task rejection tends to focus on the unfamiliar—such as financial management—it may turn also to consumer-based tasks as (1) consumers' requests become more strident, (2) the managerial requirement for service refusal is felt to be too difficult to face and (3) the techniques for refusal will not be learned. Here the believed sanctuary of professionalism, with its detached stance, may provide a temporary refuge.

Figure 5.4 portrays these three possible models of managerial attitude and behaviour. Such models are intended only to be indicators of possible behaviour. It is not intended that they should be seen as arising solely in response to consumerist demand (some, for example, may occur through change of leadership in organizations). Nevertheless, consumer-based pressures, including the need to be seen to be performing well, will be important in encouraging their development. It seems ironic that some public services—for example, local authority housing services—are now going so far in recognizing the importance of the consumer imperative as to designate particular posts as those of customer services or consumer liaison managers, with the implied danger that this could

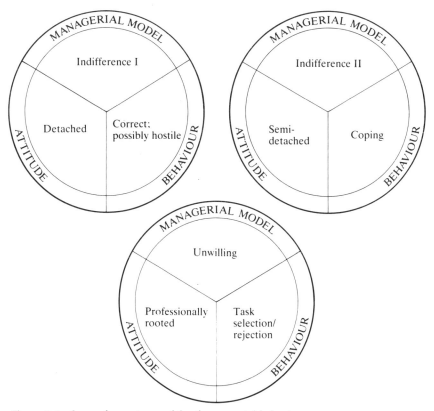

Figure 5.4 Some alternative models of managerial behaviour

identify consumer concerns as limited to particular posts, thus feeding the type of managerial indifference outlined above.

The growth of consumerism in public services is inextricably linked to the need to provide full and complex performance measures; but consumers may inevitably be seeking performance levels that are unattainable, except at the expense of other services. It is the tension promoted by work organizations' emphasis on performance targets that is identified by Scase and Goffee (1989) as a key factor in encouraging the phenomenon of 'the reluctant managers'— 'less than fully committed to their jobs . . . (with) great reservations about giving priority to their work . . .'. Through researching attitudes among 374 managers in six large UK organizations, two of which were in the public sector, and with their study, 'skewed towards middle and, to a lesser extent, senior managers', Scase and Goffee contend that such organizations contain 'substantial numbers of reluctant managers . . . (with) . . . significant impact on corporate perform- ance' (Scase and Goffee, 1989, p. 183). With all the organizations remaining unidentified in this study, more research seems necessary to pursue the extent of this reluctance and the nature and degree of impact on corporate performance it is held to have.

5.8   The collision of concepts—dynamism versus responsiveness

Whether demonstrating attitudes of engagement or indifference, public services managers are presently urged to be dynamic, yet also consumer responsive. 'Dynamic' is acceptable contemporary managerial vocabulary, signifying the pro-active manager, fearless of change and inspiring others to energetic inno- vation. Responsiveness, while laudable, in contrast to dynamism, concerns reac- tion to others. Making change through forceful initiatives raises the question of what is rightly the managerial domain, for consumer responsiveness may mean stopping change in the interests of consumer satisfaction. The language of dyna- mism suggests risk arising, for example, from ignoring excessive service demands or marketing a service so that it effectively excludes some members of the public. User responsiveness may be associated with low-risk strategies, with emphasis on fulfilling tasks that are less likely to disturb users or court criticism.

Together, these concepts give rise to conflict when managers face choices about operational preferences. Responsiveness can inhibit dynamism, especially if initiatives are limited to devices such as 'One Stop Shops', which may create a pro-consumer façade while more radical options, which would disconcert users, are shelved. Dynamism in management can open up new possibilities, with new services developed (for example, with service provision shifted to the voluntary sector) or established services remoulded so that they wean users away from over-dependence. The latter may not, however, be seen by users as in their interests and thus may be condemned as unresponsive. The public debates on proposed hospital closures regularly illustrate the dynamism/responsiveness clash.

Juggling the interests of consumers, employees and the public to achieve an acceptable balance of objectives is a paramount task for the public services manager. With many public services impinging on the public consciousness through the mass media, organizations may be managed to avoid the dissatisfaction of interested parties rather than to concentrate on effective service delivery. Whereas prisoners in public gaols may rebel against a service falling short in rehabilitation terms, sectors of the public, exercising their demands in accountability terms, may stress that custody is the prison service's prime purpose. Although customer satisfaction surveys appear to gauge dissatisfaction levels, they cannot be a final judgement, inasmuch as satisfaction itself is neither objective nor absolute. In reality, some public services may see the *dis*-satisfied user as desirable in the public interest, on the grounds of over-dependence or over-indulgence of the consumer—e.g. requests for trivial house repairs—with the implied risk that dissatisfaction also relates not to a standard norm, but to the experiences, background and knowledge of the individual user.

Many reports on consumerist development in the public services see the latter as existing to provide service, with any shortfall lying only in managing those services to customers' satisfaction. These less often stress the extent to which service professionals affect service delivery decisions, with professionals and semi-professionals setting service standards, but with managers left to carry responsibility for user satisfaction with those standards. A further area of conceptual clash occurs, therefore, where managerialist and professional approaches do not align. Managers may, for example, require organizational strategies that oppose professional standards, such as the length of hospital stays or housing standards; with both professionals and managers claiming a monopoly of user best interests.

A third area of conceptual conflict arises in relation to those criticisms of prevailing public services cultures which marginalize users—including behavioural traits such as dress, accent and vocabulary. An extreme aspect of the impact of public employees is that they are expected to identify with the consumer and to demonstrate this visibly. Increasingly, it appears that such employees are becoming atypical of a bland anonymous image and more representative of a region or district. For public services managers, this changed context of public services brings to the fore questions of staff recruitment, training and management development. Would a limited service offer be more welcome from a manager like the would-be user or from one clearly different? Can a service refusal be made more palatable if the manager identifies with or separates from the would-be user? These questions are especially central to that part of the consumerist debate which seeks advocacy by managers on users' behalf, a role which may overwhelm that of service deliverer. Varying contexts will help determine the appropriateness of user/provider similarity/dissimilarity, but here the issue of risk to be taken by managers in their staff recruitment is unavoidable.

Against a background of such conceptual mismatches the concern for managerial consumerist 'good practice' identification continues, but what is 'good practice' and which levels of public services managers have greater or lesser responsibility for its diffusion?

5.9   'Good practice' in consumer relations

Interest in consumerism is fuelled by the search for good practice models. 'Good practice' is a term well understood but rarely defined, especially by consumers themselves, except anecdotally, and then perhaps hinging upon their having received a better service than they had expected initially. Much implicit definition has stemmed from specialist professionals (not directly responsible for resource allocation) rather than from managers. In the professional literature, good practice dissemination implies accounts of activities or approaches to problems or opportunities that worked, accompanied by 'to do' lists.

The Local Government Training Board's work on management development of senior managers within social services departments, for example, contains no good practice definitions, while noting, with implied regret, that examples found were 'isolated initiatives, rather than part of a comprehensive management development strategy' (LGTB, 1987a). Yet this points to a critical good practice characteristic: its appearance is more likely to be incremental and experimental than part of a global plan. Nor is this necessarily to be regretted, since good practice proffered should be seen in time and contextual terms. As with other initiatives, the question of practice transportability arises. Indeed, it may be fallacious to seek a once-and-for-all public services definition of consumerist good practice, because of the critical variables of service context, provider and user.

Public services good practice literature stresses the thematic approach, with notions of information availability, organizational openness and the ever-popular flexibility all occurring. An alternative interpretation is that good practice is 'what is acceptable', setting some kind of 'bottom line' and keeping to it (Potter, 1988).

Learning from private sector experience may be hazardous; for example, if Peters' injunction that 'with everything up for grabs . . . we must . . . become customer-obsessed . . . routinely (looking) at the smallest nuance of the tiniest programme through the customer's eyes' has been taken to heart (Peters, 1987, p. 184). Private services publicize their consumerist techniques—such as the ordinary airline passenger, checking service standards—but analysis of consumer dissatisfaction in that sector tends to occur only when there are viable service alternatives and routes out of the problem for the staff. The value for business sectors of such obsession lies in the importance of repeat business, with the customer as an appreciating asset. For some public service areas, however, such as health services with waiting lists, repeat business is the last thing they need. If customer 'obsession' concepts have value, they may lie in making allies and supporters from among the users of public services—so that the 'customer as asset' is a service 'friend', admittedly a highly political approach to pro-consumerist development. Historically, professional institutes have defined good practice mainly by rules of behaviour and by indications of the extent of professional inputs required, or, by default, through bad practice identification. Public service literature, such as the Department of Social Security's *The Business of Service*, emphasizes the importance of accepting a service ethos as a precursor to good practice, but with such service concepts stressing user individuality, good practice notions must be inevitably shifting (DSS, 1988). Good practice, therefore, should be seen as very much self-defining for the professionals, the managers, and the users involved in each situation, and as capable of being continually redefined, with changing circumstances, users and providers.

Further, the relative importance of a particular service to the user and the provider's experience are just two important variables that may contribute towards identifying public services good practice. They explain how the same practice—for example, library opening hours and decisions on library acquisitions—is rated as good by one user and barely acceptable by another. The contributions of operational managers and staffs may prove a rich source of ideas. The involvement of a range of staffs in quality circle style groups to define what *they* mean by user-oriented good practice is likely to have more organizational validity than externally imposed good practice measures (Slinger, 1989). Within these parameters, managerial good practice in relation to consumers may be regarded as reading a situation correctly, and responding with capability and confidence. This must imply some intuitive responses (including apologizing in appropriate ways when necessary). While it requires managerial sensitivity in relation to the user's individuality, it also requires the back-up of appropriate information technology. It is hardly helpful to respond pleasantly to users' queries if the manager in turn lacks information required from higher up, or, worse, does not know where within the system to direct queries.

Good practice thus is, of necessity, incremental in nature, with motivated managers developing their own personal databases of knowledge and contacts, to help keep consumers updated. Beyond this is the issue of linking the development and use of appropriate technology to the pro-user philosophy; giving managers ready and reliable access to information for their users' benefit and a major means of encouraging a feeling of confidence in responding to queries. Appropriate technological development is thus not simply an adjunct to consumerism in practice, but is also an essential component because it helps afford user equity.

Good practice in public services contexts should also be seen to be humanizing the organization. The issue of knowledge is to the forefront. London Transport's advisers with their detailed knowledge, available to telephone callers, on the access characteristics of individual underground stations for disabled would-be passengers, are an example of a positive consumerist response, based on extending consumers' knowledge. Comprehensible signposting for major public buildings such as hospitals is now axiomatic. How much more humanizing to have people available with offers of help for the new user walking uncertainly into the building, head tilted at the angle necessary to read the signposts? Some major hospitals use volunteers for this service—an example which, in turn, raises a further issue for some public services managers about the extent to which volunteers can be encouraged to project an organization's active pro-user role.

'Humanizing' an organization may require the availability of personnel to counsel users and explore service options. This is an area where private sector comparisons are particularly unhelpful, since, to some extent, organizations in this sector may rely on and exploit consumer ignorance. Ultimately, humanizing may involve showing the organization's vulnerability, with managers sharing their organizational concerns with users. The degree of frankness will be a matter for managers to judge, given the service context. These judgements will be political, potentially engendering conflict, with a view to gaining 'friends' for the service, and the managers. At the same time the potential for a collision of concepts is clear. Where managers are very open about the limitations to their delivery potential, consumers are very well briefed and able to understand the intricacies of service delivery issues. Such openness may also, however, dampen consumer demand by capturing consumers and thus inhibiting the development of the quality debate much beyond that of 'what we'd do if we had the money'.

Certainly, humanizing a public service organization involves managerial risk-taking, not least where the non-human back-up for first-line staff is not also a focus for improvement. Management literature emphasizes the need for senior managers' leadership, to ensure staff's internalization of consumerist perspectives; but quite how that leadership can be sustained beyond the new signposting and the near-obligatory customer survey tends to be left undiscussed. In so many public services where the direct consumer/staff interface is at relatively low levels, such leadership would be seen to be more of a reality with some job rotation of, for example, reception duties. Senior managers' telephone hot lines for complainants can be no substitute for meeting the consumer face to face— even perhaps on their own territory rather than that of the organization.

One area for a managerial lead is in *self*-monitoring rather than in assessing the user-friendliness of others. Two feasible methods include using a critical incidents collection and analysis, and using encounter analysis, mapping the type of organization that the user sees as a result of the encounter. Bitner, Booms and Tretault outline the critical incidents approach in relation to service industries—hotels, restaurants, airlines—with 700 incidents, categorized from 'very satisfactory' to 'dissatisfactory'; they used students to collect data from customers who described an incident range (Bitner *et al.*, 1990). Given that these are service relationships where direct payment occurs—or has even been withheld until redress is obtained—the full portability of this approach is questionable. As a basis for *self*-development—maintaining a personal log of incidents, self-categorizing, and then comparing findings with others—this may have value (i.e. by putting the emphasis this time not on the *users'* recollections but on those of the staff).

The introduction of such an approach would require not only leadership by example, but also its confident presentation in an assuring style, to emphasize that this was not being used as part of a full appraisal system, but that staff were being trusted to record as accurately as possible. James' (1989) description of the potential use of encounter analysis in local government services does not indicate whether this approach has actually been used or with what results; but the emphasis on the encounter as the basis for service improvement is at least one that brings in the user from the periphery of the service concerns to its centre. Both these approaches may be seen very much as first stages; a complex area for managerial decision-making, subsequently, is the extent to which eventually consumerist perspectives *do* have a part to play in assessing staff performance—including the performances of managers.

User panel development and customer surveys are among particularly familiar consumerist practices, with limitations if panels over-identify with the organization. If the surveys are seen to be self-congratulatory, they are used to ward off criticism and change. Monitoring by pseudo-consumers, i.e. employees masquerading as service users, must be seen as a dubious practice. Linking provision of training to consumerist development can itself be seen to have a good practice slant, but major problems can arise here if trainers have hitherto not taken a consumerist stance. Experimenting with trainers from within various levels of staff, so that employees—particularly those facing the consumer regularly—can convey both their enthusiasms and their problems within the training process has much to commend it. Training in relation to consumerism cannot have the certainties that seem to be implied by using private sector 'customer care videos', since the most relevant training is training for uncertainty, in developing strong inter-personal skills and self-confidence in presentation. The most experimental approach here would be the use of consumers as trainers; an approach reflecting growing interest in moving consumers on from being passive recipients to active involvement in service provision, i.e. 'empowerment'.

5.10   Empowerment—consumerist and managerial implications

The term 'empowerment' is found in some public services fields where relatively weak users, particularly because of age or handicap, have had highly limited service choices. As an extension of the consumerist concept, it may be seen as radical, seeming to involve professional surrender of decision-making power on behalf of the users with a shift from professional to self-advocacy by users. Self-help groups, such as People First, emphasize the individual dignity of service users previously assigned minimal roles in decisions critically affecting their lives and regarding their capabilities; and promote self-advocacy (Crawley, 1988; Exeter Health Authority, 1986). The term challenges implicitly part of the basis of 'caring professionals' work. As an extension of the consumerist concept, empowerment requires a deliberate power shift towards users (with interesting parallels between the power shifts that some have been seeking for public services managers as against the professional staffs whom they ultimately manage), and may be seen as a moving-on even from notions of provider–user partnership. No parallel notion exists in the private sector consumerist literature.

Adopting empowerment stances requires managers to act early within policy-making cycles to ensure that opportunities for power transfer take place before too many decisions are made and resources are committed or withdrawn. Empowering consumers creates new freedom—and new responsibility—to be involved in creating policy, exercising choice and in controlling services. In effect, the burden of decision-making rests with the service user; and here users of some services so empowered may face unwelcome realities—not least receiving what they want, and subsequently discovering that this was not in their best interests. When service provision of certain kinds becomes a right, as it surely must under an empowerment philosophy, then notions of managerial discretion and of the wider problem (including employee) interest must fade. Given that service users groups are rarely homogenous, and that the existence of finite resources is a continuing fact, then moving towards empowerment of consumers may increase service provision disputes and magnify the issue of the potential for loss of equity in public service provision, as some users must inevitably be 'more empowered' than others.

In situations of empowerment (apparently still more talked about than initiated), the managerial skills of mediation may be more than ever needed, but concepts of managerial control and authority will be challenged. If some empowered users themselves become service gatekeepers, preventing development in other users' interests that are not sufficiently empowered, then the managerial role of 'guardianship' in relation to the range of consumer interests, patrician though it may sound, will be critical.

Although it is conjecture that much increased empowerment will be accompanied by an increase in intensity of disputes over service provision, the language of empowerment alone implies a growth in conflict and raises questions as to the means of dealing with users who, in the views of others if not themselves, mis-use the service. Anecdotal evidence suggests that service users *can* be among the harshest critics of each other—ward patients who criticize other patients for 'over-demanding' nursing attention, housing tenants scornful of tenants in rent arrears—but managers will know that they cannot rely on this and will recognize the very high-risk strategies accompanying any whole-scale empowerment commitment. Managerially, the incremental approach commends itself—using consumers as staff trainers, for example—but consumers embued with the empowerment language may be in too much of a hurry for such a strategy to commend itself; and some managerial resistance to empowerment may be required.

5.11   Conclusions

Much of this chapter has implied the existence of a continuum of pro-consumerist effort by public services managers, as set out below.

Placating → Informing → Satisficing → Counselling → Co-provision → Empowerment

Not only will managers and those whom they manage have different perceptions of their organization's place on the continuum (with its linkage to the openness continuum, discussed in Fig. 5.3), but politicians and their managers may differ significantly as to where the organization should stand. If organizations move along the spectrum, managerial perspectives must continue to take into account staff perceptions of their ability to respond adequately to consumer demands, as well as simply championing a consumerist cause.

During the decades of growth in public services organizations, poor images arose, primarily because of bureaucratic mechanisms and professional power, which often militated against obtaining service delivery notably in personal services areas. Growth in staff numbers fuelled resentment from individuals and from other sections of the public not directly involved. This backlog of criticism has provided much of the basis for the growth of privatized 'public' services. As this extends to the community care field, with social services departments increasingly service procurers but not necessarily service providers, it is ironic that here service users—historically among the weakest—may find it more and not less difficult to exert influence over service level and quality, as lines of managerial contact for users become less rather than more clear. How will departments ensure that the private and voluntary bodies becoming service providers have as strong a consumer orientation as they have themselves? Contract monitoring by managers should play a central part, but cannot ensure that a consumer orientation pervades these organizations. It will be essential for managers here to impose an element of bureaucracy, with monitoring procedures potentially involving the following:

- Contractual terms to activate consumerism—for example, accessibility for service managers; quality mechanisms (staff standards).
- Record keeping by service deliveries—for example, personnel (numbers,

quality, turnover); user data, including complaints and pro-active surveys).
- Inspection by public services managers—for example, random visits to service providers; utilizing service users as inspection team members.

While it appears feasible for social services departments ultimately to contract out their inspection and quality checking mechanisms in turn, to do so would be problematic. It is in this area therefore that the public services manager as consumer 'guardian' must be retained, although if the trend towards service contracting continues at its present pace, the numbers of public services managers with any *direct* experience of service provision, and memory of its management, will become rare.

As services during the past decade have increased their consumer orientation, accompanied in some areas by a decline in resources, that shift seems to have cost the public services dear, in terms of the stress imposed upon the operational middle level managers. The imposition of general management, with its apparent promise of easing situations, and creating opportunities for full managerial control, has further exacerbated this situation. In such environments, middle managers seem fair game for the consumerist critics, but in the coming decade it may be that the middle manager who has the confidence to refuse services may be more valuable than the manager who continually responds to consumer demands by coping and by papering over the inadequate resource cracks. This type of manager, who may be designated as 'resolute', seems already to be appearing, often in the decentralized public services, where middle manager learning is fast and uncomfortable; but it is a management style that may not commend itself to more senior management levels, still likely to be found making private sector-style statements as to what consumers should receive. The hypothesized existence of 'resolute managers' at middle manager level requires confirmation or refutation through research. Whether such 'resolution', if it is widespread, will be sufficient to balance the negative impact on organization performance of the 'reluctant managers' outlined above, also deserves investigation.

Consumerism will certainly persist during the 1990s in public services, but its effects may not always be towards services improvement. Contrarily, public services' contracting out may dissipate the high expectations of users. Where statements of service for users become the norm, these, realistically, may be pitched at minimal service levels. Middle and front-line managers, continuing to carry the brunt of user opinion, will grow wary of over-response to that opinion not only if it deflects from their managerial tasks but also if it damages their credibility as managers and their views of their self-worth. Their task in particular is to place the pressures of consumerism in context, despite the surge towards empowerment, and to manage service delivery in ways that recognize that public services organizations have public as well as direct-user interests as their *raison d'être*.

References

Andrew, G. H. and Thompson, B. (1988) 'Practical implications of patient satisfaction research', *Health Services Management Research*, **1** (2), 112–19.

Aucoin, P. (1987) 'Middle managers: the crucial link', *Canadian Public Administration*, **30** (2), 187–209.

Beltramini, R. F. (1981) 'Consumer–client orientation and public service marketing', *European Journal of Marketing*, **15** (4) 17–25.

Bitner, M. J., Booms, B. H. and Tretault, M. S. (1990) 'The service encounter: diagnosing favorable and unfavorable incidents', *Journal of Marketing* (54), 71–84.

Childs, F. (1988) 'Safe behind the reception desk? A study of the incidence and effects of violence in the Social Services Area Office Reception Areas in the London Borough of Hammersmith and Fulham', MSc Dissertation, CNAA, South Bank Polytechnic.

Crawley, B. (1988) *The Growing Voice—A Survey of Self-advocacy Groups*. CMH Publications, Cambridge.

Day, C. (1989) 'Marketing library services to young adults', MSc Dissertation, CNAA, South Bank Polytechnic.

DH (1989) *Working for Patients*, Cmd 555; also *Working for Patients*, Working Paper 8: *Implications for Family Practitioner Committees*. Department of Health.

DSS (1988) *The Business of Service*. The Report of the Regional Organization Scrutiny, Department of Social Security.

Durcan, A. (1984) 'A reference library talks to its users', *European Journal of Marketing*, **18** (2), 65–71.

Exeter Health Authority (1986) *People First: Day Service Users' Accounts*. Report of a conference organized by South West Regional Care Day Group Services Working Group.

Fenwick, J. (1989) 'Consumerism and local government', *Local Government Policy Making*, **16** (1), 45.

Flynn, N. (1988) 'A consumer oriented culture?' *Public Money and Management*, **8** (3), 27.

Flynn, N. (1990) *Public Sector Management*. Harvester-Wheatsheaf, Hemel Hempstead.

George, J. (1988) 'The customer—always first?', *Health Care Management*, **3** (2), 10–13.

Harrow, J. and Shaw, M. J. (1989) 'Training needs and departmental structures: development and change in local authority contexts', Management Centre Paper, South Bank Polytechnic (unpublished).

Harrow, J. and Willcocks, L. (1990) 'Public services management: activities, initiatives and limits to learning', *Journal of Management Studies*, **27** (3), 294.

James, K. (1989) 'Encounter analysis: front line conversations and their role in improving customer service', *Local Government Studies*, **15** (3), 11–24.

Jefferson, S. and Carr-Hill, R. (1989) *Family Practitioners and their Customers*. Discussion Paper 55, Centre for Health Economics, University of York.

LGTB (1987a) *The Development of Senior Managers within Social Services Departments*, Local Government Training Board, Luton, p. 21.

LGTB (1987b) *Getting Closer to the Public*, Part I, What it means, Local Government Training Board, Luton, p. 7.

Martin, E. M. (1986) 'Consumer evaluation of human services', *Social Policy and Administration*, **20** (3, Autumn), 185.

Peters, T. (1987) *Thriving on Chaos: Handbook for a Management Revolution*. Pan/Macmillan, London.

Potter, J. (1988) 'Consumerism and the public sector: how well does the coat fit?', *Public Administration*, **66** (2), 149–64.

Scase, R. and Goffee, R. (1989) *Reluctant Managers, their Work and Lifestyles*. Unwin Hyman, London.

Slinger, P. (1989) 'Moves towards a quality assurance programme for Friern Hospital', CNAA Postgraduate Diploma in Management Studies Project, South Bank Polytechnic.

Stewart, J. and Clarke, M. (1987) 'The public service orientation: issues and dilemmas', *Public Administration*, 165 (2, Summer), 161–77.

Stewart, J. and Ransom, S. (1988) 'Management in the public domain', *Public Money and Management*, 8 (3), 13.

SSI (1988) *Managing to Care: A Study of First Line Managers in Social Services Departments in Day and Domiciliary Care*. Social Services Inspectorate, Department of Health.

Stone, M. A. and Thomson, S. (1987) 'How far can marketing be applied in the further education sector?', *Quarterly Review of Marketing*, 13 (1, Autumn), 16–19.

Toffler, A. (1987) *The Third Wave*. Pan, London.

Willcocks, L. (1990) 'Information Technology in public sector settings: towards effective systems', *International Journal of Public Sector Management*, 2 (3), 15–29.

6

The manager monitored

Georges M. Selim and Sally A. Woodward

6.1 Introduction

An overview of what constitutes a public sector body, its historical development, the parameters underlying manager's work in a public sector environment have all been covered in previous chapters. The theme of this chapter is the monitoring of manager's performance and the review of his or her work for economy, efficiency, effectiveness and equity.

Defining objectives and measuring performance of the management of public sector bodies is fraught with problems since the aim of 'providing a service' is difficult to state in measurable terms, and unlike the private sector, in much of the public sector the bottom line of profit does not exist (Jackson and Palmer, 1989). As long ago as the 1970s, Anthony pointed out, in relation to non-profit-making organizations:

> The difficulty of defining objectives, or deciding on the resources required to reach objectives, and of measuring the efficiency and effectiveness with which the organisation's performance meets objectives is, I believe the most serious management problem . . .
>
> (Anthony, 1978, p. 9)

During the 1980s in government, as well as in other public sector bodies, performance measurement became a major focus in the delivery of public sector services. Please note that some authors distinguish between performance measures and performance indicators, depending on the degree of precision and ambiguity of the measure. While we acknowledge this distinction, for the purpose of clarity we have used the term 'performance measure' throughout. Earlier forms of evaluation, such as planning, programming and budgeting systems (PPBS), which were confined to intermediate outputs, and policy/programme analysis and review (PAR) introduced in the early 1970s, and management by objectives (MBO) did not achieve the comprehensiveness which the government, as an example, is trying to achieve under the Financial Management Initiative (FMI) and *Improving Management in Government: The Next Steps* (HMSO, 1988).

The FMI broadly required management of government departments to produce clearly defined objectives, a concrete measurable output plan, a measurable and compatible budget to operationalize the plan/objectives against which performance can be monitored annually, or at shorter periodic intervals.

The government, in its 'Next Steps Initiative' (HMSO, 1989) continued with the same theme of trying to encourage its executive arm (as distinct from policy advice) to deliver services more efficiently and effectively, within available resources, for the benefit of taxpayers, staff and, more importantly, their customers.

Performance measures should provide management with valid and useful information by enabling activities to be monitored regularly, at different levels within the organization, e.g. strategy/policy-making level, departmental and cost centre. The monitoring involves value for money scrutiny and the improvement of management information systems. Performance measures also provide the basis of staff appraisal and performance-related pay systems.

Managers and politicians, as well as academics, have found the use of value for money and the '4E's', or sometimes the '3E's' (omitting Equity), as convenient terms to use when talking about allocation of resources and reviewing performance. Value for money is a generic term that is popular but lacks precision. The 3E's are required for the external audit of central and local government, as enshrined in the Local Government Finance Act 1982 and the National Audit Act 1983 (HMSO, 1983b). These terms are components of a framework for devising and analysing performance measures. They are further explored below.

6.2 Economy, efficiency, effectiveness and equity

Economy, efficiency, and effectiveness are terms that are not entirely discrete but are interlinked. It is unlikely that we can discuss the review of managers' performance without including an examination of all three.

An issue that relates to economy is likely to involve, in addition, considerations of efficiency and effectiveness (see HMSO, 1983a). If we therefore attempt to categorize any measure, such as output per staff member, under one category, such as economy, it needs to be recognized that this is a simplification. However, with this limitation in mind, we shall attempt to differentiate between these terms, where possible.

Economy can be defined as the purchase and provision of service at lowest possible cost consistent with a specified quality and quantity (Klein and Carter, 1988). They point out that while, in theory, economy is a neutral term, in practice it has become an emotive term, because of the practice of equating economy with 'cost cutting'.

Efficiency is often used as both a measure and an objective of a programme. Efficiency seeks to ensure that maximum output is obtained from resources devoted to a department or programme or that only the minimum level of resources is devoted to a specified level of output.

As a measure it can be seen as a ratio of actual input to actual output, or rate at which inputs are converted into outputs.

Effectiveness aims to ensure that the impacts of a policy, i.e. customer-experienced activity, is actually meeting the policy aims. It is a measure of the relationship between intermediate outcomes/outputs and final outcomes/outputs.

Measurements of effectiveness are the most problematic to devise because of the conceptual difficulty of establishing causal relationships between outputs and outcomes relating to a specific service, especially when the impact of a policy on a service can take an unknown amount of time and a variety of environmental factors are coming into play at different times. Even where a causal relationship might be identified there are measurement problems, which can be technical and/or organizational. The choice of outcomes is normally a matter for politicians, as is the decision, in part, of what is appropriate, although the recent trend is to consider customer satisfaction, i.e. is the service providing what the customer/client wants?

Klein and Carter (1988) point out that the Treasury definition of effectiveness as 'the ratio of output to planned output' may lead to an overemphasis on economy and efficiency and an underemphasis on effectiveness.

An analogy with a printing machine can illustrate the interrelationships of these concepts. Although the machine may be uneconomic in that it costs a lot to maintain, it can still be efficient in that performance matches the design specification and this specification provides a satisfactory output in comparison with the input, i.e. raw materials, labour and power.

As mentioned above, there is an interlink between efficiency, economy and effectiveness and changes in one need to be traded off against the others. For example, a badly designed or maintained machine may consume more paper or toner (an economy issue) or it may not have the performance expected (an effectiveness issue) or both. But such a situation with extra raw material costs or unsatisfactory output can be due to inefficiency.

In other situations, additional raw material costs may be due to uneconomic practices—such as buying from a costly supplier. Unsatisfactory output may also be caused, not by inefficient operation, but by the ineffectiveness of the chosen method, such as purchasing the wrong printing machine, e.g. two colours instead of four or five colours.

A conflict between efficiency and effectiveness can be difficult to resolve and in many cases is left to the judgements of those most involved in the development of the service. The fairness/reasonableness of those individual judgements is an issue explored later in this chapter.

In addition to the 3E's, the concept of equity aims to enable the manager to include within the notion of 'value for money' a consideration of social values/needs.

All enterprises/organizations use resources in the production of their goods and/or services. This may be accomplished in an economic, efficient and effective way. But the additional consideration should be its impact on society. Is it a socially acceptable use of resources? Are the differing consumer group needs being met by the public services?

In this way, the manager is 'completing the circle', as illustrated in Fig. 6.1, by taking into account (for individual operations or for the enterprise as a whole) the social impact of taking input from, and returning output to, the environment and society.

Equity can be judged on outcome and, in addition, equity can require proper procedures so that a decision that is fair to all parties can be taken. Management need to guard against discrimination between different groups of people; for instance, a library may provide a better service to some categories of users than others.

Management need to become environmentally aware and monitor the organization's consumption of finite physical resources. In some organizations the process of converting input into output can produce harmful by-products. The planned output may enhance society in one way but management need to address unpleasant by-products, e.g. determine alternative processes and/or materials. In all cases, whether or not equity is achieved is clearly a matter of judgement.

While recognizing Klein and Carter's observations that 'the combination of conceptual ambiguity and semantic confusion reflects the contrasting objectives and uses that characterise performance measurement' (1988, p. 6), for our purposes we summarize effectiveness as a measure of *actual performance against planned performance*, efficiency as the ratio of *resource consumption to benefits produced*; economy as *the resources consumed vis-à-vis planned consumption* and equity as being the *net effect of the entity upon society and the environment*.

Having discussed WHAT we mean by the 4E's and their relationship with

Figure 6.1 The 4E's and decision-making

performance measures, we now move on to consider WHO should review, monitor and audit managers' performances. This can and needs to be carried out internally by the managers themselves and by internal auditors, and externally by review and audit bodies such as the National Audit Office and the Audit Commission.

6.2.1 REVIEW BY INTERNAL AUDITORS

The following definition, taken from *Standards and Guidelines for the Professional Practice of Internal Auditing*, issued by the Institute of Internal Auditors (IIA), describes the role of internal audit as:

> an independent appraisal activity, established within an organisation as a service to the organisation. It is a control which functions by examining and evaluating the adequacy and effectiveness of other controls. The objective of internal auditing is to assist members of the organisation in the effective discharge of their responsibilities. To this end, internal auditing furnishes them with analyses, appraisals, recommendations, counsel and information concerning the activities involved.
>
> (IIA, 1988, p. 3)

From this definition and others promulgated by CIPFA and the government in *Government Internal Audit Manual* issued by the Treasury, it would seem that internal audit is perceived as being part of the internal control system in the organization where internal auditors are employed.

The scope of internal auditing, as delineated in the statement of responsibilities of internal auditing, issued by the IIA, includes:

> . . . appraising the economy and efficiency with which resources are employed
>
> . . . reviewing operations or programmes to ascertain whether results are consistent with established objectives and goals and whether the operations or programmes are being carried out as planned.
>
> (IIA, 1988, p. 3)

The advantage of including value-for-money audit as part of the remit of the internal audit function are two-fold:

1 the internal auditor has right of access to conduct internal audits anywhere in the organization;
2 auditors can follow a system, process or operation across structural boundaries, e.g. departments, geographical locations.

While management are responsible for all aspects of managing the organization, management establish an internal auditing function and delegate to it the authority (obviously, not the responsibility) to conduct reviews. The review of value for money involves the knowledge of relevant methodologies, techniques and data.

On some occasions, a review may indicate that a system, process or operation may be good value for money in that it achieves the planned output in the most economic way, but it may also indicate a number of consequences unforeseen by policy makers, e.g. expensive, inequitable or other undesired effects. There may be other cases where problems arise because policies relate to both the objectives and the means by which these are to be achieved. Management, e.g. senior civil servants, would be expected to draw the attention of the policy makers, in this case the government, to these dysfunctional aspects of policy, and in some cases it is likely that internal audit would have been instrumental in alerting management to the situation.

Exceptionally, internal audit may report directly to policy makers if, in the internal auditor's view, an issue is not dealt with satisfactorily by management.

6.2.2   REVIEW BY EXTERNAL AUDITORS

Government spends around £200 billion each year and the Public Accounts Committee (PAC) of the House of Commons reviews about 70 per cent of that. The main aim is to ensure that money goes for the purposes intended by Parliament and that it goes to the right destinations.

The Comptroller and Auditor General (C&AG) during a disagreement with the Army Council in 1888 achieved the support of the PAC to extend examination of expenditure beyond the accepted matters of conformity with parliamentary authorization into the area of economy in contracts. Since then the C&AG has applied value-for-money audit into many aspects of financial management of government departments (Henley et al., 1989, p. 256).

In the early part of the 1980s the traditional role of the external auditor, i.e. examining the fairness of financial statements, was expanded with the introduction of value-for-money audits. For example, the Local Government Finance Act (1982, Section 15) identifies the duties of a local government auditor as:

1 ensuring the accounts are properly prepared;
2 determining whether the authority has made proper arrangements for securing the 3E's in the use of its resources;
3 reporting on matters of public interest.

The following is an extract from the National Audit Act 1983 showing the role of the C&AG and how the members of that office are expected to conduct value-for-money auditing or the 3E's:

6. (1) The Comptroller and Auditor General may carry out examinations into the economy, efficiency and effectiveness with which any department, authority or other body to which this section applies has used its resources in discharging its functions.

(2) Subsection (1) above shall not be construed as entitling the Comptroller and Auditor General to question the merits of the policy objectives of any department, authority or body in respect of which an examination is carried out.

(3) Subject to subsections (4) and (5) below, this section applies to:
   (a) any department in respect of which appropriation accounts are required to be prepared under the Exchequer and Audit Departments Act 1866;
   (b) any body required to keep accounts under section 98 of the National

Health Service Act 1977 or section 86 of the National Health Service (Scotland) Act 1978;

(c) any other authority or body whose accounts are required to be examined and certified by, or are open to the inspection of, the Comptroller and Auditor General by virtue of any enactment, including an enactment passed after this Act; and

(d) any authority or body which does not fall within section 7 below and whose accounts are required to be examined and certified by, or are open to the inspection of, the Comptroller and Auditor General by virtue of any agreement made, whether before or after the passing of this Act, between that authority or body and a Minister of the Crown.

(HMSO, 1983b)

The Act goes on to identify the bodies and/or departments subject to such an audit. These include, among others, any government department that is required to prepare appropriation accounts under the E&A Departments Act of 1866; anybody required to keep accounts under Section 98 of the NHS Act 1977 (section 86 of the NHS (Scotland) Act 1978).

Thus public audit bodies and private sector auditing firms awarded contracts for auditing in the public sector have a requirement to spend a sizeable proportion of their work on value-for-money auditing.

A discussion of the role(s) played by external auditors in the public sector cannot be complete without contrasting these roles with those delineated for the auditors of limited liability companies, where external audit is defined as the:

... independent examination and expression of opinions on the financial statements of an enterprise by an appointed auditor in the pursuance of that appointment and in compliance with any relevant statutory obligation.

(Audit Practices Committee, 1989)

Such a comparison clearly shows the limitations of the latter's role in the scope of their audit work—a role confined mainly to expressing an opinion as to whether the final accounts (Profit and Loss Account and the Balance Sheet) reflect a true and fair view of the company's operations. While this is not the place to debate the value of audit work provided by both groups of auditors, the reader will have noticed the immense contribution, through their published reports, that external auditors in the public sector (National Audit Office, Audit Commission) make to the debate, both public and private, on the management of public sector bodies.

Glynn (1986) views value-for-money auditing as a blend of some of the aspects of conventional auditing with some aspects of management consulting. The auditor makes an examination in an independent and objective way (as an auditor) using analytical models and implementation awareness (of a management consultant) to provide advice on a range of contexts and elements.

Auditors, says Glynn, act as third party intermediaries in an accountability relationship. They can give a view on whether management have done the best they can, given the resources at their disposal and the environment within which they operate. They also support management by helping to point out difficulties and advising on possible courses of action.

It is worth noting that if auditors of a local authority consider that it is in the public interest to produce a report either immediately after the discovery of an event/matter that is subject to criticism or at the end of the audit, they can do so and send it to the local authority. In turn, the authority, after consideration, must make it available to members of the public and the press.

A report in the public interest might be necessary as a result of the following:

1 Evidence of fraud or misconduct in the authority's affairs which may lead to losses.
2 Evidence of illegal activity/activities for which there is no statutory authority. A useful example of this is local authorities dealing in the SWAPS market.
3 Undue delay in preparing and/or submitting accounts.
4 Failure to make appropriate arrangements for securing the 3E's or value for money in carrying out their activities.
5 Major weaknesses in the authority's control systems.
6 Qualified audit report on the authority's accounts.

To conclude, the authors accept the premise that review bodies, both internal and external, have a major role to play in ensuring that organizations and managers are using their resources in an economic, efficient, effective and equitable manner; however, it is their belief that the first line of review is the manager who is being given an amount of resources (physical, financial, human, etc.) as part of the planning exercise. This is the person who needs to complement the cycle by monitoring and controlling his or her operations. Indeed this view was expressed by Henley and colleagues:

> The prime responsibility for achieving value for money and efficiency is the management's and not the public auditor's. Senior civil servants, and ultimately their ministers, are responsible and are held accountable for all their actions in running and managing their departments.
>
> (Henley *et al.*, 1989, p. 256)

6.3 Performance measures

Attention has been drawn in the past to the fact that a major hindrance to the effective review of management's performance is a general absence of yardsticks/standards against which to measure the performance of key operations.

Current progress in developing a performance measurement system (PMS) is providing managers, auditors and others interested in measuring performance with extremely useful tools to evaluate economy, efficiency, effectiveness and equity.

They do, however, only indicate possible, potential areas of improvement and do not of themselves offer solutions. As we show below, it is very important to ensure that only *fair* comparisons are made and that valid underlying reasons for differences are unearthed. Similarly, decisions have to be made on what is to be measured and which measures to use (e.g. economy, efficiency, effectiveness, equity). Generally, it is best to choose a number of complementary measures to enable managers to make a decision based on broader information.

The following provides an example of a classification of the main types of performance measures.

1 *Workload/demand and performance measures*   These indicate the volume of output, whether services and/or products and, when linked to measures of input of resources, give useful information on quality or quantity matters, e.g. number of claimants/enquirers served by a member of staff in a social security office in a local authority, number of books issued by a public library, percentage of first-class degrees in a university, number of home helps required in a district.

2 *Economy measures*   These measures may highlight waste in the provision of resources indicating that the same resources could have been provided more cheaply or that more resources could have been acquired at the same cost, viz. actual input costs in comparison with planned or expected input costs. Examples include, home help cost per client, cost of the personnel function per member of staff, cost of the chief executive's department per 1000 poll taxpayers.

3 *Efficiency measures*   These may highlight potential opportunities to convert, with the least possible waste, given resources to end service and/or product. These measures are computed by dividing output by the resources consumed; put another way, it is the ratio of actual input to actual output. Examples can be cleaning cost per unit area, average cost per teacher, accidents at work per 1000 staff, average cost per home help.

4 *Effectiveness measures*   These measures focus on how well objectives are being achieved, viz. actual output to planned output. Examples can be number of library users satisfied with library services, number of swimmer complaints to total swimmers of public swimming pools, number of customers of a public swimming pool.

5 *Equity measures*   These measures draw attention to present and potential unfairness by the enterprise in terms of its corporate policy and practice. Examples can be proportion of disabled employees, proportion of policemen/women from minority groups, proportion of teachers from ethnic minorities working in inner city areas with large percentage of families from these ethnic minorities.

As with ratio analysis in accounting, performance measures can be structured in a pyramid and hierarchy with macro performance measures (which describe performance of the operation in overall terms) being expanded into component micro performance measures. Each layer can give further insight to a higher measure of performance. Jackson and Palmer (1989) suggest this approach enables management to receive the degree of detail appropriate to their responsibility. (See, for example, the Audit Commission 'logic trees'.)

Performance measures can be classified as financial or non-financial. Non-financial quantitative measures will include ratios such as number of children per class, number of pupils per teacher. Financial measures will include items such as maintenance costs per unit area, return on capital employed, return on total assets.

Section 6.3.4 on page 154 presents tables from a recently privatized company (Thames Water) and an organization in the public sector (NCB) showing their performance measures in financial and non-financial terms. However, the figures for Thames Water are the last to be published. The set of accounts (Thames Water, 1988/89) produced immediately after privatization is void of any such measures!

Managers who are the subject of internal and external reviews can be seen within a systems model as shown in Fig. 6.2.

This systems-based model of managers' performance masks the fact that other blocks are not shown in this model although they are assumed to exist and will influence the different parts of the system. These additional blocks are the determination by the policy makers of the overall strategy of the organization, which in turn leads to the ascertaining of policy objectives on a macro as well

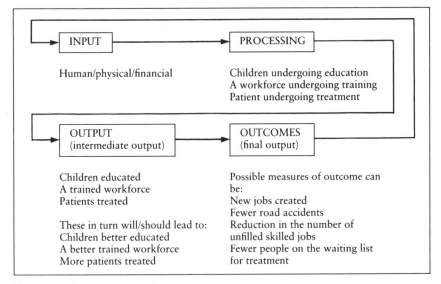

Figure 6.2   A management review system

as a micro level (manager's level). A third block, crucial and important (discussed in 6.4.3) for the monitoring of managers' performance is the management information system in use for supplying managers with the relevant information needed for performing their duties and carrying out their responsibilities.

It is worth noting that while ideally it may be useful for organizations to develop measures to cover the 4E's, the practicality, relevance and, more importantly, the learning curve that organizations need to go through in developing and using performance measures may dictate the use of a set that may not fully cover all these categories.

As an example, Holtham (1988) discusses the experience of the finance department at the London Borough of Hammersmith and Fulham in developing a set of performance measures to assess the achievements of the department against its planned performance.

Alongside the quantitative measures, a qualitative set was developed, based on a rating system for assessing quality, whereby 100 per cent represented an ideal performance measure and 40 per cent indicated little or no achievement. A rating of 120 per cent was introduced to represent excellent performance. The argument put forward by the author for introducing a rating of more than 100 per cent was:

> It was thought important in setting up the system to show that it is possible to achieve more than 100 per cent. However, the implication is that it is usually more expensive to achieve excellent performance and that this might be less important than achieving adequate standards of performance across the board.
>
> (Holtham, 1988, p. 32)

The results of the quality system used for the financial control division for the year 1986/87 is shown in Table 6.1.

Having introduced and discussed in general terms the need and the use of performance measures, the question that presents itself is what are the limitations and the shortcomings associated with the use of such measures? Are performance measures definite, non-debatable, objective and beyond manipulation as sets of figures to which all interested parties can agree and use? The answer is most definitely *maybe!!* The following subsections discuss the factors which producers as well as users of performance measures need to be aware of as they impact the validity, generalizability and applicability—in some cases— of these measures.

6.3.1   IS ACCOUNTING NEUTRAL?

The financing, investment and operational decisions of management are made conditional upon the organization's environment. This environment is the set of influences, both economic and non-economic, that determine the parameters within which organizations operate. Accounting is the language by which we seek to express in monetary terms the impact of economic influences constituting the organization's environment.

Table 6.1 Quality targets, Financial Control Division, 1986/87

Key targets	Priority	Results	Quality rating (%)
Maintain and extend credibility of MAS	Critical	Implemented new release	80
MAS enhancement:			
Cost centre enquiry	Critical	System specified	80
On line budget development	Critical	No progress 86/87	40
Downloading	Desirable	No progress 86/87	40
MAS training:			
Provide support for industrial departments	Critical	Manual monitoring developed but no demand	60
Development of GLC:			
budget and reporting requirements	Critical	Estimate prepared on super-scale, plus demonstrate applicability	100

Source: Holtham (1988), reprinted by permission.

It is a misconception bordering on myth that accounting rules are neutral and do not influence an organization's decisions. Further, there is evidence to show that, where firms have no choice over the accounting rule they employ, they will take financial or investment decisions to counteract the perceived effects of that accounting rule (e.g. where funds are allocated annually and unspent funds are not transferred to a future year, decision makers sometimes take end-of-year decisions solely for the purpose of using their funds).

In addition to the above, a lot of controversy surrounds what some people call 'creative accounting' in profit-making organizations. The term is sometimes used to cover practices which vary between permitting different entities to employ different accounting methods to account for the same type of transaction, to state-of-the-art manipulation of the organization's financial transactions, as with off-balance sheet financing (Griffiths, 1986).

The *raison d'être* behind such manipulation is an attempt to influence the users of the published accounts in their assessment of the organization's performance, both present and future.

Rutherford (1990) suggests that public sector bodies have also developed practices that fall under this heading. An example of these practices are deferred purchase schemes which involve financing by a third party of capital work undertaken for an organization, before the organization incorporates the asset and its finance in its financial statements.

The method used to finance the capital work may be appropriate and relevant as a financing tool, but the issue is that the method of financing affected the method of accounting for it: the capital asset and the source of funding it could be included in the balance sheet. The scope for doing otherwise stems from the fact that, traditionally, local authorities accounted for their capital expenditure on the basis of their funding.

6.3.2   RETROSPECTIVE NATURE OF ACCOUNTING

Analysis of the information contained in the organization's final accounts—produced as part of the financial accounting system—provides indications of the past financial performance, the soundness of the decisions made by the entity and its present strength or weakness.

Such information is vital, though wholly inadequate, to the process of evaluating the future of the organization. It may provide some signals as to the potential slide in the performance or condition of the organization. Examples can be seen in the accounts of universities, which are showing large deficits, shrinking reserves and that real financial problems are looming on the horizon. Another example can be the accounts of British Rail, which are showing the very delicate financial balance that the Board of British Rail need to maintain to ensure the organization does not turn to its paymaster, the government, for financial help and bailing out. Indeed, there is evidence that accounting information can provide such distress signals, if properly analysed and interpreted.

However, it should be noted here that management accounting and its use in the provision of quantitative (financial and non-financial) information relating to the past, present and future, does in certain cases help to remedy some of the weaknesses of financial accounting—especially for internal users.

6.3.3   COMPARATORS USED IN CROSS-SECTION AND TIME-SERIES ANALYSIS

A performance measure is only informative where there is a valid basis for comparison, i.e. a 'yardstick', a 'standard'. In central or local government, and the NHS, where similar operations may be conducted in many different locations, data can be collected for comparative purposes.

Performance of a specific operation can then be assessed for each and every location. While this statement may seem plausible if taken at face value, it is worth remembering that comparative measures/statistics may not reflect or take into account the variations in the different sources of information and the different environmental factors that will, in the majority of cases, influence and/ or distort these measures (Buttery and Simpson, 1989, p. 87)

Sources of data are numerous. Within many enterprises, comparative data may be collected internally from a number of units with similar characteristics. Targets or standards are another source of comparative data, as are data on past performance.

Analysing the performance of an organization relative to other organizations within its sector—local government, health authority, the private sector (cross-sectional analysis)—or analysing it relative to the organization's earlier performance (time-series analysis) can accomplish review objectives (Henley *et al.*, 1989, p. 154).

A third tool for measuring performance is the use of league tables. NHS, local authorities and other public sector bodies produce such tables for comparative purposes. Here again, one should remember the importance of comparing like with like. Performance should be measured against the potential of the particular unit as well as against the achievement of other units.

A report in the press (*Evening Standard*, 4 February 1991) claims that the Department of Education and Science is refusing to take environmental factors —viz. children's social class and type of housing—into account when assessing the performance of schools in public exams. The accuracy or inaccuracy of this statement is not the subject of debate here. The issue is that factors which research has proved to impact the way children perform in the classrooms and in the examinations may not be used to adjust the raw results so as to produce measures which provide for a fair comparison to be conducted across schools, authorities, etc.

6.3.4   EXAMPLES OF PERFORMANCE MEASURES

This section presents some examples of performance measures. The first is extracted from the published accounts of Thames Water. It includes a set of qualitative measures relating to the quality of water supplied to Thames' customers (Table 6.2) and a set of financial ratios for the years 1983/84 to 1987/88 (Table 6.3).

Table 6.2   Quality of water supplied by Thames Water

	1987/88 Performance against target (%)	1986/87 Performance against target (%)
Population whose resources met Thames' standards	26	32
Population receiving water at adequate pressure	98	97
Quantity of water supplied complying with certain standards of EC Directive:		
• Chemical standards	99.3	99.6
• Acceptability standards	99.9	99.8
Proportion of samples of water in supply complying with bacteriological standards of the EC Directive	> 99.45	> 99.8

Source: Thames Water (1987–88) *Annual Report and Accounts.*

Table 6.3 Performance, financial and general review of Thames Water 1983/84 to 1987/88

Item	Unit	1983/84	1984/85	1985/86	1986/87	1987/88
Water supply						
Expenditure per head of equivalent population:						
1 Operating and management expenses	(£)	10.33	9.95	9.51	10.06	9.87*
2 Current cost depreciation	(£)	2.43	2.37	2.50	2.54	2.91
3 Current cost operating profit	(£)	2.03	2.25	3.34	3.35	2.85
Percentage of water put into supply from:						
4 Ground sources	(%)	25.8	25.3	25.7	26.0	26.0
5 Surface sources	(%)	74.2	74.7	74.3	74.0	74.0
Percentage of supplies which are:						
6 Metered potable	(%)	17.1	17.9	17.7	17.1	16.3
7 Metered non-potable	(%)	—	—	—	—	—
8 Unmetered	(%)	82.9	82.1	82.3	82.9	83.7
9 Percentage of normal population on supply	(%)	99.96	99.96	99.96	99.96	99.96
Sewerage						
Expenditure per head of equivalent population:						
10 Operating and management expenses	(£)	3.67	3.63	3.54	3.34	3.42
11 Current cost depreciation	(£)	5.10	5.09	5.21	5.30	5.19
12 Current cost operating profit	(£)	0.46	0.90	1.47	1.68	1.95
13 Percentage of population connected to sewer	(%)	97.77	97.79	97.81	97.83	97.84

Sewage treatment and disposal

Expenditure per head of equivalent population:

14 Operating and management expenses	(£)	7.26	7.40	7.22	7.11	7.47
15 Current cost depreciation	(£)	3.13	2.79	2.90	2.98	2.98
16 Current cost operating profit	(£)	0.50	0.96	1.40	1.61	1.86
17 Pollution load (BOD) removed per head of population	(kg)	29.5	29.5	29.5	29.5	29.5
18 Average size works—equivalent population	(kg)	31084	31112	31377	31715	33475
19 Length of Class 3 and 4 rivers	(km)	216	270	252	234	122
20 Total length of classified rivers	(km)	2418	2418	2418	2418	2418

Environmental services

21 Expenditure per head of equivalent population	(£)	0.79	0.74	0.71	0.90	0.96

Manpower

Manpower numbers per thousand equivalent population

22 Water supply (inc. approp. part of water resources)		0.32	0.28	0.27	0.27	0.28
23 Sewerage		0.15	0.14	0.14	0.13	0.13
24 Sewage treatment and disposal		0.25	0.22	0.22	0.21	0.21
25 Land drainage		0.06	0.06	0.06	0.05	0.06

Capital expenditure

Capital expenditure per head of equivalent population:

26 Water supply	(£)	3.54	2.90	3.09	3.76	5.80
27 Sewerage	(£)	3.96	3.82	3.93	4.60	3.99
28 Sewage treatment and disposal	(£)	2.21	2.02	1.66	1.40	1.97
29 Land drainage	(£)	0.96	0.87	0.82	1.65	1.33

*£10.66 if the 'Cakebread' adjustment is excluded.

Source: Thames Water (1987–88) *Annual Report and Accounts.*

The second example (Table 6.4) relates to British Coal. The table incorporates the different performance measures published by the Board depicting the results of their operations. In addition, the annual report includes two very useful sets

Table 6.4   British Coal—performance measures 1988/89 and 1989/90

Operation (and unit of measurement)	1989/90 (53 weeks)	1988/89
Profit and loss (£m)		
Operating profit	133	498
Interest charges	(574)	(432)
Profit/(loss) after interest	(441)	66
Exceptional items	(4635)	(269)
Overall (loss)	(5076)*	(203)
Investment (capital expenditure, £m)		
Major colliery projects	177	249
Total mining capital expenditure	476	547
Safety (casualties per 100000 manshifts)		
Fatal accidents	0.08	0.07
Total accidents	27.10	29.31
Productivity (tonnes)		
Coalface output per manshift	20.5	19.05
Overall output per manshift	4.32	4.14
Output per man-year	1080	978
Output (saleable output, million tonnes)		
Deep-mined (including tip and capital coal)	7.56	85.0
Opencast	17.5	16.8
Licensed mines	2.1	2.1†
Total saleable output	95.2	103.9†
Employees (total employees at year-end)		
Colliery industrial manpower	65413	80156
Other industrial manpower	8037	10764
Non-industrial staff	11560	14125
Total employees	85010	105045
Markets (sales, million tonnes)		
Power stations	75.8	78.8†
Coke ovens	2.4	3.7
Other markets	13.5	14.2†
Total inland sales	91.7	96.7†
Exports	2.6	1.8
Total sales	94.3	98.5†

*The abnormally high overall loss arises as a consequence of British Coal's capital reconstruction under the Coal Industry Act 1990.
†Amended figure for 1988/89.
Source: British Coal Corporation (1989/90) Report and Accounts.

of statistics, viz. summary of statistics 1947 to 1989/90 and output productivity and manpower by groups.

6.3.5   SUMMARY

To summarize, the use of performance measures (in the form of ratios) is subject to the following limitations:

1 The accounting figures used in computing some of these ratios are all dependent on the accounting concepts (conventions, principles, etc.) used in the preparation of these statements, with their associated limitations and the fact that different interpretations can be attached to them (e.g. prudence, materiality).

2 The ratios produced are signposts, clues and indicators of what may be taking place in the entity. They are not answers to specific questions but merely a set of figures that can help the user to attain an answer or a conclusion to a specific query. In addition, it may be worth remembering that no deductions can be made that are of better quality than the information that was used as input to this deductive process.

3 Performance measurement needs to be conducted sensitively otherwise improvements will not occur, e.g. indirect pressures, such as induced by league tables, may be ignored. Where performance is shown as 'poor', defensive and other negative behaviours may militate against improvements, as might a rating of 'above average', which may deter striving for better results.

6.4   Reviewing and monitoring managers' performance

In the 1980s, public sector organizations faced a number of forces for change, including increasing financial pressures, privatization, increased competition, decentralization and contracting out of services. Hence, many ideas, initially conceived within the private sector during the 'Thatcher years', seem to have been transferred to public sector bodies. Notions such as leadership, mission, quality of service and reward based on performance, are contributing towards a change of culture in the public sector.

Great care needs to be taken to achieve the successful design, implementation and use of a system for reviewing and monitoring managers' performance. Flynn (1990), Glynn (1986), Holtham (1988), Jackson and Palmer (1989), Stahl (1989), among others, have identified a number of factors which essentially should be considered if success is to be achieved.

These include, firstly, considerations of significant external factors which can impact on an organizational's internal environment. For example, dynamism, hostility, technology and other factors identified by authors such as Porter (1983) and Mintzberg (1983) together with more 'traditional' factors such as multiple values and goals, ill-defined policy directives and wide stakeholder base (Harrow and Willcocks, 1990). Although these are factors over which an organization has little, if any, control, their influence needs recognition.

Secondly, certain factors internal to the organization require to be taken into account when designing, implementing and using a system of review of management performance. These include variables such as organizational culture, management style and other management systems.

6.4.1 ORGANIZATIONAL CULTURE

The culture of an organization relates to the values that pervade throughout and are the backdrop against which decisions are made and performance occurs. Because of external factors, organizations are seeking to move away from being large bureaucracies towards being organizations that can adapt quickly and respond flexibly to market and other forces. Such movement brings about a need for changes in rules, roles and relationships, and, even more funadmentally, in espoused values.

New philosophies and values underlying vision have been espoused in corporate 'mission statements'. As Drucker (1990) points out, while performance in non-profit organizations must be planned, this process starts with the mission since this defines the results.

Many organizations in the private sector have, during the 1980s, introduced a variety of total quality management (TQM) systems, based on the premise that this can provide a more integrated management approach as an alternative to more bureaucratic forms of management. It is a philosophy that aims to involve everyone—all employees, and some customers and suppliers—in providing quality and, as such, is a strong cultural change mechanism (Witcher and Wilkinson, 1990).

Within central government, for example, the 'main vehicle for the management of change in the civil service is the FMI' (Richards, 1987). A number of other initiatives can also be seen as catalysts for change. For example, Next Steps seeks to emphasize new skills and knowledge needed by civil servants in their management role and inculcate new attitudes towards responsibility and performance.

At local level, performance targets, and personal responsibility of the chief executive and others for achieving them, is central to Next Steps. Next Steps allows responsibility for the running of day-to-day operations in the civil service to the chief executive. While chief executives remain the servants of Ministers and will be accountable to them, select committees will be able to question directly the official who is responsible for the day-to-day running of an agency.

Thus, the review system should be designed to be in tune with the culture since this will be one basis for consistency of decisions across different subunits in the organization and hence can reduce the need for complex control mechanisms.

Tyson identifies one problem: the government's philosophy of 'value for money' is a symbolic term which represents a concern for efficiency and evaluation of costs and benefits. However:

> Value for money is a vague concept and is hardly likely to inspire leadership or evoke great emotional support among civil servants.
>
> (Tyson, 1990, p. 27)

Indeed, it is important that a mission statement is operational, i.e. it can be converted into specifics, otherwise it is just 'a good intention'. This enables everyone in the organization to see their contributions towards the goal.

This emphasizes the fact that change needs to be managed. This is described in the *Audit Commission Handbook* (1986/87, p. 83) as follows:

> Economy, efficiency and effectiveness do not just happen. In almost every situation changes—often uncomfortable changes, involving people doing things differently—will be involved. Those organisations in the public and private sectors which have been successful in securing beneficial changes have created an environment that thrives on challenge and change, by managing the following elements (vision, strategy, structure, systems, staffing and skills, style) in such a way as to reinforce each other.

With so many new initiatives, public sector top management need to lead and be seen to be fully supportive in order to successfully introduce and implement change within the enterprise. New systems and procedures can only be introduced successfully if top management give their authority and backing. Tyson, however, notes:

> At the heart of the difficulty of developing public servants as leaders is the question of public policy objectives. The civil service is trying to develop managers in different organisational cultures or climates in order to achieve diverse objectives. Most of these objectives are political and change as priorities change. An ideology of managerialism based on efficiency is not enough in motivational terms. There must also be commitment to the public good, because unless there is a moral purpose to public policy, it has no intrinsic worth.
>
> (Tyson, 1990, p. 30)

Part of the role of managers in public service organizations is to build in review, revision and organized abandonment of mission statements or, at least, revise the importance and priorities of objectives, as circumstances change. Much of the difficulty arises because of the number of different interest groups, each with their own objectives. A major management task is to manage dilemmas and get the various groups to agree on the long-term goals. The need is to satisfy sufficient expectations of major stakeholders to ensure continued support for the service or programme.

Although mission statements will not mobilize the human resources to get the right things done unless there is personal competence and commitment, such an approach does provide an alternative to the rationalistic ideas of planning and control.

Criticisms have been made of the totally rationalistic planning and control type system, which in this day and age is likely to be dysfunctional. Successful organizations have been found to result more from people being highly motivated, having high commitment to the selected objectives and sharing common expectations of what is required and what should be achieved.

Tomkins (1987) argues for an 'hour glass' structure of control with the focus of control on monitoring what has been achieved rather than how it has been achieved. Hence, the purposes for measuring performance must be clear and accepted by all. The structure and/or culture of an organization may need to change so as to help create an environment supporting the introduction of performance measures and in harmony with the philosophy behind it.

6.4.2   MANAGEMENT STYLE AND MANAGEMENT PERCEPTIONS

Management style influences the design, implementation and use of the review system because of the impact of managements', usually implicit, models of how people are motivated. Simplistically, managers can be placed on a continuum based on the extent to which they have an internal or external control management philosophy.

Management adhering to the former philosophy are more likely to view people as internally driven, self-directed and acting in the organization's interest. They will encourage participatively set goals, use performance measures for problem identification and solution and tie rewards to overall performance since they view performance measures as 'tin-openers'. Those managers who cluster at the opposite end of the continuum tend to view people in a more mechanistic way, imposing a more autocratic relationship, a tighter control system and use performance measures as 'dials'.

Because of the different ways that people can be viewed, and the effects on control, managers are likely to feel ambivalent towards performance measurement. From a study of six Canadian public sector organizations seen to be 'good performers' via a consensus view of senior people in government, Brodtrick noticed that the one attribute they all shared was the ability to move from bureaucracy—they had shifted from control to commitment. They recognized that 'systems alone will not give good performance; we also have to secure the motivation and commitment of people' (Brodtrick, 1989, p. 111).

Haywood, with regard to efficiency in the NHS, observes that:

> Health authorities and managers frequently justify savings/cost improvements on the basis of necessity, rather than on economic grounds. Something must be done because the Government requires it. Motivation is a mixture of duty and necessity rather than conviction.
>
> (Haywood, 1990, p. 51)

Thus, because of the way it can be used, there is a political dimension to performance measurement: performance measurement is not neutral, in many cases it is used as a weapon with which to exert control or influence (Flynn, 1986).

Managers are more likely to make effective use of performance measures—

i.e. use the system as intended—and thereby effect improvements to economy, efficiency, effectiveness and equity in the activities they control, when they concur with the purpose, need for and relevance of the system. This can only be achieved by participation and building consensus and commitment to change, which of course has implications for management development. These are explored by Tyson (1990).

Cowen and Middaugh (1990) identify four areas where management perceptions will affect the success with which the components of a planning and control system will influence their behaviour. These are: perceptions of the relevance of the objectives, targets and procedures; the relevance of the performance criteria; the clarity of the performance–reward relationship; and the nature of the rewards.

If managers do not see the established objectives and targets (at whatever level, individual, group, unit) to be relevant and fair, then managerial behaviour may 'take the form of system circumnavigation, game playing, alliance building and other tactical responses as a safeguard against being hurt by the system' (Cowen and Middaugh, 1990, p. 80). In such cases managerial effort is misdirected and non-optimal decisions may occur.

Closely related to the relevance of objectives and targets is management's perceptions of the relevance of performance criteria. For example: Do they actually measure what they purport to measure? Are they valid? Similarly: Are they accurate, i.e. reliable? To what extent do they incorporate an element of subjectivity? Do the measures really reflect performance? What is the relationship between management effort and the performance dimension measured? Where managers see a performance measure to be 'accurate' and credible they will more likely accept the findings.

Managers will not feel motivated if they are held accountable for performance in areas for which they have no responsibility. Performance measures, therefore, can only be allocated to managers for activities over which they have some control. Frustration may occur otherwise.

In some cases management is encouraged to use performance measurement as an incentive, by linking it to a reward system and an appraisal scheme. A report, based on research carried out by Incomes Data Services for Coopers and Lybrand, found that the main reason for introducing performance-related pay was 'to foster a performance culture'. For example, performance-related pay is becoming more common. In some agencies, health authorities and government departments, the chief executives, senior managers and senior civil servants are receiving additional payment subject to their organizations' achieving performance targets. Some units are developing group performance bonus schemes based on 'profit' made above targets.

However, a performance-based incentive scheme can only be used successfully where a clear relationship exists between the individual's/group's behaviour and the performance measure, and managers should not be praised or rewarded for positive outcomes that can be due to extraneous factors, or vice versa.

Rawlinson and Tanner (1989, p. 81) believe that correctly designed performance-related pay schemes will serve to increase motivation and enhance job satisfaction. However, they threaten: 'Inadequately designed and insensitively applied, the reverse will happen and local government may not achieve another decade of service, let alone another century!'

Sometimes performance rewards are in conflict with the way managers perceive organizational objectives to be prioritized. In many situations, differences occur between what is stated as the basis for rewards and what is used for reward determination. To overcome this, top management needs to state explicitly the organizational objectives and ensure that (a) these objectives are communicated to all levels of management and (b) the performance appraisal and reward systems are based on managers' contribution to the achievement of key organizational objectives.

Another consideration when measuring performance is that it can cause the emphasis to be placed on short-term performance. In situations in which promotion depends upon performance, managers may concentrate on achieving short-term improvements in performance. This means that there might be an under-investment in long-term strategic areas such as innovation, training and quality improvements. However, a bias towards the short term can be corrected when top management link performance measures to long-term or strategic planning and assess a manager's performance in terms of his or her contribution to meeting objectives to achieve these long-term aims.

Thus, where the purpose of performance measurement is multi-fold there are problems with competing requirements (see, for example, James, 1988; Stewart and Stewart, 1987). Where measurement is used consistently, creatively, constructively and positively to help managers improve their performance, implementation and use is more likely to be a success. If systems are designed and used punitively, managers may cheat and, in Glynn's words, 'Deviancy is a result of the nature of the rules, not of delinquent tendencies by managers' (1986, p. 112).

6.4.3   OTHER MANAGEMENT SYSTEMS

In all cases there is a need to align organizational, subunit and individual objectives and reflect this in the review of management performance. Similarly, there is a need to align the performance review system with other management systems. For example, at central level, the Treasury and Civil Service Commission have been working together to develop financial, personnel and reward systems that will complement the attempts to increase unit efficiency and management accountability. This reflects the importance of what we mentioned earlier—the need for all systems to reinforce each other by ensuring consistency and coherency across the organization.

Management who use performance measures to review performance by the

4E's need to consider whether existing information systems will provide the quality and quantity of information required. Data errors, missing values and abnormal distributions can affect the value of a performance measure, rendering any interpretation of its relationship with other measures suspect.

While public sector organizations operate financial procedures that tell them how much they have spent and on what activity—i.e. information relating to inputs and outputs—differences occur in the extent to which their information systems can provide qualitative data to indicate performance to predetermined activities and objectives, i.e. information relating to outcomes and quality.

Varying progress has been made in different parts of the sector and some of this has been covered earlier in this chapter, but the greatest concentration has been on producing quantifiable input and output performance measures that utilize existing information. However, even in this area, as Flynn (1989) points out, most of these measures have been devised to help scrutiny by people outside the organization, e.g. auditors, select committees and others, for external accountability purposes. In many cases, managers need different measures to help them assess performance in their own terms, i.e. for managerial efficiency purposes. Flynn (1989, p. 106) suggests: 'What is interesting for managers are measures which help rearrange the inputs to the service in such a way that the outputs can be improved.'

This, of course, also relates to a possible area of conflict, where operational management of units has been devolved to one level, yet resource allocation is left at a higher level. Managers need sufficient authority to make strategic changes in direction that might be required. Accountability needs to be focused towards responding effectively to the 'market' for services rather than merely keeping budgets under control (Metcalfe and Richards, 1987). Where this is not the case, managers need presentational skills and powers of persuasion to ensure that information provided by the feedback loop, in the management review system (see Fig. 6.2) is acted upon.

Management who are focusing on performance require new information systems that not only utilize existing databases, but will generate additional data on likely outcome performance measures that can provide some—albeit crude—monitoring of impact. Banks (1990) draws attention to the importance of considering the measurement of final output for both managers and policy makers. It is important to show, through analysis, that policies are 'good' and hence that the service provider is 'doing the right thing'.

Yet, management also needs to consider the cost of producing additional data in relation to the benefits derived from the improvements in efficiency and performance and guard against overload in providing the basic information from which the performance measures are compiled and in the number of measures considered. Hence, when deciding what to measure, selectivity is crucial and only key areas should be the focus of measurement (critical 'success' factors). Since some information needs are likely to change relatively quickly, units may take on responsibility for designing systems as required, with IT professionals providing advice and support.

6.5   Conclusion

Scarcity and competition for resources in today's environment compels managers, as well as the top decision makers, to ensure on the macro as well as the micro levels (units, divisions, local authorities, government departments, etc.) that resources are being used within the parameters of the 4E's.

The planning and controlling cycle requires managers to develop and use standards/yardsticks as measures to assess performance. The feedback from comparing actual with expected is essential if the organization is to stay on course to achieve its original objectives or to change and adapt these objectives so as to meet the changes in the environment in which it operates.

Performance measures (whether internally or externally generated) have been and are being developed continuously. The myriad number of these measures highlights the need to ensure that their development is not becoming an end in itself but the means to help managers assess, and where needed, improve their performance.

We have described in this chapter a number of advantages provided by performance measures. A survey conducted by Jackson in 1988 and reported in Jackson and Palmer (1989, p. 2) found similar advantages, such as they:

- enable comparison of actual performance against planned performance, past performance or against the relevant performance of others
- highlight areas of interest and difference
- provide a comprehensive view of a service
- indicate trends over time
- enable the development of local benchmarks or norms.

However, it is also worth emphasizing that there are a number of factors that should essentially be considered for the successful design, implementation and use of a system for appraising and monitoring managers' performance.

As mentioned earlier, one of the major factors for managers who are considering introducing a performance review scheme is the importance of fit. Fowler (1988, p. 50) describes this as follows: 'Managers . . . must start with an analysis of their local authority's objectives, style and values and tailor a scheme to fit. Buying in a scheme "off the shelf" or copying a neighbouring authority's scheme is a recipe for failure.'

Other important attributes for a system to work successfully include:

- its leadership by top management
- its application to all staff
- a focus on key corporate objectives and values
- the inclusion of qualitative performance measures

- purpose for measuring is clear and communicated
- objectives set for individual accountabilities (including consideration of personal development goals)
- quality/price and other trade-offs are made explicit
- periodic review of performance, including discussion and revision and setting of new objectives.

Once implemented and in use, management need to be aware of the risks that the establishment of comparative data may create. Arguments can develop as to whether or not the comparison is valid. The ideal way forward for managers, as well as auditors, is to identify the opportunities to improve the 4E's. This can be achieved by a thorough examination of the methods and means used to achieve the objectives of the unit/department and endeavour to make recommmendations based upon observation and judgement that will help improve the performance of the unit/department.

Stewart (1990, p. 62) usefully draws our attention to the importance of the 'art of judgement'. For him: 'Judgement is at the heart of management in local government: professional judgement and political judgement intertwine in many decisions.'

In all parts of the public sector, managers and policy makers are required to make judgements about the management of equity, of risk, of time, of discretion and with regard to rationing. Different judgements will occur and these can be assisted by analysis and management information systems to inform political management; in addition, widened management development approaches (Maclagan, 1990) and debate, discussion, argument and advocacy (open communications) can be used to inform professional judgement.

Management is about getting things done through people, and good managers focus on getting the right things done excellently. As mentioned earlier, performance measures are not a panacea; they need to be reviewed and revised at regular intervals. Performance measures are but one way of helping management monitor, review and thereby improve performance.

Fowler (1990) has drawn attention to a number of problems with some current schemes for performance measurement in local government. These include schemes where:

- total emphasis is placed on statistically measured task performance
- too much reliance is placed on objective setting and review as an annual event rather than as an ongoing and informal management activity
- administration is too complex, e.g. one authority has an 8-page appraisal form and a 48-page management manual.

Other problems result from systems that are too hastily introduced and in confusing situations where TQM and PMS are both in existence.

If this chapter has provided managers with some thoughts on what is required to introduce and manage a successful system of performance review and identified some of the pitfalls, then we will have met our objectives.

References and further reading

ACAS (1988) *Employee Appraisal*. Advisory Booklet No. 11, ACAS, London.

Anthony, R. N. (1978) *Financial Accounting in Non-business Organizations*. Financial Accounting Standards Board, Stanford, Conn.

Audit Commission Handbook, updated annually.

Banks, T. (1990) 'Performance measurement: the needs of managers and policy makers', *Public Money and Management*, Summer, 47–9.

Beeton, D. (1988) 'Performance measurement: the state of the art', *Public Money and Management*, Spring/Summer.

Beeton, D. (ed.) (1988) '*Performance Measurement: Getting the Concepts Right*'. Discussion paper No. 18, Public Finance Foundation.

British Coal Corporation (1989/90) *Report and Accounts*.

Brodtrick, O. (1989) 'The attributes of well performing organisations', Chapter 10, in Beeton, D. and Terry, F. (eds), *Evaluating Public Service Peformance*. Discussion Paper No. 31, Public Finance Foundation.

Broussine, M. (1990) 'Across the sectoral divide: how managers see each other', *Public Money and Management*, Spring.

Buttery, R. and Simpson, R. K. (1989) *Audit in the Public Sector*. Woodhead Faulkner.

Chambers, A., Selim, G. and Vinten, G. (1990) *Internal Auditing* (2nd edn.). Pitman, London.

Corby, S. (1991) 'Civil service decentralisation: reality or rhetoric?', *Personnel Management*, February.

Cowen, S. S. and Middaugh, K. J. (1990) 'Matching an organisation's planning and control system to its environment', *Journal of General Management*, 16 (1, Autumn).

Dopson, S. and Stewart, R. (1990) 'Public and private sector management: the case for a wider debate', *Public Money and Management*, Spring.

Drucker, P. F. (1990) *Managing the Non-profit Organisation*. Butterworth–Heinemann, Oxford.

Everwijn, S. E. M. *et al.* (1990) 'Commitment and competence in solving work performance problems', *European Management Journal*, 8 (4, December).

Flynn, N. (1986) 'Performance measurement in public sector services', *Policy and Politics*, 14 (3).

Flynn, N. (1989) 'Public sector services', in Jones, P. (ed.), *Management in Service Industries*, Pitman, London.

Flynn, N. (1990) *Public Sector Management*, Harvester Wheatsheaf, Hemel Hempstead.

Fowler, A. (1988) *Human Resource Management in Local Government*. Longman and LGTB, London.

Fowler, A. (1990) 'Performance management: the MBO of the '90s?', *Personnel Management*, July.

Fry, G. *et al.* (1988) 'Symposium on improving management in government', *Public Administration*, 66 (Winter).

Glynn, J. J. (1986) *Value for Money Auditing in the Public Sector*. Prentice-Hall International, London.

Griffiths, I. (1986) *Creative Accounting*. Sidgwick & Jackson.

Hardcastle, A. (1990) 'Financial accountability and reporting in central government', *Public Money and Management*, Summer.

Harrow, J. and Willcocks, L. (1990) 'Public services management: activities, initiatives and limits to learning', *Journal of Management Studies*, 27.

Haywood, S. (1990) 'Efficiency and the NHS', *Public Money and Management*, Summer.

Henley, D., Holtham, C., Likierman, A. and Perrin, J. (1989) *Public Sector Accounting and Financial Control* (3rd edn). Van Nostrand Reinhold (Int.), London.

Holtham, C. (1988) 'Developing a system for measuring departmental performance', *Public Money and Management*, Winter, 29–33.

HMSO (1983a) *Efficiency and Effectiveness in the Civil Service*. Cmnd 8616, HMSO, London.

HMSO (1983b) *National Audit Act 1983*. HMSO, London.

HMSO (1988) *Improving Management in Government; The Next Steps*. HMSO, London.

HMSO (1989) *The Financing and Accountability of Next Steps Agencies*. Cmnd 914, HMSO, London.

ICAEW (1989) *Auditing and Reporting*. Institute of Chartered Accountants.

IIA (1988) *Standards and Guidelines for the Professional Practice of Internal Auditing*. Institute of Internal Auditors.

Jackson, P. and Palmer, B. (1989) *First Steps in Measuring Performance in the Public Sector: A Management Guide*. Public Finance Foundation.

James, G. (1988) *Performance Appraisal*. Work Research Unit, Occasional Paper No. 40, ACAS, London.

Jones, R. and Pendlebury, M. (1988) *Public Sector Accounting*. Pitman, London.

Kessler, I. (1990) 'Personnel management in local government: the new agenda', *Personnel Management*, November.

Klein, R. and Carter, N. (1988) 'Performance measurement: a review of concepts and issues', in Beeton, D. (ed.), *Performance Measurement: Getting the Concepts Right*. Discussion paper No. 18, Public Finance Foundation.

Lengnick-Hall, C. and Lengnick-Hall, M. (1988) 'Strategic human resource management: a review of the literature and a proposed typology', *Academy of Management Review*, 13 (3).

Lewis, P. (1991) 'Peformance-related pay: pretexts and pitfalls', *Employee Relations*, 13 (1, Spring).

Lewis, S. (ed.) (1986) *Output and Performance Measurement in Central Government: Progress in Departments*. Treasury Working Paper No. 38, HM Treasury.

Maclagan, P. (1990) 'Moral behaviour in organisations: the contribution of management education and development', *British Journal of Management*, 1 (1).

Masters, S. (1990) 'Financial accountability and reporting in the NHS', *Public Money and Management*, Summer.

Metcalfe, L. and Richards, S. (1987) *Improving Public Management*. Sage, London.

Mintzberg, H. (1983) *Structure in Fives—Designing Effective Organizations*, Prentice-Hall, Englewood Cliffs, CA.

Porter, M. E. (1983) *Cases in Competitive Strategy*, Free Press, New York.

Rawlinson, D. and Tanner, B. (1989) *Financial Management in the 1990s*. Longman and LGTB, London.

Richards, S. (1987) 'The financial management initiative', in Gretton, J. and Harrison, A. (eds) *Reshaping Central Government, 1979–1987*. Policy Journals, Newbury.

Rutherford, B. (1990) 'Towards a conceptual framework for public sector financial reporting', *Public Money and Management*, Summer.

Stahl, J. (1989) 'Innovative approaches to critical policy and management issues', in Beeton, D. and Terry, F. (eds), *Evaluating Public Service Performance*. Discussion Paper No. 31, Public Finance Foundation.

Stewart, J. (1990) 'Local government: new thinking on neglected issues', *Public Money and Management*, Summer.

Stewart, V. and Stewart, A. (1987) *Practical Performance Appraisal: Designing, Installing and Maintaining Performance Appraisal Systems*. Gower, Aldershot.

Storey, J. and Fenwick, N. (1990) 'The changing face of employment management in local government', *Journal of General Management*, **16** (1, Autumn).

Thames Water (1987/88) *Annual Report and Accounts*.

Thames Water (1988/89) *Annual Report and Accounts*.

Tomkins, C. R. (1987) *Achieving Economy, Efficiency and Effectiveness in the Public Sector*. Kogan Page, Edinburgh.

Tyson, S. (1990) 'Turning civil servants into managers', *Public Money and Management*, Spring.

Witcher, B. and Wilkinson, A. (1990) *Total Quality Management in the United Kingdom*. Occasional Paper No. 9072, Durham University Business School.

7

The manager as technologist

Leslie Willcocks

7.1 Introduction

Information Technology (IT) is now very big business in UK public administration. According to the Trade and Industry Select Committee (1988; see also
1989a, b) central government IT spend for the financial year 1987–88, excluding Ministry of Defence operational equipment, was £1800 million and rising.
This represented 1 per cent of total public expenditure and a rise of 16 per cent
over the previous year. Within this total picture the Department of Social Security (DSS) is spending £1749 million between 1982 and 1999 on its Operational
Strategy, though this figure has a history of being revised upwards (National
Audit Office, 1989a). The National Health Service (NHS) spends about 1 per
cent of its total budget—around £130 million in 1988–89, on IT; conservative
estimates for 1990–91 were around £230 million, an amount expected to rise
in subsequent years (Haughton, 1990; National Audit Office, 1990). Local
government expenditure was £407 million in 1988, anticipated to rise to £613
million in 1990 (Audit Commission, 1990; ICL, 1989). There are also some
very large-scale computer projects in public administration, for example the
1980s computerization of PAYE within the Inland Revenue at an estimated
cost of £340 million at 1987 prices (Lamont, 1989). This massive and rising
expenditure is paralleled in the private sector, where it is now about £12 billion,
and averages 1.2 per cent of annual turnover (Kearney, 1990; Price Waterhouse,
1990). All this pushes IT above the parapet in organizations. By 1992 senior
managers and policy makers in both public and private sectors were increasingly
wanting to question what the return is from such investments, whether the IT
route has been and will be a wise decision, and, if not, how IT practice can be
improved.

What can IT be used for in public administration? The 1980s and early
1990s saw considerable interest in the potential of computer-based systems for
delivering economy, efficiency and effectiveness at all staff levels in UK public
sector organizations. More recently there has been increasing emphasis on
improving the responsiveness of public sector organizations to customer requirements through how IT is applied (Taylor and Williams, 1990). A related, larger
concern has been to improve management across the public sector. A vital

170

element here has been perceived as information for managerial decision-making. Improving management has thus tended to become tied in with and highly dependent upon the provision of faster, more flexible, integrated and comprehensive financial and management information systems—made possible mainly by the application of IT.

But if IT is to deliver on these several purposes, then that delivery itself is dependent on management practices on several fronts. Does the public sector face an IT management Catch 22 where an improvement in its management requires good management in the first place? What have been the problems with computerization so far? Can the UK National Health Service cope with IT, and from its experience and prospects what lessons can all public sector organizations learn about how to implement IT? There is considerable evidence to show a dearth of informed strategy on IT in UK public administration and service organizations. Frequently what are termed 'implementation problems' are in fact the results of inadequacies in policy and planning, as will emerge particularly from the Department of Health and Social Security (now Department of Social Security—DSS) and NHS experience discussed below.

However, while such points need to be made, many of the policy decisions and plans developed at national and local political levels have to be lived with, and implementation practice remains an area where emergent, possibly different policies can, and may need to be developed. However, there is also the possibility of developing intermediate strategy on IT; this will direct implementation practice while also upwardly influencing policy and decision makers at higher levels, for example, elected local government representatives and Ministers of State.

In this chapter the principal concern is to discuss these issues and possibilities. Utilizing the research evidence of the author and others, the chapter draws out lessons on implementation practice for public sector organizations undergoing or anticipating advanced technological change. The chapter concludes by offering a broader perspective on IT implementation with detailed pointers for future management practice.

7.2 IT implementation: emerging problems

Information Technology investment has been, so far, a high-risk, hidden-cost process in both private and public sectors. This is a difficult area about which to generalize. However, research studies suggest that about 20 per cent of UK IT expenditure is wasted, and that between 30–40 per cent of IT projects realize no net benefits whatsoever, however measured (Eason, 1988; Kearney, 1984, 1987; KPMG Peat Marwick Mitchell, 1990; Willcocks and Lester, 1991; Wroe, 1986). A 1990 survey of some 400 organizations measured IT performance on objective criteria, and found only 11 per cent of the sample to be successful users of IT (Kearney, 1990).

There is much evidence from both private and public sectors that the major problems experienced in computer projects in the 1980s have stemmed from underestimation of the time needed to get a new installation operational (Kearney, 1984, 1987; Price Waterhouse, 1987). This source of problem has been closely followed by difficulties in getting the original definition right for the software required, and in recruiting and retraining high-quality staff (Kobler Unit, 1987; Strassman, 1985). A 1989–90 survey of over 130 private and public sector organizations by the SOMIT (Study of the Management of Information Technology) group at City University Business School suggest these problems are still recurring, though some change in emphasis occurs between organizations with different lengths of experience of implementing IT. This became particularly true with the setting of time scales, with these becoming more realistic along with an organization's greater IT experience. The major exceptions to this were where such time scales were externally imposed. This point is made because government imposition of deadlines has been a particular feature in IT implementation in the public sector—for example, between 1989 and 1991 in the cases of local government information systems for poll tax management, and IT for the Resource Management Initiative (RMI) in the NHS.

A range of research studies show common problems and weaknesses across public and private sector IT practice. Managements have been marked by confusion about the potential of IT, lack of awareness of new developments, and an absence of IT know-how at senior management levels (Daniel, 1987; Griffiths, 1987; Willcocks, 1989). In practice the predominant managerial tendencies in many IT projects may be summarized as limited choices, financial, short-term focus together with technocratically driven perspectives and outcomes (Boddy and Buchanan, 1986; Buchanan and Boddy, 1983; Clegg and Kemp, 1988; Kearney, 1987, 1990; Rowe, 1984; Willcocks, 1989). In a review of the research, Willcocks and Mason (1988a,b) show different, often conflicting objectives at different managerial levels in an organization. Additionally, human resource issues such as planning, pay levels, recruitment of IT-related staff, training and development and industrial relations rarely receive high priority; IT projects are often abandonded to systems professionals; and personnel managers are involved, if at all, only at very late stages of computer projects.

Specific studies of public sector computerization throw up a range of implementation problems. In the 1980s the National Audit Office produced several reports highly critical of IT applications in the Inland Revenue, the social security system, the National Health Service and the civil service generally. They show a lack of applied IT strategy, inadequate IT project management skills, inadequate evaluation and control mechanisms, training and staffing in major projects (National Audit Office, 1987, 1989a,b, 1990). As one example, in the Inland Revenue a major computer project was abandoned in 1985, leading to losses of £16.5 million. The failure was blamed on weaknesses in project management, design and staffing. Particular problems emerged in the management of human resources. Thus the Inland Revenue underestimated the number of staff needed to complete the project successfully. A general shortage of staff with IT skills was also identified. This shortfall was met by using consultants who, on average, charged over four times the rate of equivalent revenue staff, but whose specialist skills were rarely fully utilized (National Audit Office, 1987). These problems, though experienced to different degrees, emerged as fairly typical of public sector IT projects in the mid and late 1980s. Thus in a general review of the IT performance of government departments the major problem areas were identified as: a 25 per cent critical shortfall of specialist data-processing staff; lack of IT strategy; civil service managers ill-equipped in IT project management skills; lack of IT training for existing staff; underestimation of the difficulties in implementing large-scale IT projects; lack of ways of consulting unions affected; and problems deriving from inter-departmental politics (HM Treasury, 1984).

It is clear that many of these problem areas continued into the late 1980s and early 1990s. The Welsh Office, for example, experienced a three-year overrun, to 1990, in developing a management information system to give a detailed account of where its £3.5 billion budget goes (National Audit Office, 1989b). A 1990 survey of 23 central government departments found problems with human resource and financial shortages, management of user expectations, technical issues and standards, the considerable pace of change, unsatisfactory performance of external consultants and implementation delays (Bacon, 1991). A 1989 Coopers and Lybrand report on implementing IT in the Passport Office showed that performance requirements laid down in the specification were insufficient; a more radical look might have produced a better solution; implementation was both premature and untimely—coming during the pre-holiday peak; there was insufficient management and staff involvement and insufficient participation in vetting procedures. In a demonstration of the strong links between IT management and industrial relations issues, one outcome was a 1989 strike at Liverpool Passport Office holding up thousands of passport applications (Smith, 1989).

Some problem areas, particularly shortages in IT specialist staff and inadequacies in IT project management skills, far from having been managed out or down, have partially contributed to greater use of consultants in the public sector, contracting-out and, sometimes, privatization of computer departments. What has received too little attention, however, is how these solutions can themselves engender fresh problems. Firstly, these may not represent the most cost-effective route, but can result in large increases in costs, especially given the lower relative pay levels for IT staff in the public sector. This has been particularly found in the case of major projects in the Inland Revenue and DSS (National Audit Office, 1987, 1989a,b). Interestingly Conservative-run Northamptonshire County Council abandoned competitive tendering in 1991, claiming that users have not always been getting the best systems. Privatization of the computing department at West Wiltshire District Council also folded in the same year (Gibbs, 1991). Secondly, in-house IT staff are not always anxious to join the private sector, as found for example by NHS Trent, and North West Thames Regional Health Authorities in their 1989 plans to privatize computer services. Subcontracting can also encounter problems from the limited control over contractors, lack of organizational commitment and knowledge from contract staff, and problems of quality where, after a year to 18 months, good contract staff may be moved on to service new contracts elsewhere. These possibilities need to be considered carefully and it may well emerge that abandoning good IT implementation practice to the private sector instead of improving in-house performance on computer projects is by no means always the most economic, efficient and effective approach.

7.3   The DSS: managing an operational strategy

Many of these issues emerge from considering the history of the Operational Strategy at the Department of Health and Social Security (DHSS, subsequently divided into the DH and DSS). In 1982 the DHSS devised this 15-year strategy to computerize the recording, assessment, calculation and payment of all UK social security payments. Among the major gains would be more efficient delivery of DSS services and £700 million savings on operating costs by 1995. However, a range of weaknesses in planning and implementation practice emerged (Willcocks and Mason, 1986). The plans were not flexible enough to take in the long time scales, unpredictabilities in environment and government policy and the massive size of the project—the largest civil computer project in Europe; they were also very technically focused. There was a lack of skill and experience in managing large IT projects; moreover, implementation began in the mid-1980s as unemployment surpassed 3 million and a massive increase in social security payments work occurred. Furthermore, computerization was made more difficult by existing complicated manual regulations and procedures that received little simplification but many government-sponsored policy changes in the 1980s.

Additionally, the operational strategy ran into industrial relations problems —over how implementation was managed and the fact that the major savings from the project were to come from displacing 25000 DHSS staff by 1995. Lack of industrial relations foresight and the adoption of a confrontational style in the face of staff opposition in a highly unionized environment led to a 7-month strike at the key Newcastle computer centre in 1984 (Willcocks and Mason, 1987a). This severely delayed the computerization project, irretrievably soured the industrial relations climate and incurred costs approaching £200 million. The outcome for the late 1980s involved even tighter time scales, mutual distrust between management and employees, increased use of consultants and impending privatization of computer centres. So far, in an all too familiar scenario on the long path from IT planning to implementation, the ever-rising costs of the project have become more evident as its benefits are reassessed downwards.

A particular feature of this computer project has been the mismanagement of the human resource issues surrounding IT implementation. An alternative perspective could see the computerization process as a vehicle for displacing labour and reducing the power of the civil service unions. This may well be facilitated by 1990s moves to executive agency status, a decentralized computer centre structure, relocation of back office work to the regions, supported by IT, and the privatization of most computer centres (see Fig. 7.1). However, such criteria for success must also be measured against the massive and rising costs of implementing the operational strategy (on 1992 estimates, over £2 billion) and the constant reassessment of net savings downwards—net present value has been estimated by the DSS at £175 million to 1998–99, but this figure crucially depends upon the level of staff savings being achieved. As the National Audit Office (1989a) comments: 'A 17 per cent shortfall in the estimate could reduce the value to nil and put the financial viability of the Strategy at risk.' One must also point out that to recover time lost and to deliver systems quickly, from the late 1980s the DSS has deferred a number of low-priority functions, while some less important projects have been postponed indefinitely. Furthermore, based on their own research evidence from internal documents and interviews on the reliability and functionality of what has been delivered, particularly in the software field, Margetts and Willcocks (1991) put a note of caution against the short- and long-term appropriateness, technical robustness and daily availability times of the implemented systems. An even more pressing problem area, pointed to by the National Audit Office (1989a), has been the lack of user know-how and training on the new systems, though this would seem to be receiving increased attention in the early 1990s (Dyerson and Roper, 1990).

7.4 Implementation in the National Health Service

The NHS provides a highly pertinent case for examining the problems experienced in implementing IT in public administration and services. Here the Government has promoted major radical changes in the 1980s, and for the 1990s, all highly dependent on the delivery of IT to the organization. These include the attempt to establish a common framework of data sets and practices across the NHS (the 1982–84 Korner reports); the introduction of general management at every level (the 1983 Griffiths Report); the 1986 Resource Management Initiative (RMI) to use financial and management information to match use of resources with their cost (DHSS, 1986); and the January 1989 White Paper whose major changes are heavily dependent on the success or otherwise of the RMI being implemented and utilized by at least 260 hospitals by April 1991.

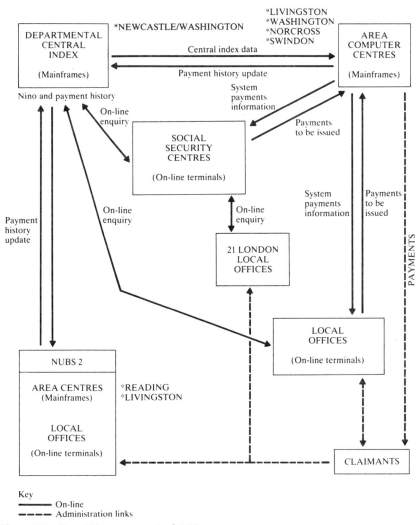

Figure 7.1   Post-1991 computerized DSS system

In practice, the NHS has experienced a number of general problems in its management of the IT aspects of these changes. These will be discussed here as a prelude to reviewing more detailed research findings on IT implementation in the NHS.

The fast pace and substantial volume of change demanded by Government from NHS management and information initiatives have in themselves created extensive IT implementation difficulties. Furthermore, from 1986, many interest groups within the NHS have increasingly questioned the high priority, expenditure and relevance of the IT vehicle of these initiatives in the light of the primary activity of the NHS of delivering patient care, together with the tight budgetary constraints operating elsewhere in the service. In the NHS, IT as a basis for new financial and management information systems shows few short-term benefits and has become increasingly identified with a rush to implement Korner and the RMI as ends in themselves. The fact that many interested parties have come to question the credibility of IT does not help its implementation and the achievement of managerial and information targets. It may be that, by 1988, the time had come in the NHS for a period of consolidation and reflection (Willcocks and Mark, 1989); since then, however, the urgency from the centre seems to have increased, not abated, even though the 1989 White Paper itself admitted that its deadlines for the IT-based RMI represented an ambitious timetable (Department of Health, 1989, p. 16).

A further recurrent problem is the high IT funding implications of recent legislative change and the extent to which central government, health authorities and hospitals are able and willing to meet these. According to the Society of Information Technology Managers in Local Government (SOCITM), the RMI will cost over £250 million, computerization of GP services £100 million or more, medical audit procedures over £150 million and hospital and information support services £1400 million plus (Audit Commission, 1990). Such computerization has enormous training and development implications, but while a strategy for staff training and development has been produced (NHS Training Authority, 1989), it does not clarify precisely how the four-year training programme was to be funded. In practice, the national training strategy budget of £4.5 million for 1989–90 was underspent by £2 million, due to the time needed to establish training projects and recruit staff in the first year. However, the National Audit Office (1990) indicates among health authorities continuing doubts at future funding availability feeding into continuing IT skills shortages and low priority given to information management and IT training.

One fundamental weakness in implementation practice has come from the treatment of the management and information policies as 'initiatives' and events rather than evolutionary processes that would grow along with the organization. There may be many reasons for this, including centrally imposed deadlines and a lack of identification with the emergent aims by some influential interest groups. However, and ironically, a key influence has come from the introduction of general management and the assignment of finite tasks and targets for general managers through the annual performance review and short-term programmes. Unfortunately, one major outcome for managers has been the need to deliver results short term in the NHS, thus cutting through more appropriate time scales and activities for IT implementation.

A further range of problems involves the politics of computerization. Information creates a number of dilemmas for organizations—for example, who controls it?; what sort of information will be collected?; to whom will it be made available? As Bourn (1987) argues, not all interested parties in the NHS will identify with the specifically managerial purposes and the collection of data for mainly managerial objectives, as in the case of the IT initiatives we are discussing. Furthermore, as Willcocks and Mason (1987a) argue, the status of IT as a resource, its creation as a social product, its cost and human resource implications and its ability to create winners and losers all raise additional organizational problems for large-scale implementation and operation of computer-based systems. A further set of implementation activities is necessary for NHS general and project managers—what has been called 'a polits track' (Willcocks and Mason, 1988b). However, while the need for such activities and related skills has often been acknowledged within the NHS, in practice the need has not always been addressed at managerial levels appropriate to the tasks; and frequently, at local levels, technical issues (together with deadlines imposed from above) have left the behavioural and organizational aspects of managing technological change neglected. This becomes a serious omission in an organization as 'political' as the NHS and will receive further attention below.

7.5   Implementation: an NHS region 1986–91

A greater feel for emerging IT problems in the NHS can be given from ongoing research following through several computer projects in one region in the south of England. Earlier detailed interim findings were reported in Willcocks and Mark (1989). The situation within the region is illustrated in Fig. 7.2.

The NHS Information Advisory Group produced at national level a strategic framework for information management. However, within the region studied its prescriptions were found to be impractical and largely irrelevant to regional, district and hospital needs. At regional level the long-term strategic objective in the period studied was to obtain comprehensive and integrated IT applications operating in districts on computers generally located in districts. However, to meet pressing information requirements, the immediate implementation of 'first generation' systems was encouraged, provided that they were 'useful, reliable and pay for themselves in terms of benefits'. This pattern was fairly typical throughout NHS regions at this time.

At regional level the prime movers tended to be the scientific officer, systems specialists, and clinicians who sat on the relevant committees. Not surprisingly, the direction of computerization at hospital level tended to follow their perceptions of, and priorities in, IT needs.

Though the whole thrust of the stated regional strategy has been towards district computing—in terms of computer location, control of IT and district determination of regional priorities—in practice, for many reasons, IT priorities, decisions and the determination as to which systems were actually implemented have largely remained in the hands of regional bodies. A common reason for this throughout 1986–87 was that either general managers at district level had not been appointed, or that, as recent appointees, they had enough to do

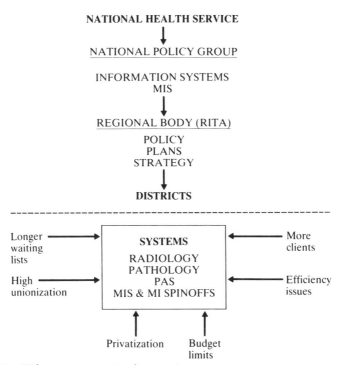

Figure 7.2   IT from strategy to implementation

without embarking on computer projects in an area in which they often had little experience. Many groups were also reluctant to contemplate the further reorganization and activity implied by computerization against a backdrop of already overstretched resources, staff shortages, other policy changes and reorganizations, rising patient waiting lists and a variety of funding problems at district and hospital level. A further factor was considerable scepticism at the ability of new computer systems to deliver on their specific local information needs. This largely derived from bitter experience with the imperfections of existing computer systems.

One major weakness with the regional strategy under review was that it was in reality a list of application and computer projects. It confused strategy with applications. The true strategy questions—for example: What would the hardware/software environment look like across the region? Will there be district mainframes? What would be run on those mainframes? Which systems should be at district level and which at region? Where are you going to get the skilled IT staff from? Should the key people be at district or should they be at regional computer centre?—were rarely asked, at least up to early 1988, let alone addressed. This weakness, driven by the rush to implement Korner and to be seen in the mid-1980s' climate to be 'doing something about IT', tended to filter through into implementing a mosaic of poorly matched IT projects being imposed upon, or partially displacing, existing, largely unrelated computer-based systems. It is upon this inheritance that further computerization, including the RMI, has to be built. In the face of such computer development, the dissatisfaction with, puzzlement at, and scepticism about computerization often encountered in user departments at local levels within the region was not always surprising. Subsequent developments suggest a much improved strategic approach by 1991, but its efficacy will be tested by user scepticism accumulated through the IT history described above, and the wider constraints, pressures and problems common to health authorities, and indicated in the previous section.

7.5.1   POST-IMPLEMENTATION REVIEW

To ascertain the impacts of implementation practice in the research region, in 1989 detailed post-implementation reviews were carried out, including two on computer projects in radiology and pathology departments. The results appear in more detail in Willcocks and Mark (1989). These revealed that systems were suboptimizing because many groups were untrained in IT, and training largely ceased once the systems specialists were off-site. It also later emerged that additional training would be a local responsibility and financed out of existing local budgets. This had the practical outcome of largely discouraging further movement on training. One consequence of inadequate user involvement in analysis, design and implementation was that 67 per cent of hospital doctors surveyed disapproved of the new systems. Furthermore, it emerged that an unpredicted 20 per cent of the new system workload came from community GPs—who had no training or involvement during systems development. This created large inputting problems and false expectations about the systems. Systems development was partial because it was largely left to specialist staff, and hospital user representatives participated while carrying out their normal full-time work with no extra reward or time made available. This dependence on staff goodwill continued hazardously into the implementation phase. When one system went down, no back-up system had been put in place, the working of the whole hospital was threatened, and staff goodwill gained system reinstatement. With so little thought given to the human aspects of computerization, a question mark must be placed against how long such goodwill would continue to support system running.

The positive side to such review information is that it can be fed back to improve present systems operation, and be applied to avoid similar problems in future computer projects within the organization. However, in our research we have noticed little tendency for this to be countenanced in the formal methods adopted, let alone operated in practice, in IT projects in the NHS. This is reinforced by the extensive survey by the National Audit Office (1990), which showed few post-implementation reviews being performed and therefore little dissemination of the lessons learned.

7.6   Politics and information systems

This case illustrates some of the IT implementation problems—many of which are, at root, political in nature—that have been experienced at regional, district and hospital levels within the NHS. Politics breed in times of technological change and it is worth considering how this is the case in some detail, using the NHS as the illustrative example. A major influence here is the limited power bases that the relatively new general managers have formed, and their over-dependence on formal position even where those managers have been recruited from within the NHS. As a result, they have rarely been able to act as a countervailing force against, and indeed most often have to work with, the grain of existing power structures, whether these are of a central versus local dimension, or consist of other powerful groupings and vested interests, in particular clinicians. The result is that, whatever policy is, in practice the needs and priorities of groups like clinicians, or of groups at regional rather than district level, are the first to be embodied in what has actually been successfully implemented so far in the NHS.

This political focus is supported by the findings of a number of studies of computerization in the NHS. Stocking (1985) found IT innovations difficult to introduce and maintain because of the bureaucratic nature of the organization and the entrenched power structure. When change occurred it depended on power, not rational decision-making; required powerful champions; had local appeal; did not cause conflict; was adaptable; and needed few resources. These criteria rarely applied in IT projects. The only one that frequently did and facilitated change was 'the need to do something', a kind of 'desperation' syndrome' (Stocking, 1985, p. 65). Wright and Rhodes (1985) studied a high security mental hospital and also found that successful computerization depended on a 'crisis'—in this case the questioning of the quality of patient care, an issue to which the professional elements in the NHS are particularly sensitive. IT implementation was successful because it provided an answer to this crisis; that is, addressed a problem perceived to be very real by those affected by and involved in IT operation. Additionally, Wright and Rhodes found that line authority was required, particularly for the introduction of integrated systems that cut across a number of interest groups. They also found that a leader or agent of change was needed to push through and maintain the momentum of change: and that in a political system like the NHS collaboration between change agents and users, and the active support of senior management, must be encouraged to reduce resistance to change.

Willcocks and Mark (1989) addressed the issue that—despite remarkable unanimity across all regions and districts in the NHS as to the benefits of adopting integrated hospital information systems, and the fact that the technical difficulties are not great (for some evidence see Faulkner et al., 1987; Sweeney and Mason, 1987)—such systems have been rarely implemented in the NHS. Research on a technically proficient system called PROMIS (Problem-Oriented Medical Information System), commercially available from the late 1970s, reveals the importance of human and political issues surrounding computerization. PROMIS makes available on-line up-to-date information to any staff member able to input into the system a recognized password (see Fig. 7.3). In fact, in enhancing skill levels and discretion of other hospital staff and making doctors' work more visible, PROMIS threatens the strong political positions of most doctors in hierarchically organized hospitals. Furthermore, as Child (1986) establishes, clinicians have such strong power bases in hospitals—expert knowledge, direct responsibility for patients undergoing high personal risk, strong occupational organization and senior formal positions in hospitals and in institutional decision processes—that few computer systems can be introduced into the NHS without being vetted for their impact on the position of doctors.

The problem with PROMIS and other integrated hospital information systems is that they presuppose the existence or the creation of a health care team that is problem- and patient-oriented, and dependent on shared expertise and information easily accessed by every member of the team. PROMIS has low acceptability in hospitals and clinics that are hierarchically structured, with more rigid demarcations and traditional relationships between doctors, nurses, ancillary and other professional staff. Two trends may favour systems like PROMIS: firstly, the increasing move towards training health care practitioners,

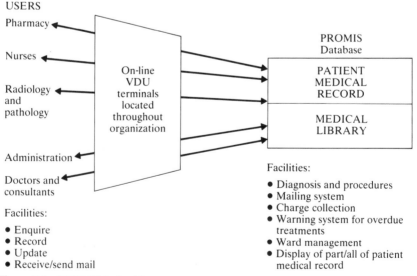

Figure 7.3 PROMIS in health care

including doctors, in a more task- and patient-centred approach. Systems like PROMIS tend to have much more support among groups already functioning along these lines; and, secondly, the growing, if belated recognition across all interest groups in the NHS of the need for and value of integrated computer-based information systems. However, with the attempted return to hierarchical forms of management, as embodied in Griffiths, such developments may well be frustrated by, or at least be in conflict with, managerial struggles to establish leadership in their organizations.

The search for legitimacy, feasibility and support required for any policy initiatives to become operationalized has been well described by Hall *et al.* (1975). Such a search is still in progress in the NHS in relation to the three issues of managerialism, information and Information Technology. The problem becomes how to tie IT stakeholders into supporting the implementation and subsequent operation of specific systems while achieving, in the case of management for example, managerial objectives. As Willcocks and Mason (1988b) have argued, the solutions are not easy but one area requiring attention in *all* IT projects is the need for more political, less technically focused approaches to IT implementation. From the analysis put forward here this is particularly the case for the NHS of the early 1990s.

7.7 From IT to information systems management

Many of the problems experienced in implementing IT in public adminis-tration relate strongly to environmental pressures and constraints. To take the example of local government, there have been budget constraints, contin-ual central government intervention and legislative changes (for example, the Community Charge), other new policies (for example, EEC Directives), together with immediate environmental and community needs to be delivered on. There have also been skills shortages, labour market pressures and restrictions on changing pay and reward systems. Furthermore, Community Charge, Compulsory Competitive Tendering and Local Management in Schools have tended to create additional pressures as service managers look specifically to IT to deliver the solutions (Audit Commission, 1990). Additionally, ideological stances of local councillors may change, there may well operate manufacturer or hardware lock-in, and at the same time, as found by Kraemer *et al.* (1989) in investigating US local governments, different political structures within an organization may determine the shape of computing—that is, whether it is oriented towards technical advancement, administrative or service objectives or policy ends.

It may well be that the size of IT investment appears low in comparison to the private sector, though it should be noted that investment size bears little relationship to the effectiveness of IT usage (Kobler Unit, 1990; Strassman, 1990; Willcocks and Lester, 1991). It may well be that IT departments are overwhelmed with current tasks, the maintenance of old applications, the scramble to meet new legislative requirements. It is clear, as shown in the case of the NHS, that much of this may need central government action in permitting a period of consolidation, and a reconsideration of IT funding throughout public service organizations. However, the poor IT management inheritance must also be given due weight. A 1990 survey of 23 government organizations shows a more encouraging picture on how far information systems strategies were being developed, but comments that many are still in the early stages of implementation (Bacon, 1991). To take again the example of local government, the Audit Commission (1990) notes: inadequate organization culture (e.g. departmentalism and élitism, lack of clear policy direction by members); poor top management attitude to IT (e.g. failure to tackle glaring track record of poor productivity); lack of IT strategy; low IT staffing and skills; inadequate IT management arrangements; inappropriate IT costing/charging systems; low performance of IT resources and little monitoring thereof; no agreed priorities in systems development; user abdicating their 'client' role. From this, and the evidence and arguments detailed elsewhere in this paper, it is clear that the management of IT can be improved upon. In fact a major shift is required, from IT to Information Systems (IS) management. This implies also new management divisions of labour.

IS management can be usefully divided into strategic, project and operational levels. In addition to those enumerated above, frequent observable problems in both private and public organizations include: failure to establish clarity in the managerial arrangements and responsibilities at and between these levels; lack of a strategic dimension linked with business/organizational objectives; IS professionals dominating the management processes in practice: poor user manager–IS professional liaison; lack of integration between the different levels of management (Ernst and Young, 1990; Macdonald, 1990; Rockart and Short, 1990; Scott Morton, 1989; Willcocks and Mason, 1987b; Willcocks, 1991). One way forward here is to see the strategic dimension as aligning objectives and plans with those of the organization, establishing management structures, resource allocation, monitoring and financial evaluation. Project management could then be seen as the development and delivery of systems to defined requirements within time and budget, user liaison and the management of systems staff, while operational management would be primarily concerned with the detailed management of routine operations, managing systems staff and user liaison.

Case research and active participation in IT projects would suggest a number of points. At the operational levels IT professionals need to look after detailed technical operations while taking responsibility for user liaison, support and much more user IT education than is commonly provided. Specific IT projects are often better managed by those with business and organizational skills rather than IS professionals. To endorse the findings of Beath and Ives (1988), champions, with power and resources, are needed at the project management level, as well as the strategic level, to ensure that projects maintain momentum on a daily basis. Experience also suggests that mixed project teams tend to produce better long-term results; there should also operate succession planning for key project staff, including project champions, both to encourage IT and management learning, but also to ensure that project time, and valuable learning, is not lost when key skilled staff are, as often happens, attracted into other work or organizations. It is the cross-fertilization of skills and the creation of opportunities for learning that should be built into the way IS management operates as a process. At all levels this means regular review to learn from mistakes inevitably made in what are often high-risk activities; at the strategic level it means a mix of skills, cross-learning and IT professionals actively involved in senior management decision-making. Much of this implies that IS management by its practice should be in itself a learning process, and this would seem to be one way of addressing the limitations in general and IS professional management practices detailed above.

However, if it ever could, IS management can no longer be seen as merely operating at these three levels. Figure 7.4 illustrates some major issues that will form a fundamental part of the agenda that IS managers need to address in the

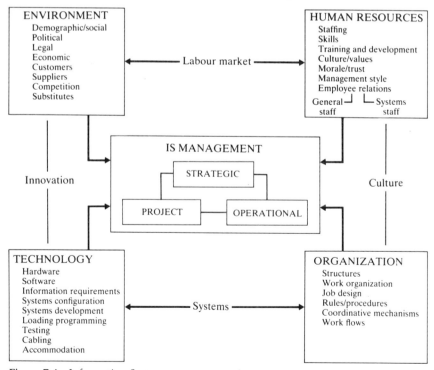

Figure 7.4 Information Systems management: issues

1990s. What is clear from the 1980s experience in both the private sector and in public administration is that the major managerial emphasis has fallen on the IS management–technological relationship. The major questions and issues that tended to be addressed were techno-centred—for example: the reliance on technical know-how in the face of IS professional staff shortages; the level of innovateness required by the industry; the technical systems required by the organization. More recently a great deal more emphasis, at least in the literature, has fallen on the Environment–IS Management–Organization axis, particularly on the degree of organizational openness to its environment (see, for example, Holtham, 1989; Jackson, 1989; Rotemberg and Saloner, 1990).

However, what remains true is that IT-based systems have too frequently been designed, introduced and run with little concern for the social, organizational and political contexts in which they are supposed to operate (Eason, 1988; Scott Morton, 1989; Willcocks and Mason, 1987b, 1990). Perhaps this has contributed to the situation highlighted by the most recent evidence, showing that the major perceived problems in IS management are now human and organizational, not technical in nature (Kearney, 1990; McKersie and Walton, 1990). Our 1989–90 SOMIT research reinforces this evidence. The major problems perceived by those responsible for computerization have been, in order of importance: shortage of IT specialist staff, inadequate definition of initial software requirements; time scales greater than planned; lack of top management support; disappointing equipment performance; user resistance to IT systems; installation costs exceed budget; recruitment/retraining of other staff for computer literacy. The reasons for suboptimization in systems development and operation are complex, but it is noticeable how far many of the actual problems experienced are traceable back, ultimately, to human resource issues.

This discussion raises a number of points. It is clear that IS management in the 1990s needs to be a complex multifaceted set of activities. Not only will it be necessary to manage on the four fronts—technological, environmental, human resource and organizational—at the same time, giving each due emphasis, but the interrelationships between these four fronts will also need to be managed. Traditional management divisions of labour will probably no longer be adequate to the tasks in hand. This issue will be dealt with in more detail below. For the moment it is imporant to point out that one thing Fig. 7.4 establishes is the likely IS management education and development agenda. In particular, it more than ever highlights the need to redress the balance by managing from the human resource corner. This means managing 'culture', 'know-how' and labour market issues, as much as technical issues.

7.8 IS implementation: improving the practice
From the evidence and arguments put together in this chapter, a number of criteria for success emerge for IT projects in public administrative and service

organizations. These are summarized in Fig. 7.5. At the level of planning and strategy, particular attention would seem to be required throughout the public sector with developing the skills of senior management in formulating IT strategy in the light of organizational objectives, and testing the practicality of the ensuing plans. A major aspect here is a much greater degree of involvement of line management and end-user representatives at early stages in the strategy and planning processes. It is accepted that tight time scales and inaccurate, inflexible funding have often occurred at these stages due to government and departmental political exigencies, policies and pressures. However, it has become clear from the experience of the 1980s that these factors need to be counterbalanced, even if this slows up decision-making and implementation, if effective systems are to be delivered.

There is some evidence that moves to Executive Agency status have speeded up these developments in the organizations involved, at least in the area of formulating strategy (Bacon, 1991), and there is no shortage of useful guidelines available—for example, as produced by the CCTA and the Audit Commission (1990). To a great degree, however, and as in private sector organizations, management education for IT needs fresh thought and funding. One useful development is the recent emphasis on producing 'hybrid' managers; that is, link personnel with business, IT and organizational skills (Palmer, 1990). However, these are no panacea, take a long time to produce, and it is most helpful to see their development as a part of a process of formulating a new division of labour for managing IT. Earl (1990) suggests one way forward. Several roles may need to be developed for comprehensive information management, each with different skill emphases in the organizational, business and technological areas. *Professionals* will be experts in the technical domain, but need further

---

- Users and implementors involved in planning and policy process
- Strategy exists; not just a list of applications and projects
- Realistic time scales and contingency plans
- IT as evolutionary process, not 'initiative' and 'event'
- Ensure IT-organization structure fit
- IT perceived as necessary at point of product/service delivery
- Sufficient investment in human resources as well as equipment and software
- Flexibility between capital and expenditure
- Continuity of project personnel and expertise
- Consultants gain understanding of how organization works
- Political contingencies management approach
- Powerful project champion(s)
- User involvement in systems design development and implementation
- Development of supportive IT culture from project initiation, if not before
- Opportunities for organizational learning on IT
- Post-implementation reviews
- New roles for information management
- Senior management development for strategy formulation and the 'extended implementation' process

Figure 7.5   Managing Information Systems: effectiveness criteria

education in the other two areas. *Hybrids* operate in the user/doing domains with abilities across the three skill areas, while *Leaders* will be needed in the user/driving domains and are particularly strong in business/organization skills. Finally, *Impresarios* are needed at senior IS levels and operate in the specialist/ driving domains. This classification implies that 'hybridization' cannot really be restricted, as a process, merely to those called hybrids in Earl's classification. Holtham (1990) and Willcocks (1991) endorse this conclusion by finding from research that IT and general management skills need considerable development across all types of role holder if effective information management is to happen. Holtham also identifies a fifth role, that of *Architect*, a vital part of project management in the construction industry, but not present yet in the majority of IS projects.

Major problems have occurred in maintaining continuity of personnel and expertise on IT projects due to shortages of such staff, failure to be flexible on incentives, and widespread use of consultants on tightly drawn, time-bound contracts. At the same time, IT implementation has rarely been treated as a long-term evolutionary process that grows along with the organization. These patterns need to be modified. Because many IT projects have been imposed from above, there has tended to be little investigation into what the real needs of local management and end-users have been, and inadequacies in ensuring that IT is perceived as addressing critical problems at the point of product/service delivery. Consequent scepticism at local levels creates forms of resistance that necessitate the constant support for the project of a powerful champion to engender commitment, to demonstrate that bottlenecks and difficulties are sur-mountable and to maintain project momentum. Even without such resistance, a range of research has demonstrated that IT product champions are important keys to effective IT implementation (Beath, 1988; Ehrlich, 1985; Land *et al.*, 1989). A common finding from the author's own research in the public sector is that such roles are customarily held by managers at too low a level in the organization to make a significant difference to the course of implementation, and that practical constant senior management support is lacking (Willcocks and Mark, 1989).

The other major success factors delineated in Fig. 7.5 relate strongly to the human, social and organizational aspects of computerization, neglected in IT projects in both the private and public sectors alike. It is particularly crucial to understand an organization's political structure and how different types and levels of computerization will relate to political activity. The development of such understanding needs to be the first step in planning and implementing computer-based systems in any organization (Willcocks and Mason, 1988b). It becomes especially relevant in organizations as 'political' as the NHS, local government, or DSS for example, where people share power, differ about what must be done, and where these differences are of some consequence.

A political perspective implies the possibility of resistance and the need to gain organizational acceptance for computerization. Resistance should not be seen merely as a problem to be solved so that the original system can then be installed as intended. Resistance can be used more positively in systems development. In fact it provides a good clue as to what is going wrong and what can be done about it. The narrow determination to see a certain systems design up and running will inhibit useful analysis of resistance—as is all too typical of dominant systems design practices in both the private and public sectors. This process can be seen at work, at least in the 1980s, in the DSS Operational Strategy (discussed above), which countenanced 25 000 redundancies as a result of IT use, but made no provision for the consequent human resource issues surrounding implementation. In fact resistance needs to be viewed in relation to the general results and outcomes required from a computer system. This is where a political contingencies management approach comes in; that is, being prepared to adapt the system to the political circumstances prevailing, while also being willing and able to operate in and change those circumstances. In the case of the DHSS Operational Strategy and its difficulties, it is interesting to note the lack of such a perspective—for example, new technology agreements with the key civil service unions were allowed to run out precisely when the first equipment and software were being installed.

The need for something called 'user involvement' has become almost a platitude in IT projects. However, it is still most noticeable by its absence, the low priority assigned to it, and a lack of understanding among managers and systems professionals as to what it should amount to, and its possible benefits. As one example in the NHS, the frequent lack of involvement of all likely users of the system in forming objectives, selecting equipment and software, and in the design of systems, too often had the outcome of lack of identification with the specifically managerial purposes of much data collection that followed the Korner recommendations. People who collect data of little use to themselves, but that might serve managerial purposes in assessing their performances, are unlikely to have a high degree of commitment to IT implementation, or to their data collection tasks and IT tools, when systems are up and running. This is a danger that the RMI has also encountered. What is needed here is a much wider definition of who are to be the users of a given system. These people then need to be involved more meaningfully in the decision-making, systems design and development that are likely to affect their working lives, or, if they are patients, their health care.

A more general point, but also linked to the need to develop more political approaches to IT implementation, is the way in which implementation is too often identified quite narrowly with the installation of the technical system. However, implementation should also be concerned with the institutionalization of its use in the ongoing context of jobs, formal and informal structures, and personal and group processes. Keen (1984) puts it succinctly: 'Installation does not guarantee institutionalization.' Willcocks and Mason (1987a) and Walton

(1989), in work based on case studies, identify the need for an 'extended implementation' process. The extension would be in several directions. Firstly, the development of strategy would not end the role or responsibilities of senior managers. Strategy means little if it cannot be implemented; and the two are not separable. For Walton (1989) senior management have responsibility for ensuring that systems strategies are aligned with organizational needs, that systems become owned and that the necessary skills and competencies to exploit the IT are mastered. Willcocks (1991) makes the same point, in detailing how ownership and mastery can be achieved through building an appropriate IS culture within the organization.

The second extension, as implied above, is in managing the human and organizational aspects of bringing in IT-based systems. In much of public administration and services the over-technical focus in most computerization projects seems to derive from a number of factors:

- as an inheritance from traditional (and still dominant) systems design practice;
- a shortage of skills in computer project management leading to projects being driven essentially by systems specialists whose strengths and preferences do not lie in analysing behaviour and organizational context;
- the widespread use in projects of private sector consultancy and computer firms who understandably are rarely at home with the behaviours and politics produced by organizations so complex as those found in public administration;
- the time scales for implementation tend to take over (as happened in the implementation of Korner in the NHS for example, and happened again in the RMI) and technical delivery receives priority, and indeed may exclude altogether the behavioural processes of managing change.

It should be pointed out that most of these factors, and an over-technical focus, are not peculiar to public administration and services, but are noticeable features in many computerization projects in private sector firms (Kearney, 1990; Kobler Unit, 1990; Willcocks, 1991). Thus the management of the political and behavioural aspects of computerization need much more attention than they are receiving at the moment if systems are not only to be proficient technically, but are also to receive productive, efficient and preferred use in practice.

As a development of this point, a further problem area has been the tendency to overcommit funds on the technical side of IT systems while skimping on the people who will use IT and make it work. Yet, as Strassman (1985) has shown, people are and should be a major cost in successful IT projects. Arguing from case studies, Hochstrasser (1990) estimates that indirect human and organizational costs might well have to be up to four times as high as direct technology and equipment costs, but are consistently undervalued or even omitted in how IS investment feasibilities are evaluated. This is supported by research into 50 private and public sector organizations by Willcocks and Lester (1991). Also, following the strictures of the National Audit Office (1989a, b, 1990) on poor financial planning and control in many projects investigated, this would argue for improved IS evaluation methodologies leading to improved funding of human resource areas.

Thus a common finding in public administration is that funding is focused around hardware and software development, and budgets pay little attention to building in such costs as those of organizational learning, gaining user acceptance, appropriate reward systems, and of ensuring sufficient staff are available for secondment from their full-time jobs. A frequent symptom of this approach is to see limited 'hands-on' training by itself as constituting adequate training and development. Unfortunately this scenario is all too typical of standard practice wherever IT is being introduced, and is not a problem unique to public administration; indeed, in some respects, especially with the widespread use of consultants, it has been inherited by public services organizations from private sector practice itself. In complex public services organizations, especially where there are severe shortages in required IT culture and skills, the problems need a thorough-going approach. A major way forward is building an IS culture. This can be defined as:

> the shared/sharing of: norms, values and understanding, skills/competencies, continuous learning related to IT needs, cooperative relationships with IS professionals, and commitment—supportive of existing and required IT usage at organisational, departmental, group and individual levels.
>
> (Willcocks, 1991)

The main elements of such an approach have been described in detail elsewhere (Willcocks, 1991). However, it means seeing people as integral drivers of information systems and an integrated approach to management education and development, formulating strategy, human resources management, systems design and development methods, restructuring, job design and work organization, employee relations, designing environment and workstation, change management, and technology (see Fig. 7.6). Much of the evidence now available about the 1980s shows that implementing IT has freqently led to few pay-offs for the organization involved. Spending more on IT in public administration is a necessary but still an insufficient condition for building effective systems, especially if the money continues to be routed mainly into hardware, software and equipment. The way forward requires considerable changes in perspectives, practices, organization and know-how at all management levels, as delineated in this chapter. The alternative approach—of subcontracting work to private sector agencies then limiting the IS public management role to managing the contract—can, of course, run in parallel rather than to the exclusion of in-house IS development. However, the abdication of IS management to private sector organizations to a large extent merely passes on the problem of skills shortages,

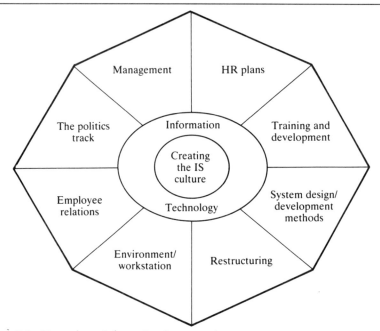

Figure 7.6   Towards an Information Systems culture

brings no guarantees of appropriate IS management practice, or understanding of how public sector organizations work, and whether or not these virtues are prevalent may, in many cases, prove considerably more costly than the in-house option into the 1990s, as a number of reports have already shown about the 1980s' experience (for example, National Audit Office, 1987, 1989a,b, 1990).

7.9   Conclusion

Three eras can be discerned in the recent history of informatization of public administration and services in the United Kingdom. These are variously existent, and, temporally, may exist in parallel with one another in different organizations, or in different sections of the same organization. The first, that of 'Implementation', has seen fragmented, underfunded, frequently poorly focused, technocratically-oriented efforts to bring in IT within turbulent environments in the face of rapid and large-scale legislative change and tight deadlines established by the centre. The second, that of 'Strategy', has seen attempts from the centre, and sometimes at middle levels within public service organizations, as well as various agencies, notably the CCTA, to develop strategic frameworks based around information as well as IT needs. This has attempted to focus IT implementation much more on organizational and user needs. It would seem that in UK public administration and services, the 'Strategic' era is very much the one now being moved towards in the early 1990s. The 'Management' era exists very patchily and in parts of public administration at lower levels in these organizations, but rarely forms a coherent, integrated approach as delineated in this chapter. There are islands of good practice along the 'Management' era lines that remain exactly that. However, they are there to be learned from, as are those better IS management practices found in private sector organizations.

As computer-based systems penetrate to the core of organizational functioning, thus bringing more users on-stream, and as technology costs get driven down, against IS labour supplies being in continual shortage, the 'technical-efficiency' approach, typical of the 'Implementation' era becomes ever less appropriate. In particular, IS management in public administration needs to be driven as much from the human resource and organizational, as from the technological and environmental fronts. Cook (1990) suggests a strong economic rationale for this new emphasis. Previously computer equipment was optimized by suboptimizing people. It has now become cheaper to optimize human resource skills and competencies by exploiting the flexibility of IT-based equipment as much as possible. The key to IS management in both public and private sectors will be delivering usable effective systems through developing people willing and able to exploit IT to achieve business or organizational advantage. Where computerization in public administration and services is built around this type of focus, and the practices it implies, it will then be moving into the 'Management' era, as delineated in this chapter.

References and further reading

Audit Commission (1990) 'Preparing an Information Technology strategy: making it happen', Management Paper No. 7, February, HMSO, London.

Bacon, N. (1991) 'Information systems strategies in government—recent survey evidence', Journal of Information Technology, 6 (2), July.

Beath, C. (1988) 'The IT project champion', Paper delivered at the Oxford PA Conference on Information Management: The Performance Dimension, 27–29 September.

Beath, C. and Ives, B. (1988) 'The Information Technology champion: aiding and abetting, care and feeding', in Sprague, R. (ed.), Proceedings of the Twenty-First Annual Hawaii International Conference on Systems Science, Vol. 14, pp. 115–24.

Boddy, D. and Buchanan, D. A. (1986) Managing New Technology. Blackwell, Oxford.

Bourn, A. (1987) 'Fighting truth decay in the NHS', Accountancy, September, 120–1.

Buchanan, D. and Boddy, D. (1983) Organizations in the Computer Age. Gower, London.

Child, J. (1986) 'New technology and the service class', in Purcell, K. et al. (eds), The Changing Experience of Employment. Macmillan, London.

Clegg, C. and Kemp, N. (1988) 'Information Technology—personnel where are you?', Personnel Review, 15 (1).

Cook, P. (1990) 'The application and management of IS globalization within business', Paper presented at the 11th International Conference on Information Systems, Copenhagen, Denmark, 16–19 December.

Daniel, W. (1987). Workplace Industrial Relations and Technical Change. Pinter/ACAS/PSI, London.

Department of Health (1989) Working for Patients. HMSO, London.

DHSS (1986) *Resource Management (Management Budgeting) in Health Authorities.* DHSS, HN(86)34.

Dyerson, R. and Roper, M. (1990) *Implementing the Operational Strategy at the DSS: From Technical Push to User Pull.* Technology Project Papers No. 8, December, London Business School, London.

Earl, M. (1990) 'Education: the foundation for effective IT strategies. IT and the new manager conference', *Computer Weekly/Business Intelligence*, London, June.

Eason, K. (1988) *Information Technology and Organisational Change.* Taylor & Francis, London.

Ehrlich, K. (1985) 'Factors influencing technology transfer', *SIGGHI Bulletin*, 17 (2), 20–4.

Ernst & Young, (1990) *Strategic Alignment Report: 1990 UK Survey.* Ernst & Young, London.

Faulkner, J., Orr, J. and Burdett, D. (1987) 'The road to an integrated hospital information system', *Hospital and Health Services Review*, 83 (2), 57–61.

Gibbs, C. (1991) Reports in *Computer Weekly*, 31 January and 7 February.

Griffiths, P. (ed.) (1987) *The Role of Information Management in Competitive Success.* Pergamon Infotech, London.

Hall, P., Land, H., Parker, R. and Webb, A. (1975) *Change, Choice and Conflict in Social Policy.* Heinemann, London.

Haughton, E. (1990) 'Can a new-look NHS take the strain?', *Computer Weekly*, 2 August, 16–18.

Hepworth, M., Dominy, G. and Graham, S. (1989) *Local Authorities and the Information Economy in Great Britain.* Newcastle Studies of the Information Economy, Working Paper 11. Centre for Urban and Regional Development Studies, Newcastle.

HM Treasury (1984) *Information Technology in the Civil Service. IT Series No. 5.* HMSO, London.

Hochstrasser, B. (1990) 'Evaluating IT investments: matching projects to techniques', *Journal of Information Technology*, 5 (4), December.

Holtham, C. (1989) 'Information technology management in the 1990s. A position paper', *Journal of Information Technology*, 4 (4), 179–96.

Holtham, C. (1990) 'A practical approach to executive education. IT and the new manager conference', *Computer Weekly/Business Intelligence*, London, June.

ICL (1989) *Local Government in Britain: An ICL Report on the Impact of Information Technology.* ICL, London.

Jackson, I. (1989) 'Information systems planning and alignment: a progress assessment', *Journal of Information Technology*, 4 (4), 216–29.

Kearney, A. T. (1984) *The Barriers and Opportunities of Information Technology—A Management Perspective.* Institute of Administrative Management, Orpington.

Kearney, A. T. (1987) *Corporate Organisation and Overhead Effectiveness Survey.* Price Waterhouse, London.

Kearney, A. T. (1990) *Barriers 2—Barriers to the Successful Implementation of Information Technology.* DTI/CIMA/A. T. Kearney, London.

Keen, P. (1984) 'VDTs as agents of change', in Bennett, J. *et al.* (eds), *Visual Display Terminals.* Prentice Hall, London.

Kobler Unit (1987) *Does Information Technology Slow You Down?* Kobler Unit for the Management of Information Technology, London.

Kobler Unit (1990) *Regaining Control of IT Investments—A Handbook for Senior UK Managers* (Hochstrasser, B. and Griffiths, C. (eds)). Kobler Unit, London.

KPMG Peat Marwick Mitchell (1990) Quoted in *Datalink*, 12 March, p. 1.

Kraemer, K., King, J., Dunkle, D. and Lane, J. (1989) *Managing Information Systems—*

Change and Control in Organizational Computing. Jossey-Bass, San Francisco.

Lamont, N. (1989) House of Commons Reply, *Hansard*, 27 January.

Land, F., Le Quesne, P. and Wijegunartne, I. (1989) 'Effective systems: overcoming the obstacles', *Journal of Information Technology*, 4 (2), 81–91.

Macdonald, K. (1990) 'An introduction to processes for development and alignment of business strategies deriving from changing patterns of interfirm competition and collaboration and IT-induced business reconfiguration, in Scott Morton, M. and Forrester, J. (eds), *Management in the 1990s Research Program, Final Report.* Massachusetts Institute of Technology, Sloan School of Management, USA.

McKersie, R. and Walton, R. (1990) 'Organizational change and implementation, in Scott Morton, M. and Forrester, J. (eds), *Management in the 1990s Research Program, Final Report.* Massachusetts Institute of Technology, Sloan School of Management, USA.

Margetts, H. and Willcocks, L. (1991) 'Information technology as policy instrument? Trends and prospects in the UK social security system', Paper at the EGPA Conference: *Informatization in Public Administration.* The Hague, Netherlands, 29–31 August.

National Audit Office (1987) *Inland Revenue: Control of Major Developments in the Use of Information Technology.* HMSO, London.

National Audit Office (1989a) *Department of Social Security: Operational Strategy.* Session 1988–89, HC 111. HMSO, London.

National Audit Office (1989b) Reported in *Datalink*, 13 March, p. 1.

National Audit Office (1990) *Managing Computer Projects in the National Health Service.* HMSO, London.

NHS Training Authority (1989) *Information Management and Technology (IMT) Strategy for Training and Staff Development.* NHS Training Authority, Bristol.

Palmer, C. (1990) ' "Hybrids"—A critical force in the application of information technology in the nineties', *Journal of Information Technology*, 5 (4), 232–5.

Price Waterhouse (1987) *Information Technology Review 1987/88.* Price Waterhouse, London.

Price Waterhouse (1990) *Information Technology Review 1990/91.* Price Waterhouse, London.

Rockart, J. and Short, J. (1990) 'IT and the networked organization: toward more effective management of interdependence', in Scott Morton, M. and Forrester, J. (eds), *Management in the 1990s Research Program, Final Report.* Massachusetts Institute of Technology, Sloan School of Management, USA.

Rotemberg, J. and Saloner, G. (1990) 'The changing patterns of interfirm competition and collaboration', in Scott Morton, M. and Forrester, J. (eds), *Management in the 1990s Research Program, Final Report.* Massachusetts Institute of Technology, Sloan School of Management, USA.

Rowe, C. (1984) 'The development of computer systems in a brewery', *Information Technology Training*, 2 (4), November.

Scott Morton, M. (1989) 'Management and IT in the 1990's', in *Innovation through Information Technology: Managing Change.* Amdahl Executive Institute, London.

Smith, J. (1989) 'No faith in the passport gospel,' *Datalink*, 19 June, p. 7.

Stocking, B. (1985) *Initiative and Inertia, Case Studies in the NHS.* Nuffield Provincial Hospitals Trust, London.

Strassmann, P. (1985) *Information Payoff—The Transformation of Work in the Electronic Age.* Macmillan, London.

Strassmann, P. (1990) *The Business Value of Computers.* The Information Economics Press, New Canaan.

Sweeney, J. and Mason, A. (1987) 'Integrated hospital information systems', *Journal of the Royal College of Physicians of London*, **20** (2 April), 102–4.

Taylor, J. and Williams, H. (1990) 'Themes and issues in an information polity', *Journal of Information Technology*, **5** (3), 151–60.

Trade and Industry Select Committee (1988) *First Report—Information Technology*, Vol. 1, 23 November. HMSO, London.

Trade and Industry Select Committee (1989a) *Information Technology, Minutes of Evidence, 26 April*. HMSO, London.

Trade and Industry Select Committee (1989b) *Information Technology. Minutes of Evidence, 12 July*. HMSO, London.

Walton, R. (1989) *Up and Running*. Harvard Business School Press, Boston.

Willcocks, L. (1989) *Information Technology and Human Resources Management: In Search of Strategy*. Working Paper No. 94, January, City University Business School.

Willcocks, L. (1990) 'IT and the new manager', *Journal of Information Technology*, **5** (3), June.

Willcocks, L. (1991) 'Building an information systems culture—How to get to there from here', Paper at the AMED/AMRG Conference: *Individual and Organisation Development: Conflict and Synergy*. Ashridge Management College, 3–4 January.

Willcocks, L. and Lester, S. (1991) 'Information systems investments: evaluation at the feasibility stage of projects', *Technovation*, Autumn.

Willcocks, L. and Mark, A. (1988) *Information for Management? A Review of Progress on Information Technology and General Management in the UK National Health Service*. Working Paper No. 92, April, City University Business School.

Willcocks, L. and Mark, A. (1989). 'IT systems implementation: research findings from the public sector', *Journal of Information Technology*, **4** (2).

Willcocks, L. and Mason, D. (1986) *The DHSS Operational Strategy 1975–86. Business Case File in Information Technology*. Van Nostrand Reinhold, London.

Willcocks, L. and Mason, D. (1987a) *Computerising Work: People, Systems Design and Workplace Relations*. Paradigm, London.

Willcocks, L. and Mason, D. (1987b) 'Computerising: lessons from the DHSS pensions strike, *Employee Relations*, **9** (1).

Willcocks, L. and Mason, D. (1988a) 'New technology and human resources – the role of management', *Employee Relations*, **10** (4)

Willcocks, L. and Mason, D. (1988b) 'Managing technological change: the politics track', *Sundridge Park Management Review*, **2** (2), 32–40.

Willcocks, L. and Mason, D. (1990). 'Managing new technology and workplace relations', *Employee Relations*, **12** (3), 3–11.

Wright, M. and Rhodes, D. (1985) *Managing IT! Exploiting Information Systems for Effective Management*. Pinter, London.

Wroe, B. (1986) *Contractors and Computers: Why Systems Succeed or Fail*. PhD thesis, Loughborough University of Technology.

8

Management in the National Health Service
Annabelle Mark and Hilary Scott

8.1 Introduction

Changes to the National Health Service since its inception have been accelerated by pressure from both inside and outside the organization. The effect of these changes is still a matter for interpretation, and this chapter provides only one perspective of events, but it is hoped that these views will encourage understanding and analysis of a complex situation.

By 1990 the health service was grappling with the implications of three major white papers: *Promoting Better Health* (DHSS, 1987), which addressed the future of family practitioner services; *Working for Patients* (DHSS, 1989a), which looked at the organizational structure of the health service with particular reference to hospital services; and *Caring for People* (DHSS, 1989b), which considered the future arrangements for care of elderly people, people with a mental illness or handicap and others living outside the hospital environment. What becomes plain—as the pattern of thought behind the introduction of managed competition, and payment by results, unfolds within all three documents—is that none of them could have been proposed if they had not been preceded by the introduction of general management into the National Health Service (NHS) (Griffiths, 1983). Griffiths identified four key problems in the NHS:

1 Individual managerial accountability could not be located: '. . . in short if Florence Nightingale were carrying her lamp through the corridors of the NHS today, she would almost certainly be searching for the people in charge.'
2 '. . . the machinery of implementation is generally weak . . .'—a lack of motivation to initiate and implement change.
3 A lack of performance evaluation of either management objectives, economic evaluation, clinical practice or health outcomes.
4 A lack of responsiveness to the consumers.

The consequent change in culture or 'system of shared meaning' (Robbins, 1988) within the organization, from administrative to managerial, has been characterized by Stewart (1985) as a change, for those involved, from being the 'oil in the wheel to the grit in the oyster'. The new culture means the explicit allocation of personal responsibility for purposeful action in pursuit of defined objectives; as such it also attempts to alter the way that all staff perceive their work and that of the NHS. As an idea it goes beyond mere cost consciousness to something that may yet emerge, if Strong and Robinson (1988) are correct, as a better understanding of the way health care is delivered, and the impact that its public sector context can have.

Anyone looking for evidence of the change from administration to general management might be tempted to review the success of 'management initiatives' that were so much a part of the NHS in the 1980s Thatcher years. These initiatives, for example Rayner Scrutinies (DHSS, 1984), Performance Indicators (DHSS, 1985b), Performance Related Pay (Personnel Memorandum, 1986), are however, good illustrations of the point that Willcocks and Harrow make in the Introduction of this book, which is that labels are not always a good guide to content. The initiatives, presented as managerial activity, were in fact policy changes from government.

8.1.1   RAYNER SCRUTINIES

The Rayner Scrutinies, which have begun within the central government process (Metcalfe and Richards, 1990) were extended to the NHS in April 1982. Their purpose was to scrutinize through intensive study a particular area of expenditure (DHSS, 1982a) under the guidance of the managing director of Marks & Spencer, Sir Derek Rayner, who was acting as part-time efficiency adviser to the Government. The areas chosen were vacancy advertising, the storage of supplies, catering costs, the cost-effectiveness of meetings, NHS residential property, the recovery of aids loaned to patients, ambulance service control systems, collection of income due to health authorities and the administration of project briefs for hospital building schemes (DHSS, 1982b). The scrutinies did make some useful suggestions although implementation sometimes led to unforeseen consequences, for example, the rush to sell nurses residential accommodation which sent this low pay group into the unsubsidized private sector market. This proposal was later quietly dropped because of the outcry and the fear of losing these valuable, if still lowly paid staff, from the service (Crabbe, 1989).

Such scrutinies, with their short, sharp, shock methods exemplify the effect of what has been described as the 'commando raid' approach to management, contributing nothing in the longer term to the integrated management approach needed in these organizations (Riseborough and Walter, 1988). Other criticism has focused on those areas avoided for scrutiny, for example, anything likely to have an adverse impact on doctors (Harrison, 1988).

8.1.2   PERFORMANCE INDICATORS

Performance indicators were introduced as a 'practical and useful tool for management' to 'provide pointers and signals to areas which appear to merit further investigation' (DHSS, 1985a). They are also, perhaps more significantly, part of the attempt to introduce more central control of expenditure (Small, 1989). Their scope covered manpower, finance, estate management, ambulance services and all areas of clinical activity. Their development has not passed without criticism of their purpose (Small, 1989), quality (Yates, 1985; Allen *et al.*, 1987) and usefulness (Pollitt, 1984) and there is evidence that their original purpose of merely indicating areas for further investigation has changed to one of setting targets and achieving success (Allen *et al.*, 1987).

8.1.3   PERFORMANCE-RELATED PAY

The introduction of performance-related pay works on the assumption that individuals will work harder if they gain extra reward for doing so. Unfortunately, this simplistic approach is not always appropriate; many people within the health service, with its relatively low financial rewards, stay with the service for other reasons (Riseborough and Walter, 1988; Williams *et al.*, 1991). It is also suggested that this form of incentive reward system can be divisive, demoralizing and conflict with the public services ethic. Furthermore, evidence from the US shows that such schemes run out of steam; staff become systematically marked at higher levels each year; and thus the link between performance and reward is progressively weakened (IDS/Coopers Lybrand, 1989).

In examining the origin and role of some of the management initiatives and their part in changing the culture, it becomes apparent that the problem lies in distinguishing between the policy process which initiated them, and indicators of real cultural change in management and service provision following implementation. Making management action and policy decisions interchangeable terms, as the term 'management initiatives' implies, or changing labels as discussed in the Introduction, can be the road to discord, confusion and disillusionment.

How, then, can a review of changes in the organization be undertaken? To start, it is appropriate to establish when and how the idea of general management came to the NHS, and then it may be useful to pose the following questions:

- How has the NHS interpreted general management so far?
- Is it a correct interpretation?
- Can we ensure future success by rethinking this interpretation?

8.2   Origins of managerialism

Although Griffiths was not even appointed until early in 1983 to review the NHS, the beginnings of this form of managerialism appeared early in the eighties. Davidson (1987) points out '1982 became, with hindsight, the year when management and managerial preoccupations took over the NHS and began to set the parameters within which we now think about public healthcare'.

Before identifying factors that may illustrate this change, it is important to look at the way in which general management arrived in 1984, challenging 40 years of administrative culture.

A brief summary of events leading up to the appointment of Griffiths in 1983 indicates that the central concepts behind the Griffiths Report (1983) had not burst upon an unsuspecting service. As early as the 1950s the Bradbeer Report (1954) recommended the establishment of a chief executive role. The idea continued through the 1960s and 1970s in the policies of both Labour and Conservative governments, culminating in what Haywood and Alaszewski (1980) have described as a period of managerialism leading up to the General Election in 1979. The absence of planning and management within the NHS had been recognized early on by the Guillebaud Report in 1956 (MH, 1956). The climate of reform, however, took another decade to emerge within the NHS, and not until the 1968 Green Paper was it proposed that '. . . senior officers would act as an executive directorate with the chief administrator acting as Managing Director' (MH, 1968). A change of government in 1970 may have affected the detail of arrangements for the new NHS structure (DHSS, 1970) implemented in 1974, but the proposals for restructuring the service remained (Klein, 1989). They were based on the introduction of consensus management, but remained within the prevailing agreement between all political parties for greater control by central government over resources. The methods chosen to achieve this were through better and more centrally led planning and management of the service, as set out in the Grey Book; this outlined in detail the structure, roles and process for running the service (DHSS, 1972).

The reasons for the emergence of consensus management as the preferred model of managerialism in the 1970s are four-fold.

Firstly, they represent what MacKenzie (1979), using Paretos ideas, described as the 'residues' and 'hangovers' from previous states of organization. This is confirmed more recently by Leathard (1990) in her comment that 'the NHS had had a tradition of consensus management (Merrison Report, 1979, p. 314) in which a form of shared managerial responsibility, between doctors, nurses and administrators had been based on a perceived need and demand for considerable professional autonomy'.

Secondly, it was the result of negotiating with a medical profession that had no thought for any limit on the exercise of clinical autonomy which, in the early seventies, as Tolliday (1978) suggested, gave 'doctors their right to unmanaged status'.

Thirdly, and as a consequence of the second point, a method was needed to involve doctors explicitly in the process of rationing health care at an organizational as well as an individual level. The situation until then was well summed up by Cooper (1975) who explained 'rationing, however, has never been explicitly organized but has hidden behind each doctor's clinical freedom'.

Lastly, and perhaps of greatest significance, was the organizational context of the period in both public and private sectors, which favoured consensus teams as shown in Pettigrew's (1985) major study of ICI, 'Consensus decision making was the key theme in discussion of the management board culture of the 1970s'.

8.3   Obstacles to a new form of managerialism

The major stumbling block to cultural change in the NHS was the historical power of professionals (Perkin, 1989), in particular the doctors. Growing professionalization by all groups, as described in 1964 by Wilensky, had further increased the role of professions in public sector policy-making in the 1970s, be it teachers' control of the curriculum, social workers' control of social services departments or doctors' control of health services. Wilding (1982) concluding that as a consequence of this

> decisions made serve professional interests rather than the public interest . . . lead to services organized according to professional skills and ideas rather than according to client need . . . mean that certain elements and interests within the professions are able to dominate decision making because of their greater prestige and status.

All aspects of this view are confirmed by Klein (1989) as being present in the negotiations and implementation of the 1974 reorganization. In using the consensus model of management, the status quo was maintained for the professions, as it was seen, particularly by the clinicians, as no challenge to their existing power of veto over decisions.

The relative economic calm of the period preceding the 1974 reorganization (DHSS, 1972) had allowed the consensus management approach, similar to that described in the 1974 Vroom and Yetton contingency leadership model, to develop. A slow form of decision process was allowed to evolve which relied on the criteria of 'time investment' (Vroom and Yetton, 1973), the pay-offs occur long term through developing those individuals involved in the decision process by allowing them to participate in it fully. The impact of the oil crisis that began in 1973, together with a move later in the decade towards a policy led by individualism as described by Flynn (1989)[1] in the post-1979 election era, brought external pressures to bear on the fragile consensus team model. Forsyth (1983) has noted that 'both post '74 and '82 reorganizations were immediately followed by a much reduced rate of growth', the first because of the economic climate and the second because of government policy to reduce public spending. In such environments the contingency leadership approach (Vroom and Yetton, 1973) provides for alternative forms of leadership style that move away from the former slow democratic or consultative style of consensus decision-making towards a faster more autocratic model. In this context individual managers are required to use a 'time efficient' decision process, the pay-off for this style is short term, providing quicker and more efficient decisions that may not stick. In the post-1974 era individualism and an autocratic decision style in organizations were not the favoured methods, thus adding to the problems of the consensus teams who were unable to respond rapidly, as the contingency model implies, to fast-changing circumstances; after 1982 it soon became apparent that the pluralistic leadership found in the consensus team was now also seen as inappropriate to policy needs, and consideration of chief executive led and business-orientated organizations was back on the agenda.

In retrospect, the cultural change since *Patients First* (DHSS, 1979) is best exemplified by the inappropriate simplicity of the statement that it is the medical profession 'who provide the care and cure of patients . . . it is the purpose of management to support them in giving that service' (DHSS, 1979). Management in health care, as in many other UK organizations (Barsoux and Lawrence, 1990), is now no longer seen in only this supportive role, but has moved to the forefront of activity, perhaps less in support of the professions and more in support of government policy as Harrison (1988) has suggested. The professions meanwhile were generally in retreat from a government intent on controlling their former power (Perkin, 1989).

8.4   Reinterpreting management—a new political context

The new spirit of individualism outlined by Flynn (1989)[1] in his analysis of the role and methods of the 'new right' suggests that '. . . individualism and individual choice should take precedence over collective choices and planned provision'. This applied not only to the Government's view of individuals but to their view of organizations as well. Within this approach, and in the attention paid to the consumer in those parts of the Royal Commission Report (Merrison Report, 1979) accepted by the Government, were the seeds of another new aspect of policy called consumerism; this was initially addressed by the Government in their first NHS White Paper *Patients First* (DHSS, 1979).

Further evidence for the consolidation of this business approach combined with an emphasis on individuals and consumerism was the appointment by Mrs Thatcher in 1983 of an individual, Roy Griffiths, deputy chairman and managing director of Messrs J. Sainsbury, as leader of a small team exclusively from the business sector with a remit to advise her on the way to change the NHS.

The problems of managing the NHS are at root political and philosophical, but the response to them has invariably been structural change. The arguments over the degree to which strategy determines structure (Chandler, 1962) had little chance of taking place because strategy has so often been the prerequisite of the politicians rather than the managers in the NHS. The most telling evidence of this was the degree to which a planning strategy influenced the NHS structure, in the post-1974 era, as set out in the Grey Book (DHSS, 1972) and explained in one of Mintzberg and Waters strategic types, as follows:

Strategies originate in formal plans: precise intentions exist, formulated and articulated by central leadership, backed up by formal controls to ensure surprise free implementation in benign, controllable or predictable environments.

(Mintzberg and Waters, 1989)

Unfortunately, whatever the intentions and interpretations of central leadership, it was soon apparent that the environment was neither benign nor surprise free. Griffiths took a broader view in identifying the need for cultural change. Initially, however, the Government and the NHS reacted traditionally and again structural change swept the service, not least because of a lack of understanding of managerialism (Metcalfe and Richards, 1990) and the Government's pressing need for a clear command structure. Where the understanding of managerialism has grown, mainly within and between the new managers, this has not so far been adequately communicated to the other parts of the organization or to government. After the initial structural impact of the Griffiths changes, there was a tendency to revert to old habits (Williams *et al.*, 1985); the cultural change proposed by Griffiths was thus delayed by the primarily structural response of the organization to the proposals.

The cultural or organic changes required by the Griffiths Report (1983), as expressed in the Burns and Stalker (1966) theoretical model where organizations are seen on an organic/mechanistic continuum, did not lessen the degree of mechanical changes required of the organization by the Government; they were rather seen as a way of speeding up further structural change, which ran contrary to Burns' interpretation of hospitals as more organic collaborative systems (Burns, 1981). The mechanical/structural changes embodied in the latest White Papers (DHSS, 1987, 1989a,b) would have been inappropriate in 1979 to the forms of organic change proposed by the Royal Commission (Merrison Report, 1979). The difference is that these mechanical/structural changes now rest for their success on the degree to which the organic or cultural changes, brought about by the introduction of Griffiths' form of managerialism, have permeated the body politic of the NHS.

8.5   The managerial role and its policy purpose

The search for this new organizational form for the NHS was initially motivated by three overt objectives:

1 The need to deal with obvious variations in volume and quality of activity across the country, perhaps by some sort of command structure.
2 The need to deal with the increasing complexity of health service delivery arising from changes in technology and population structure.
3 The need for economy in the context of government commitment to reduce public expenditure while retaining a public commitment to a National Health Service.

General management was thus set objectives which no previous organizational form had dealt with successfully: Griffiths' suggested solution to this mixture of problems did seem somewhat simplistic. As a general approach, in some ways, it exhibited parallels with the 1974 reorganization that had already been criticized by the Royal Commission (Merrison Report, 1979) as 'a one dimensional structural solution to the problem'. However, the simplicity of the formula was deceptive: the reality was a sophisticated process for changing perceptions as well as the organization.

8.6   The arrival of general management in the NHS

The speedy production and implementation of the Griffiths proposals indicated the new pace at which government wished to address the conflict of values represented by the collectivism embodied in the NHS, as set against a government ideology centred on individualism.

General manager appointments were made during 1985/86; many administrators believed they were applying for their own jobs. Some, who had grasped what it was to manage a public sector organization, were; the rest were to suffer personal and intellectual pain in making the discovery that they were not appointed. As Leathard (1990) has confirmed, 'by 1987 there had been a 5% turnover of general managers. The departures were largely explained by a misunderstanding over the nature and culture of the job.'

The change in activity from administration to management has been researched elsewhere, notably by Stewart (1987/88) and Harrison (1988). More recent research in the field (Harrison et al., 1989a) identified current issues requiring attention if management was to improve; problems are identified in relation to the agenda for general managers:

- the size of the agendas is too large
- the relevance of the content is not clear
- agendas are dominated by finance
- clinical performance is not on the agenda
- there is a lack of clarity about the role of the Resource Management Initiative (explained elsewhere in the chapter)
- consumerism is a marginal issue and not a driving force behind change.

The outcomes for the introduction of the managerial culture in the NHS is open to interpretation, and the further changes proposed in the three White Papers (DHSS, 1987, 1989a,b) suggested at least two of them. Either general management had not been able to deliver adequate solutions quickly enough to meet the three key objectives we have already outlined, or, as Alford (1975) has suggested, the Government's new proposals confirmed his point that 'constant administrative juggling is a sign of inability to put together a functioning coalition of power and resources'. A third option is, of course, that general management was simply a prerequisite for the introduction of a 'market economy' to the NHS which represents the third phase in Flynn's (1989) analysis of the introduction of change by the 'new right'[1]: the political timetable demands that the next stage is embarked upon before the first, the introduction of a management culture, is sufficiently advanced.

8.7   Limits to management

If, therefore, the introduction of the White Papers (DHSS, 1987, 1989a,b) was a response to the limited success general management has had in securing policy objectives so far, it is important that the limiting factors are identified. Two major areas stand out, political expediency and failure to change perceptions.

8.7.1   POLITICAL EXPEDIENCY

It was expedient to *blame* the lack of economy and variable quality on the management of the service. Many managers believed this and tried to change their own behaviour . . . macho management and a retreat to tribalism were examples, but as Klein (1984) has pointed out, 'if governments seek to centralize credit in times of economic growth—the 1974 model of the NHS—it would seem that they try to diffuse blame when recession means that there is only bad news? The failure on the part of the managers is to recognize that sometimes they are being used as scapegoats to explain current crisis for policy makers and professional service providers. As Alford had suggested in 1975, 'crises are usually creations of specific interest groups seeking to make political capital out of a situation which has existed for many years, and which will continue to exist after the crises have disappeared from public view'. Furthermore, many of these interest groups are glad to have individual managers to whom blame can be passed for failures in the system, whether or not these managers are responsible, as it often has the added advantage of locating responsibility away from the real cause.

Expectations of the *pace* at which improved results could be delivered were too high; for example, it led to great pressure for a change in the timetable for the major reform proposals outlined in *Working for Patients* (DHSS, 1989a) as reported by Moore and Sheldon (1990), and led to real postponements for the introduction of *Caring for People* (DHSS, 1989b).

Another major example of misunderstanding of the pace at which change can be successfully implemented is the Resource Management Initiative (RMI), as set out in HN(86)34 (DHSS, 1986). This seeks to involve doctors in the direct management of their resources. Ham and Hunter's study of progress in managing clinical activity in the NHS warned Ministers against proceeding too quickly with the RMI. This warning was given because the concept of RMI required a long-term change in the clinical as well as the managerial culture if it is to succeed (Ham and Hunter, 1988). However, this did not prevent Ministers from proceeding with the proposals to expand the RMI (DH, 1989a) before receiving results from the six pilot sites. As a consequence, disillusionment has set in; for example, Dr John Roberts, former Unit General Manager for Arrow Park Hospital, one of the six pilot sites, has said, 'Initially we sold the idea of RMI to our colleagues as a way of improving patient care. Increasingly it looks like a way of controlling expenditure irrespective of quality of care' (Tomlin, 1990). The reason for this is that the motive of RMI has changed from developing the organization towards a managerial culture to implementing the political agenda set out in the changes required by *Working for Patients* (DHSS, 1989a).

Management-led changes of a different kind also give cause for concern; for example, the need for both policy makers and managers to find adequate outcome measures for the NHS. This was identified by both Mrs Korner in her proposals for a new information system in the NHS (Korner Steering Group, 1982) and Roy Griffiths (Griffiths Report, 1983). Over half a decade later little progress had been made (Social Services Committee, 1988); and this may not only be because of the difficulty of the task, as suggested by Flynn *et al.* (1988), but also because, as Flynn *et al.* (1988) go on to point out, defining objectives and measuring them may result in the politically unacceptable result of 'bad news' and 'the barriers against doing so are as much structural and political as technical' (Coulter, 1991). Substitutes for outcome measures have therefore been promoted in the form of the waiting lists initiatives. To enable this approach to succeed, money was top sliced from existing budgets, reducing management's ability to develop good outcome methodologies and improve quality while maintaining the quantity of work undertaken. Robbing Peter to pay Paul, and reducing the flexibility available to managers to determine their own rate of progress, is not conducive to management motivation and is confirmed by research (Dopson and Stewart, 1990) which found that 'there was a feeling that managers were given the responsibility but not the power to meet specified targets'. More recently in identifying key tasks for managers for 1991/92, Duncan Nichol the chief executive of the NHS demanded reductions in waiting lists with the warning that managers' performance-related pay would be judged on waiting times (Sheldon, 1990). The motives for this were identified by Maureen Dixon, retiring Director of the Institute of Health Services Management, as attempts at 'responding to what one expects are politically motivated concerns' (Sheldon, 1990). Pam Charlwood, her successor in the role, has further confirmed this in highlighting Duncan Nichol's message to the Institute of Health Service Management 1990 conference, that the public (in the run up to the general election) will judge the proposed health reforms embodied in *Working for Patients* (DHSS, 1989a) by the effect they have on waiting lists (Sheldon, 1990).

In spite of this side tracking into a politically expedient but inadequate form of outcome measure as provided by waiting lists, it would be relevant for policy makers to reflect on the very slow progress on outcome management made in the business-orientated health systems of the USA as reported by Ellwood (1988); this shows that work in the USA has only recently been undertaken, between the New England Medical Centre and researchers from the Rand Corporation, on health status and quality of life outcomes to patients after discharge (JAMA, 1990). Recent comparative information from the UK and USA has confirmed the particular problems of the UK systems in concentrating on process at the expense of real outcome measures (Coulter, 1991; Roberts, 1990) indicating furthermore that where information does exist it fails to reach managers (Roberts, 1990).

Event management is the process by which politicians, both nationally and locally, target an objective for delivery by managers as proof that action has been taken. It leads to the measurement of success in short-term goals rather than concern with shaping the longer term future (HSMR, 1989). This approach has been discussed by Willcocks and Mark (1988) in relation to Information Technology (IT) initiatives in the NHS, but applies equally to the waiting list initiative where little attention had been paid to finding a means of preventing waiting lists returning to former levels, except by targeting managers' pay. However, recent research would suggest that using waiting lists as a surrogate for outcome is very misleading anyway as the increase is more significantly due to people waiting for treatments that were impossible 40 years ago (OHE, 1989).

Targeting waiting lists in this way provides a focus for action by managers, and relieves the pressure to address the politically unacceptable solution of providing extra resources. The frustration that this causes was summed up by the District General Manager with the worst waiting lists in England in 1990: 'We have been through all the other reasons. Our surgeons are workaholics. We have come down to a lack of resources. These are not excuses but reasons' (Sheldon, 1990). Such pleas for time, resources and closer analysis were given added weight by the resignation in 1991 of the John Yates team from their contract with the Government as their 'leading specialists in cutting waiting lists' (Renton, 1991). Yates considered the Department of Health target of ensuring no one waits more than two years after March 1992 as 'just crazy' and 'totally unrealistic'. What is also apparent from these events is that when they go wrong, as with the resignation of the Yates team, the failure becomes an event in itself and is a lead item for the national press rather than something that can be consigned to the back page of specialist journals.

8.7.2 FAILURE TO CHANGE PERCEPTIONS

The second area for concern is the failure to turn what had become a cliché in management circles pre-Griffiths ('Doctors spend money, not administrators') into an effective force for change in the new management environment. Doctors were encouraged into management for three reasons:

1 To combine power with responsibility for use of resources by the doctors.
2 To reduce what MacKenzie (1979) has described as the 'antinomy between the power and responsibility of medical care in action at the periphery, and the power and responsibility for resource allocation at the centre', with the manager acting as go-between.
3 As a concession to Wilding's description of the professions need to 'dominate decision making' (Wilding, 1982).

The fear from the professions that the new general managers had been given the power, through increased pay, prestige and status in the organization to dominate decisions could only be checked by granting the doctors a number of management posts. Furthermore, the changes for the professionals also carried with it the risk of deprofessionalization (Haug, 1976)[2] associated as it is with a greater degree of consumer power (Elston, 1991), or, worse still, proletarianiz-ation (Oppenheimer 1973)[2] (McKinlay and Stoeckle, 1988) of doctors[2] which envisages the transformation of doctoring into a management task as part of the more general process of social change. As it transpired only 9.5 per cent of appointments went to the medical profession, as reported by Alleway (1985), perhaps either because of their poor understanding of management or their reluctance to accept the new organizational culture. Nevertheless, making doc-tors into managers has been a key objective since then. As an objective it should also be seen in the wider context of the time in which it began; as Butter and Mejia (1987) pointed out, it was one of oversupply of doctors worldwide, leading to suggestions of the need for redeployment in other spheres, manage-ment of health systems being a prime candidate.

8.8 Role change—from clinician to manager

The emergence of clinicians willing and able to make the conceptual leap towards managerialism was patchy and variable. The pace of change was again at fault. Too little attention was paid to the problem posed by clinicians' percep-tion of management activity, and their own skills in relation to it. Like many administrators, some clinicians confused administering the service with manag-ing it; others, all too aware of the reality of the managerial role, saw a conflict of interests. Slow progress, or perhaps progress at the right pace, is now taking place in the education of clinicians—for example, in the publication of books like Allen and Horsley's (1990) *A Management Handbook for Doctors* or the introduction of an in-house management training programme for doctors in the North Western RHA (NHSTA, 1990), which uses the general management training programme developed by the Open University and the IHSM for the National Health Service Training Authority (OU, 1990). Clinicians who recog-nize that their case and patient management skills could equip them for service management are growing, not least because leaders within the clinical field are showing the necessity for involvement if the future of medicine is to retain its validity and credibility (Jennett, 1986). Some doctors also welcome the opportunity to exercise the considerable influence that comes with this different kind of responsibility, and as Elston (1991) suggests, 'it may turn out that it is the "corporate rationalisers" (Alford, 1975) WITHIN the profession who are in the ascendant in Britain'.

8.9 Locating management

As a consequence of the concentration of management development on this group of staff (Horsley *et al.*, 1990) it becomes apparent that there is a need to redefine the location of management within the NHS. Mumford (1989) has suggested a spectrum of doctors' involvement in management (Table 8.1), and this variety in possible models of involvement has been confirmed in more recent research (IHSM, 1990). The managerial label applied almost exclusively to lay persons who have been responsible for administering and managing the service is no longer appropriate. The managerial role is now explicitly acknowledged to exist elsewhere in the organization and may in the longer term be more likely to meet policy objectives from these new perspectives. Indeed, Tap and Shut (1987) have suggested that it may prove to be essential, in times of consolidation

Table 8.1 A spectrum of doctors' involvement in management

	Free agent	Practising medical audit	Specialty/ multi-specialty manager	Medical adviser/ representative	Part-time general manager (unit/district)
Patient perspective	One to one	Retrospective studies of patients	Prospective view of potential patients	Whole population	Whole population
Financial perspective	Minimal interest, peripheral limitations	From nil to limited impact, greater impact anticipated in the white paper	Range from awareness of cost to full responsibility for managing within a cash limit	Individually nil, but accountable as part of team	Accountable for managing within a cash limit
Sphere of influence	Traditional relationship with other professions	Self management required and possibly needed to influence colleagues	Colleagues, partnership with support manager, other profession managers	Colleagues and management team	Senior managers, professional heads of department, colleagues

Source: Mumford 1989
Reproduced with permission from *Health Services Journal.*

rather than expansion, to unite responsibility for resource allocation and patient care under one head, in what they describe as the physician executive or the UK may know as clinical directors.

Pioneering work in this field was first undertaken at Johns Hopkins Hospital, Baltimore, USA (NEJM, 1984). It set out a new pattern of management within the organization, first adopted in the UK at Guy's Hospital, London, and now spreading throughout the country. The model decentralizes management within the organization to Clinical Directorates. Managerial responsibility rests with the director who is preferably a doctor, and the administrative tasks are undertaken by lay staff sometimes called 'business managers'. A variety of models have appeared since its introduction (IHSM, 1990) according to the individuals and organizations involved. After the first enthusiasm for this model subsided, a number of concerns have appeared about its acceptability in the UK—for example, in relation to the RMI it brings into sharp relief clinicians' accountability and has been described by clinicians in at least one RMI pilot site as 'intolerable' (Tomlin, 1990). Another group with good reason to voice major concerns about it are nurses (Dean, 1990) who, under the model, have their power over resources and input to senior management levels removed. As IHSM (1990) points out, with something approaching astonishment, 'nurses have even been appointed to the post of clinical director, either because no consultant was willing to take on the role or because the senior nurse was seen as the best person for the job . . .' (IHSM, 1990), confirming Clay's (1987) view that, in managerial terms, for the most part in the post-Griffiths NHS 'nurses were deemed monumentally unimportant'.

8.10   Medical managerialism

This new managerial form, which is termed medical managerialism, has profound implications for both present managers without clinical qualifications and future lay recruits to management in the NHS. The anecdotal evidence of lay managers leading from behind, in support of their clinical director colleagues who accrue the credit, is supported by the IHSM research (IHSM, 1990). Such organizational signals are already affecting the ability to recruit and retain high-quality 'lay' managers, particularly those performing the 'business manager role' (IHSM, 1990) where rapid turnover is giving rise to a loss of continuity. Consideration of the past experience of administrators should not be forgotten; the sometimes poor reputation of NHS administration was not simply a function of low pay and poor training within the NHS, but was also a function of the secondary role played to professional decision makers in the organization.

A cultural schizophrenia for lay managers similar to the schizoid style of organization described by de Vries and Miller (1984)[3] will again emerge if it is not made clear where their jobs, in whole or in part, are administrative rather than managerial, and what consequences this has for progress through the managerial hierarchy. The clinical directorate structure also implies an increase in administration/management as each directorate has a business manager. This will not go unnoticed if the media or other interested parties need to find a whipping boy for any potential failures in the performance of the clinical directorate structures.

What can be concluded from these new arrangements is that the administrative task still exists but is now seen to exist both within the managerial and clinical hierarchies.

8.11   Locating roles

The Institute of Health Services Management has broadened its base to all potential recruits to management across the spectrum of professionals working in health care. This change is essential to the newly recognized and divergent location of the management role within the organization. However, if the clinical talents of professional staff are not to be wasted by attracting too many of them full time into management roles, clearer indicators for the future career paths of lay managers are required as well as a clearer definition of the scope and power of the clinical director's role. One step that has been suggested is consideration of a new form of training for managers working in health to incorporate some elements of clinical training (Royce, 1988–89). The idea is a further development of the work of the Institute of Health Services Management programme of *Medicine for Managers* (IHSM, 1988), which has been run successfully in conjunction with the Royal Colleges and has developed an understanding by managers of the dilemmas that face clinicians. There is another factor that may also affect the future scope and availability of managers from the medical profession: the level of doctor supply. Fluctuations from periods of over-to-under-supply in the UK have occurred before because, for example, of reductions in training, the growth of the private sector or migration in both its forms (Abel-Smith, 1976; Parkhouse, 1990). A reversal in the over-supply of doctors, as described by Butter and Mejia (1987), means that recruits from the medical profession to full- or part-time management may become more difficult; their role may revert to one of only professional advice or veto to managers' decisions. There is a need, therefore, for practising clinicians as well as medical managers to gain a greater understanding of the role of management in the organization, if they are to remain as clinicians and accept 'lay manager' as well as clinical director decisions (Moore, 1990).

Such understanding may well need to begin at student doctor level, as suggested by Fox (1989), if mutual understanding is to become the norm rather than the exception within the organization.

A further somewhat different interpretation can be made if individual career paths rather than organizational needs are taken as the starting point. Research from INSEAD (Evans, 1990) suggests that individuals from both the managerial and professional groups may opt for 'layered careers'. Within the NHS this implies perhaps setting out as a doctor, then after 10 years or so of practice looking for a new challenge and moving over to management for 5 or 10 years, finally moving back to a strategic professional role for the last years of working life. From this perspective the implications for training and development to meet organizational needs may be very different from those being pursued at the present time.

So far we have established that management in the NHS has a long history of development, culminating in its most overt form in the Griffiths Report (1983). This report was a specific statement about a form of managerialism that focused the decisions onto individuals and away from teams. We have yet to see if, as Hunter (1986) suggests, this shows how 'reformers have failed to recognise the NHS's power structure'. The arrival of management after Griffiths was thus a victory in the long-running battle for its introduction into the NHS. The interpretation of this form of management has been adapted, firstly, as a structural change, and more recently into medical managerialism which provides a way for clinicians to reassert their decision-making power within the organization, or, viewed from the policy maker's or manager's perspective (Scrivens, 1988), to enable responsibility for resource use to be located with the real user, the clinicians.

Government appointment of an adviser from the private business sector meant that the new culture of management used a private sector model to bring about change within a public sector organization. The same attraction to external sources for new ideas has been used to inform proposals for the new structure outlined in *Working for Patients* (DHSS, 1989a), most notably the work of Enthoven on internal markets (Enthoven, 1985). This envisaged the separation of roles within the NHS into purchaser (e.g. District Health Authorities) and provider (e.g. hospitals) organizations where the purchaser acts in the provider's market on behalf of the community to ensure effective and efficient provision of service within the context of 'market forces'. However, government interpretation and implementation of ideas often conflict with the methods originally proposed. Enthoven, for example, originally saw it as essential to pilot a change to internal markets (May, 1989a), but the Government wished to go straight into full implementation (DH, 1989a). More recent reports suggest that after 'a whirlwind tour to meet supporters of the reforms', Enthoven is now persuaded of 'the positive response by NHS managers' (Davies, 1991). The interpretation of proposed changes can therefore be seen to be influenced by the perception of the interpreter or, as Kouzes and Mico (1979) explain, 'we are what we observe, and what we observe is certainly tinged by our theoretical windows to the world'.

Changes to the interpretation of managerialism in the NHS have occurred since its inception in 1948, and these interpretations have depended significantly on the beliefs of the party in power and their interpretation by Whitehall civil servants. In general, recent such interpretations have been 'very dated' (Metcalfe and Richards, 1990) and have been in danger of dragging any part of government affected, including the NHS, 'kicking and screaming back into the 1950s' (Metcalfe and Richards, 1990) in terms of the developments in management theory. Supporting any of these interpretations of management have been sets of value systems, but providing some understanding of what these values are has proved more difficult. However, whatever the changes the NHS has been undergoing may be, they follow McKevitt in Chapter 2 in that they are common to public organizations across Europe where appropriate concepts of management for public organizations have yet to develop (Kooiman and Eliassen, 1987). In addition, these changes also reflected the emergence in the Thatcher era of management in general as a more respectable profession in its own right: 'managers are no longer down trodden, nor do they have to justify their existence 1970s style . . . this development is not unique to Britain. But it does make a particularly striking change to what went before' (Barsoux and Lawrence, 1990).

8.12   Domain theory

Some explanation of this new cultural environment within the United Kingdom's NHS, is clarified with the aid of domain theory, as outlined in the Introduction to this book. As a way of looking at the organization, domain theory helps to 'clarify roles and relieve tensions' (Kouzes and Mico, 1979) within the new approach now required.

This theory has been further explored by others in relation to the NHS, notably Smith (1984), Thompson (1985) and Edmonstone (1986). At a more critical level, as an image, it falls within what Morgan (1986) describes as the organization as a political system where a plurality of interests hold power. As such, its strength, Morgan (1986) suggests, lies in a number of areas:

- in acceptance of the reality of politics in organizational life;
- in exploding the myth of rationality in so far as it poses questions about whose goals or interests are served through efficiency and effectiveness;
- in so doing, it also questions the concept of organizations as unified systems, and highlights understanding of the political nature of human behaviour within organizations and within the sociopolitical context of the organization in its interaction with the wider society.

Conversely, the interpretation may lead to over-politicization of the organization, a tendency that has been observed as particularly prevalent in British managers (Barsoux and Lawrence, 1990). This means seeing politics everywhere, through finding hidden agendas where none exist, which leads to the development of cynicism and mistrust as the only mode of operation. The danger is to ignore what Morgan highlights as the Aristotelian role of politics as a constructive force in the creation of social order, and to 'overstate the power and importance of the individual and underplay the system dynamics that determines what becomes political and how politics occurs' (Morgan, 1986).

Domain theory, however, offers a persuasive explanation for much of the discord and uneven development of ideas and action within the NHS because of the separateness of the domains. To derive the greatest benefit from this interpretation of the development of the NHS, it is necessary at the outset to think about the activity and scope of the organization.

NHS activity is a compromise between the demands of public health policy, the level of expenditure perceived to be acceptable for the public to contribute through tax towards local budgets, and the prevailing medical view of the needs of the service, or, as Waldegrave has put it, 'the interacation between the political process, the professions and the public' (DH, 1990b). These activities led Thompson (1985) to ascribe to each a domain: political, administrative and practitioner respectively. This was further developed by Edmonstone, following the Griffiths changes, who describes them as political, management and professional domains (see Table 8.2).

What becomes clear from Edmonstone's work is that a closer analysis of the domains, and the responsibilities that are vested in each, gives clues to some of the problems that block organizational awareness and success in anyone's terms —clinician, manager or politician.

Various parts of the NHS are evolving at different rates into this new organizational culture. The different time scales involved will affect the acceptability of managerial values. The NHS is in reality made up of a number of different kinds of organizations; for example, of Regional Health Authorities (RHAs) and District Health Authorities (DHAs) with forms and structures appropriate to the relationships and command structures that exist within the differing parts of those organizations. It also includes Family Health Service Authorities (FHSAs), the former Family Practitioner Committees (FPCs), whose organizational form and history have been very different, based as they were on the administration of the GPs as independent contractors. The form previously found in FPCs was also made subject to policy changes, including the introduction of managerialism and its progress now within the FHSAs will necessarily be different from the road already taken by the RHAs and DHAs. In some respects, as Mark and Willcocks (1989) have suggested, the FPCs (now FHSAs) may more easily adapt to methods from the private sector because of their familiarity in dealing with what can be termed the small business culture of general practice. The problem, therefore, is to ensure that the context, culture and changes proposed are appropriate to the different parts of the organization. However, if differences between the parts prove so great, in future it may be more appropriate not to think of the NHS as an organization at all, but rather, as Mintzberg has suggested, 'Maybe the NHS should be viewed as a policy, not an organization' (Spry, 1989) operating through the concept of a policy network

Table 8.2 Domains in human service organizations

Management	Professional	Political
Attempts to mirror the image of industrial management; emphasis on comprehensive, rational view of the world and on hierarchical control and coordination	Professional autonomy; self-governing experts with the competence to respond to the needs and demands of clients	Parliamentary (i.e. representative) democracy; emphasis on consent of the governed
Information	Professional status	Respect for the law
General managers, administrators	Professional representative machinery; professional boards and committees	Health authority chairman and DHA members
Increased rationality, cost-efficiency and effectiveness; value for money	Professional standards; quality of care, etc.	Equity—just, impartial and fair policy decisions
Bureaucracy	Collegial, individualized client-specific problem-solving	Representation
Conformity to rules	Non-conformist individuality	Acceptable public disagreement

Source: Edmonstone 1986
Reprinted with permission of MCB University Press Limited.

which is described by Benson (1982) as 'a complex of organisations connected to each other by resource dependencies (particularly in the post White Paper purchaser/provider world) and distinguished from other complexes by breaks in the structure of resource dependencies'.

Notwithstanding these problems, what is common to all parts of the NHS, whether it is one organization or a series, is the existence of its three domains.

The existence of the three domains could therefore be said to reveal the common values that underpin such human service organizations (HSOs). Edmonstone has gone further in showing how we can interpret the new domains in the post-Griffiths era be they political, professional or managerial. What becomes important thereafter is translating the theory into a model that helps to explain past, present and future changes. The questions which then arise are: Can we establish:

- the continued existence of each domain?
- the changing location of groups between each domain?

- the interrelationship between the domains?
- the location of issues within or between the domains?

8.12.1   THE CONTINUED EXISTENCE OF EACH DOMAIN
Why should these three domains, which have behaviours incompatible to each other, continue to exist? Kouzes and Mico (1979) state that 'they act together as an organizational check and balance system' and in so doing they meet the 'multiple needs of human communities'.

The new right's interpretation of the world, as set out by Flynn (1989)[1] leads to the conclusion that the Thatcher government had problems in accepting the concepts of communities and societies and their collectivist organizations; this view was most cogently expressed by Mrs Thatcher herself in 1987 in her often quoted statement: 'There is no such thing as society. There are individual men and women and there are families' (*Woman's Own*, 1987). It is not surprising, therefore, to find that the concepts underpinning *Working for Patients* (DHSS, 1989a) rested on a dominant managerial model of a board of directors to whom individuals within the organization are responsible, but whose local political or community accountability is substantially reduced (NAHA, 1988). Further-more, the role of the Community Health Councils (CHCs) as community watch-dog, already changed by *Patients First* (DHSS, 1979), was further disregarded in the loss of its automatic rights of representation on the new health authority boards (DHSS, 1989a). This effectively begins the transfer of the organization from a public to a private sector model as defined by Ranson and Stewart (1989), the private organization having only customers, while the public organization is more accountable through the broader concept of citizens as its audience. The loss of these parts which make up the political domain at a local level, would upset the balance between the domains in each DHA. Furthermore, it would not only mean the loss of a domain, but also may imply that one of the other domains would usurp the role; the manager or professional as politician.

The professional domain is vulnerable to further developments in depro-fessionalization (Haug, 1976, 1988) and proletarianization as originally defined by Oppenheimer (1973),[2] for any of the professional groups working in the NHS. This implies the absorption of a profession into the organization with the consequent removal or transfer of the controls and values particular to that domain. This may occur through the influence of another domain, for example the Resource Management Initiative (DHSS, 1986), as the influence of both the political and managerial domain over the professional domain; or for other reasons, for example the introduction of new technology. However, of the three, the professional domain may prove the strongest if, as Turner (1987) suggests, 'professionalization can be seen as an occupational strategy to maintain certain privileges and rewards'; especially as its activity is not directly answerable to other groups—as the managerial is to the political domain, and as the political is to its constituents—but is answerable only to itself within the broad context of the wider society.

The managerial domain, the youngest of the three, has proved the most vulnerable of all so far, with the appointment in October 1986 of the senior politician Mr Tony Newton, Minister of Health, to be in charge of the NHS Management Board. This demonstrates the political domain in the process of usurping the role of the managerial domain, and occurred too soon for comfort after the Griffiths' managerial challenge to 40 years of professional domination of the NHS (Petchey, 1986). Subsequent changes, involving the creation of a policy board chaired by the Secretary of State and a subsidiary Management Executive chaired by a chief executive Duncan Nichol, working with a board of executive and non-executive directors, has not reversed this situation. Further evidence of the consequences of these changes was provided by the obvious personal involvement of the then Secretary of State Kenneth Clark in the ambulance workers' dispute of 1989/90 (BMJ, 1990), despite the fact that the 'management side' response should have been the sole prerogative of the chief executive. Later controversy over the linking of waiting lists to managers' performance-related pay (Sheldon, 1990) has reinforced this view and led one manager to comment 'Duncan Nichol is doing this because he has been told to' (Davies, 1990) by his political masters. It must be concluded, therefore, that so far the managerial domain has failed to establish a shared set of values within the domain, which can both resist the pressure from the other domains and form the basis for a shared interpretation of management in the context of public service organizations.

8.12.2   THE CHANGING LOCATION OF GROUPS BETWEEN EACH DOMAIN

Arguably, the manager as partially trained clinician (Royce, 1988–89) and the clinician as manager (Horsley et al., 1990) provide evidence of the very positive steps now being proposed for groups to change domain. Other research, however, suggests that little is in fact changing (Harrison, 1989) and that both groups 'continue to inhabit a shared culture of medical autonomy in which only rarely do managers challenge clinicians'.

The most effective managerial challenge to clinicians occurs when the manager is a clinician. When such a challenge fails, as it did with the resignation in May 1990 of Professor Elaine Murphy as general manager of Lewisham and North Southwark Health Authority (Glassman, 1990), the consequences for all domains are substantial. The credibility gap for the management and political domains is made worse when doctors retreat in this way to the professional domain to pursue once again a clinical career; domain retreat is not available to managers or politicians in quite the same way. Similarly, the professional domain looks too much like a safe haven for those only playing at management, even if they are in agreement, as Professor Murphy was, with the objectives of the political domain. The later resignation of Dr Stephen Jenkins as district general manager of West Lambeth Health Authority (Sheldon, 1991) came after the six senior doctors, all with clinical directorates, advised the chairman that they might resign if Dr Jenkins' future management role was not curtailed. What was not clear is whether the senior doctors were acting in their role as professionals or as medical managers or both, in appealing to the political domain, represented by the chairman. Whichever it was, it seems likely that their 'advice' (Sheldon, 1991) was received as primarily from professionals and only secondarily as managers. Furthermore, some doubt was cast on the availability of domain retreat for Dr Jenkins within his own clinical specialty at St Thomas's, perhaps, because, as his clinical colleague put it, of the 'huge distance' in management terms that he was seen to have moved the organization. The lesson from these two examples seems to be that professional clinicians who undertake a management task survive more successfully than managers who formerly were doctors, especially when they find close allies within the political domain; so medical managers are safest sticking ultimately to the values of the professional rather than the managerial domain.

The problems of locating groups between the domains are most forcibly demonstrated by a group who have consistently fallen between the domains and suffered as a consequence—that is, the community physicians, or public health doctors as they are now known.

Their significant planning role, as perceived in the 1974 reorganization (DHSS, 1972), located them within the managerial domain and no doubt contributed to the continuing problems in attracting new recruits from the medical profession. In 1988 the specialty had a 21.5 per cent vacancy rate as against an average 5 per cent in other specialties (Harvey and Judge, 1988). Furthermore, in the post-1979 era, their emphasis on communities as their patients was out of step with the emphasis on individualism (Flynn, 1989) coming from the political domain, and did not seem nearly so attractive as the focus on individual patients of their clinical colleagues. Their location in the management or administrative domain since 1974 also contributed in part to the propensity of newly appointed district general managers to attempt to abolish the district medical officer role in the post-Griffiths reorganization (Alleway, 1987). The clear signals were: you are a doctor/professional and no longer have a managerial role at this level of the organization. The disquiet that this caused led to a review of the role of public health following the introduction of general management (Acheson Report, 1988); the research papers prepared for the review showed evidence of the role and domain confusion experienced by this group. The review reported in January 1988, and revealed acceptance of the view that public health should be located in the professional domain. Furthermore, not only were general managers to be involved in appointments, indicating an increase in managerial control over this group and intervention in the professional domain, but the successors to the district medical officers, the new directors of public health, had their direct access to another overtly political domain, provided by their responsibilities to local authorities, curtailed. As a group they currently are back on the periphery of the professional domain, but with a developing role in providing information on populations and disease patterns for the new purchaser/provider authorities. As such, their role can be seen as serving management decisions by the use of their professional skills in epidemiology.

Another major professional group substantially affected by the change to managerialism were the nurses. Like the public health doctors they fell victim to general management implementation. However, they were even less successful than the public health doctors in redressing the situation. As Banyard (1988) has noted, only a third of all districts retained a chief nursing officer post, a third combined it with other duties (as if representing the work of 50 per cent of the workforce was not enough) while the remaining third abolished the post altogether. Glennester's study confirms how nurses feared role conflict, brought about by the separation of management control and professional advice (Glennester *et al.*, 1986); in the post-Griffiths world, confusion over domain location was thus seen as a potential problem. Later studies (Robinson and Strong, 1987) suggested giving nurses a greater role in providing professional advice, implying a very definite confirmation of their place in the professional rather than the management domain. More recently a more positive view of the nurses' role in management has emerged (Strong and Robinson, 1988), but as Leathard (1990) points out, by 1989 there were still only six district general managers with a background in nursing, and Dean (1990) suggests that the move to clinical directorates is a further threat to nurses as both managers and professionals. Many other examples of the problems being faced by the changing location of groups could be illuminated by the application of domain theory, but what seems important for all of them to recognize is their place in an existing domain, as well as an understanding of the possible consequences of moving to another.

8.12.3   THE INTERRELATIONSHIP BETWEEN THE DOMAINS

Problems arising from the interrelationship between the domains in the NHS have been explored by Smith (1984), who characterizes them in the following manner:

1 'The tenuous and often antagonistic relationships between the separate domains.' This he suggests is symptomized by reciprocal scapegoating, a recent example of which is the reinterpretation by government of the 1987 funding crisis into a problem of poor management.
2 'Poor communication and the failure to develop successful corporate planning', for example the collapse of the much heralded Communications Programme (Moore, 1990) which resulted in the *Health Services Journal* editorial

concluding 'the irony is that the root of this débâcle is the centre's own appalling record of poor communication' (HSJ, 1990).

3 'Each domain is characterized by different values, which lead to a lack of interest in the other domains, now somewhat ameliorated by some joint activity between the domains', e.g. the joint publications between the Institute of Health Services Management (IHSM), the British Medical Association (BMA) and the Royal College of Nursing (RCN) (Bosanquet, 1985; Maynard and Bosanquet, 1986; O'Higgins, 1987) or the Medicine for Managers courses previously mentioned (IHSM, 1988).

4 'Occupants of the various domains collect information to suit their own needs and purposes alone'; an example of this is the substantial problems in defining the information base for the NHS in terms of whose interests are served— clinicians, managers or policy makers (Orr, 1990).

5 'The existence of the domains implies an inbuilt conflict within the NHS' which, as we know from Kouzes and Mico (1979), is an integral part of their domain theory.

The most notable victim of this conflict and the problems of the interrelationship between domains was Victor Paige, the first chairman of the NHS Management Board as it then was, who resigned after only 18 months in office because, as Leathard (1990) suggests, he had 'a disagreement with Ministers over his right to manage. Frustration mounted over priorities between management and politics'. Even later the problems of interrelationships shifted to the professional and political interface; as Leathard (1990) goes on to say, it was because an 'explosive public row erupted amongst health professionals and politicians over inadequate resources' late in 1987, that the Government was forced to act and so set up a further review of the NHS (DH, 1989a).

The development of a fourth domain has been recommended by others (Thompson, 1985); this Thompson then goes on to describe erroneously as the role of general management. Such a misinterpretation of the theory does, however, provide a further way of coming to terms with these problems of inter-relationship through the use of a fourth domain, and while such a domain may take many forms—for example, the Health Advisory Service or the use of outside consultants—as a strategy it seeks to deny the very creative tension to which the three domains give rise by virtue of their existence. Those who cannot live with this tension or dynamic conflict and put it to good use are failing to understand the environment that exists in HSOs.

8.12.4   THE LOCATION OF ISSUES WITHIN OR BETWEEN THE DOMAINS
Locating issues within or between the domains demonstrates how each domain responds to issues, and how such issues are changed or affect the domains.

Of the recently arrived issues on the NHS agenda, quality has shown itself to be a sufficiently flexible concept to be interpreted differently, but in the interests of each domain. There is, so far, little evidence of NHS management having methods to assess the quality and reliability of patient services (Best, 1989), or the quality of clinical practice (Harrison *et al.*, 1989a). The primary interest in the subject came from the professional domain where the issue is most convincingly located. However, even within this domain the various groups have different approaches; for example, the doctors through clinical audit as demonstrated since the CEPOD Report (Buck *et al.*, 1987) and the nurses through measures of care (Kitson, 1990). Initially, managers looked at quality in areas over which they had direct and legitimate control, like hotel services. Only more recently have they become involved in quality issues as they directly affect the care and treatment of patients. Managers have, however, found it hard to draw clinicians into management on the basis of a partnership for quality when, firstly, many clinicians do not want such explicitly shared responsibility, and, secondly, those who might be willing and able, fear being used to legitimize underfunding of the NHS. An example of this problem was found in practice by one of the authors of this chapter through the introduction of medical audit into general practice (DH, 1989b). The proposal focused on care audit as a means of improving clinical decision-making. However, the role given to the FPC (now FHSA) was regarded by the profession as a means of policing GPs: the consequent concern felt by the doctors may have resulted in a setback to the systematic review of practice (Metcalfe, 1989). Service providers regarded managerial involvement as an intrusion into clinical territory, based on the premise that managers were only concerned for economy. Policy makers treated the abreaction as evidence of clinicians' resistance to any form of visible accountability, and it was left to the managers to negotiate a solution in the face of scepticism from both. Efforts focused on the idea of medical audit as the heart of clinical and service audit. This required a partnership between managers, doctors and policy makers, all of whom had an interest and contribution to make to the improvement of services. A key to understanding was the acceptance of the idea that audit would be incomplete without the mutual support of these three groups.

A second, new, issue that has so far failed to find the right lead domain or 'product champion' is consumerism. Progress in making the service consumer sensitive is slow (Harrison *et al.*, 1989a). Why should this be so? The first problem for the NHS is in identifying the customer: is it the patient or the doctor acting on the patient's behalf? Winkler (1987) has suggested that once again interpretation is at fault. Viewed from a domain theory perspective the problem may tell us more about the inability of the three groups to relate their activities to the external environment or to undertake what the commercial sector knows as 'environmental scanning' (Gunn, 1989). Flynn *et al.* (1988) argues that environmental scanning is more difficult in the public sector because of the perennial uncertainty as to which specific issues will in practice become politically significant. Alternatively, it may be because—unlike commercial concerns, which look for market-and profit-related trends—public services have difficulty in defining their purpose and thus isolating the information they require and also what they are scanning for (Gunn, 1989). They are instead absorbed by the complex interrelationships that exist between the three domains in the internal environment, as described by de Vries and Miller (1984), in relation to their schizoid organizational type.[3] The consumer thus remains part of the external environment and in the post-internal market organization, as Klein and Day (1989) and Green (1990) agree, it will continue to be the GP or DHA as purchaser, rather than patient as the consumer, who will make choices about which services are used—once again excluding the consumer's voice.

However, the most obvious location for the issue is within the political domain because the patient/consumer as a constituent of that domain has the ability to withdraw support from the group currently leading that domain; being voted out is not, however, a very pressing problem for the domain except within a very short period before an election. At a local level, without the constituents' ability to vote out those residing in the political domain (members of health authorities are, and will be, appointed not elected), their voice is not heard. This issue has been seen by Government as a conflict in role between the political and managerial domains. Their way of resolving it at a local level has been in favour of the managerial model by removing political influence on health authorities as set out in the White Paper *Working for Patients* (DHSS, 1989a), and not requiring the boards of directors who are replacing health authorities to meet regularly in public. Within Whitehall itself there has been little attempt to impose the managerial model on the administrative civil service working with Ministers, and rather than seeing this as a discrepancy (Maynard, 1991) domain theory would suggest that the reason is because they form part of the political and professional, but not managerial, domains.

At a national level, the Government is more aware of consumers as constituents; it has therefore directed the domains to become more responsive to consumer needs, in the managerial domain it has issued the waiting list imperative in the lead up to the next election (Davies, 1990), in the professional domain there are the directions to GPs contained within *Promoting Better Health* (DHSS, 1987).

Perhaps the final test of consumer sensitivity at a national level will be the extent to which the Government accepts consumer concerns about their reform programme. In following the trend of looking to America for policy answers— for example, clinical directorates (NEJM, 1984) or internal markets (Enthoven, 1985)—a recent study at Harvard (Blendon and Donelan, 1989) may be instructive in identifying the consumer view of proposed reforms. The study undertook surveys in the UK but also included a review of 20 national surveys of public opinion in the UK between 1983 and 1989; it concludes that the public:

- oppose the reform proposals
- oppose substituting the existing UK systems with anything resembling the US system
- oppose the idea of an internal market
- agree with the increase in private sector provision but oppose any form of subsidy for it from central government (like the recently introduced tax concessions for the elderly (DHSS, 1989a)).

Such concerns from the consumer are mirrored in the professional domain and may also reflect fears in the management domain, but at present no reliable data have been allowed publication (Moore, 1991).

In conclusion, the examples explored are an attempt to locate issues within and between the domains, and demonstrate the need for each domain to look for and understand the appropriate responses, as a lead or following domain, to issues as they arise within the internal and external environments.

8.13   Locating domain theory

In establishing evidence to support the relevance of the four questions discussed above, it becomes apparent that a revised model of domain theory is emerging from its further application to the NHS. This new approach relies more on what Morgan (1986) would describe as the organization as an organism—a perspective also now favoured by Drucker (1989). In so doing it describes the nature of relationships between the domains and the external environment (see Fig. 8.1)

One of the strengths of this view is that in placing the organization in its external environment, as an image it shows more clearly the possibilities, which are currently absent (Gunn, 1989), for environmental scanning. Furthermore, as an image it also highlights the desirability of looking at the needs of the interacting processes within the organization (Morgan, 1986). The organic nature of the model is demonstrated by the permeability of the walls that surround both the domains and the HSO itself. The points where the domains touch each other and the external environment can, as has been demonstrated by an examination of some of the issues, give rise to cooperation or conflict. This will be determined by the answers to such questions as: Who owns the issue? What benefit or threat does the issue hold for the occupants of each domain? Will the issue penetrate in either direction between the permeable walls of the domains and/or the external environment? Essential to this model is the tension created by the boundaries around each domain and their proximity. The tension in itself sustains the very existence of the internal environment, the HSO. The domains are seen to act together in times of cooperation, but often with two cooperating in conflict against the third, as, for example, in the collaboration between the IHSM representing management and the BMA and RCN

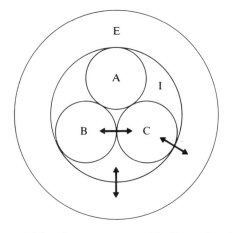

A = Managerial domain   E = External environment
B = Professional domain   I = Internal environment
C = Political domain

Arrows indicate the movement of issues, groups and individuals between internal
and external environments and any of the domains. Each domain also has reference
points for its value system or parts of it within the external environment;
e.g. professionals have the professional organization and/or those working in other
organizations in the same role.

Figure 8.1   Movement of issues between external and internal environments

representing the professions, in their joint reports exposing their conflict with
the political domain over funding (Bosanquet, 1985; Maynard and Bosanquet,
1986; O'Higgins, 1987).

Solutions to the problems for new managers working in the post-Griffiths
NHS, using domain theory, have been explored by others: for example, Thompson (1985) and Smith (1984) in their suggestions for a fourth domain to unify
the separation that exists between the three domains. In so doing they make the
mistake of perceiving and using one of the main limitations of seeing organizations as organisms—that is, that unity and harmony can and should be achieved
in organizational life (Morgan, 1986). Such an interpretation is not so much a
limitation bound by the image used, but more likely an indicator of the lack of
knowledge in general about the tensions and conflicts within organisms that
enable change and growth to take place. In visualizing domain theory as both
political and ecological images we are provided with more 'theoretical windows
to the world' (Kouzes and Mico, 1979) which enable us to begin to understand
the strengths and weaknesses of the NHS and public sector organization in
general.

8.14   Developing value systems

As an essential part of understanding the problems currently being faced within the NHS as an organization, much of the evidence we have explored suggests that the NHS management domain does not yet seem to have developed a set of shared values, and is therefore not able to communicate those values to the external and internal environments. Meanwhile, the development of a communications strategy by the political domain (DH, 1990a), in part to redress this problem, has had almost predictable consequences viewed in the light of what domain theory has shown. Following the introduction of the communications strategy it soon became clear from the results of the survey, undertaken as a first part of the strategy (NHS Executive, 1990), that an unacceptably high level of mistrust still exists even within the management domain itself. Such a problem confirms the lack of shared values within the domain and makes it vulnerable to pressure from each of the other domains and the external environment. The political domain had already grasped this and had sought to usurp the situation by implementing a communications strategy (DH, 1990a) which imposed a top-down approach to implementing the changes that arise from the political domain, namely the three White Papers (DHSS, 1987, 1989a,b): 'it is essential that NHS managers at all levels should be fully aware of the changes taking place and should communicate effectively with their staff' (DH, 1990a).

In so doing it not only misinterpreted the form that this strategy should take as a simplistic public relations exercise (HSJ, 1990), but it also usurped once again the role of the management domain. In this instance, however, the management domain did manage to reassert itself by rejecting the first programme, as demonstrated by the 16 managers who threatened to walk out (Moore, 1990) if changes were not made to the programme; this was followed by a subsequent cancellation and review of similar programmes (Moore, 1990).

8.15   Conclusion

In conclusion the evidence seems to suggest that confusion about the success or otherwise of the introduction of general management (Harrison *et al.*, 1989b) may rest on several factors, which are clarified by looking at the organization with the aid of domain theory.

In answering the questions with which we began (see section 8.1):

- How has the NHS interpreted general management so far?
- Is it a correct interpretation?
- Can we ensure future success by rethinking this interpretation?

it seems that general management was initially misinterpreted as a structural rather than a cultural change; then, when reinterpreted as a cultural change, it was shown to be too simplistic an approach as it was taken from a less complex environment (Gunn, 1989).

The way forward requires a much closer examination of both management in general and within the public services and the NHS in particular, as Metcalfe and Richards (1990) suggest:

> the development of new concepts and methods in public management is especially important now, because we are probably reaching the limits of imitation of business management by government.

This view was echoed by the first post-Thatcher Secretary of State when he said:

> I think we have overdone the language of commerce in relation to the health service . . . it just bears saying straight out: the NHS is not a business; it is a public service, and a great one.

> (DH, 1990b)

Interpretation of management, particularly in the public sector, is itself problematic, as Stewart and Ranson (1988) have suggested. Management in both the public and private sectors is also under discussion more generally as a much more informal, interpersonal, unplanned and unsystematic approach (Kotter, 1982; May, 1989a) than previously thought. There is thus no correct interpretation as such but only one suitable to the organization's tasks and environments involved; where these are unclear perhaps because of hidden agendas—for example, the idea that the political domain in the UK has a hidden commitment to change the NHS into a series of private sector organizations—it is more difficult to communicate a shared idea of managerialism.

The future success of the NHS in the UK is therefore dependent on a shared knowledge and understanding of both the purpose and objectives of the political, managerial and professional domains. Further research across all aspects of the process is essential but this may be hampered by a lack of cooperation from the interests under investigation as well as the methods chosen to investigate them (Pollitt *et al.*, 1990). This will be particularly true in the era following *Working for Patients* (DHSS, 1989a), where, as has been suggested, different sets of interests and coalitions will arise with the purchaser/provider split necessary to the new internal markets (Harrison *et al.*, 1990).

A higher level of organizational learning than is currently revealed is also required as argued in Chapter 3, and a more positive indication that the purpose of the political domain is not to attempt to transform the organization without the knowledge of the other two domains. Furthermore, management, as one of the three domains, has yet to establish and communicate its values and role to the other domains, so enabling the creative tension that should exist between the domains to reassert itself and move the organization into a creative and dynamic future. Once such dynamic tension has been re-established it is more likely that the NHS can become a learning organization 'which facilitates the learning of all its members and continually transforms itself' (Pedler *et al.*, 1988).

To facilitate the future success of these developments, and after examining a number of issues with the aid of domain theory, three activities have been identified as essential for learning to take place within and between all three domains:

1 *Identification* of the domains and the location of individuals, groups and issues within and between the domains and the external environment.
2 *Interpretation* of the responses to and by individuals, groups and issues within and between the domains and the external environment.
3 *Communication* in general and about specific issues between individuals and groups, both between the domains and the external environment.

The new management domain, therefore, has much to do if it is to ensure a successful future for itself. As a domain it is frequently placed as interpreter and negotiator between the other two domains; without the confidence to retain this role it will remain vulnerable to, or dominated by, the professional and political domains.

Notes

1 Norman Flynn (1989)—Elements of ideology are:
  • market mechanism—even when imperfect—takes precedence over planning, rationing and allocation
  • competition between providers aids efficiency and consumer orientation: consumers choose public/private/voluntary
  • individuals and individual choice take precedence over collective choice and planned provision
  • State provision at a minimum to encourage self-reliance; help should be provided by families.
Process of implementation:
  • contain public expenditure
  • weaken opposition by restructuring
  • implement new policies.

2 Haug (1976)—Deprofessionalization takes place because:
  • there is a growth of bureaucracy where professionals working in bureaucratic settings often find their professional autonomy undermined by the hierarchical structure of rules and authority
  • the very process of socialization and development of knowledge may bring about a fragmentation of a profession into quite distinctive groups
  • there is pressure from new professionals and para-professionals to take over and encroach upon the domain of the most prestigious and established professions.

Oppenheimer (1973)—Proletarianization occurs when there is:
  • an extensive division of labour in which a worker performs a limited number of tasks
  • the conditions of work, the nature of the workplace and the character of the work process are set and determined by a higher authority rather than by the worker
  • the wage is the primary source of income and this is determined by the marketplace rather than by individual negotiation

- the worker, in order to be proctected from the transformation at work, has to form some association or union to bargain collectively for improvements.

3 The Schizoid Organization—extract from de Vries and Miller (1984):

The schizoid organisation, like the depressive one, is characterised by a leadership vacuum. Its top executive discourages interaction because of a fear of involvement. Schizoid leaders experience the world as an unhappy place, populated by frustrating individuals. Perhaps because of past disappointments, they believe most contacts may end painfully for them. Consequently, they are inclined to day dream to compensate for a lack of fulfilment. In some organisations the second tier of executives will make up for what is missing from the leader with their own warmth and extroversion. This complementarity among executive personalities can sometimes overcome certain deficiencies of the leader. Frequently, however, the schizoid organisation can become a political battlefield. Members of the second tier see in the withdrawn nature of the top executives an opportunity to pursue their own needs . . .

The divided nature of the organisation thwarts effective cross functional (and where relevant inter-divisional) coordination and communication. Information is used more as a power resource than as a vehicle for effective adaptation. Very real barriers are erected to prevent the free flow of information. But this is not the only shortcoming of the information system. Another is the absence of environmental scanning. The focus is internal—on personal political ambitions and catering to the top managers desires. Second tier managers find it more useful to ignore objective environmental phenomena that might reflect poorly on their own past behaviour or might conflict with the wishes of the detached leader.

References

Abel-Smith, B. (1976) *Value for Money in Health Services.* Heinemann, London.

Acheson Report (1988) *Public Health in England.* The Report of the Committee of Inquiry into the future development of the Public Health Function. HMSO, London.

Alford, R. R. (1975) *Health Care Politics: Ideological and Interest Group Barriers to Reform.* Chicago University Press, Chicago.

Alleway, L. (1985) 'No rush of new blood into the NHS', *Health and Social Service Journal,* 12 September.

Alleway, L. (1987) 'Decline and fall of the DMOs', *Health Service Journal,* 98 (5034), 89.

Allen D., Harley, M. and Makinsin, G. T. (1987) 'Performance indicators in the National Health Service', *Social Policy and Administration,* 21 (1, Spring), 70–84.

Allen, D. and Horsley, S. (1990) *A Management Handbook for Doctors.* Macmillan, London.

Banyard, R. (1988) 'More power to the units', *Health Services Journal,* 4 August, 882–3.

Barsoux, J. L. and Lawrence, P. (1990) *The Challenge of British Management.* Macmillan, London.

Benson, J. K. (1982) 'Networks and policy sectors: a framework for extending interorganisational analysis', in Rogers, D. and Whitten, D. (eds), *Interorganisational Coordination.* Iowa State University Press, Ames.

Best, G. (1989) 'Exciting journey into the unknown', *Health Services Journal,* 99 (5137), 166.

Blendon, R. J. and Donelan, K. (1989) 'British public opinion on NHS reforms', *Health Affairs,* 8 (4, Winter).

BMJ (1990) News: 'Ambulance dispute', *British Medical Journal,* 300 (6717), 69.

Bosanquet, N. (1985) *Public Expenditure on the NHS—Recent Trends and Outlooks.* Joint Report of the British Medical Association, Royal College of Nursing and the Institute of Health Service Managers. IHSM, London.

Bradbeer Report (1954) *The Internal Administration of Hospitals.* Report by a Committee of the Central Health Services Council. HMSO, London.

Buck, N., Devlin, H. B. and Lunn, J. N. (1987) *A Report of the Confidential Enquiry into Perioperative Deaths.* Nuffield Provincial Hospital Trust, London.

Burns, T. (1981) *A Comparative Study of Administrative Structure and Organisational Processes in Selected Areas of the NHS.* SSRC Research Report.

Burns, T. and Stalker, G. H. (1966) *The Management of Innovation.* Tavistock, London.

Butter, I. and Mejia, A. (1987) 'Too many doctors!', *World Health Forum*, Vol. 8. WHO, Geneva.

Chandler, A. D. (1962) 'Strategy and structure', in *The History of Industrial Enterprise.* MIT Press, Cambridge, Mass.

Clay, T. (1987) *Nurses: Power and Politics.* Heinemann, London.

Cooper, M. H. (1975) *Rationing Health Care.* Croom Helm, London.

Coulter, A. (1991) 'Evaluating the outcomes of health care', in J. Gabe *et al.* (eds), *The Sociology of the Health Service.* Routledge, London.

Crabbe, G. (1989) 'Slum sweet slum', *Nursing Times*, 85 (29) (19 July).

Davidson, N. (1987) *A Question of Care: The Changing Face of the NHS.* Michael Joseph, London.

Davies, P. (1990) 'PRP: the carrot becomes a stick', *Health Services Journal*, 100 (5214), 1206 (16 August).

Davies, P. (1991) 'No need to fear the market of the wild west', *News Focus, Health Service Journal*, 31 January.

Dean, D. (1990) 'Doctor's orders', *Health Services Journal*, 100 (5214) 1215 (16 August).

de Vries, M. K. and Miller, D. (1984) *The Neurotic Organisation.* Jossey-Bass, San Francisco.

DH (1989a) *National Health Service Review Working Papers.* HMSO, London.

DH (1989b) Draft HC(FP)89, NHS Review: *Working for Patients. Medical Audit in the Family Practitioner Services.*

DH (1990a) 'Duncan Nichol announces new communications programme with NHS managers and staff', Press Release 90/144, 19 March.

DH (1990b) Trafford Memorial Lecture given by William Waldegrave, Secretary of State for Health, at Royal College of Surgeons, 12 December. Secretary of State's Office Department of Health, Richmond Terrace, London.

DHSS (1970) *National Health Service: The future structure of the National Health Services.* HMSO, London.

DHSS (1972) *Management Arrangements for the Reorganized National Health Services.* (The Grey Book.) HMSO, London.

DHSS (1979) *Patients First.* Consultative paper on the structure and management of the National Health Service in England and Wales.

DHSS (1982a) 'New look at NHS performance: Sir Derek Rayner to advise on scrutinies'. Press Release No. 82/90, 1 April.

DHSS (1982b) 'Nine new Rayner scrutinies in the National Health Service'. Press Release No. 82/240, 30 July.

DHSS (1984) *The Next Steps: Management in the Health Service.* DHSS, London.

DHSS (1985a) *Performance Indicators for the NHS.* DHSS, London.

DHSS (1985b) HC(85)23: *Health Service Management Performance Indicators.* DHSS, London.

DHSS (1986) HN(86)34: *Resource Management (Management Budgeting) in Health Authorities*. DHSS, London.

DHSS (1987) '*Promoting Better Health: The Government's Programme for Improving Primary Health Care*. Cmd 248, HMSO, London.

DHSS (1989a) *Working for Patients: The Health Service Caring for the 1990s*. Cmd 55, HMSO, London.

DHSS (1989b) Caring for People: *Community Care in the Next Decade and Beyond*. Cmnd 849, HMSO, London.

Dopson, S. and Stewart, R. (1990) 'Public and private sector management: the case for a wider debate', *Public Money and Management*, Spring.

Drucker, P. (1989) *The New Realities*. Harper & Row, New York.

Edmonstone, J. D. (1986) 'If you're not the woodcutter, what are you doing with the axe?', *Health Services Manpower Review*, **12** (3), 8–12 (November).

Ellwood, P. M. (1988) 'Outcome management: a technology of patient experience, *New England Journal of Medicine*, **318**.

Elston, M. A. (1991) 'The politics of professional power', in Gabe, J. *et al.* (eds), *The Sociology of the Health Service*. Routledge, London.

Enthoven, A. (1985) *Reflections on the Management of the NHS*. Nuffield Provincial Hospitals Trust, London.

Evans, P. (1990) 'International management development and the balance between generalism and professionalism', *Personnel Management*, December.

Flynn, A., Gray, A., Jenkins, W. *et al.* (1988) 'Accountable management in British Central Government: some reflections on the official record', *Financial Accountability in Management*, **4** (3, Autumn).

Flynn, N. (1989) 'The "new right" and social policy', *Police and Politics*, **17** (2), 97–109.

Forsyth, G. (1983) 'Background to management', in Allen, D. (ed.), *Management for Health Service Administration*. Pitman, London.

Fox, N. (1989) 'Will my examiners ask me about management?', *Journal of Management in Medicine*, **4** (1, Summer), 61–63.

Glassman, D. (1990) 'News focus—disillusionment riding on the flagship of reform', *Health Service Journal*, **100** (5203), 31 May.

Glennester, H. *et al.* (1986) *The Nursing Management Function after Griffiths: A study in the North West Thames Region*. The London School of Economics and NWTRHA, London.

Green, D. (ed.) (1990) *The NHS Reforms: Whatever happened to consumer choice?* Institute of Economic Affairs, London.

Griffiths Report (1983) *NHS Management Inquiry*. DHSS, London.

Gunn, L. (1989) 'A public management approach to the NHS', *Health Services Management Research*, **2** (1), March.

Ham, C. and Hunter, D. (1988) *Managing Clinical Activity in the NHS*. Kings Fund Institute, London.

Harrison, S. (1988) *Managing the National Health Service—Shifting the Frontier?* Chapman and Hall, London.

Harrison, S. (1989) 'General management and medical autonomy in the National Health Service', *Health Services Management Research*, **2** (1), March.

Harrison, S., Hunter, D., Marnoch, G. and Pollitt, C. (1989a) *The Impact of General Management in the National Health Service*. Report No. 1. Nuffield Institute for Health Studies, University of Leeds and the Open University, Milton Keynes.

Harrison, S., Hunter, D., Marnoch, G. and Pollitt, C. (1989b) *General management in the National Health Service: before and after the White paper*. Report No. 2, Nuffield Institute for Health Service Studies, Leeds.

Harrison, S., Hunter, D. J. and Pollitt, C. (1990) *The Dynamics of British Health Policy*. Unwin Hyman, London.

Harvey, S. and Judge, K. (1988) *Community Physicians and Community Medicine*. Kings Fund Institute, London.

Haug, M. R. (1976) 'The erosion of professional authority: a cross cultural inquiry in the case of the physician', *Millbank Memorial Fund Quarterly*, **54**, 83–106.

Haug, M. R. (1988) 'A re-examination of the hypothesis of deprofessionalization', *The Millbank Quarterly*, **66** (Suppl. 2), 48–56.

Haywood, S. and Alaszewski, A. (1980) *Crisis in the Health Service*. Croom Helm, London.

Horsley, S. D., Vaughan, D. H., Hessett, C. and Allen, D. E. (1990) 'Management for consultants', *Journal of Management in Medicine*, 4 (4, Spring).

HSJ (1990) Comment: 'The £4M flop', *Health Services Journal*, **100** (5214), 16 August.

HSMR (1989) *Health Services Management Research*, 'General management in the NHS: three views from the trenches', **2** (1), March.

Hunter, D. (1986) *Managing the National Health Service in Scotland: Review and Assessment of Research Needs*. Scottish Health Service Studies No. 45. Scottish Home and Health Dept, Edinburgh.

IDS Public Sector Unit/Coopers Lybrand (1989) *Paying for Performance in the Public Sector: A Progress Report*. IDS Public Sector Unit, London.

IHSM (1988) *Medicine for Managers*. Pilot course run jointly with the Royal Colleges. Institute of Health Services Management, London.

IHSM (1990) *Models of Clinical Management*. Institute of Health Services Management, London.

JAMA (1990) Editorial: 'The prospective payment system and quality—no skeletons in the closet', *Journal of the American Medical Association*, **264** (15), 17 October.

Jennett Bryan (1986) *High Technology Medicine*. Oxford University Press, Oxford.

Kitson, A. (1990) 'Managing the quality of care', in Fielding, P. and Berman, P. C. (eds), *Surviving in General Management—A Resource for Health Professionals*. Macmillan Education, London.

Klein R. (1984) 'Britain's National Health Service in the 1980s', *Millbank Memorial Fund Quarterly/Health and Society*, **62** (1).

Klein, R. (1989) *The Politics of the National Health Service*. Longman, Harlow.

Klein, R. and Day, P. (1989) 'NHS review: the broad picture', *British Medical Journal*, **298** (11 February), 339–40.

Kooiman, J. and Eliassen, K. A. (eds) (1987) *Managing Public Organizations—Lessons from Contemporary European Experience*. Sage, London.

Korner Steering Group (1982) *Health Services Informtion*. HMSO, London.

Kotter, J. P. (1982) *The General Managers*. Free Press, New York.

Kouzes, J. M. and Mico, P. R. (1979) 'Domain Theory, an introduction to organizational behaviour in human service organisations', *Journal of Applied Behavioural Science*, 15 (4), 449–69.

Leathard, A. (1990) *Health Care Provision Past, Present and Future*. Chapman and Hall, London.

MacKenzie, W. J. M. (1979) *Power and Responsibility in Health Care—The National Health Service as a Political Institution*. Nuffield Provincial Hospital Trust, Oxford University Press.

Mark, A. and Willcocks, L. (1989) 'The secret of success', *Health Services Management*, **85** (December).

May, A. (1989a) 'A guru vexed by his government disciples', *Health Services Journal*, 21 September.

May, A. (1989b) News Focus: 'Wind of change rustles in the ivory towers', *Health Services Journal*, 99 (5176), 9 November.

Maynard, A. (1991) 'Practise what you preach', *Health Services Journal*, 100 (5), 7 February.

Maynard, A. and Bosanquet, N. (1986) *Public Expenditure and the NHS—Recent trends and future problems*. Joint report of British Medical Association, Royal College of Nursing and Institute of Health Services Managers. IHSM, London.

McKinlay, J. B. and Stoeckle, J. D. (1988) 'Corporatization and the social transformation of doctoring', *International Journal of Health Services*, 18 (2).

Merrison Report (1979) *Report of the Royal Commission on the National Health Service*. Cmnd 7615, HMSO, London.

Metcalfe, D. H. H. (1989) 'Audit in general practice', *British Medical Journal*, 299, 1293–4 (25 November).

Metcalfe, L. and Richards, S. (1990) *Improving Public Management* (enlarged edn). Sage, London.

MH (1956) *Report of the Committee of Enquiry into the Cost of the National Health Service* (Chairman C. W. Guillebaud). Cmnd 9663, HMSO, London.

MH (1968) *NHS Services: The Administrative Structure of Medical and Related Services in England and Wales*. HMSO, London.

Mintzberg, H. and Waters, J. A. (1989) 'Of strategies, deliberate and emergent', in Asch, D. and Bowman, C. (eds), *Reading in Strategic Management*. Macmillan, London.

Moore, G. T. (1990) in Costain, D. (ed.), *The Future of Acute Services: Doctors as Managers*. Kings Fund, London.

Moore, W. (1990) News: 'Communications drive collapses after mutiny', *Health Services Journal*, 100 (5214), 16 August.

Moore, W. and Sheldon, T. (1990) 'DoH to put brakes on pace of reform', *Health Services Journal*, 29 March.

Moore, W. (1991) News: 'Survey kept under wraps', *Health Services Journal*, 101 (5234), 17 January.

Morgan, G. (1986) *Images of Organisation*. Sage, London.

Mumford, P. (1989) 'Doctors in the driving seat', *Health Services Journal*, 99 (5151), 18 May.

NAHA (1988) *The Nation's Health: A Way Forward*. National Association of Health Authorities, Birmingham.

NEJM (1984) Special Report, *New England Journal of Medicine*, 310 (22), 31 May.

NHS Executive (1990) *Unit Communications Survey, National Results Summary*. Commissioned by NHS Management Executive and published to General Managers in the NHS, 2 April.

NHS Executive (1990) *Unit Communications Survey—National Results Summary*. National Health Service Executive, London.

NHSTA (1990) *Points* (July). National Health Service Training Authority.

OHE (1989) *People as Patients and Patients as People*. Office of Health Economics, London.

O'Higgins, M. (1987) *Health Spending—A way to substantial growth*. Joint report of British Medical Association, Royal College of Nursing and Institute of Health Service Managers, IHSM, London.

Oppenheimer, M. (1973) 'The proletarianisation of the profession', in Halmos, P. (ed.),

Professionalisation and Social Change. Sociological Review Monograph, 20. University of Keele.

Orr, J. S. (1990) 'Management power and information technology', *Health Services Management*, **86** (3), June.

OU (1990) *Managing Health Services.* Open University, Milton Keynes.

Parkhouse, J. (1990) *Doctors' Careers.* Routledge, London.

Pedler, M., Boydell, T. and Burgoyne, T. (1988) 'Towards the learning company', *Management Education and Development*, **20** (Part 1, Spring).

Perkin, H. (1989) *The Rise of Professional Society—England since 1880.* Routledge, London.

Personnel Memorandum (1986) PM (86) 11: General Mangement—Arrangements for the Introduction of Performance Related Pay. DHSS, London.

Petchey, R. (1986) 'The Griffiths reorganisation of the National Health Service: Fowlerism by stealth?', *Critical Social Policy*, Issue 17, Autumn.

Pettigrew, A. (1985) *The Awakening Giant—Continuity and Change in ICI.* Blackwell, Oxford.

Pollitt, C. (1984) 'The quality and the width', *Health and Social Services Journal*, **94**, 1415.

Pollitt, C., Harrison, S., Hunter, D. J. and Marnoch, G. (1990) 'No hiding place: on the discomforts of researching the contemporary policy process', *Journal of Social Policy*, **19** (2), 169–90.

Ranson, S. and Stewart, J. (1989) 'Citizenship and government: the challenge for management in the public domain', *Political Studies*, No. XXXVII, 5–24.

Renton, A. (1991) 'NHS waiting list team quits over "crazy" target', *The Independent*, 14 February.

Riseborough, P. A. and Walter, M. (1988) *Management in Health Care.* Butterworth, London.

Robbins, P. (1988) *Management Concepts and Applications* (2nd edn). Prentice Hall International, Englewood Cliffs, New Jersey.

Roberts, H. (1990) *Outcome and Performance in Health Care.* Discussion Paper No. 33, Public Finance Foundation, London.

Robinson, J. and Strong, P. (1987) *Professional Nursing Advice after Griffiths: an interim report.* Nursing Policy Studies Centre, University of Warwick.

Royce, R. G. (1988–89) 'Clinical training for general managers?', *Journal of Management in Medicine*, 3, 17–25.

Scrivens, E. (1988) 'The management of clinicians in the National Health Service', *Social Policy and Administration*, **22** (1), 22–34.

Sheldon, T. (1990) 'Bid to cut waiting lists attacked as "political"', *Health Services Journal*, 9 August.

Sheldon, T. (1991) 'Casualty of a hospital's need for new blood', *Health Service Journal*, 31 January.

Small, N. (1989) *Politics and Planning in the National Health Service.* Open University Press, Milton Keynes.

Smith, G. W. (1984) 'Towards an organisation theory for the NHS', *Health Services Manpower Review*, **19** (3).

Social Services Committee (1988) *The Future of the National Health Service.* Fifth Report, HMSO, London.

Spry, C. (1989) 'A look at the future', in 'Management in the 1990s', *Health Services Management*, **85** (4), August.

Stewart, R. (1985) 'From administration to management', *Health Service Week*, 2 October.

Stewart, R. (1987/8) *Templeton Series on District General Managers: Issue Studies 1–9*. NHSTA, Bristol.

Stewart, J. and Ranson, S. (1988) 'Management in the public domain', *Public Money and Management*, Spring/Summer, 13–19.

Strong, P. and Robinson, J. (1988) *New Model Management: Griffiths and the NHS*. Nursing Policy Studies Centre, University of Warwick.

Tap, H. J. and Shut, F. T. (1987) 'Escaping from the dual organisation: physician self governance', *International Journal of Health Planning and Management*, 2, 229–42.

Thompson, D. (1985) 'District general managers: the fourth coalition?', *Hospital and Health Services Review*, 81 (4) July.

Tolliday, H. (1978) 'Clinical autonomy in the health services', in Jaques, E. (ed.), *Health Services*. Heinemann, London.

Tomlin, Z. (1990) 'RMI pilots fear collapse of clinical directorates', *Health Services Journal*, 14 June.

Turner, B. S. (1987) *Medical Power and Social Knowledge*. Sage, London.

Vroom, V. and Yetton, P. W. (1973) *Leadership and Decision Making*. University of Pittsburgh Press, Pittsburgh.

Wilding, P. (1982) *Professional Power and Social Welfare*. Routledge & Kegan Paul, London.

Wilensky, H. L. (1964) 'The professionalisation of everyone', *American Journal of Sociology*, 70 (2).

Willcocks, L. and Mark, A. (1988) 'Information Technology in the NHS: from strategy to implementation', *Public Money and Management*, Autumn.

Williams, C., Soothill, K. and Barry, J. (1991) 'Love nursing, hate the job', *Health Services Journal*, 101 (5238), 14 February.

Williams, D. *et al.* (1985) 'Piecing together the jigsaw', *Health and Social Services Journal*, 668–70 (30 May).

Winkler, F. (1987) 'Consumerism in health care—beyond the supermarket model', *Policy and Politics*, 15 (1), 1–8.

Woman's Own (1987) Interview with Margaret Thatcher, 31 October.

Yates, J. (1985) 'In search of efficiency. When will the players get involved?', *Health and Social Services Journal*, XCIV (4957), Centre Eight.

Managing social services in the 1990s

Gill Smith and Peter O'Hara

9.1 Introduction

This chapter focuses on social services and suggests that it provides an extreme case of three sets of problems that have yet to be clearly diagnosed in public services organizations. The first has to do with social policy and legitimacy; the second with running service organizations; and the third with stimulating and managing change.

In order to examine the effects of these three problems, the chapter describes the current situation in social services and analyses the management techniques that are available to cope with such situations. Several key issues are highlighted and discussed in detail, notably, the question of management leadership, organizational style and definition of service. A case study of one department is explored to illustrate the use and relationship of management and Information Technology (IT) strategies before concluding with a suggested management agenda for revitalizing social services organizations.

Not only does social services provide a good model to explore a set of general problems encountered by all public services organizations, but it is also passing through a period of uncertainty and stress that began with the Wagner (1987) and Griffiths (1988) reports and unfolded with the National Health Service and Community Care Act (DH, 1989a) and the Children's Act (DH, 1989b) and may be followed by more shocks as the Government applies its many leverages to change the face of personal social services in the 1990s.

9.1.1 HISTORICAL ANTECEDENTS TO CRISIS MANAGEMENT

Within the welfare state, social services is the child among the other family members of housing, education, health and income support, not being established till the 1970s, some 25 years after the others. Still in its early twenties, social services has not been without its growing pains and has yet to clearly define its role, identity and purpose within local government. Rather than exhibit the confidence and exuberance of youth, it sometimes resembles more an organization that finds every step forward painful.

The early exuberance that was ushered in by the Seebhom Report (1968) saw the pulling together of widely disparate services into a single unified department within local government. It was a period of high expectations and confidence at the ability of these new personal social services organizations to bring about fundamental change in individuals' lives and communities. This optimism of the early 1970s, which saw annual growth rates in double figures, was soon overtaken by the dual challenges of the 1980s' 'new realism' in its fundamental questioning of the role of public services and the doubts raised through a series of highly publicized child care tragedies.

Social services holds a unique position within public services organizations as the catch all for the problems left unresolved by other parts of the welfare state. It is the initial point of call for people with complex problems that cannot easily be categorized as health, housing, education, and income related, or perhaps the point of last resort for people who cannot make the system work for them. This is not to ignore the specific statutory duties of social services, but by the nature of its clients this legislative framework is less specific than it might seem and is strongly associated with social need for which there is no simple solution or definition. Thus social services has no specific instruments at its disposal to resolve the problems experienced by its clients; rather it has to rely on its ability to work with other public services organizations, and to deploy its own resources to investigate, advocate and provide support to individuals.

It is perhaps not surprising that social services has not fulfilled the anticipations of its founders. Following on from the post-war tradition, and in line with the corporatist views prevalent at the time, the social services departments within local government were established as large centralized and bureaucratic organizations—a design that was seen as essential to achieve the necessary economies of scale for the delivery of personal social services in preference to alternative models. Departments were initially organized along the functional lines of day care, residential, domiciliary care and fieldwork with a hierarchy of managers within each to control and organize the delivery of services. It took the Barclay Report (1982), and much internal debate, to reassert the primacy for a community centred focus to social services activity, one which needed to be backed by the adequate decentralization of resources and decision-making.

By the late 1980s a new and more responsive form of specialism was asserting itself and the locus of the majority of departments turned to centre on specific client groups within the community—a shift that has had a powerful influence on structures and service within departments (Banford, 1990). However, the growing pains of many reorganizations, government enquiries and public scrutiny in each of the decades that have followed its birth since Seebhom, have done little to help social services assert a distinct and easily identifiable focus for itself, which is understandable given the wide and disparate activities for which departments are responsible.

Many of the services grafted on to social services in the beginning were largely institutional in nature, commanding a large amount of resources that had to be maintained throughout the early years. This slowed down the development of new, more responsive community-based services—a change that was further stalled by the pressures arising from the resource constraints of the 1980s at the same time as major external changes were taking place among its constituents, e.g. rising unemployment, hospital closures, homelessness, sexual abuse, increasing elderly population, etc.

With such a turbulent history its very existence and relevance was to be questioned from both the left and the right. Its role and purpose were first challenged by Brewar and Last (1980), and more recently by Banford (1990). The ability of social services organizations to secure a future by responding positively to the challenges of the 1990s and shaking off the bureaucratic strait-jacket will be severely tested as it grapples with the social policy agenda set by a radical Conservative government and the changes that have occurred in British society as a whole.

9.1.2   INHERENT PROBLEMS AND DILEMMAS

Because of its requirement to take a holistic view of human/social need (and achieve meaningful outcomes for individuals), social services has an immediate difficulty in the contested terrain of social policy. Moreover, given the range of needs to which it is required to respond, it has an inherent difficulty in articulating what it is and what it is trying to achieve. Further difficulties in managing the organization are caused by the anomalous position of social services in the governance framework (Fig. 9.1), whereby it is relatively autonomous and free of central control, but relatively powerless and positioned at the confluence of some awkward flows of funding which bring it into the battlefield of local government expenditure and inter-agency collaboration. Additionally the range of organizations with varying degrees of responsibility for community care give rise to a complex set of inter-agency relationships which departments have to strive to maintain in pursuit of their objectives.

Social services is an awkward entity in governance terms, caught in the crossfire of socio-economic change and political ideology. It is typically servicing client needs arising from human disadvantage, but with no specific instruments to address underlying reasons for disadvantage. Additionally, it tends to a bureaucratic model, which creates inherent stress and conflict, excites external criticism and adverse comparison with the private sector, while limiting its responsiveness to change.

The current legislation has done little to address the underlying problems of social services organizations. Further demands and expectations have been created, without providing the negotiating framework, information, or resources to fully satisfy them.

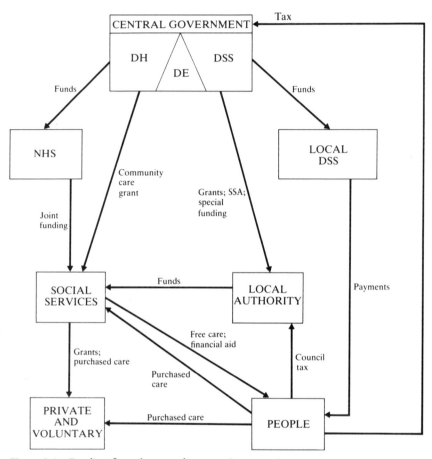

Figure 9.1   Funding flows between key agencies

As Banford (1990) has pointed out, there has been a recurring theme inhibiting the development of social services organizations since their founding. Continued resource pressure, an emphasis on informal care based on various social policy models of the role of the family, a strengthening of a pluralistic model of welfare provision, together with a hostility to public bureaucracies and a determination to apply market disciplines to welfare even when these are less efficient.

We can add to this list the challenges that all organizations need to address, but which are particularly critical to social services at this period in its development. These arise from changes in the external environment, the nature of the organization and is culture, human resource management and the changing nature of communications technology. Such issues establish an agenda for social services management to fulfil as guardians of an organization's future.

9.2   Environmental change: the management challenge

In many respects it could be argued that social services has been moving towards community care since its birth and the recent legislation is a reassertion of its primary role within local government (DH, 1988). However, the ideology that underpins this initiative is firmly grounded in a free market approach to welfare provision. The ability of social services organizations to turn this initiative on its head and achieve meaningful change for the people it serves is the main challenge of the 1990s.

Recent legislation has once again brought social services into the arena of public debate. However, clarity of the debate has been impeded by two factors: the failure, as yet, to establish the social policy goals as a key element of the debate, and the unresolved questions surrounding recent child abuse events.

Social policy determines the value system on which decisions are made and against which facts are analysed. The value system, which seems to underpin current initiatives in health and social services, places an emphasis on the citizen as consumer and purseholder, with public services acting as agents for rationing and allocating a finite level of resources. Though social services is foremost in championing a move from some of the paternalistic and bureaucratic attitudes associated with welfare provision, it is also concerned that a purely cost-led approach can preclude proper consideration of social need and models of care. This point can be illustrated by examining some of the arguments in recent years.

The White Paper, *Caring for People* (DHSS, 1989), stated that gross expenditure had risen by 60 per cent between 1980 and 1988, although, with respect to community care, 'Progress has, however, been slower and less even than the government would like . . .'. Ironically, while social services departments were espousing the importance of locally based community services, the number of elderly persons in residential accommodation increased by over 100 per cent, from 52 438 to 109 607, between 1979 and 1986—a growth pattern that has carried on through the 1980s and early 1990s causing a cost explosion that has pushed community care to the forefront after a decade of indifference.

Failure to react to demographic trends and provide alternative resources in a timely manner has created a situation for which there are no quick fixes. The inefficiencies and lack of clear responsibility for planning and responding to needs was highlighted by the Audit Commission (1986); as they noted at the time, 'The one option that is not tenable is to do nothing about present financial, organizational and staffing arrangements.'

One form of popular opinion, propounded by some, argues that no one is really deprived in modern Britain, and that there are plenty of opportunities for people who are prepared to take them. Social services should, therefore, service the small number who are in real need.

This belies a mountain of statistics which show an increasing demand for the wide range of services provided by departments. Single local authority studies highlight major levels of unmet need in the community, e.g. '16.5% of people have long-term health problems or difficulties with daily living' (London Borough of Camden, 1988).

Dean (1990) challenged a claim by a former Secretary of State (John Moore) that 'absolute poverty' has been abolished in the UK. Those in poverty (having 50 per cent or less of the average national income) number 10 million; homelessness has been exacerbated by the 2 year postponement of community care funding (which would have added £15 to the average poll tax bill); and the Social Fund, justified on the grounds that it reduces 'welfare dependency' of people, has increased the levels of deprivation in many communities.

The absence of a more positive public image for social services is in part due to the lack of an open debate on the social policy issues facing the UK throughout much of the 1980s. The marginalization of such issues as poverty could be cynically ascribed to the fact that not all have been losers during the decade of opportunity. As Dean states, the average couple are 23 per cent better off, but in contrast every retired couple is losing £18.95 a week with the abolition of the earnings related index of pension in 1980 (for 1990 alone that represented a 'saving' of £4 billion). However, the inability of social services departments to stimulate debate on the social questions with which they grapple daily says much for the state of those organizations today.

9.2.1   COMMUNITY CARE: THE OPPORTUNITY TO CHANGE

The current legislative changes, Community Care and the Children Act, seem to have been framed by a government hostile to public services in general, and local government in particular. However, it is a framework which endorses a historical commitment to locally based services and provides the opportunity for departments to become key shapers in developing responses to the many issues of social policy that remain to be addressed in Britain during the 1990s. The question is whether the existing social services model can be redesigned to provide a more appropriate range of relevant and responsive quality services beyond the 1990s. It is a question of survival since governments of this decade may choose alternative vehicles to achieve their social policy goals and increasingly marginalize the largest organization in personal social services in Europe.

It would be useful at this stage to summarize the key elements of the recent legislative changes affecting social services in the 1990s as a prelude to a more extensive analysis of the organizational models and approaches that could be adopted.

The basic requirements of the National Health Service and Community Care Act (DH, 1989a) are that social services should:

- maintain and publish a wider range of appropriate service available to the community

- stimulate alternative local sources of service provision rather than be direct delivery services
- assess people's needs and develop packages of care that are designed to optimize client choice, participation and personal achievement
- demonstrate that services are targeted to the needy and subject to proper financial management and quality control.

The Children Act (DH, 1989b) embodies the same general principles but adds specific directives on:

- more focused use of the courts to address children's needs while preserving family ties and parental responsibility
- duties towards children at risk, and their families
- provision for under-5s, under-8 school children on holidays, and young people who leave care.

Such changes, far from being a radical departure from the past, provide social services the opportunity to move along a path of continuity, building on its models of good practice and value base as an organization. The legislative framework reasserts the key elements of a community, externally focused public services with:

- an emphasis on needs-led, rather than service-led approach
- a holistic view of people's situations, including recognition of needs for education, leisure and employment opportunities for people being cared for
- recognition of people's rights and the legitimate voice of family and friends (including, importantly, their rights to be supported as carers)
- a belief that prevention is more effective than intervention
- recognition of the need for effective structures to improve multi-agency working, including training for courts, special roles (e.g. guardian ad litem), obligation to notify (e.g. when children leave care), joint responsibilities
- the importance of ensuring and enabling client participation and empowering their roles in service planning
- the need to define standards and improve the management of quality.

However, there are two main tasks facing managers at this juncture in the history of social services. Firstly, to satisfy themselves about their key concerns, e.g. to clearly establish the boundaries between statutory duties and permissive powers within a coherent policy framework, and hence their scope for manoeuvre. Secondly, to identify, derive and enact appropriate strategies for change that will enable them to respond positively to the challenges they face and ensure that social services is a powerful influencer in the shaping of social policy.

9.2.2   COMMUNITY CARE: THE RESPONSE TO DATE

At the end of 1991 there had been three main areas of activity in responding to the legislative changes: firstly, a debate on the principles of the Acts; secondly, a search for defining and acquiring adequate information systems; and, finally, disagreements on the implementation and funding arrangements. The last is currently a lost cause with the Government failing to adequately elucidate how the transfer of funding will take place and its last-minute delay in implementing community care from 1991 to 1993.

The debate on principles is also highly contentious within and outside social services. Some argue strongly that the Community Care and the Children Acts are very different, requiring different organizational responses. Others have argued the common aspects of both pieces of legislation, and propose service strategies that will position departments as responsive organizations able to provide appropriate care in a range of situations.

A variation of the twin organization argument can also be identified in the debate over the purchaser/provider approach to care management and services. How far the coercion towards a mixed provision approach will occur is still unclear. The level of buyer and supplier roles that a social services department could theoretically perform, ranges from active promotion of the private and voluntary sector, through outsourcing all service needs and providing funding/ training incentives, to adopting a detached stance of purchaser and enforcer of standards (or even to steering contracts towards their own staff or opted-out services). How this potential conflict is to be squared by those proposing separate organizations for children and family services has yet to be answered. However, the separate purchaser/provider model envisaged by the Government is being pursued despite warnings (Flynn and Commons, 1990) of the dangers and constraints that tight contracts would impose on social services departments.

The causes of such divisions in approaches are not hard to find. Social services departments embrace a wide range of people trying to address a multitude of needs. The communication problems, boundary issues and wide spectrum of values lead to conflict.

As Kouzes and Mico (1979) point out, handling conflict is an important area of management activity, and managing conflict at the boundaries of domains is something which Harrow and Willcocks (1990) describe as characteristic of public services management.

An example drawn from our case study will help illuminate the inherent tensions within social services organizations. In 1988 the London Borough of Camden social services department commissioned an IT strategy study using consultants from a large 'blue chip' company. The primary aim was to help the department elucidate its current stance and direction, in response to impending major legislative change and internal pressures, and identify the systems (human, organizational and computer based) that would be needed to support its aims into the 1990s. Extensive debate, at times highly emotive, about values, policy, practice, professionalism, structure, rules, responsibilities, internal conflicts and contributions were stirred up and brought to the top of management's agenda by the strategy study's focus on the primary objectives, critical success factors and key performance indicators which needed to be elucidated to facilitate the organization's moving forward and facing the challenges of the future with strength.

It appeared that the exposure of the boundaries of conflict, coupled with high anxiety about futures, was blocking the necessary actions and rethinking that were needed to address those very futures. A particular reluctance to embrace aspects of planning and performance was exhibited due to its connotations and association with a 'business culture' despite the importance of these elements to the future well-being of the organization.

The examples from other case studies known to the authors demonstrate the tendency for bureaucratic work environments to create patterns and behaviours in which 'abilities function as inadequacies or blind spots', Merton (1940). Much reframing of the thinking within social services is required in the 1990s if, as organizations, they are to reassert their role and overcome the current blockages that are preventing them from articulating their primary objectives of measuring their performance in terms of 'human outcomes'.

Finally, the progress in selecting and developing appropriate information systems to support the organizational changes envisaged by the legislation has yet to prove successful. As with other organizations, a technology-led approach appears to have been adopted, emphasizing the acquisition of hardware with the objective of automating discrete parts of current operations. Little attention has been paid to the strategic nature of such investment and the importance of proper design of systems to provide relevant tools to staff who have to be organized around new methods of working to support community care.

9.3   Management techniques available to social services

9.3.1   DEFINING AN APPROPRIATE ORGANIZATIONAL MODEL

Hadley and Young (1990) give an interesting analysis of the perceived short-comings of administrative (or bureaucratic) organizations. They suggest that four alternative styles are emerging for social services. The first aims to cut public services provision to the bone; the second to prune back to a core specialist services; and the third to create business units that are financially viable and efficient. Only the fourth alternative, the responsive organization, appears to be pro-active rather than reactive.

The range and severity of issues confronting social services indicates an urgent need for management to review their organization, its purpose and vitality, even without the stimulus of legislative change.

In times of pressure, there is a tendency for organizations to adopt attitudes that are essentially reactive: to try harder, and cling to past glories, to base plans on perceptions that are already out of date (and sometimes corporate performance figures that are years old), or to embrace uncritically a current panacea, such as is apparently offered by the private sector management model.

In these circumstances, it would not be surprising if social services resorted to the residual, defensive or business paradigms identified by Hadley and Young (1990), even though this could be seen as fighting tomorrow's battles with yesterday's weapons.

To take the fourth option identified by Hadley and Young, and set out to create a responsive organization will require the courage and innovation needed in 'breakthrough' situations. It poses a radical challenge to social services to rediscover and refine the best of public services management.

It is undisputed that the area of social care and policy is highly political, but the ability of social services to influence the debate is first and foremost a question of how effective its organizations are. The challenges are there, but

> implementing changes that are required in this sphere is primarily a managerial task. It is about regrouping a set of resources, money, buildings and people in a new pattern of services by a given date. And that is a managerial job.
>
> (Warner, 1990)

To do this managers in social services need to develop the necessary knowledge, understanding and skills to:

- define policy and practice
- articulate social theory and policy
- develop strategic thinking
- regularly scan the external environment
- apply relevant techniques to improve quality and add value to their organizations
- apply relevant measures of the organizations' performances
- manage change and overcome bureaucratic resistance.

Social services managers need to address these challenges as well as managing the more traditional competencies of the management curriculum, e.g. budgeting, industrial relations.

Handy et al., (1988) suggests that 'business education is not, by itself, a qualification for management, only a prelude to it'. In addition, social services organizations should have an explicit strategy and means of implementing an ongoing management development programme: the personal development of individuals through experience, training, education and secondment to better fulfil their current or next job. The required skills span a wide range of knowledge, classified as technical, human and conceptual and require practice through placing the individual early on in 'situations where responsibility may exceed competence' (which will require a high degree of trust).

That management education in this country has been 'too little, too late, for too few' (Handy *et al.*, 1988) is also reflected in organizations like social services. The lack of management skills was considered so dire that the Government announced a £2 million programme in 1990 to support departments that initiated development programmes. At the same time, a self-development package for social services managers, Transitions, was released by the Department of Health. While these initiatives were welcome, the scale of the problem would lead one to conclude that it was also too little, too late.

9.3.2   THE IMPORTANCE OF STRATEGY

The key management responsibilities and required skills for carrying social services into the community care era revolve round developing and sustaining organizational strategy. The aim should be to build a responsive organization, one that is characterized by the receptiveness, willingness and capability to make sense of change and to do those things that tend towards real solutions. Key factors in building a responsive service organization can be summarized as

- a strong vision of success based on principles of quality and value
- nurturing of strategic thinking and creativity within the organization
- support structures for pathfinders, decision makers and implementors
- sustaining shared values of the organization through enabling styles of management
- positively approaching and resolving conflict
- adopting risk analysis to support risk-taking.

Many of the issues of strategy in public services organizations were discussed in Chapter 2. Here we shall discuss two aspects, as they affect social services. The first is an example of a strategic planning framework (Fig. 9.2) and the second of an issue management model (Figs 9.3a and 9.3b). The planning model is adapted from Bryson (1988) and the issue model from Willcocks (1991a).

The recommended contingency approach requires that we address strategic issues within the framework of an overall plan for the organization. The first task is to establish direction (Bryson's steps 1–3). We have mentioned the use of aims, objectives and critical success factors (CSFs) to represent what social services is and where it is going (an example is included here as Fig. 9.4). Once the direction is established, management can begin to identify means to measure progress in critical areas. These are the key performance indicators (KPIs), which, because they are central to the organization's success, will be few and subject to change as priorities alter over time.

The value of the technique is that it invites participants to question assumptions, ambiguities and contradictions, seek consensus and gain insights. CSFs represent issues that directly affect the achievement of objectives, but consideration of each CSF will yield additional strategic issues or contributing factors, e.g. situations, risks, weaknesses and obstacles that must be addressed if the chosen organizational direction is to be achieved.

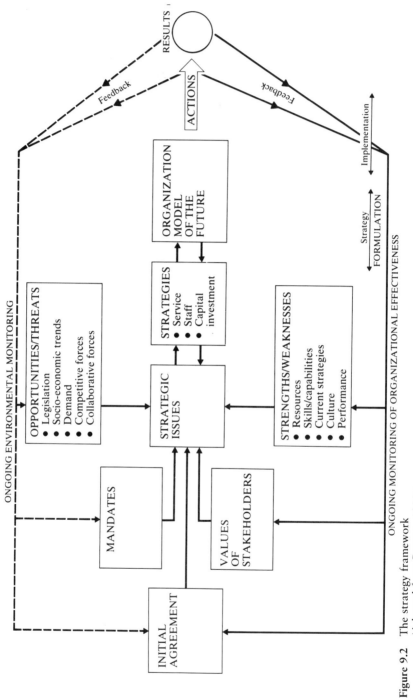

Figure 9.2 The strategy framework
(Adapted from Bryson, 1988.)

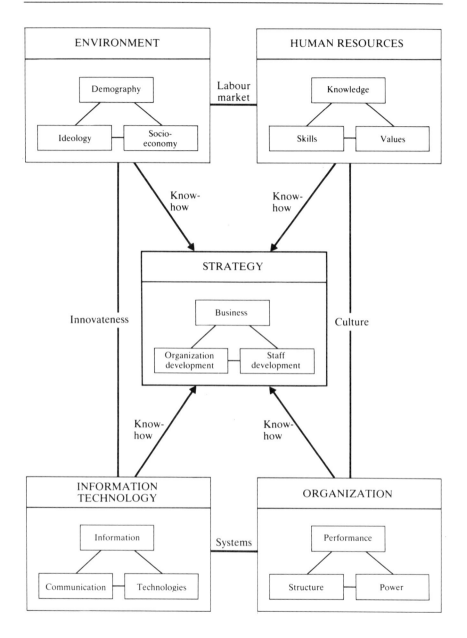

Figure 9.3a   Issue management—the process

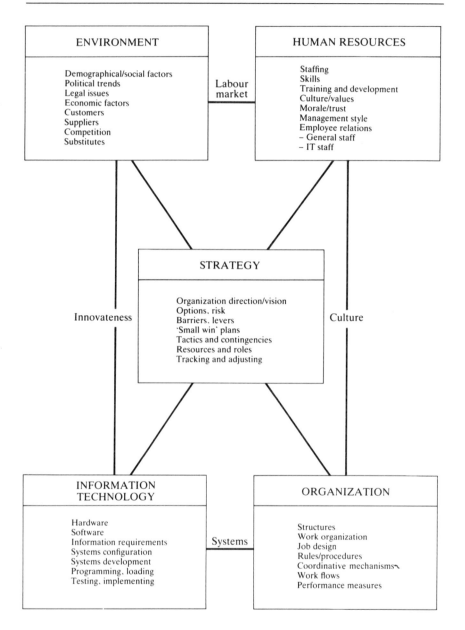

Figure 9.3b Issue management—the content

AIM	OBJECTIVE	CSF
To empower individuals to seek and gain the safety, help and opportunities needed to fulfil their potential and sustain quality of life.	1. To provide the means for the elderly to live safely at home or in a homely setting 2. To protect children in need and young people in trouble, as far as possible without recourse to the court 3. To encourage parental responsibility and nurture caring relationships within families 4. To provide a range of community facilities to stimulate the isolated and relieve their carers 5. To provide help, advice, training and support in a pre-emptive way, to minimize the need for intervention 6. To foster multi-agency links for the better support of clients and sharing of information	*General CSFs for a public services organization* 1. Understanding of needs and range of ways to address them 2. Access to resources (direct or indirect) to mobilize services 3. Effective channels to receive, assess and direct clients to appropriate services 4. Acceptable models for assessment and targeting of resources (so that clients know the eligibility rules, practitioners believe in them, funders approve the investment) 5. Goodwill of other agencies in the field *CSFs specific to Social Services at this time* 6. People committed to responsiveness and constant search for improvement 7. Organization and mechanisms to harness new attitudes and show results 8. Ability to project results and obtain confidence of public and influential bodies

Figure 9.4   Techniques to chart organizational direction

Bryson's next steps (4 and 5) are to do a strengths, weaknesses, opportunities and threats (SWOT) analysis, often represented as a grid:

(+) Strengths	(−) Weaknesses	Internal analysis
(+) Opportunities	(−) Threats	External analysis

The general idea is to maximize strengths, address weaknesses, and hence overcome threats and achieve opportunities. However, factors can often be linked in more complex ways. For instance, a social services organization may have a core team of competent professionals (planners, social workers, advocates, etc.), but its very strength causes weakness in the corporate culture—a tendency for the organization to polarize into two camps, with a corresponding threat to shared values, communications and team work. SWOT analyses, like CSFs, represent issues which directly affect the organization's well-being: even strengths and opportunities need to be managed to best effect, and not allowed to create an imbalance in the organization. Once again close consideration of SWOT analyses will often yield further issues: for instance, the reason for a polarization between two sets of staff may be the reward system, a difference in management styles applied (e.g. more freedom for professional staff) or even differential access to favoured communication channels (e.g. representation at senior management meetings).

At this stage, there will be lists of issues, but we still need to use the strategic issue scanning process shown in Figs 9.3a and 9.3b to ensure completeness. Particularly where opportunities or threats are strongly suggested, there is a tendency to focus on the obvious area (typically those that have been significant in the past) and miss an important contributory or facilitating factor. For instance, there are probably few social services organizations who yet fully realize the potential of systems to shape their future to support service delivery and how essential they are to fulfilling community care goals.

Bryson's steps 7 and 8 consist of an iterative process of working through issues, guided by the 'vision of success', to arrive at and test possible scenarios for action. Since this is an incremental approach, the chosen actions will be small enough to allow timely feedback and refinement of the strategic planning process, so that adjustments can be made to maintain direction even in situations of unpredictable change.

9.3.3   ORGANIZATION STRUCTURES TO FACILITATE STRATEGY

The responsibilities of management to nurture an appropriate organizational model is generally accepted. Much of the considerable body of work on this subject is still based on the original findings of Burns and Stalker (1966), who over 30 years ago introduced a dual classification of organizations into mechanistic (stable, control-oriented) and organic (evolving, informal).

The mechanistic model suits organizations which, because of size and uniformity of operation, need a high degree of central control and emphasize process. The organic model is appropriate in organizations seeking a dynamic response to a range of challenges and needing to emphasize outcomes. The nature of social services activity would tend to push it towards an organic structure.

The relationship between structure and work flows within an organization was demonstrated by Kilmann (1987). Analysing the tasks in a process can show three different patterns of dependency. Sequential task flows involve a series of steps; reciprocal flows involve frequent interaction between tasks to produce useful output; and pooled flows represent the situation where tasks can be carried out in parallel, sharing information at any point to create 'added value'.

The optimum organizational structure involves defining units that encompass sequential and reciprocal task flows, and provide the means to facilitate pooled flows between units. However, these arrangements for operational efficiency will not support the organization in all situations, and will become increasingly 'out of touch' as the environment changes. To ensure effectiveness, Kilmann advocates a 'collateral structure': a potential shadow organization that can be deployed to address dynamic situations and can even take over, and instigate restructuring activities, when required.

The collateral structure is a set of informal groups (task forces, cross-functional planning teams, special interest groups, performance evaluation units) derived by periodic sampling of staff expertise, interest and desire to be involved in missions that arise in the organization. Kilmann describes the partnership between operational units and the collateral structure as the Problem Management Organization: 'the best 2 punch combination for aligning strategy and structure in today's world'. Such an approach was adopted by a number of social services departments, familiar to the authors, in response to the challenges of the Community Care and the Children Acts.

9.3.4   USING IT STRATEGIES TO STIMULATE CHANGE

Information Technology (IT) has the potential to deliver immense benefit through its production and service processes. It can also act as a change agent, by enriching debate and facilitating the move to states of greater organizational capability. Its prime role is to make available the information that enables people to take responsibility. We shall call this informating the organization. Willcocks describes how it comes about through the creation of an Information Systems (IS) culture (Willcocks, 1991b). This is very different from automating processes, and represents a stage in the maturation of IT where, communications technology (computers, networks, etc.) are used to increase the capabilities of people rather than as number crunchers. It is particularly important in a service organization like social services to find the most appropriate application of technology to add value and improve productivity.

Part of the approach is to use IT to initiate debate, champion the change process, and involve stakeholders, so that the organization is moved forward on the back, or at the forefront, of new strategic information systems. This approach will provide opportunities for IT to assist in identifying task flows and dysfunctional work boundaries. It can act as a facilitator in feeding back issues, and supporting initiatives to address problems. Finally, in participative development of new systems, IT creates collateral structures (user teams) which can provide cross-functional views and new insights into the organization's future.

If IT is to play a significant role as an enabling strategy for social services, there will need to be sufficient funding for quality staff, freeing of user time to participate in systems development, and training/education.

Investment is the means to improve current or future capability and hence sustain or enable cost-effective growth. In the private sector, IT investment has been variously justified through cost reduction (e.g. enabling labour displacement, increased productivity or better control), through better products and services (e.g. improving design, timeliness and customer responsiveness), and through 'return on management' (e.g. encouraging better planning, decision-making and organizing). These add up to competitive advantage, which explains the continuing investment, currently running at approximately 0.9 per cent of turnover in large organizations (over 1000 employees) and up to 13 per cent of turnover in small ones (under 200 employees).

Social services is arguably one of the most neglected areas of IT investment in local government and hence starts from a strong bargaining position, even without the exhortations of the White Paper. The average spend on IT in social services in 1991 was estimated at £100 000 with an average of three staff employed to support implementation (CIPFA/ADSS, 1990); this represents less than 1 per cent of the average department's budget, which is far from adequate given the level of investment required.

It is a strong candidate for all the benefits of computerization listed above, suggesting a return on investment will be impressive. In particular, IT should provide improved design of services, enhanced productivity and increased effectiveness through use of information and tools.

In order to protect this investment, the use of IT will need to be managed. It is essential:

- that IT works closely within the strategic framework
- that IT builds on its legitimacy with stakeholders by identifying points for maximum return on investment, and providing balanced programmes of development
- that IT provides returns for management and staff by enhancing skills, promoting vision of success and delivering value
- that IT specialists develop diagnostic and facilitative skills throughout the organization
- that IT has sufficient revenue budgets as well as capital investment (e.g. to cover training).

Good IT management will need to be reinforced by measuring the contribution of IT to the quality of services delivered to clients.

Considering its cost and the considerable influence on an organization's performance, it is a strange fact that most IT projects are not formally justified, and even fewer are reviewed to establish whether they achieved the expected benefits. This apparently tolerant attitude is not in the interests of either the organization or IT: it creates risk of over-reaction in either direction (unjustified euphoria or understated credit) and it reduces the value of IT's educational role in helping the organization focus on CSFs and KPIs.

However, accountancy based measures of value will usually understate IT's contribution. They can reflect increases in productivity or efficacy of cost control measures, but they are of little use in the wider assessment of the enabling effects of IT on skills development, management effectiveness and the achievement of strategic goals. Strassman (1985) argues that 'whether a society is productive or not can ultimately be determined only by consumers' and suggests a market assessment of the business package (a strategy and its IT component). It should not be costed except in the context of business planning and delivery: for instance, it is inappropriate to cost e-mail as a 'consumer item' when it is part of a strategy to improve an organization's communications, which may in fact, involve changes in roles, organization structure and management style.

Similarly, costing welfare benefit systems *per se*, without acknowledging that the strategy is to create 'information middlemen' from social workers and protect clients from time-consuming, costly and depressing treks around a variety of agencies, would be to deny the system's enabling benefits.

9.3.5   SUSTAINING AN IS CULTURE WITHIN AN ORGANIC STRUCTURE

Willcocks (1991b) argues the need for IT usage to become embedded in organizational values and know-how. In addition to the good management practice described above, effective IT usage needs to be supported by attention to six broad areas: strategic and project management; human resource planning; design and development; job design and work organization: environment and workstation; and the politics track. Given the current level of underdevelopment of IT within social services, close attention will need to be given to all these elements by management wishing to ensure that relevant systems are implemented to support the organization through the 1990s. This will require a shift of emphasis away from current thinking, which focuses attention on the technology, towards strategies that emphasize information and the systems of working for the organization to be responsive to clients.

9.4   Managing a service organization: strategies for social services

Service organizations exist to satisfy customer needs—efficiently enough to make good use of resources and avoid criticism from their stakeholders, and effectively enough to sustain demand. The essential process of a service organization can be illustrated diagrammatically, as in Fig. 9.5.

Whereas both efficiency and effectiveness are important, the approach involved with each concerns different attitudes and practices, and management

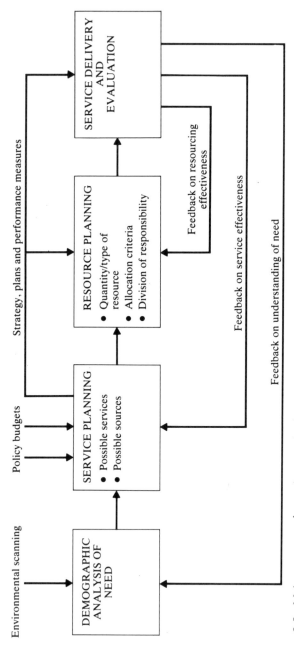

Figure 9.5 Main processes of a service organization

needs to make explicit trade-offs and to provide clear guidelines. Table 9.1 illustrates the differing perspectives of both.

Table 9.1   Characteristics of efficiency and effectiveness

Aspect	Efficiency model	Effectiveness model
Main principal	Conversion of A to B in the most cost-effective manner (process driven)	Achievement of a desired outcome (which may not be completely defined at the outset)
Critical success factors	Precision, standardization, tight control, 'systems' approach	Understanding of desired outcome (empathy with customer), flexibility, skill, commitment to task
Process	Reductionist approach: break work into small units and concentrate on rationalizing the process, reducing variability	'Big picture' approach: consider units of work in relation to the whole, evolve or adapt methods using toolkit
Inputs	Inputs are selected on the basis of conformity and contribution to reduction of work	Inputs are accepted if they contribute to the desired outcome, even though they may be highly variable and even problematic
Outputs	Outputs are specified in quantitative terms, e.g. 'a system which will process 1000 invoices a day'	Outputs are specified in qualitative terms, e.g. 'a system which provides the capability to reduce outstanding debt'
Benefits	Benefits are expressed in terms of conversion ratios, e.g. reduced input, increased output, price/performance, profit	Benefits are expressed as value achieved in terms of desired outcome, increased capability, position, opportunity
Control	Control is process-based. Metrics are often used to control work within parameters of acceptable time, cost and defect rate	Control is outcome oriented. Interim results are evaluated for possible outcome, to allow work to be steered towards high-value options
Management approach	Narrow focus, short time horizons. Tends towards mechanistic solutions	Wider focus, longer time scales. Tends to more innovative, socio-technical solutions

Being primarily a service organization, social services departments need to be continually addressing four main questions.

1 What needs are social services aiming to address?

The nature of social services activities results in a lot of talking about people's needs without applying the analytical clarity necessary to address this fundamental question. Service organizations, in general, typically spend a great deal of time monitoring the needs of their customers, since needs are not always obvious and shift frequently in response to external events and changes in market perception. In social services a model based on client groups has been widely adopted against which need levels are prescribed and services planned.

There is a danger, when defining the organization's purpose, of trying to short cut needs analysis, and define requirements for a service instead. This is exacerbated by the difficulty of categorizing needs in a social services context, arising as they do from the complex social problems presented by some clients.

2 What resources do we have for meeting needs?

The absence of a viable set of need categories is an immediate problem. Ideally, we want fairly high-level statements which enable us to look at a wide range of resourcing options, e.g. 2000 people will require a level of support for daily living tasks, due to age, infirmity, disability or mental health problems. Statements of this sort encourage consideration of the choices with respect to resources, thus facilitating examination of more strategic options for meeting requirements.

3 How shall we control resources?

Management control incorporates the acquisition, management, allocation and evaluation of resources. It is common practice to divorce the first two aspects from the last two. For instance, line managers acquire and manage staff, but functional managers deploy them. For community care, a similar model has been suggested: resource managers provide and care managers draw upon resources. There are many issues in this approach, such as who will take the credit (or blame) for a particular performance level. There are also potential strengths to the approach, in creating flexible task-based structures, that have been shown to work in organizations that have a strong sense of purpose and a supportive culture.

4 How can we measure performance?

The ultimate test of performance has to be 'satisfying the customer'. The manner in which social services performs also needs to be measured to ensure that resources are effectively deployed, that decisions can be justified and that commitment can be focused on a constant improvement of services.

There is a danger of confusing planning and research data with performance (results) data, and creating a monster that does little to guide practitioners through the everyday dilemma of 'how to do better' for this client or group. To keep a clear focus on the purpose of performance measurement, it should be incorporated in the culture of the organization through such means as quality management intiatives and a commitment to define and review what each part of the organization is trying to achieve, using such tools as objectives, critical success factors, and key performance indicators.

9.4.1 STIMULATING AND MANAGING CHANGE: THE NEED FOR STRATEGY

It is commonly accepted that managers not only control the organization, but do so within some 'grand plan'. A coherent and flexible strategy is particularly vital for steering the organization during times of change, when the danger is to respond reactively, resulting in the organization losing its sense of direction.

For our purposes, we shall adopt a pragmatic definition of strategy; the consistent direction adopted by an organization over a long period of time. We shall define 'policy' as the set of rules applied in achieving the stated direction, the 'what to do' and 'how to do' model for organizational behaviour.

Ohmae (1983) provides a more visionary description of strategy as an 'idiosyncratic mode of thinking in which company, customers and competition merge in a dynamic interaction out of which a comprehensive set of objectives and plans for action eventually crystallises'. This 'way of thinking' appears to be a better start point for organizations that want to emulate Japanese success than the usual practice of importing 'intellectual products' such as 'Just in Time' supply and quality circles. It is also close to the paradigm of the responsive organization.

9.4.2 DEVELOPING STRATEGIC SERVICE UNITS

In order to ensure the strategic direction of the organization as a whole it is important to establish, firstly, the level and size of units that can have a discrete set of responsibilities. Such units should be able to plan, manage resources and serve a market, with relative independence from the rest of the organization.

This concept was introduced by Porter (1985), who defined the strategic business unit (SBU): a discrete business line within the organization which serves a particular market and has distinct primary activities (though sometimes sharing support activities with other SBUs).

In social services, we should redefine SBU as strategic service unit (SSU): a discrete set of services which serve a particular client set or 'market' and which therefore has a cohesive set of primary activities. This is fundamentally different from the current shape of social services organizations, which are divided into functional areas to serve client groups. The concept of SSUs is closer to the original ideals of 'community social services' envisaged in the early seventies, avoiding stigmatization, and employing a more holistic approach to service development.

It is not easy to define SSUs, partly because a high level of professionalism and inter-agency working creates and maintains current boundaries associated with client groups and specialisms. However, we would suggest that an emphasis on 'client markets' gives us two potential ways to group services, which are not based on purely descriptive qualities, e.g. age, disability, etc.

1 Services designed to respond to a client situation. Such a situation might include:
- poor physical health
- housing or financial problems
- conflict or breakdown
- discharge from hospital or institution
- special needs or heavy dependency
- frailty
- disability
- emotional problems
- economic deprivation.

2 Services designed to respond to need/capability. Such needs might include:
- support with living tasks
- nurturing
- social skills
- extended capability and confidence
- protection and security.

A person's situation can give rise to a variety of needs around which services can be organized, providing focus and direction in achieving meaningful outcomes. This approach provides interesting possibilities for scoping services around mixed client groups. For instance, one permutation of needs/situation includes clients who are temporarily in need of intensive support due to physical or emotional damage, discharge from hospital or absence of a carer. A service combination of this kind would concentrate on normalizing the situation, extending the client's capabilities and finding long-term solutions that provide more independence and stability.

We can begin to use this approach to provide a more strategically focused model for responding to the challenges of the 1990s. Figure 9.6 illustrates a possible matrix of the 'needs/situation' of a client of social services and develops appropriate responses for a cluster of client sets or markets. It is also a challenge to existing professional models of managing 'individual cases' and moves the organization on towards managing 'care services' for a wide range of people in the community. Such a model provides a means for social services to move away from labelled 'client groups' towards a more responsive and flexible organization designed around SSUs.

(a) Diagnostic model (to derive client/service clusters)

Needs/situation	Poor health	Housing problem	Family breakdown	Income/ financial
Domestic help	×			
Social skills			×	×
Protection	×		×	
Advice/information	×	×		×
Mobility assistance	×			×
⋮				

(b) Resource template (based on client/service clusters)

Client set/ services units	Transport	Adaptations	Home help	Counselling
A1	×	×	×	
A2	×			×
A3	×	×		
⋮				

Figure 9.6   Client needs/situation

This approach gives a clearer focus to social services activities and presents major challenges to organizations that are rigid through their functional focus. It requires a more flexible organization that can respond to the changes in people's lives, and ensures that resources are directed to achieving particular outcomes dependent on a client's needs/situation at particular times. Such a model can facilitate the power of the client by putting control in his or her hands to identify the type, range and level of services required.

Defining and developing SSUs within the social services will contribute to asserting the need for social policy and planning within local government as a whole. It will enable performance to be measured in terms of 'people outcomes', e.g. improved mobility, increased economic activity, independence, etc., instead of the normal measurements of 'process outcomes', e.g. economy, efficiency, etc.

The effectiveness of social services as a whole can be measured in terms of social policy goals, thus:

$$\frac{\text{Change in client set}}{\text{SSU input}} = \text{Effectiveness}$$

It will mean reshaping social services to enable it to respond to client 'market' needs in a more flexible and distinctive way. The dominant profession within departments, social work, will itself have to change its role from that of gate-keeper of resources to that of a more distinct service provider within each SSU.

Figure 9.7 suggests levels of the social services organization where strategies may be appropriate (including cross-functional, or enabling strategies). Figure 9.8 shows Porter's concept of the SBU as a unit within which activities can be analysed for their contribution in adding value to the outcome, applied to social services in the form of SSUs.

9.4.3   NURTURING A RESPONSIVE CULTURE

We have noted that social services management are facing external threats to their organizations, internal dissensions on the way forward and a large agenda of change.

There is a paradox that moving to the responsive organization will encourage managers to develop skills, wisdom and leadership, but without sufficient of any of these from the outset the move cannot be accomplished. We shall conclude this section by looking at some of the ways to give leverage to management skills and tide the organization over until the move is well under way.

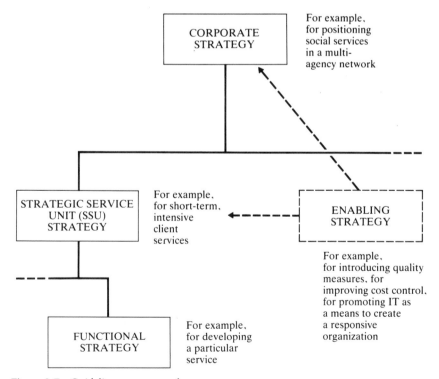

Figure 9.7 Guidelines on scope of strategy

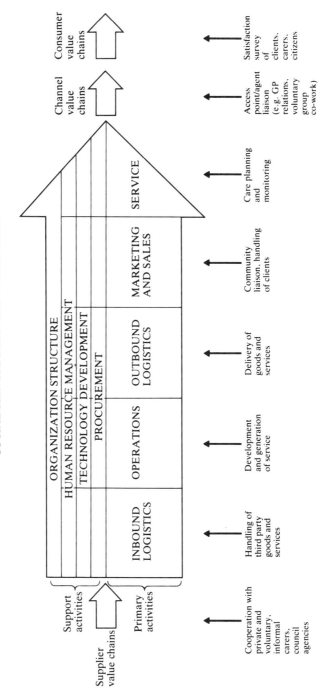

Figure 9.8 Value chain concepts applied to social services

Firstly, competent managers need to be deployed and recruited for those parts of the organization where change is likely to be greatest, most rapid or most resisted.

Secondly, a management style needs to be fostered that focuses on performance measurement in an open creative manner so that attention is concentrated on improving the quality of services by all staff.

Thirdly, management should actively promote success within and outside the organization in order to build confidence and commitment to the change processes.

Finally, management should be supportive of staff embarking on the identified changes in order to overcome resistance positively. The 'small win' approach will help, but it is also vital for management to be sensitive to positive or negative trends, using situations as they arise to unblock resistance or encourage new norms. Moss Kanter (1989) describes renewal initiatives in USA organizations and change mechanisms used to overcome resistance.

9.5   Developing a responsive IT strategy: Case study 1986–1991

Our case study, on the use of IT for attaining strategic leverage within social services, is drawn from the experience of the London Borough of Camden social services department during a five-year period. Metaphors to express the 'ebb and flow' of their incrementalist approach are borrowed from Lynch and Kordis (1989) to illuminate the key elements from this case study.

Wave 1: Glimpsing the future

In 1986, the department identified that the Government was likely to address social services in the context of NHS reforms and that computer systems could be vital in preparing for impending change. The project manager strongly believed in IT as an agent of change, and determined that IT for social services in Camden would be user led, with a high degree of staff involvement to facilitate the process of skills development, to stimulate debate and to evolve creative strategies for moving the organization forwards as a result of conceptualizing required systems.

It was a particularly inauspicious time to launch a major initiative like an IT strategy. Because of current and anticipated cut-backs, Camden was going through a drastic and painful restructuring exercise, with replacement of the director, most of the second-tier managers, changing roles for all of the third-tier officers, and the complete reshaping of the organizational structure. At the start the impending legislative changes could only be guessed at, and the absence of a firm framework made the creation of vision very difficult. The organization was to a great extent paralysed by fear of the future and distress at the present, but, as we noted above, the greater the challenge, the more necessary it is to engage and address it urgently. Besides IT was hitherto centrally administered by the central IT department and very underdeveloped in social services, so there was a grudging and somewhat cynical interest in what might transpire from this new thing of a department IT strategy; the project manager at least had an audience.

In order to position IT (and the computer liaison team) in this role of catalyst for community care, the project manager had to create and sustain a vision of success and mobilize key players at council, management and staff levels to support the strategy. The processing of tenders for an IT supplier afforded the opportunity to educate those involved, and empower them to make choices about values, approach and options that had never previously been articulated. This mind-stretching exercise reinforced the vision of success; it effectively coalesced the energies of several smaller waves to create sufficient momentum to launch the IT project.

Wave 2: Establishing a strategic framework
From a number of potential suppliers, one was the chosen partner to provide the energy source for the next wave. In the last quarter of 1988 an IT strategy study was commissioned, but the terms of reference went beyond technical deliverables to include a brief to reflect the organization back to itself in such terms that it would be galvanized into seizing the vision of success and setting about the task of evaluating strategic options and identifying strategic issues. Figure 9.9 describes the process that has continued every year since 1988.

During the four months of the IT strategy study, staff and management were again comprehensively involved. Various challenges arose; management had a clear idea of mission, but when asked to define objectives, critical success factors and key performance indicators, two forms of behaviour emerged. One was to debate (and dispute) value systems, and the other was to express dismay and disinclination for the task of defining quantitative goals or measures.

It appeared that this particular wave had faltered; it had taken the staff to new heights of awareness and excitement about pursuing the promises of new techniques and the concepts for community care that were emerging. But the same wave was in danger of washing management back towards eddies and whirlpools which the organization was not yet strong enough to face. The decision was to recommend a joint programme of organization and system initiatives, and aim to use the next wave as a real breaker, to sweep all before it. The first system to be developed (client interface system—CIS) was to pioneer a new corporate awareness (via generic systems to be used across the board) and hinting of the intention to challenge current functional preoccupations by integrating client and resource systems. The report also invited management into the driving seat through listing issues, suggesting areas for attention (e.g. structure and responsibilities, planning, communications, training, etc.) and offering alternative routes through the organization in terms of different systems which addressed different priorities (e.g. cost control, efficiency of service deliv-

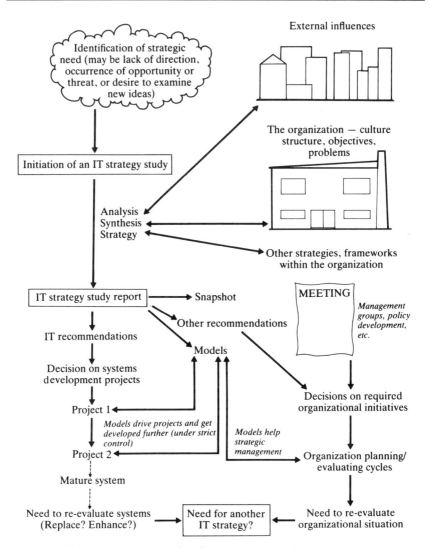

Figure 9.9 Using strategy as a catalyst for organizational change
Source: Camden IT Strategy (1988), London Borough of Camden.

ery, understanding of needs, service development, staff development, agency liaison, work load management).

Wave 3: Creating momentum
During 1989, a joint team of users (design teams) and consultants prototyped, found and resolved issues, shared the process and results through a series of open days and built the first block of the integrated system—CIS. The design

team was excited; the hundreds of people within and outside Camden who saw and discussed the prototype were stimulated and started to create their own visions of what IT could do for them and, sometimes, of where the process could take the organization; but management were distant. As the project manager commented at the time 'the incubation period for a system is only 9 months, and we are ahead of the organization in our thinking'.

This was a big issue: the organization initiatives recommended as an integral part of the strategy had not been fully followed through, and without management being fully involved a few problems became evident:

- Implementation on the ground would be difficult. (Managing change on the ground takes considerable time, energy and resources—more than the computer liaison team could undertake.)
- The desire to be part of the IT project that had arisen in the open days could not be satisfied: the next set of user design teams for adapting/enhancing CIS and sponsoring subsequent systems should already be being prepared.
- The purpose of the system (to endorse the vision of the new Camden, under community care) was jeopardized by the lack of development work on objectives, KPIs and new methods of working. At best, the system could only hope to support staff operationally, and perhaps stimulate innovation through access to data and support of generic processes (such as event recording, care package negotiation).

There was power in the wave, but it was going to be deflected by hidden obstacles that the team knew only too well. Should they stop the wave, or let it break and hope some of the energy would carry through to start new movements?

Wave 4: Turbulence

CIS was delivered, on time and under budget. Figures 9.10a and 9.10b illustrate the framework for aligning the IT strategy to the organizational development process. However, the real impact came when attempts were made to implement the system in the home help service in line with agreed priorities. The problems of managing change were apparent, as were the penalties for underestimating the tasks involved. Staff insecurity, lack of leadership among key managers, inadequate operational planning, the potential impact on work organization and other functions were just a few of the hurdles encountered. The computer liaison team decided that the turbulence was a necessary learning experience for the organization, which had had no previous experience of implementing large systems, and that although the organization was not yet ready for the results, the development work should continue as a vehicle for continued education and vision building, and to ensure that the department could be ready to support community care.

PROVIDING A SOCIAL SERVICES SYSTEM
DESIGNED BY SOCIAL SERVICES

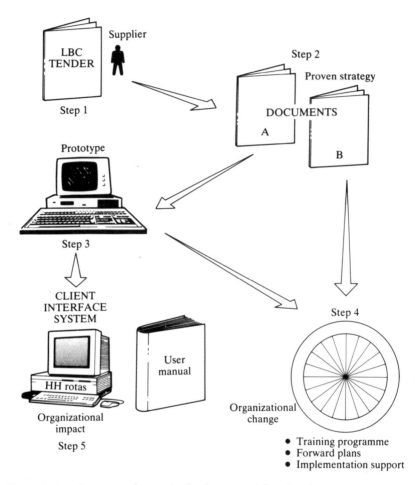

Figure 9.10a   Summary of stages in development of first Camden system
Source: Camden IT Strategy (1989), London Borough of Camden.

Wave 5: Wider waters
The next system to be developed through 1990 (Resource Management) was
conceived as the first of a series of core systems that would build on the foundation system (CIS). It was designed to extend the base of data and the use of
generic systems into the realms of carer recruitment, resource allocation, child
protection, quality inspection and client monitoring. The project team knew
that this last item raised immediate issues about social work practice in formaliz-
ing the process of monitoring warnings, assessing risk and running the child

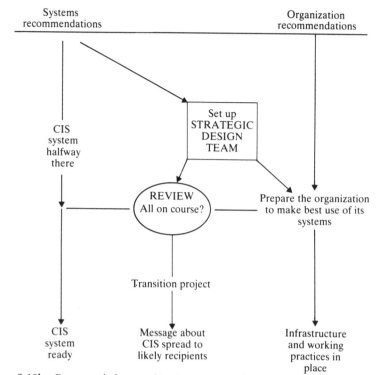

Figure 9.10b Framework for coordinating system and organizational change
Source: Camden IT Strategy (1989), London Borough of Camden.

protection register, and undertook consultations and prototyping exercises with those involved. The waves were tremendous! The concepts were good, the implications for service organizations were challenging and, to some, unacceptable. Others saw the need for small changes (submitting to using a system), and some saw much wider visions (including the possibilities for a shared system with other agencies, hospitals, etc.). It is in these waters that the Camden experience is still currently swimming. There is a whole range of new potential waves (based on visions that go far beyond the next planned systems, which are after all only change agents). Some of these are gathering force (for instance, a quality assurance initiative using available technology was launched on the back of the IT strategy).

Playing with the waves has its exhilarating and dampening moments but because we believe that change is an evolutionary process, it is necessary to be patient. A great deal has been, and continues to be, achieved at Camden:

- The foundation system Client Resource Management, was developed in two years, on time and under budget, with a participative approach involving staff at all stages.

- It is forward in its thinking, with an optimum design for current needs and future flexibility and invites a creative approach in those who use it (enabling, not dictating).
- A successful IT strategy has opened the possibility for other staff to engage in the process of organizational renewal. As we noted above, an incrementalist approach optimizes learning, and, most importantly, releases energy and resource flows to bring about a snowball effect of small wins.
- New initiatives, using technology to assist management in understanding the processes involved in service delivery that affected quality, were launched in 1990.

Despite difficulties, the renewal process has begun for Camden who have developed a balanced IT strategy to facilitate the move to the paradigm of the responsive organization. However, these are difficult times, and we are reminded of Ohmae's advice that there has to be strategic insight, but strategy also requires attention to reality, ripeness and resources.

9.6   Lessons from Camden case study

We shall highlight three aspects of the events between 1986 and 1991.

1 The positioning of the IT project in 1988, and indeed the IT strategy itself, involved substantial environmental scanning and analysis of mandates and values (Bryson's steps 1–5).
2 At all times, the identification of strategic issues (Bryson's step 6, amplified by Willcocks) was seen to be vital. Time was spent considering the impact of new ideas, the likely behaviour of dominant coalitions, the anxieties about work organization and required skills and the possible routes to leverage support and resources.
3 The biggest issue in terms of the received wisdom on strategy is that the Camden work is 'bottom-up'; essentially an 'enabling' strategy trying to stimulate a corporate strategy (part of which would be to define SSUs and initiate business strategies). The triggering event was the perceived need for information systems to support the Community Care and the Children Acts. The desired corporate strategy was effectively a renewal exercise to create the responsive organization, from which the new ideas on services, resources, clients and quality would arise to stimulate reframing of the existing organization and its functions.

9.6.1   SUMMARY OF CAMDEN STRATEGY 1986–1991

The process in the preceding sections can be expressed as a series of milestones, controlled within a change management programme. Figure 9.11 shows how activities in several different areas of responsibility can be coordinated by a series of dependent milestones which act as a focal point for the stakeholders,

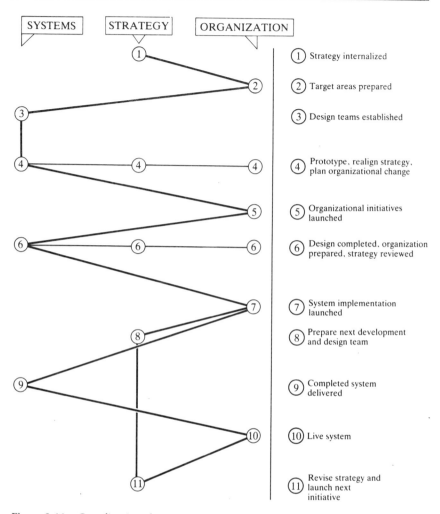

| SYSTEMS | STRATEGY | ORGANIZATION |

1 — Strategy internalized

2 — Target areas prepared

3 — Design teams established

4 — Prototype, realign strategy, plan organizational change

5 — Organizational initiatives launched

6 — Design completed, organization prepared, strategy reviewed

7 — System implementation launched

8 — Prepare next development and design team

9 — Completed system delivered

10 — Live system

11 — Revise strategy and launch next initiative

Figure 9.11   Coordinating change

but leave the management of the work to those concerned. ⊤ ᵥe main areas of responsibility, as shown, were strategy, systems development and organizational preparation. In the course of the IT strategy and systems development work the project team strayed into corporate and business domains to share insights and nurture the vision of success that would provide the required energy to embark on corporate strategy.

Although hardly ideal, it is not uncommon for this 'bottom-up' process to occur, and is a style that has been familiar in other departments known to the authors. Clearly, it is hard to keep a perspective and recognize the initial work for what it is (the means to an end, and not an end in itself), but this is essential if the work is not to become a barrier to strategy development within the organization. For instance, in Kraemer *et al.* (1989), it appears that the 'management states' deriving from IT locus of control and interest served were often perversions of the initial intent to use IT in the service of the organization: lack of understanding, obstacles and political expediency often overtook events, and the course of IT was seen to be divorced from the environmental events that shaped the organization. Kraemer *et al.*'s 'management states' were described as strategic, services or skill biased (in other words predominantly aligned to supporting management control, operating efficiency or the desire to exploit technology). The project team resisted the temptation at Camden to support any particular lobby, aiming instead to provide a broad operational system (concentrating on data and generic processes) from which strategic benefit may be gained, and which employs technology of appropriate sophistication to do the job (which may vary across applications). However, Camden's increments were perhaps of too large a size and too frequent for the organization to assimilate fully, particularly given that it was a greenfield site, struggling to cope with organizational change and not yet confident enough to believe that IT could be a strategic partner in the process.

The likely outcome is hard to gauge. The organization will implement its systems and intends to continue meanwhile to the next phase of development. It may be that the vision of success will suddenly gain momentum and the earlier modules that were built will suddenly seem a small step compared with the expanding possibilities. Each new phase of development also widens the base of users involved in the conceptual dialogue and develops individuals who are not afraid to question, interact and try, while at the same time increasing the level of organizational know-how. With generic systems, the concepts themselves are used over again in an expanded scope or through different user perspectives and thus become more familiar.

By these approaches, the strange analytical language of modelling (see Fig. 9.12) will gradually become institutionalized, and prototyping and debate will become a recognized way for users to drive the development process. Although users accept that systems analysts can never 'know' their jobs as intimately as the users, they nevertheless have a valid perspective that makes them a useful sounding board when the organization contemplates change. Working together, analysts and users can establish a constructive dialogue to talk about community care in conceptual terms. Staff and managers at Camden were surprised to discover that models could illuminate problems and illustrate options in a way that often circumvented emotional issues, and organizational and political blockages.

9.7 Conclusion

In the absence of active debate on social policy during the 1980s, social services may be deemed to no longer have an inherent justification for existence. There

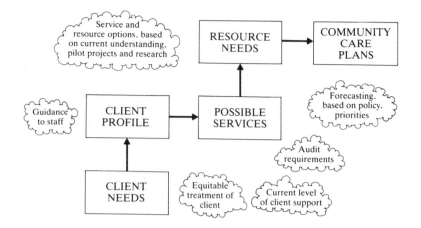

**'Soft' modelling techniques to explore
requirements at the conceptual level.
Example is Needs Based Resource Planning**

If we understand client needs, we could provide a means of categorizing them
(a client profile), such that we can assess any client and make a judgement as to the
profile they most closely fit (which will then help us in planning suitable services).

In assessing client needs, we must be careful to ensure we are treating clients
equitably (i.e. behaving consistently, not using methods that could disadvantage
some clients). We must also balance needs against current level of support to assess
the most 'deserving cases'. Client profiles could be a valuable tool for guiding staff
in choosing appropriate services, but tools should never override human judgement
(and the effectiveness of profiles will have to be continually monitored).

However, support for proper service choices will be useful in demonstrating
targeting of services, for performance measurement.

Once client profiles are relatively well established as a means to predict possible
services, then demographic analysis will enable us to predict resource needs. This
will also depend on policy and priorities: for instance, eligibility criteria may be
shifted within a range, to accommodate various situations of anticipated resource
constraint.

Figure 9.12   Example of modelling approach
            Source: Camden IT Strategy (1989), London Borough of Camden.

are certainly many challenges ahead, and new ways to be found to respond to
old problems. The 1980s may have produced a lot of winners but there remain
unacceptably high levels of losers with increasing poverty, deprivation, child
abuse, and dependent citizens. That there is a need for a unified personal social
services organization is unquestionable to many in the field, but the drive for a
more pluralistic and competitive environment for these services will not disappear. To survive and fulfil the original mission envisaged by Seebhom, social

services departments will have to develop strategies that will establish them as responsive organizations providing quality services.

The strengths to survive against the prevailing winds are to be found in social services' historical roots, which stretch back to the Victorian campaigners for social justice. As Banford (1990) says:

> The continuity lies in the duality of concern for social policy and social planning on the one hand and for individuals and groups in need of care on the other. It is seen in the continuing emphasis on the community and the support which it can offer to supplement the input of the professional helper. It is evident in the stress on the maximum possible participation of citizens in decisions which affect them . . .

But the move into the paradigm of the responsive organization rests with managers in social services. Unless they stimulate a progressive debate through the clear articulation of value systems, and show the determination to promote and enact policies in the public domain, then the debate will turn from purpose to politics, leaving social services in great danger in its struggle against a cost-led Government strategy and imposition of an impoverished style of so-called private sector management. The ultimate losers will once again be the clients for whom social policy has a very real meaning.

Social services must therefore determine what it is and where it is going, create appropriate strategies and implement them effectively in such a way that it is seen to be serving the various stakeholders. An incrementalist approach within a strategic planning framework driven by a strong sense of vision is required.

The many issues and questions raised in this chapter will need to be defined and tackled by social services managers if they are to steer their departments out of the current confusion towards a more confident and effective organization in the decade ahead.

Throughout we have emphasized the leadership qualities required to enable social services to achieve a breakthrough into the new paradigm of the responsive organization. The management skills required for such a breakthrough involve understanding the external environment, developing appropriate organizational structures, nurturing a culture that embraces all stakeholders in the change processes, and finally developing the techniques and technologies that support the implementation of strategic goals. These skills, when fostered within the culture of a responsive organization, can create a self-reinforcing movement for organizational renewal, which is at the heart of 'thriving on chaos'.

The SSU, coupled with adequate IT investment, can be a powerful lever to move the organization towards the responsive model, since together they establish dialogue, facilitate change and provide the information that is essential to effective action.

Social services is not alone in requiring the urgent application of education and management development. However, it can exploit the sources available, including reciprocal training and secondments with other organizations. It can also embrace the route to an IS culture as being a significant step in empowering individuals and increasing organizational know-how.

Last, but not least, it can rediscover the public sector management strengths which, in the past, created and sustained the vision of the welfare state, and the small wins of many social services personnel in serving their clients and communities over the past 20 years or more.

Through these efforts, social services can address the three sets of problems that are currently behind many of its difficulties: the need to re-establish social policy and legitimacy; the need to understand the essentials of a service organization; and the need to manage change effectively.

References

Audit Commission (1986) *Making a Reality of Community Care*. HMSO, London.

Banford, T. (1990) *The Future of Social Work*. Macmillan, London.

Barclay Report (1982) *Social Workers, their Roles and Tasks*. Bedford Square Press, London.

Brewar, C. and Last, J. (1980) *Can Social Work Survive?* Temple Smith, London.

Bryson, J. (1988) *Strategic Planning for Public and Non-Profit Organisations*. Jossey-Bass, London.

Bryson, J. and Roering, W. (1987) 'Applying private sector strategic planning to the public sector', *Journal of the American Planning Association*, 53, 9–22.

Burns, T. and Stalker, G. (1966) *The Management of Innovation*. Tavistock, London.

CIPFA/ADSS (1990) *Financial Partnership—An Information Strategy*. CIPFA, London.

Dean, M. (1990) 'The poor state of Major's nation', *The Guardian*, 5 December.

DH (1988) *Indicators of Local Authority Social Services*. Social Services Inspectorate, London.

DH (1989a) *National Health Service and Community Care Act*. HMSO, London.

DH (1989b) *Children Act 1989*. HMSO, London.

DHSS (1989) *Caring for People*. HMSO, London.

Flynn, N. and Commons, R. (1990) *Implementation Documents: Contracts for Community Care*. SSI Project Group, HMSO, London.

Griffiths Report (1988) *Community Care: Agenda for Action*. HMSO, London.

Hadley, R. and Young, K. (1990) *Creating a Responsive Public Service*. Harvester Wheatsheaf, London.

Handy, C. (1985) *Understanding Organisations*. Penguin, London.

Handy, C., Gordon, C. and Randlesome, C. (1988) *Making Managers*. Pitman, London.

Harrow, J. and Willcocks, L. (1990) 'Public sector management: activities, initiatives and limits to learning', *Journal of Management Studies*, 27 (3), May.

Kilmann, R. (1987) *Beyond the Quick Fix—Managing 5 Tracks to Organizational Success*. Jossey-Bass, San Francisco.

Kouzes, J. and Mico, P. (1979) 'Domain theory; an introduction to organisational behavior in human service organisations', *Journal of Applied Behavioral Science*, 15 (41), 449–69.

Kraemer, K. King, J., Dunkle, D and Lane, J. (1989) *Managing Information Systems*. Jossey-Bass, San Francisco.

London Borough of Camden (1988) *Camden Survey of People with Disabilities and Long Term Health Problems*. Camden, London.

Lynch, D. and Kordis, P. (1989) *Strategy of the Dolphin*. Arrow Books, London.

Merton, R. (1940) 'Bureaucratic structures and personality', *Social Forces*, **18**, 560–8.

Moss Kanter, R. (1989) *When Giants Learn to Dance*. Simon & Schuster, New York.

Ohmae, K. (1983) *The Mind of the Strategist*. Penguin, London.

Porter, M. (1985) *Competitive Advantage*. Free Press, New York.

Seebhom Report (1968) HMSO, London.

Strassman, P. (1985) *An Information Payoff—the Transformation of Work in the Electronic Age*. Free Press, New York.

Warner, N. (1990) 'Action by social security departments', in *Community Care from White Paper to Action*. Public Finance Foundation, London.

Willcocks, L. (1991a) 'Critical issues for information systems management', Paper at ITAP 1991 Conference, Open University, Milton Keynes, 12–13 April.

Willcocks, L. (1991b) 'Building an information systems culture', Paper at AMED/AMRO Conference, Ashridge Management College, 3–4 January.

10

Management and the usefulness of information

Everton Dockery

10.1 Introduction

Over the last decade, the managerial significance of issues in the public sector has matched that of issues in the wider business environment. Thus like large-scale business organizations, public services have responded to new institutional pressures with Information Technology (IT) playing an important role in almost all functions. As expected, IT is beginning to affect the fabric of organizational structure at all levels; in particular, as indicated in Chapter 7, the technology can be used to alter the managerial processes and the mechanism by which managers control the flow of resources and manage activities. In these and other respects, little explicit attention has been paid to how managers in public services organizations obtain information both for use in management control and decision-making. To that extent, a number of studies on business organizations suggest potential cause for variations in information-seeking behaviour from an end-user perspective. For instance, in an ideal situation, decision makers have been viewed to select information from those sources perceived to proffer the highest quality information. Typically, therefore, information quality would be high if the information was relevant or specific to problems being addressed, accurate, reliable and timely—as noted by Zmud (1979). But, as suggested here, quality of information merely allows a decision maker to justify the basis of the decision to others by arguing that if the information used is timely, accurate and reliable, then any decision made is likely to be good. It should, however, be noted that quality of itself is not an objective dimension, as perceptions of the accuracy and reliability of information from a management information system (MIS) may vary according to the decision maker's experience, goals or personal predilections. Although quality should be related to all aspects of the use of MIS information, thus, it is not *de rigueur* that all managers will acquiesce on the quality or indeed the usefulness of MIS information.

The usefulness of information is by all accounts an important and timely issue since computer-based information systems (CBISs) are being increasingly relied upon to improve the quality of management decision-making. Such systems are designed to process selectively the growing body of information (financial and non-financial) confronting local government. But to what extent is this information useful for management control purposes? This chapter raises two important conceptual and practical questions. First, and perhaps more fundamental: To what extent is MIS information useful or accurate enough to enable effective monitoring and control of performance? Second: Can management control effectiveness and efficiency be enhanced through better flow of MIS information? These critical questions require much research from different perspectives. We have chosen to focus on these issues by conducting research in actual settings where these issues are being played out. The setting is the study of a finance department in a local authority, which, for reasons of confidentiality, we shall refer to as local government X. One objective of the division was to introduce new MISs into certain management processes, this being made possible with the advent of more sophisticated CBIS technology within organizations.

The research method is interpretive, and follows the work of Daft and Weick (1984) who attempted to establish a theoretical link between organizational context and interpretation at the organizational level of analysis. This research has suggested that the information from an environment (i.e. the economic, political, social and technological factors) that managers attend to and the meanings they attach to that information are, in part, functions of frameworks inveterate in organization level contextual factors. These modes of interpretation (Daft and Weick, 1984, p. 289) affect the situations and events to which managers will purposely attend, those they will seek to ignore, and those they will perceive as having a strategic impact on their organizational setting. Research data and subjective judgements were obtained from senior, middle, and lower level managers of the finance department and, in some cases, from important team members who were knowledgeable about the functions of the local government's MIS. The research involved 30 managers. Data were collected from all the chief decision makers within a number of cost centre units.

10.2   Local government X and the role and use of information systems

One of the benefits of detailed, case study research is that it allows us to probe more deeply into the reality behind strategic initiatives designed to adapt organizational structures in line with the broad requirement of the organization, and thus into the reality behind the implementation of a formal MIS, and to see how managers respond to the information they receive for such routine activities as planning and management control. In such a situation, one is able to determine the relative fit between the MIS and its environment and the degree to which the system is able to achieve its goals as a benchmark of system effectiveness, as suggested by Guimaraes (1984), Srinivasan (1985) and Rivard and Huff (1988). Ideally one would like to assume that when a good fit is achieved, and the goals are being met, there is a high probability that the system is widely used, thereby making it possible for judgement to be made regarding system efficacy and success in addressing a multiplicity of organizational requirements.

The organization in our case study is a small inner London borough, noted for its innovative approach to local government management. In the early 1980s the authority embarked on a process of management change which culminated in organizational restructuring, and developments in organizational systems. Part of that restructuring involved the implementation of a management accounting information system (hereinafter the management information system) which, it was viewed, would not only revolutionize the way in which the authority managed and controlled resources, but also would achieve greater efficiency and effectiveness in public services delivery. Over a number of years, the authority has been involved in a process of integration and modification—most of it concerned with supporting the process of making decisions, and with trying to integrate different aspects of information systems that were fragmented throughout the organization. These changes have also made it possible for managers to have at their command a wide range of data-processing and information tools—consequently enabling managers at all levels of the department structure to draw on computer-based on-line information to monitor, and thus control, expenditure across areas of immediate responsibility. This means that for any given functional task spanning the basic operation of the finance division, the control information flowing through the system is expected to authorize managers to compare predetermined budget standards against actual results, detect deviations from planned objectives, and to induce managers to take timely corrective action as and when circumstances dictate a response to confronting problems.

The MIS comprises a network of computer terminals operating through a central computer. In the finance department (see Fig. 10.1) a number of terminals are distributed among accountants, and middle and lower level managers responsible for the overall performance of subunit activity encompassing a broad range of specialist functions.

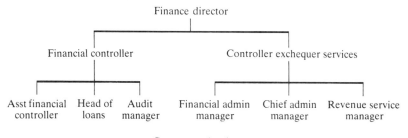

Figure 10.1   Plan of finance department structure

In these units, computer terminals are used by managers to check budget levels, to record payments and all similar procedures concerned with the flow and control of resources through cost centres. However, because information is so intrinsic to this type of control, the system is generally considered to improve the administrative efficiency of cost centres by virtue of its ability to provide specific and timely information in such performance criteria as budget standards and the level of spend on operating budgets. Consequently, there is a degree of expectation on the part of managers interacting with the system (McLean, 1979; Rockart and Flanery, 1983) that an MIS application's utility in management control decision is enhanced when the systems output meets the basic information requirement of managers (see Bailey and Pearson, 1983).

In its current form, the MIS collects data from feeder systems such as salaries, wages, creditors and income, and stores, analyses and reports on events of an economic and quantitative nature. It also produces detailed monthly reports of expenditure under all headings, notably on salary and income, with breakdowns to individual cost centres. These are generated by the computerized information system for income, payroll, *inter alia*, which also means that managers across a number of specialist functions have virement between expenditure categories. The results of this activity are management control reports (or information retrieval capability in an on-line system) that are utilized for several purposes, namely the monitoring of budget, cost containment and performance evaluation. It is worth noting, however, that since MIS is effectively a subset of the management accounting system (MAS), data that are journalized through the MAS flows through the MIS, while other information sources forming part of the overall information processing activity of managers is processed through a number of informal channels, such as, for example, management action plans and service profile. Both sources are of great importance to the achievement of broad user objectives encapsulating:

- the coordination of and advice on budget strategy
- the provision of comprehensive advice and information service to the council, its committees and departments
- independent review monitoring and advice to all spending departments that systems and procedures (a) achieve high standards of stewardship and public accountability, and (b) promote and achieve economy, efficiency and effectiveness in the use of resources.

Since most of these activities are broadly centred around the acquisition of information or transfer of information in various forms in progress towards the achievement of objectives, managers are invariably the targets of a cluster of information. In typical fashion, decisions are communicated by passing information to managers who have delegated responsibility for performance achievement. Under this system, managers are required to perform their tasks in accordance with the pre-established standards against which their activity, cost and performance are measured and are in the main reliant upon information to keep them abreast of ongoing changes to budget levels. As a preliminary to what follows in the next sections, one senior manager explained the role of the MIS and, in turn, the usefulness of information to his area of responsibility thus:

> What I think MIS does is to make us more professional in what we do as a unit. It does that by releasing more time for us to spend on matters concerned with the running of the unit instead of chasing information. Personally, I as a manager have become more efficient as a result of the increased flow of information, and I suppose I am probably more motivated towards achieving results because I am now more confident with the level of information I receive.

He went on to further note that:

> ... on another level, I do think that speed of information and a quick and clear interpretation of that information is important. So there is really no point in having MIS information unless you can comprehend and use it. We are all aware of the major issues that affect us, and can see things happening in that we can spot trends and develop from that an appropriate strategy for the following weeks or months ahead that will either maintain or improve upon present circumstances. We have a breakdown of all our spending every month of where we are on the budget. And I regard that information as being a useful warning signal, or indeed, for spotting potential problems. I see that as being of great benefit to what I do ...

In the context of the foregoing perspective, the MIS, in line with Ackoff's (1967) thinking, is an adaptive learning control system in that it has been continuously modified to fit the structure of management during the time in which the organization has been undergoing a period of structural and management change. Like Ackoff's management system, the MIS has been designed to

• store and retrieve large amounts of information more quickly
• identify problems
• communicate information pertaining to the problems identified
• facilitate the decision to be made
• monitor the implemented control decision
• accurately combine and refigure information in order to create new information
• record and retrieve information about the content and nature of activities carried out.

Notably, as the organization has risen in experience with the MIS, much emphasis has been placed on efficiency and effectiveness as objectives of the system. This, as Baroudi et al. (1986) point out, is recognition that ease of use is of particular importance in facilitating managerial use of inquiry or decision support. The implied view is that ease of use will lead to increased usage rather than usage inducing satisfaction.

At the time of writing, the system was broadly considered to reflect the organization's structure and specific related characteristics: viz. its specialist functions, its size and complexity of operation and degree of decentralization. As a result, the system is now expected to help managers cope with the broad practices of management and constraints operating on areas of responsibility through the provision of information on total financial position, though much of its current role is now clearly seen in terms of buttressing the two basic and routinized functions of planning and management control to which we now turn our attention.

10.3   Application of MISs to local government: monitoring and controlling performance

At this juncture, discussion of MISs in the local authority studied has to proceed on the basis of its extensive experience in the process of management control. This is made possible by utilizing the MIS framework developed from Gorry and Scott Morton's (1971) rearticulation of Anthony's (1965) seminal work on planning and control systems. In that framework, Gorry and Scott Morton mapped out that an organization's MIS must furnish information to managers with three levels of responsibilities in mind: strategic planning, management control and operational control. In keeping within the main arguments of this framework, the MIS is proclaimed to purvey a variety of information specific to the requirement of the management and control function of the finance department in total. Therefore, in addressing the usefulness of information, it is worth noting that a diverse range of information is prepared formally and communicated via on-line computer-based terminals to address the information requirement of different users. Such information is generally considered to allow various managerial levels the opportunity to monitor budget levels and the relative performance of spending departments. In effect, managers are able to procure from this source of information an indication of those activities that seem to deserve special attention at any given time, or verification that progress in all aspects of activities for which they are responsible are functioning according to what is required at corporate level—readily observing any deviations—with some indication of their relative significance. But bearing in mind that formal information is produced in ever-larger volumes, it was important to discover the extent to which information for control purposes is appropriate and useful to the requirement of management control and decision-making. This is reflected by the comments of one manager who noted that:

> I receive regular reports via MIS on all activities where I have a personal involvement. The reports are just summary levels of where departments stand on current expenditure, so I can get a feel for whether or not there is a problem. Generally I . . . access information via the system when there is a need to know how progress is in terms of budgets. I find that useful as it enables a timely response to events occurring elsewhere in the organisation.

Many middle managers whose tasks Anthony (1965) describes as being primarily concerned with management control, found themselves consciously relying on information so as to enhance the process of financial control. Managers reported that whenever they had a problem to address, they invariably relied upon MIS information. This was further seen as reinforcing the confidence designers of the system placed on the usefulness of information in meeting the information requirements of managers, which seem to prejudice claims from middle managers outside the remit of financial management control that MIS information was not sufficiently timely for effective performance monitoring. Clearly, the discrepancy over the usefulness of information as viewed by middle managers originates from deep-seated instincts concerning the appropriateness of the MIS to management, and accordingly the relevance of information to emerging problems. From these concerns, the findings indicate that organizational pressures are rarely wholly absent, especially when middle managers are wrestling with financial uncertainty over aspirations within the revenue programme. For although management may be given information to substantiate what it has already decided to do, it was observed that, as decision makers, managers outside the remit of financial management control tend to have very different temperaments and will react to emerging problems and respond to ambiguity in ways conflicting with the flow of information. These managers tended to interpret their information in the light of what they perceive as an acceptable pattern of behaviour. Consequently, the usefulness of information was determined by the degree to which they found themselves able to interact with the system directly and to utilize information (Sprague, 1980). The view was that if information is to be regarded as useful, it must be timely and appropriate to effective management control decisions. As one manager commented:

> In terms of how the system has been set up to fit in with the overall structure of management accountability, the information we receive is only useful in that it provides a detailed and overall picture of what is happening. Though there are other areas which I do feel the system ought to be developed to address.

It is instructive, therefore, that middle managers should utilize a MIS for monitoring purposes, especially when information is fairly current and specific to the problems requiring a decision action. As viewed from this perspective, the usefulness of information refers to performance in the intrinsic elements. What is intrinsic is service delivery, and so middle managers' use of information is primarily concerned with how progress in the intrinsic elements are in relation to targets. It was observed that managers' need for information was driven by the desire to improve the quality of financial management control decisions, and by the need to obtain information in order to ensure that operations were performing according to planned objectives. One reason for this was due to pressures on managers to achieve objectives within expenditure guidelines, coupled with external pressure to deliver services within planned resources. This in turn forced managers to make further claims on the MIS so that they could make timely decisions to ensure that activities for which they were responsible performed within the boundaries of resource levels. This is captured in the following comment from one manager:

> The organization's sensitivity to current resource constraints does pose some problems, particularly where services are concerned. What that means is that we have to be more cost conscious in terms of how we consume resources, which also means that we have to constantly monitor how we are doing on the budget. To do that, I generally try to keep on top of the situation by making use of on-line information which, since the system has been in operation, has proved to be rather effective in enabling me to perform my tasks.

Generally, middle managers found information supportive to everyday management control and/or decision-making. They typically expressed this support as 'MIS information is useful in enabling me to manage my area of responsibility'. This, and similar perceptions, would seem to lend support to the emerging theory that MISs simply buttress the manager's function by maintaining its potential for management decision-making, and therefore remain markedly consistent with the theoretical view emanating from the literature that information becomes valuable when its relevance is precise to decision-making (Ein-dor and Segev, 1978; King and Epstein, 1976). Though arguably, events underpinning the nature of change, as indicated by the way in which middle managers were observed to adapt themselves to shifts in priorities and changing goals, tend to suggest that information facilitates the management control process mainly by enabling middle managers to verify significant changes to expenditure levels, for a given change in resource allocation. Such findings are in accordance with the arguments delineated in Fig. 10.2.

Figure 10.2 shows that managers' attitudes towards MISs represent a key factor in influencing its overall effectiveness to the process of decision-making, management control, and in turn user satisfaction and system utilization. This is based on the strict assumption that the attitudes of public sector managers to a set of goals or objectives are likely to play a key role in inducing their behaviour towards it. In support of this proposition, the evidence reported by Lucas (1978), and Robey (1979) found user attitude to be positively correlated to computer usage. Similarly, Rivard and Huff (1988) found that user attitudes are positively related to user satisfaction in total. However, it should be said that the complexity and uncertainty of the decision are imperative determinants of system success as measured in terms of its overall usefulness to managerial work; see, for example, Cheney and Dickson (1982) and O'Reilly (1982).

10.4   The use of information in operational control

Operational control at cost centre level is characterized by monitoring activities composed of short-time horizons, such that management control decisions are

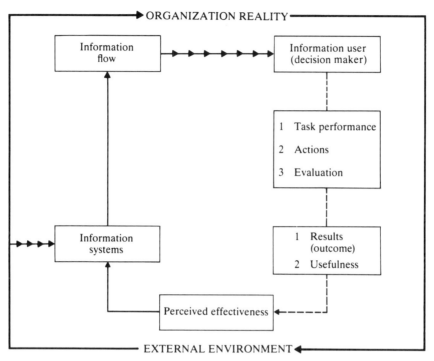

Figure 10.2   Management Information Systems user environment

invariably very routine and somewhat repetitive. As a result, very little ambiguity was found to impinge upon the decision-making cognition of cost centre managers. An indication of this was observed in the activities in which cost centre managers were involved. The findings indicate that the main preoccupation of cost centre managers was primarily with operational control, and a concern for budget levels. Moreover, because managers were invariably concerned with operational control, a great deal of emphasis was placed on the MIS to provide information that is situationally specific to what they do. At this level, the flow of information was found to be not only specific to the level of resources associated with the operation of cost centres, but was also specific to the cost centre managers accountable for controlling performance. Specifically, all appropriate performance data were retrieved through MIS, and analysis was performed by managers, sometimes with the help of accountants responsible for the transmission of budget reports to cost centres. Thus, as far as the activities of cost centres were observable, it was observed that when current data flowed out of the unit, fairly up-to-date and practical information, sufficient for the effective execution of task activity, flowed back simultaneously. As one cost centre manager remarked:

... with regards to performance monitoring, the information flowing through the system on exact spend is fairly current and has played a crucial role in keeping the budget down within prescribed allocation, as well as within allocation to particular categories where there's a need to keep costs to a minimum.

As implied above, there is an effective feedback of information which allowed managers to address themselves to varying problems as and when they arose. A recognized dimension of the feedback process is its directional and motivational impact on the management control and decision-making processes encountered in the unit of analysis, for it was found from discussions with managers that the MIS was instrumental in directing their behaviour by providing information for corrective action, and motivational in the sense that the information communicated motivated management control decisions. Most managers stressed the corrective assistance that the MIS afforded to the management control process, primarily as it was seen to provide valuable information when it was required to correct expenditure levels when they were observed to deviate from their desired standards (Lawler, 1976). This is supported by March and Olsen (1976) who suggests that the feedback of information process is both a re-examination and clarification, a form of rationalization that coexists and conditions prospective decision-making in most organizations. It is, however, in this strict sense that the work of March and Olsen (1976) furnish an interesting lead to the understanding of information, and the usefulness of MIS information in management control decisions, as illustrated by the following comment:

A lot of what we do in this section is very routine, and as you might expect, most of that work is divided up into routine tasks which are themselves concerned with our main task of administering financial control over department spend . . . The mere fact that we employ the MIS to carry out that function is indicative of the extent to which we rely upon the system to provide information about the correctness, accuracy, and effectiveness of resource utilization.

As the testimony shows, managers are reliant on information to provide guidance to management control decisions. And in that reliance on MIS information, managers consider feedback to promote effective monitoring and performance. And as suggested here, the appropriateness of information to management control decisions primarily depends on the extent to which it enables a timely response to organizational problems. Ilgen et al. (1979), for example, suggests that effectiveness of feedback information in affecting organizational behaviour rather depends on its quantity, timeliness, understandability, specificity, relevance to task, and the sign of feedback—that is, for a given information request, whether the information communicated is positive or negative. But as related to the usefulness of MIS information, it was found that the information characteristics enunciated by Ilgen et al. (1979) broadly reflect the general expectations that managers have of the essential attributes of an information system. In that meaning, the efficient functioning and usefulness of MIS was viewed by managers as contingent on a number of Ilgen et al. (1979) characteristics for it to be considered useful in its overall function. Indeed, our findings would seem to indicate that the value of information depended in no uncertain terms on the information's accuracy and timeliness to management control decisions.

Regarding the value of information, the MIS was perceived to have value when information could be used in management control decisions. In that regard, managers repeatedly indicated that when the MIS information was timely control decisions were in accordance with problems being addressed. And since managers were always able to utilize information, it was found that emphasis on timeliness as an expectation of the MIS had more to do with the personal goals of managers and their desire to achieve task goals. Thus, in a climate characterized by financial constraints and demands for greater efficiency and effectiveness, many managers supported the view that decision-making and management control decisions will be considered good when MIS information enables effective monitoring; in particular, when managers are under pressure to deliver the public good within strict expenditure limits. This concern over expenditure gave rise to demands for specific information that would enable control over the cost of delivering public services within defined guidelines. This is illustrated by the following comment:

> With the tightening of revenue resources, there is a slight suspicion that certain parts of the budget will be more certain than others. Therefore, in the drive to protect all services, it is a natural response, in terms of financial control, to continuously monitor certain categories of expenditure which are particularly sensitive to changes in our overall priorities. That is the reason why there is a demand for certain types of information for controlling what needs to be controlled.

Our findings suggest that managers who displayed their commitment by performing their task in a cost-conscious way (in terms of the amount of time spent on budget analysis) were immersed not only in the management network, but intellectually supported the financial management order of things. These managers were viewed to have a more professional outlook, and tended to be concerned with a MIS more as a management device than as a mechanistic system. The findings noted here would seem to bear close parallel with the work of Ouchi and Maguire (1975), who, in their discussion of various types of control strategies used in economic organizations, note that quantitative results, such as budget information, may be utilized as much for justifying the functional activities of cost centres as they are for controlling the idiosyncratic behaviour of workers. Our findings suggest that managers in their endeavour to monitor and thus control the task for which they are accountable were only concerned with receiving information that allowed them to maintain effective control over spending levels. This is illustrated by the following response of one manager:

> In this department, I have total responsibility over what we do. And without that responsibility, I very much doubt if we could have responded to the demands of the unit as we do now. My job is to maintain control over the unit, and I get plenty of

information via the system to enable me to do that, as well as information from the monthly reports I receive.

One of the more interesting findings that emerged from our study was that besides making use of formal information provided by MIS, most managers at this level (as did middle managers) relied on their own source of informal information, which they perceived as a buffer to effective management control and/or decision-making. Naturally, there may be particular reasons why some managers continue to maintain informal information systems. Though it is instructive to note that the use of informal information is a fundamental characteristic not only of local authorities; Hopwood (1974), Argyris (1977) and Clancy and Collins (1979) have reported their wide use in economic organizations. In that regard, it was observed that the informal information generated by managers consists of a series of records that are housed in well-managed files that are easily accessible and relate to financial details of an economic nature. In the majority of cost centres, the records were kept by managers or supporting team members who had recourse for using the information, either because the information they required was not held on-line or because the information was considered too basic for a MIS to hold. Thus, one of the reasons given for the preponderance of localized information at subunit level was that it gave certainty to decision-making in both planning and control. But as Clancy and Collins (1979) note, one other reason why cost centre managers maintained informal records was that the actual process of assembling data keeps them in contact with the process they are managing. Our findings do seem to support this claim, as well as the claims of Argyris (1977), as it was found, albeit for a few cases, that informal information furnished a more solid and accurate record of expenditure of each cost centre situation than the formal MIS. These informal systems allowed managers to establish and to protect themselves when questions are raised about the current operational state (Hedberg and Jonsson, 1978). As one manager remarked:

> As well as making use of information in the system I also make use of information on areas of the work with which I am involved. The information in these files is mainly for my own use, and is mainly there as a support to what I do on the capital side.

Similarly, another manager noted that:

> It is often the case that in devising our strategy that we will require information on the extent to which we are meeting our objectives . . . not only in terms of overall budget, but also in terms of actual service delivery performance. As it stands, the present system does not provide information which tells us precisely of the outcome of decisions taken. Consequently, we have devised our own system of collecting and processing information that supports the overall management of the unit, which, of course, enables us to give a timely response to both planning and control matters.

The foregoing is consistent with the findings reported by Kmetz (1984), even though his findings relate specifically to the development of buffers in VAST workshops (in Navy Aircraft Electronics). In Kmetz's study it was observed that when buffers were maintained they facilitated the task of subunits in the short run, although, in the long run, they ran the risk of being maladaptive as they were seen to frustrate feedback and, as a consequence, cause adjustment to the larger system. From this it can be reasoned that the information buffers that Kmetz postulates were devised primarily because of internal divisions concerning the adequacy of information. If formal information is technically deficient in its quality, then, in order to maintain a reasonable flow of information capable of facilitating their task activities, managers may have to accommodate themselves by devising information buffers incorporating the information that is perceived as being adequate to varying situational problems. As such, it is noticeable that the buffers reported by Kmetz were found to facilitate workflow in decision-making by way of decoupling performance monitoring information from workflow control information.

In that light, it is to be noted that the information requirements of managers were also apparent. That is to say, managers required information about the operating performance of their units, and in particular the need to ensure that functional objectives were consistent with predetermined plans. Nearly all of the managers could elicit information adequate for decision-making and control. But, although not interpreted in the same way as cost centre managers and supporting team members who maintained a system of localized informal information, managers were openly creating information buffers that were freely available. Noticeably, in the study reported by Kmetz (1984), VAST workshops created buffers for their own requirements, albeit illegitimately. Thus, from the findings reported here it can be seen that cost centre managers buffer themselves by processing information that could be relied on to maintain their effective functioning and, if required, could readily transmit all information that is appropriate to support the larger system. In the case reported by Kmetz, subunits were found to buffer themselves by accumulating information they required, but at the same time were not prepared to transmit to the larger system.

10.5   Computer-based information and the link with managerial work

This section considers how management functions are evolving with the use of computer-based information systems (CBISs) and further illustrates the extent to which management attitudes are being affected by the use of information systems technology. Its objective is to show that there are similarities and core influences between managers in public services and private sector organizations, and that there is a high degree of commonality of issues of critical importance to the future use of information systems in managerial work.

Viewed from the broader perspective, the evidence from the previous section seems to underpin the general experience of managers and their use of a CBIS and its product information in the private sector. In that respect, studies of private sector organizations by Dockery (1991) throw up a range of issues pertinent to the use of CBISs at senior management levels which parallels the experience of managers in local government. Many of these issues emerge from considering the impact of CBISs on managerial work at both senior and middle managerial levels of responsibility of which the findings, notwithstanding the wide use of computers by middle management, overwhelmingly point to an increasing use of information systems at senior management levels.

As in the case of local government, private sector organizations acquire and process information in order to carry out the critical functions of strategic planning and management control. In many cases, this effort requires the processing of large amounts of information, conveying messages critical to the tasks of what senior managers do on a day-to-day basis. In those 26 organizations in the study, senior managers had, in the main, preconceived attitudes—i.e. beliefs, values and expectations—regarding the impact a CBIS and its product information would have on their work. At most sites studied, these attitudes were expressed towards perceptions of the capabilities of and need for CBIS in giving value to the specific, and sometimes routine, functions of senior managers. They emphasized the need for CBISs to facilitate what senior managers do on a daily basis. This view is of critical significance, illustrating that the issues we are discussing are of similar concern to managers in public services. More importantly, however, it shows the extent to which there are convergences of managerial requirements of information systems between public services and private sector organizations, suggesting therefore that there are good managerial practices which share a common interest in systems directed towards what managers do on a day-to-day basis.

In most firms, the installed base of CBIS reflects current strategies on business and information systems strategy. The general consensus seems to be that if firms were not taking full advantage of current developments in technology, they might well find themselves at a competitive disadvantage with their competitors, particularly as many of their competitors were perceived to have gone into computing in a major way—especially in the computerization of work roles where there had previously existed a high level of fixed costs. For many firms, however, a CBIS was seen as a way of improving overall effectiveness in business communication, while for others, investing in CBIS technology meant more than just improving the flow of information, but the means through which greater efficiency in operation could be achieved. Therefore, we can see elements of this finding supporting the evidence reported in our earlier discussion on local government management use of information systems. There it was shown that managers placed particular emphasis on specific organizing qualities of the system in order to facilitate what they were doing when they were planning or controlling activities. Further evidence within the sites studied illustrates that an increasing number of information systems were being deployed to buttress decision-making. For example, in the area of software, most firms typically had one or two packages for the major business applications of spreadsheet, word-processing, database management, and in some cases, communications. Thus, for the range of packages available for specific organizational use, CBISs were used to facilitate a very wide range of managerial activities over and above the needs of forecasting, sales and marketing.

From a managerial standpoint, senior managers have become direct users of CBISs in several ways. One has been based on their need to capture, inquire of, and retrieve specific kinds of information relating to their work; the second emerges from their desire to have timely and current information; while the third has grown from the need to analyse financial data and develop forecasts or projections, models and numerous 'what if' modus operandi methods. Simultaneously, demands for information to perform analytical tasks have grown out of the strategic planning and management control side of managerial work. The heavy proportion of senior managers who use spreadsheets and other software applications are an indication of the level of usage. At most sites studied, examples of these applications include financial projections, developing budget reports for corporate meetings, cost reporting for specific cost centres and other internal communication flow. In many respects, the select ways in which managers in these firms used CBISs mirrors managers in local government, and would seem to demonstrate the degree of congruence between the ways in which managers at the same level were observed to use information in managerial work. Most striking, however, are the similarities between management use of information in both the private sector and the public services, which would seem to suggest the coming together of management function and behaviour, possibly illustrating the extent of management learning from private to public management.

As in the case of local government, the introduction of CBISs at senior management level was triggered primarily by an implicit demand for such application. Though it is interesting to note the dimension of one piece of software application, notably spreadsheets. Indeed, nearly all the senior managers in the sites studied used spreadsheets either primarily or almost exclusively. And as they acquire greater individual dexterity, they develop further applications as they become more confident with the technology. This is exemplified by the following response of one senior manager who noted that:

> The way in which the PC helps me in my job is several fold. Firstly, in the actual day-to-day running in terms of the monitoring of expenditure, budgets, etc. And, secondly, in financial planning and control. So I use it quite heavily from that point of view, and it's much better than having to make use of paper.

Another senior manager commented that:

> I can do things more quickly in terms of day-to-day budgeting matters, primarily because of the flexibility that I have with the use of the system which actually speeds things up.

As can be seen, senior managers were more likely to claim that CBISs had increased their overall effectiveness. And, for the most part, the findings hitherto appear to corroborate those claims. It is, however, instructive to note that senior managers' perceptions of more specific aspects of their work—namely, strategic planning and management control—seem to be significantly affected by their use of CBISs. This rather suggests that senior managers were encouraged by the introduction of these systems to their function and as a consequence became more satisfied with the degree of effectiveness achieved with information systems as a result. In that regard, quite a number of senior managers saw concrete changes and, in turn, positive benefits resulting from the impact of CBISs either to themselves or their work. Almost without exception these changes are seen to be in the direction of making their work less strenuous. As a result of the benefits proffered to managerial work, senior managers agreed that they now have more time to concentrate on other tasks, owing to the amount of time saved on more routine tasks. In that regard, the findings reported here seem to suggest that the quality and value of information to managerial work has improved task effectiveness markedly. This is further supported by the claims of senior managers that CBISs have led to increases in effectiveness and efficiency, both in their own work and in the work of their individual departments and organizations. As one senior manager commented:

> Since we had the system installed, we have become more effective in the way we conduct our business. And as a result, we are now looking at ways in which we can use the system to enhance the individual responsibility of managers.

In the context of the foregoing, what we can learn from the study of senior managers' use of CBISs and their roles in managerial work is that they can be most useful for freeing managerial time, especially in those organizations where time is considered to be a precious commodity. A major managerial implication from this finding is that managerial work is related to user satisfaction, perceived effectiveness and information systems usage. The realization that managerial attitudes had a significant effect on the success and effectiveness of what senior managers do, validates the important role of attitude emphasized in the work of Rivard and Huff (1988). Thus, the findings, if interpreted as outlined here, suggest that information systems, in terms of their influence on managerial work, can have similar impacts upon the work roles of managers in local government.

As a final note, it is worth drawing attention to the fact in both the private sector and the public services, all users tended to certify that CBISs had supported and enriched their work. This corroborates the idea that there may be a strong relationship between managerial perceptions and attitudes on IT and its eventual usage. Certainly non-users and infrequent users of IT among the managers surveyed tended to have less positive views on the value of the information technologies available to them.

10.6   Conclusion

This analysis does not provide easy recipes for public services management on how to manage the complexity represented by MISs. But it underscores the importance of studying the factors that influence success in the use of MISs and their product—information—in managerial work. In that regard, the importance attached to the usefulness of information stems primarily from the contribution it makes to the coordination and control of finance-related and other administrative activities. The information produced by MISs was found to provide managers with a basis upon which they could readily assess performance against pre-established targets, and is therefore seen as an essential aid to management work, more so because information is considered to help alleviate situational problems seen to impinge upon the choice of managers. Our findings suggested also that MISs have proved to be successful in facilitating the planning and management control processes. But apart from extending the capabilities of managers by providing them with an instantaneous information retriever and analyser, the findings indicate that when considered in its conceptual setting, an MIS supported the operating functions of managers purposively. In that regard, the evidence from both the private sector and public services illustrates that task activity influences MIS usage, user satisfaction, perceived usefulness, and effectiveness. The findings also demonstrate that task achievement is related to user satisfaction, perceived usefulness and MIS usage. However, one should also recognize that there are innumerable repetitive tasks that have benefited from MISs. In an effort to increase the effectiveness of MISs, public services management may use this finding to stress the importance of CBISs to managerial work. The findings that attitudes of MIS users had a significant effect on the success of MISs and perceived changes in task effectiveness confirms the important role of attitudes emphasized in prior studies of MIS (Lucas, 1978; Rivard and Huff, 1988). Viewed from this perspective, it is important to recall that some managers did not always find the MIS responsive to all their requirements. For while managers found information useful in planning and control, in the sense that control information triggered off what was perceived as control decision, it was observed that some managers generally maintained localized informal information which buffered activities. The reason why managers construct and use informal systems is because they act as a cushion to the formal MIS. Such systems are not, however, untypical, since there is evidence in the literature which suggests that informal information assists the management process (Clancy and Collins, 1979). However, from the point of view of MIS planning, there is a final learning point from the analysis. It is that more attention should be given to prioritize the broad use of information among managers who deal with local authority business characterized by ambiguity and variety.

References

Ackoff, R. C. (1967) 'Management misinformation systems', *Management Science*, **14** (4), 147–56.

Anthony, R. N. (1965) *Planning and Control Systems: A Framework for Analysis*. Graduate School of Business Administration, Harvard University, Boston.

Argyris, C. (1977) 'Organisational learning and management information systems', *Accounting, Organisations and Society*, **2** (2), 113–23.

Bailey, J. E. and Pearson, S. W. (1983) 'Development of a tool for measuring and analysing computer user satisfaction', *Management Science*, **25** (5), 530–45.

Baroudi, J. J., Olson, M. H. and Ives, B. (1986) 'An empirical study of the impact of user involvement on systems usage and information satisfaction', *Communications of the ACM*, **29** (3) 232–8.

Cheney, P. and Dickson, G. B. (1982) 'Organisational characteristics and information systems success: an exploratory investigation', *Academy of Management Journal*, **25** (1), 17–184.

Clancy, D. K. and Collins, F. (1979) 'Informal accounting information systems: some tentative findings', *Accounting, Organisations and Society*, **4** (2), 3–13.

Daft, R. and Weick, K. E. (1984) 'Toward a model of organizations as interpretation systems', *Academy of Management Review*, **9**, 77–82.

Dockery, E. (1991) *The Use of Information Systems in Managerial Work: Perspectives on Senior Management Use of Information*. Working Paper No. 109, City University Business School, London.

Ein-dor, P. and Segev, E. (1978) 'Organisational context and the success of management information systems', *Management Science*, **24** (10), 1064–77.

Gorry, G. A. and Scott Morton, M. S. (1971) 'A framework for management information systems', *Sloan Management Review*, 55–70.

Guimaraes, T. (1984) 'The benefits and problems of user computing', *Journal of Information Systems Management*, **1** (4), 8–9.

Hedberg, B. and Jonsson, S. (1978) 'Designing semi-confusing information systems for organisations in changing environments', *Accounting Organisations and Society*, **3** (1), 47–64.

Hopwood, A. G. (1974) *Accounting and Human Behaviour*. Haymarket, London.

Ilgen, D., Fisher, C. and Taylor, M. S. (1979) 'Consequences of individual feedback on behaviour in organisations', *Journal of Applied Psychology*, 349–71.

King, W. R. and Epstein, B. J. (1976) 'Assessing the value of information', *Management Datamatics*, **5** (4), 171–80.

Kmetz, J. L. (1984) 'An information processing study of a complex workflow in electronics repair', *Administrative Science Quarterly*. **29**, 255–80.

Lawler, E. E. (1976) 'Control systems in organisations', in Dunnette, M. (ed.), *Handbook of Industrial and Organizational Psychology*. Rand McNally.

Lucas, J. C., (1978) 'Empirical evidence for a descriptive model of implementation', *MIS Quarterly*, **2** (2), 27–41.

March, J. G. and Olsen, J. P. (1976) *Ambiguity and Choice in Organisations*. Universitetsforlaget, Bergen, Norway.

McLean, E. R. (1979) 'End users as application developers', *MIS Quarterly*, **3** (4), 37–46.

O'Reilly, C. H. (1982) 'Variations in decision makers use of information sources: the impact of quality and accessibility of information', *Academy of Management Journal*, **25** (4), 756–71.

Ouchi, W. H. and Maguire, M. A. (1975) 'Organisational control: two functions', *Administrative Science Quarterly*, **20**, 559–69.

Rivard, S. and Huff, S. L. (1988) 'Factors of success for end user computing', *Communication of the ACM*, **31** (5), 552–61.

Robey, D. (1979) 'User attitudes and management information systems use', *Academy of Management Journal*, **22** (3), 527–61.

Rockart, J. F. and Flanery, L. S. (1983) 'The management of end user computing', *Communications of the ACM*, **26** (10), 776–84.

Sprague, R. H. (1980) 'A framework for the development of decision support systems', *MIS Quarterly*, **4** (4), 1–26.

Srinivasan, A. (1985) 'Alternative measures of system effectiveness: association and implications', *MIS Quarterly*, **9** (3), 243–53.

Zmud, R. (1979) 'Individual differences and MIS success: a review of the empirical literature', *Management Science*, **25** (10), 966–79.

11

Police: changing management

Terence Grange

11.1 Introduction

This book discusses the nature and special problems of managing in the public services. It has attempted to demonstrate the uneasy mix and complexity of importing alleged good management prescriptions from the private sector into the public. A decade ago such a discussion may have appeared premature for the public services; it is unlikely that the police and its management would have been included in the discussion. In the past ten years, however, the police service has not been exempted from the political, societal and technological changes that have affected other public services. The views of central government upon the role of the public services and their limits, their demands for greater efficiency and value for money, a more volatile, demanding and questioning consumer of police services and the rapid advance of information technology (IT) upon a management not properly aware of its benefits and difficulties; all these have affected the police as they have the other public services—though their effects may have been more obvious in the education and health services—and they have affected both the content and style of management of the police.

Following the theme developed earlier, the police service has been subjected to the rigours of the Government's Financial Management Initiative (FMI) and its concomitant Rayner style efficiency scrutinies, has struggled with IT and striven to develop performance measures that provide full and not merely financial analyses of performance. In company with other public services the police have seen structural reorganization as one solution and sought to alter structures, systems and latterly cultures to meet the challenge of change. With the other public services, the police may anticipate further pressure for change in the next decade. For police this may entail alterations to the national structure, removal to agency status of support functions such as the Forensic Science Service, a process already under way, privatization of other non-core functions and continuing civilization. The prospect of external managers being forced upon the service is also present. The police may also anticipate continuing financial stringency and a government examining the competence of police management with an increasingly jaundiced eye.

This chapter seeks to pursue the thesis that many of the management prescriptions brought from the private sector sit uneasily within the public services, concentrating upon changes in the management of police. It will show how closely the changes in police management parallel those that have taken place in the other public services and how policies and strategies chosen have mirrored those adopted elsewhere in the public sector. In doing so it will suggest that management of the police belongs within the genus public sector; that the challenges facing us all are generically similar and that resolution or partial resolution has been found in similar philosophies and management strategies. Though there has been a great deal of change affecting all levels of the police service it is the management strata, the superintending ranks, that have taken the major strain of changes in the past decade. That is not to argue that pressures upon operational officers at the front line have not grown; they have grown markedly, but for police managers the change has been more complex, involving new conceptions of their roles and areas of responsibility, and the added disciplines of managing more complex organizations.

For police managers the major change has involved increasing levels of uncertainty. The uncertainty begins with the management styles now needed. Plumridge (1989, p. 113), in discussing his studies of police managers at the Police Staff College, suggested that the change required

> was from a top-down controlling style in which managers behaved largely as supervisors implementing bureaucratically imposed policies to a supportive style in which the different levels in the hierarchy carried out different functions but encouraged and developed a learning climate within the organization.

Bureaucracy and policy imposed from above provides certainty. To foster a learning environment involves following criticism, even from below, and that in itself is an uncertainty police managers could be claimed to be averse to. Managers, now required to formulate local policy and carry it through in open discussion with the public, and their operational officers, have discovered that financial management, rostering personnel for duty, choosing between available strategies when under internal and external pressure, and carrying through change in the traditional imposed style can, in a more openly critical internal and external environment, prove very difficult. The now almost obligatory openness and public consultation is bringing into public view the policy-making processes, and publicly presenting police managers at all levels with decisions that carry elements of risk and uncertainty. Foremost among these is the style of policing to be adopted. There are, for instance:

> on one hand pressures to develop sensitivity through 'community policing', on the other hand there are forces pushing in the direction of para-military operations in order to contain public disorder.
>
> (Plumridge, 1989, p. 115)

For the police the judgement at this level is between forms and even philosophies of policing. In the inner cities, for instance, a balance must be found between demands for increased foot patrolling which Waddington (1990), commenting in the *Police Review*, suggests is the most appropriate strategy to deal with the major concerns of the majority of the public, it being 'yobbery and not robbery' that induces fear of crime, and the dangers that may follow an omnipresent and apparently overpowering police presence which may reduce 'yobbery' but induce the tensions that lead to confrontation between police and a population resenting that police presence. For the police manager the costs of the wrong choice of strategy are not merely financial; they are counted in more personal terms in injuries, crime and damaged property. Conversely, success may pass unnoticed.

The past decade has produced empirical examples of these choices being made: in Bristol in 1980 where a police raid on a café became the trigger for major public disorder (Weigh, 1980) and in Brixton, where a police operation to deter street robbery was claimed to be the trigger for more major disorder (Scarman, 1982). These are perhaps dramatic examples of risk-taking, whether or not the risk was appreciated. In the years following those incidents the risks involved in strategy choice have been well learned. At this level the decisions and analysis in support of them, though not obviously carrying the financial element upon which the literature on risk management concentrates, may be seen as analogous in that the risks of alternative choices must be balanced and predicted outcomes judged so that the most beneficial risk can be taken. At a less dramatic level choices as to which areas will receive priority for police patrols or the level of police effort put into particular crime investigations, which became a matter of policy under an initiative known as crime screening, have been made. The latter choice resulted in damaging publicity for the force concerned. Uncertainty can therefore be seen in the relationship with the consumer, a matter not previously considered, and in consulting staff, a consideration of which police managers had little experience.

In seeking to explore how police management has altered to cope with uncertain environments and risk-taking, this chapter commences with a brief explanation of the structure of the police service; how a force is organized and the effects of that organization upon its personnel, their attitudes, cultures and perceptions of the organizational reality. From that brief discussion follows application of the domain theory suggested in the Introduction to this book against the historical structure and later the developing structure of police organizations. To set the scene for discussion of the management initiatives and their impact, intended and unintended, on the events and incidents of the past decade, the legal and political changes are then introduced to explain how the police came to their present position before the most important of these changes are explored more deeply. The choice of those factors is personal and open to challenge by colleagues and students of police. The closeness of these strategies to those adopted elsewhere in the public sector are noted, as are the consequences of prevailing internal tensions and cultures. The problems of importing initiatives into contradictory environments are shown, as are the complexities of introducing into an organization and management culture that has made a virtue of bureaucracy, the more organic and entrepreneurial styles of management that these initiatives demand. Then the future is tentatively suggested, together with the types and contents of future management roles. What then is a police organization?

11.2 Police organization and cultures

Modern police organizations in the United Kingdom were formed in the nineteenth century, their structures being basic command and control systems, with no specialist or detective units. Through the twentieth century, government policy upon standardization and amalgamations has created the present structure. There are 43 police forces in England and Wales, ranging from the 43 000 strong Metropolitan Police to the small county forces like Warwickshire and Northamptonshire, some 1400 personnel. It is argued by McKenzie and Gallagher (1989, p. 69) that there are no typical organizational structures: 'the relative autonomy and independence of the chief officer enables him to devise and supervise a unique organisational structure'.

This perception is accurate; the size and nature of area policed, the community, problems and other special features will dictate to some extent the formal structure of a force, as will the philosophies and strategies of the chief officer. The Metropolitan Police is unique in its Royalty and Diplomatic Protection Department whose sole function is protection duties. Other forces have centralized traffic departments, or have decentralized them, as policy. Even so, certain features are common across the organizations. All possess some specialist units; there are 247 special squads in the 43 forces (OPR, 1990), and most forces appear to be structured into three or four major groupings: Operations, Support and Personnel/Training. It is under the Operations title that the vast majority of policing effort seen and experienced by the public is gathered. Within Operations are found the majority of police managers and operational personnel and a range of specialist squads and departments formed to deal with specific problems. Within the other departments are found training officers and police officers involved in research, communications provision, community relations policy and work and a range of other supportive functions. However, it is within the Operations department that inter-organizational incompatibilities and links induce much of the pressures that have helped form the cultures noted and reported upon by outside students of police.

The organization chart shown in Fig. 11.1 suggests the separation. Within this type of structure the gap between the specialist and high profile central units and the uniform groups and community constables on subdivisions, where communities are policed, may be defined. Together the central units comprise less than a fifth of the personnel of any force. Units such as the Task Force or

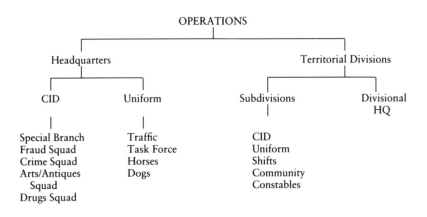

Figure 11.1   Organization chart

special patrol groups are high profile, highly trained personnel tasked to deal with public disorder, and their training and control is more military than any other part of the police system. There are inherent tensions in such an arrangement, Brogden *et al.* (1988, p. 78) suggesting that:

> the problems of upgrading specialist tasks can be compounded in a number of ways. The specialist training involved, separateness, camaraderie, all contribute to a feeling of superiority.

The use of upbeat titles reinforces such concepts and encourages attitudes and perceptions of the police role quite different from that of the core of the police effort, the uniform shifts and community constables. Similarly, detectives may see their career path and loyalties resting in their ability to impress detective headquarters and not their local managers.

Police officers on shifts are also bound together, not by specialism but by the clock. They work and often play in groups and can come to perceive the world from that closed group. The aggregation of the cultures formed in these groups is what to outside observers is the prevailing police culture at operational levels. Within these groups formal management roles are carried out by sergeants and inspectors, planning, allocating and monitoring the activities of their personnel. Theirs is an important role in the development of new recruits and promising personnel. Such groups can become claustrophobically self-concerned, viewing the world from behind self-created walls, sometimes joined there by their immediate managers. The introspection and defensiveness of that outlook is expressed in one comment noted by Reiner (1985):

> We're a tightknit community. We've got to stand by each other because we're getting it from all angles. We get it from outside, the general public, from solicitors, we get it from our own bosses.

This last comment is the most telling. How does management affect operational officers and what do police managers do? Plumridge's comments, noted earlier, provide an understanding. Historically police managers have imposed, through layer upon layer of supervision, the policies of the chief officer. From junior through middle manager, inspector to chief superintendent, there has been little separation of activities. The overriding function has been that of supervision of the results of the activities of junior personnel. Thus the major discretionary activity and responsibility has rested at the bottom of the organization while managers have concentrated upon supervision of post-incident reports. Arrest reports, accident reports, papers prepared for courts, property records, all were examined by layer after layer of supervisor to reduce the possibility of error and to ensure a correct decision. Thus, in one force at 8 a.m. a chief inspector would examine records, to be followed by a superintendent at 8.30 a.m., and possibly a chief superintendent at 9 a.m., all examining the same records. At divisional command level studies by Males (1983) of the roles of superintendents and chief superintendents produced evidence that the activities of both were identical, many force reorganizations using that premise as a starting point for job redefinition, and the recasting of roles discussed later.

For police officers at all levels the major requirement has historically been that of compliance with the rules. For junior levels—possessing the greatest discretion and, in their eyes, the most responsibility—Kelling et al. (1988, p. 2), discussing the American experience, suggests that:

> strain between the realities of police work and the command and control systems creates problems for administrators. The discontinuities between organisational perceptions and work realities are not lost on police officers, the results are considerable role strain on officers who are portrayed as professionals on one hand but treated as recalcitrant employees on the other.

Smith (1983), in his research among police in England, reports finding in London an alternative culture among operation officers antithetical to that of their management, and Reiner (1985) suggests that the experience of America reported by Kelling et al. is replicated here, and that the consequences are similar. McKenzie and Gallagher (1989, p. 111) report that

> in 1983 a series of workshops on police stress in England and Wales chose to categorise sources of police stress under four major headings; management style, management structure, management systems and traumatic incidents.

The costs are insidious and debilitating. As Kelling et al. (1988) suggest, creativity and productivity may go unrewarded, potential is left untapped and a culture characterized by suspiciousness, isolation, fear and internal solidarity becomes a norm. Such a culture is not unusual, and may be recognizable to others in the public sector. However, its ability to frustrate and deny change in the face of compelling evidence of need cannot be underestimated. For police managers a similar picture may be drawn, concentrating upon supervision and seeking to retain command and control through application of rigid rules, the authority of rank and a formal discipline code, their time concerned with examination of papers, sometimes dozens of interviews to conduct the formal staff appraisal system and constant rehearsal of the events of the past day.

From this picture of antithetical cultures and interests it is possible to examine the police through the domain theory suggested in the Introduction. The domain theory of Kouzes and Mico (1979) suggests that human service organizations (HSOs) may be seen through three domains, each with its own set of governing principles, success measures and work modes that are incongruent with the others. It suggests a policy domain, a management domain and a service domain. Recent developments in police management and management structures and roles may permit application of that theory, as will be discussed later. Within the historical structure there have been three clear groupings: the Association of Chief Police Officers, the Superintendents Association and the Police Federation representing the lower, service levels. However, the theory suggests that the three domains will acknowledge the difference and separateness of each other and that does not so clearly apply to the police. The service level may argue that there are only two domains, theirs and management, which would include all those not in their perception of the service group. The management strata would possibly seek to claim to be police officers obliged by their rank to supervise, but nevertheless police officers. Given that difference, the tensions and area for conflict between the two, the differing views upon success and differing principles by which they seek to govern themselves, appear to exist.

This section has briefly discussed the formal structures of police forces and the effects they have upon operational police officers and the roles and activities of police managers. The cultures that have evolved within the structure were suggested. This is, for many forces, a historical and no longer applicable picture, indeed it is a picture that is of necessity somewhat broad brush. The changes to the laws within which the police work, in requirements of management for more efficiency and in policing philosophies, have begun to alter those cultures. In the next section the events, incidents, legal and managerial changes that have wrought these alterations will be introduced prior to discussing those that have had the most impact.

11.3   1974 to 1990—preparation for change

The police service enters the 1990s facing an apparent crisis of public confidence and increasing debate as to the quality of its management and leadership. From what incidents and changes has this decreasing confidence in police developed? Albeit artificially, a history of the changes may have begun in 1974 when the last major police force restructuring created the present 43 force structure. The next few years saw major public disorder in Notting Hill at the 1976 carnival, repeated in 1977. This was followed by the death of Blair Peach in Southall in

1979. Both produced concerns as to police ability to deal with this level of disorder. The Guildford 4, the McGuire 7 and the alleged Birmingham pub bombers were convicted. By 1991 all these groups had successfully challenged their convictions in the Appeal Courts, adding to the concerns on police management. The police service suffered from low morale and high wastage through poor pay and conditions, culminating in the Edmund Davies report of 1979 which radically improved police pay and became latterly a source of discontent among other public services employees. The 1970s were not good years for the police: a series of scandals raised debate about the conduct of police; there was concern that police were not only unaccountable but in some areas deviant; and the relationship between the police and ethnic minority populations became increasingly sour. The 1980s were little different—a period in which change appeared to be the only certainty, and the role of the police service came under increasing and acrimonious scrutiny following a series of major civil and industrial disturbances (Weatheritt, 1989, p. 6). There appeared ever-present public disorder and industrial strife, the major disorders being:

1980 St Pauls, Bristol
1981 Toxteth, Brixton, Handsworth
1984 The Miners' Strike
1985 Wapping, Broadwater Farm, Brixton

These incidents also provided an internal backdrop against which changes in policing styles and legal and other changes sought by government were examined. The disorders produced a more militaristic style of policing and debate upon the need for a separate force to deal with riots. From dustbin lids in 1976 the police now possess a wide range of protective equipment and a well-trained reserve of officers to deal with disorder. Alleged failings in police command and control at these incidents produced internal tension and external criticism of the competence of police commanders.

11.3.1 LEGAL CHANGE
The 1980s produced two major pieces of legislation affecting police powers:

1984 The Police and Criminal Evidence Act, which introduced wide ranging changes in police powers and practice in the detention, treatment and questioning of prisoners, giving specific legal responsibilities to sergeants, inspectors and superintendents. It also formalized consultative arrangements between police and the public, and the powers of the Police Complaints Authority.
1985 The Prosecution of Offences Act, which introduced the Crown Prosecution Service, and removed the prosecution process from police control.

Though the law and repetitive incidence of public disorder, the two major industrial disputes and the Hillsborough tragedy have radically affected police training and attitudes towards the role of many police managers and operational officers, it is the government-inspired changes in management practice, and the initiatives that followed, that have most affected management roles. The causes and initiatives are listed in Table 11.1.

Towards the end of the decade the police at all levels felt under challenge. The continuing pressures upon police, and fears as to the consequences for the future style of policing, produced in 1990 the *Operational Policing Review*, a document commissioned by the three Police Staff Associations. The review (OPR, 1990) discussed the Home Office Circulars mentioned in Table 11.1 and their costs to the police in terms of seeking the quantifiable results favoured by the Home Office and the initiatives that have followed. It also discussed and researched the views of the public and serving police officers on styles and priorities of policing, what they should be and what should take priority. The seductive nature of managing by numbers and the resultant loss of quality of service were brought to public debate more fully in the document than hitherto, and the results of the public and police surveys presented clear evidence of the problems facing police managers. While the public seek more foot patrols and community-orientated policing, given a choice between a 'caring community constable' and a 'firm law enforcer' they naturally chose the former; they also require immediate response to calls for police in emergencies, which raises the question of: Who defines an emergency? They also require offender detection and arrest and crime investigations in full. Police officers saw responding to emergencies as the primary role and were very ambivalent and almost dismissive of the concept of community orientated or soft policing (OPR, 1990, sections 5 and 6). The contrast in views is not surprising but it begs questions as to the ease with which police managers will successfully change policing styles.

Within these surveys is found the major dichotomy posed for police managers

Table 11.1   Government changes in police management

Home Office Circular	Initiative
114/83: on manpower, efficiency and effectiveness	Policing by objectives (results orientated policing)
105/88: on civilianization programmes	Civilianization of front offices and control rooms and senior posts
106/88: on increasing establishments	Crime management (whether or not to investigate)
35/89: on changing capital budget arrangements	Decentralization and devolvement of authority, including budgets and efficiency scrutinies
87/89: on equal opportunities	Force reorganizations (fewer senior managers)

in seeking to produce effective policing strategies through the confused signals received from the public. This single issue may separate the police most from other public services, where public expectations of the role may be more clear. The fundamental issue for police and public is whether the police is a service or a force; should the community-orientated service, seen in the uniformed officer on foot patrol seeking to meet the needs of the community from within, take precedence, or should the crime fighter, using modern technology, police the community? The public appear to wish the former in general and require the latter when they call police, speed of response being a measure of police performance in such circumstances. Maintaining a facility to provide swift response in a time when calls for police are increasing exponentially annually militates against increased foot patrols. From within, the issue is equally unclear; the desired ethic of many is that of crime fighter—a form of heroic/technologically equipped specialist in combating crime and criminals with no concern for non-crime matters—with community-orientated service policing being seen as a soft form of policing best left to community officers. Within this argument may be found the view that crime-fighting is the major police role and that they, as professionals, should be left to get on with it. Also the confusion caused by signals received may provide excuses or alibis for alleged police reticence to involve the public in setting policy, for they are not clear as to what they want, or in involving the public in discussion of policing strategy or priorities. Proponents of this view within the police are able to subordinate individual and community concerns over minor matters to those more important demands of real crime that the 'professional' perceives as the real issue. The 1980s have brought the choice of policing style, whether it be community-based or independent crime fighter, and the accountability of police firmly into the public domain. The next section seeks to examine both issues and what the police functions are, and the difficulties facing police policy makers in introducing 'management' as a concept. These questions feature heavily in further discussion of the role of the police manager and the relationship between police managers and the public.

11.4   Who is in charge?

The views of some policy makers in policing are clear on this issue. Sir Peter Imbert, Commissioner of the Metropolitan Police, the largest constabulary in the country, stated at the International Police Exhibition in September 1989 that

> Police sometimes quite wrongly assume the monopoly of good ideas on good community relations and good policing . . . the public have a right to be actively involved in determining how policing is developed.

He went on to say that his philosophy would be one of 'Openness, access, power sharing and the sharing of responsibility' (*The Guardian*, 1989, 8 November). Should this statement of philosophy be followed through it will have a major impact upon police managers, those whom it is suggested already bear the brunt of change, for it is at the local level that openness becomes a reality and impacts upon the police/public relationship, as will be demonstrated. The comments of Sir Peter Imbert touch in a sense upon the most contentious areas of policing, those of accountability and public involvement in policing, equity and probity, all of which are familiar to other public services. Police accountability has long been a vexed issue; a tripartite structure as between the Home Office, local police authorities and chief constables. This structure is most recently embodied in the Police Act 1964. The Act provides for clear and separate roles for the three members of this tripartite arrangement, and gives chief police officers a level of operational autonomy unique in the public services. A police authority has 'a duty to secure the maintenance of an adequate and efficient police force (Section 4.a) and to keep themselves informed of the manner in which complaints made by members of the public against the force are dealt with by the chief constable (Section 50)'. Chief constables have a duty to 'direct and control' their forces (Section 5 (1)), enforce the law and submit annually a written report to the Home Secretary and the police authority on the policing of the area (Section 12(1)). The Home Secretary has powers to make regulations as to the government, administration and conditions of service of police forces, and to 'act in such a manner as appears to him to be best calculated to promote the efficiency of the force' (Section 28). This arrangement is argued by government to provide a proper balance of power between the chief officer, local political authority and central authority. In matters of operations the chief constable is to be free from political direction.

It is argued that the present structure provides too much independence to chief officers and power or control to government at the expense of local political representatives (Simey, 1988) and that the stewardship form of accountability, which the tripartite system follows, with the chief officer annually giving an account of how stewardship of the area has been conducted, denies power to the local people most affected by the stewardship (Jefferson and Grimshaw, 1984; Lustgarten, 1986). This argument, followed by Brogden *et al.* (1988) and others, provides one of the mainstream literatures upon police. Others examine sociological perspectives of policing or concentrate upon organization, the classic of the latter type being O. W. Wilson's *Police Administration* (1950), which argued for an independent professional police force led by highly qualified police administrators. Another form may be taking shape in discussions that seek to marry the separate literatures and produce from them a synthesis that may stimulate further debate. Bradley *et al.* (1986) in *Managing the Police* provide what may become a seminal contribution. They suggest the first and major problem for public, police policy maker, police manager and police operator is that the goals of policing are not only complex, they are ambiguous, contradictory and often mutually incompatible. Outlining six broad goals:

1 The maintenance of law and order and the protection of persons and property.
2 The prevention of crime.
3 The detection of criminals.
4 Controlling of road traffic and advising local authorities on traffic questions.
5 Carrying out certain duties on behalf of government departments.
6 Befriending anyone who needs help and being available at any time to cope with minor
   and major emergencies.

(Bradley *et al.*, 1986, p. 65)

Bradley *et al.* demonstrate how strategies to impact one goal can affect another adversely. They also suggest how complex predicting and planning can be—a possibility of which many police critics appear unaware. It is suggested by Brogden *et. al.* (1988) that a proper construct of police management can only be formulated from an understanding of Bradley *et al.*'s argument that police goals are ambiguous and often incompatible. While this argument suggests that the police face special and unique problems, managers in the health service might be able to draw analogies. Police managers also face equally pressing issues such as motivating a discrete group of 'professionals' possessing their own codes and mores and measuring and monitoring their performance—issues that hospital and social services managers will find familiar. The imperatives of efficiency and attempts to ration service, which the recent 'crime screening' strategy was, and the problems of measuring outputs and lack of choice of customer are similar across the organizations.

For the police the internal environmental issues suggested by Ianni (1983) and Smith (1983), and supported by research upon proposals to alter working rosters conducted by the author (Grange, 1988), provide for difficulties in introducing change, which other services will also recognize. They may also recognize the 'reluctant police manager' of Bradley *et al.* (1986, p. 35). This conception of the management function as irrelevent, unnecessary and unwelcome—especially to officers whose preferred role is that of some form of 'police street leader' to operational personnel, and who find the problems of constructing and monitoring performance measures, planning according to budgets and having to confront what are essentially management rather than policing or professional issues—is noted by Bradley *et al.* but must be familiar to professionals in the social services, education and health. The new management/leadership abilities, leading and managing change, together with open consultation with the public upon previously internal professional issues may be those that are seen as unacceptable and, along with budgeting and performance measurement, those that produce the reluctant or indifferent manager. How this reluctance or indifference will be overcome may be one of the issues for the public services in the next decade. This issue is unlikely to go away; police personnel and police managers cannot be removed to assist the processes of change as can and does occur in private industry. The new chief executive cannot sweep away the immediate team nor can middle management be retired, at least not yet; they have to be brought into the change process and those managing change must include in their deliberations the costs of ignoring these powerful groups or seek to utilize their abilities.

It may be seen that the environment within which police managers are working is complex externally and internally, and occasionally hostile. The issues they face are those familiar to all modern management, rapid and constant change, performance measurement and financial stringency, probity, equity and increasing and more diverse forms of demand and accountability. The sources of these issues are now discussed, and their impact explored, beginning with legislation.

11.5   The Police and Criminal Evidence Act 1984

It has been suggested that the issues of accountability, equity and probity are constant issues for police. The major source of change in these areas during the 1980s is found in the Police and Criminal Evidence Act 1984. The PACE Act laid down formal guidelines as to the arrest and detention of persons detained or in police custody, their questioning and rights; it also encouraged consultative procedures (Section 106) between police and local communities. This change has had potentially the most radical effect upon police management. One consequence has been the strengthening of one of the management roles undertaken by police sergeants. They have two main functions; one involves the supervision of their constables, a Fayolian prescription of planning, allocating, motivating and coordinating their activities. The role altered by the PACE Act, that of custody officer, makes them the guardian of the rights of the temporarily dispossessed, the person in custody:

> At the immediate end he will be the executive officer of the law, the guardian of police station procedures and a defender of civil liberties. His judgement will be crucial and his decisons vital.
>
> (Eldon Griffiths, MP)

This can bring them into conflict with investigating officers whose imperatives are different and whose previous ability to control aspects of the detention process to their advantage has been lessened if not removed. The role of custody sergeant is both complex and demanding, and possibly unwelcome:

> You ask any young probationer what is the worst job in the police service, he'll say Custody Officer. They absolutely hate it. Because if anything goes wrong the buck will definitely land in your lap.

This quote from a police sergeant in Roger Graef's *Talking Blues* (1989, p. 284)—a volume of quotations from serving police officers—neatly encapsulates one view on the role. The need for scrupulous maintenance of custody records and occasional conflict with colleagues who find difficulty in coming to terms with this protective role does little to encourage its acceptance. The custody sergeant's role as guardian of the rights and liberties of the client/

prisoner goes unseen and unremarked yet it is a signal increase in responsibility which, if not well conducted, permits those acts that are inequitable or lack probity, and fosters the deviant practices that allegedly underlie present public disquiet. Conversely, its proper conduct instils in those carrying it out a respect for legal procedures and probity that can be brought to their other supervisory role, which in a period of increasing consumerism will be a healthy development. Their position in the earliest management role is particularly invidious, placing them in positions of personal responsibility far greater than their more senior managers. Comparisons may be found in the roles of hospital unit managers and custody officers, both are in potential conflict with experts seeking to impose their long-held practices in a changed environment.

The sergeant custody officer is, for police, the first line of service maintenance and quality assurance and is in direct contact with those who most feel any failures in quality, i.e. the public who are detained. The role is almost hidden from public view, though lay visitor schemes permitting selected members of the public access to police cells have sought to examine it in operation, yet through its conduct public perceptions of police are altered and reinforced. Its importance should not be underestimated.

Other parts of the PACE Act had some origins in the Scarman Report, which suggested that local consultation could forestall the distrust and disenfranchisement felt by many inner city residents and others (Scarman, 1982). The consultative arrangements are based upon local communities, and though there is some debate as to their success (Morgan, 1987), they can cause police superintendents to examine critically their policies and priorities. They have clearly demonstrated the gaps in perceptions of policing priorities between police professionals and the consumers of the service. One such instance may be seen in the differing definitions of vandalism, which the public perceive as dumped cars, litter and noisy youths or drunks wandering in their area, while the police perceive it as acts of criminal damage. The consultative process can influence police behaviour and strategy: a survey by questionnaire recently conducted under the auspices of the local Police Liaison Committee among 1000 residents of Kingswood, Bristol, who had sought police assistance, disclosed high levels of satisfaction with the service provided but also criticism of police failure to inform callers of the results of their calls, and dislike of police officers treating service calls (non-crime) as being unimportant or trivial (Brooks, 1989).

Public fora such as these, despite Morgan's (1987) criticism that they are dominated by the well-meaning and middle classes, provide the primary interface between police managers and their public. They place police superintendents at the front of debate, albeit only locally, on the priorities and objectives of policing and the policing styles, attitudes and results of their officers. Current trends towards decentralization may have origins in this initiative and will place more emphasis upon this forum, as conversely would moves towards regional or national control of police organizations; the more central and distant the control, the more local power would have to be devolved. They present difficulties for police superintendents; much of the debate can centre upon the inadequacies of other local arrangements for clearing streets of litter, dumped vehicles and unwelcome outsiders, inviting criticism of other social agencies. It can also centre upon inadequate resources or lack of support for local police strategy from the centre or other organizations. There is a temptation to use them to find 'friends' of the police and to seek to use those friends to press the police view on local matters or forward the local police view of police matters to force headquarters. There are limits to the potential for such strategies being deployed. The police are part of the judicial process and the social process. Other organizations, the courts, social services, education service, Crown Prosecution Service (CPS), probation service and health service, have roles also. The gathering of friends to press the police view can on occasion be to the detriment of relations with these organizations, and may place police managers in positions where their friends have unrealistic expectations that cannot or should not be met. For instance, removing itinerant travellers is an expectation that cannot be met unless the law allows it—a matter seldom understood by local friends of the police. Within these constraints, with which many may disagree, the police manager should see the local consultative group as a forum for open discussion, inviting criticism, gathering support and friends. Doing so may require a more open and approachable face than the studies cited above suggest has been shown by some.

The PACE Act has had its effects upon police at all levels, but police managers in their role as local policy makers and strategists have felt its demands for more open consultation and explanation more keenly than other levels. Alongside this change the introduction of independent prosecutors and the Police Complaints Authority have had their effect. It is the local police manager who conducts liaison with the CPS over matters of local prosecution policy and difficulties or disputes over decisions made by the CPS. Other developments include the encouragement by central government of a wider and more strategic approach to crime (Locke, 1990). Arguments for this wider approach criticize the present responses as being fragmented and lacking the collaborative coordination among the various social agencies involved in the criminal justice system that would enable a comprehensive strategic approach to the problem of crime. The inability of police to surrender the lead position in such strategic teams is particularly criticized and remains possibly the most difficult issue for police to come to terms with. The equal partnerships Locke suggests as necessary must include a freer exchange of information and greater intra-organizational trust, which may be difficult to achieve and would excite the concerns of professionals in the separate organizations, and civil liberties organizations. There have been attempts to form widely based collaborative groups to create joint strategies to deal with crime, the Metropolitan Police multi-agency approach was one (Newman, 1983), and the Home Office continues to encourage more attempts, though successful attempts have been few. The PACE Act has, as has been shown, altered perceptions and the realities of managerial roles in the police, and increased the contact between police managers and the public. Linked to this pressure for increased contacts have been government circulars upon police manpower, efficiency, effectiveness and economy and the results police managers should seek to achieve, though there are few numerical measures of success. It is to these that discussion now turns, and their impact upon police management and operations.

11.6   Efficiency and the police

The Financial Management Initiative (FMI) has had major effects. Concomitant with its introduction, forces have reorganized the roles of their superintending ranks, introduced decentralized responsibility and authority encouraged by Her Majesty's Inspector of Constabularies, and in some cases introduced local financial management based around superintendent command unit subdivisions. For the police service FMI is found in the Home Office Circular 114/83 on 'Manpower, efficiency and effectiveness', a seminal document in the changes that have occurred in the last decade, though some forces rightly claim to have adopted their programmes earlier, Northampton commencing theirs in 1981.

The circular informed chief constables and police authorities that future bids for resources would be subject to clear evidence that all present resources were being deployed efficiently and effectively. To that end chief constables were advised that the Home Office would expect police priorities and activities to be subjected to analysis from which would flow measurable goals and objectives and that performance measurement would become a standard tool of analysis. The circular brought police spending firmly under central government control, producing de facto central control, which recent circulars on capital spending, giving the Home Office a prior veto on spending plans, have reinforced.

Supporting 114/83 have come Circulars 105/88 and 106/88 on police manpower and civilianization, both of which pursue the central thesis that increased use of civilians should be a major efficiency target and that previously acknowledged measures of demand for increased police establishments, such as increased population, no longer apply. These circulars, which have as their focus efficiency then effectiveness, have been buttressed by evidence culled from the works of such as the Police Foundation on police experiments (Weatheritt, 1986), the Audit Commission studies on police vehicle fleets, administrative procedures and systems and training (Audit Commission Papers on Police, Nos 1 to 3) and Home Office Research and Planning Unit papers on police foot patrols and criminal investigations which have challenged many long-standing beliefs as to the efficacy of these arrangements (Clarke and Hough, 1984). More recent criticism of police management may be found in The Economist:

Imagine a company whose shift rotas are determined a year in advance and whose workers, in return for accepting last minute alterations, demand large bonuses—yes its the police.

(*The Economist*, 10 February, 1990)

These arrangements are legally binding and have caused one police manager in London to inform his two local professional football clubs that matches may no longer be arranged at short notice, the cost to his budget being excessive.

From 114/83 have flown Rayner style efficiency scrutinies into subjects as diverse as police bands, communications and overtime—implications of the latter being examined shortly—and value-for-money initiatives that include restructuring organizations. The initiatives have been varied, but all appear to centre upon results-orientated policing and the management of policing towards achieving defined results. It is that change that is now discussed.

11.7   Management by results?

The strictures of Circular 114/83 demanded that the purposes of police forces be articulated by chief officers through updated mission statements, clear force goals and objectives flowing from them, and then the setting locally of objectives from which action plans could be prepared, conducted and analysed through the use of specific and agreed measures of performance: in essence, rational management; analysis of role; and presentation of a newly defined mission statement, the philosophy from which objectives and local plans could be constructed. The police systems all appear to be derived from the works of Lubans and Edgar (1979) on *Policing by Objectives* (PBO), a derivative at some remove of the Management by Objectives (MBO) concepts of Drucker (1955). PBO demands a clear analysis of demands and statements of priorities by the chief constables—missions and goals—followed by analysis at all levels down the organizational pyramid upon objectives, demands, plans and evaluations of plans in action. Its success was theorized to be founded upon the involvement of officers at all levels, from which commitment to the process would inevitably follow, and a comprehensive planning cycle. Locally, superintendents are the managers of the system and are responsible for its implementation and success.

By its very nature and that of the police organization, PBO began as a massive paper bureaucracy and a major producer of meetings, action groups, working parties and evaluation exercises. The belief that involvement would engender enthusiasm is challenged by the studies in New York of Reuss-Ianni and Ianni (1983, p. 113):

Whilst we assumed that headquarters was well intentioned and expected the MBO program to improve efficiency, at the precinct level supervisors as well as street cops ridiculed as well as resented the fact that they were being asked to come up with numbers which were meaningless to them in terms of actual precinct work.

That similar views are held by police managers and operational officers in this country has never been seriously challenged, and presents a major difficulty in the early stages of implementing such a strategy. The works of Burrows and Lewis (1988), which suggests that constables—those who carry out the action plans—resist attempts to set goals and that their activities are guided more by their own backgrounds and personal interests than by management's wishes, presents clear evidence of another factor acting against the MBO style of management. Similarly, operational officers who take a jaundiced view of their management are unlikely to provide quick, uncritical support. Empirical evidence within two forces suggests to the author that the process had other major problems to overcome before acceptance. The process is rational and scientific. Its early introduction was fostered by guidelines and advice that was couched in specifically management terms, in jargon that was for many long-service senior and middle-ranking officers almost unreadable. The police culture tends to the use of plain language, albeit it becomes somewhat stylized, and the initial guidance was neither plain nor in language that was easily understood, which delivered a serious wound to the concept before it began.

Implementation also commenced with the removal of operational officers from street duties to provide the analytical teams necessary to its functioning —an event that encouraged sceptics to question how the time lost to operational work would be replaced. In effect the management strata charged with its implementation was in some cases lacking the commitment necessary, as suggested by the 'reluctant manager' syndrome noted earlier and the cultures at lower levels were not immediately receptive. Many of these problems have been overcome and a more fluid system now exists with less time committed to the supporting structure of the process. There were, however, other problems. The process invited operational officers to produce action plans to meet local objectives, and also through the consultative processes could involve the local population in suggesting targets for action. Objectives and plans so conceived can require changes in spending plans or priorities or in operational policy. The majority of police forces in the early 1980s were essentially centralist in character; authority for policy change or finance resting at the centre, and the 'experts' overseeing the new management systems were also at the centre. Local managers occasionally found that lower level enthusiasm could be diluted through realization that what they thought were simple decisions required central authority, which could be a long time in generation. In addition, previously acceptable measures—that is, acceptable to operational officers—such as arrest rates, were seemingly replaced by efficiency measures: how much will the operation cost and will the results justify the cost? Cost was not at that time seen as relevant to a culture that had no dealings with finance. In a financial environment in which costs will play a major role in determining the ongoing commitment to a murder enquiry, as suggested by reports on 22 May 1990 into a murder in Gloucestershire (Points West, BBC), the change is radical and clearly one of balancing the risk that the public will take a dim view of such a choice against the increasing costs of what may appear a continuing and fruitless enquiry. An equally interesting point is that the police went public.

PBO suffered from its rationality, it assumed that given rational analysis and clear specification of targets, operational personnel would support it. The humanist perceptions appeared to be ignored and the internal cultures and values that bind operational officers together were apparently neither properly understood nor used to assist in the introduction of the new order. It is argued that to date it has not been the success that was hoped for. Studies conducted by McGregor in 1989 and reported in the *Operational Policing Review* (1990) suggest that, in one force studied, less than 20 per cent of operational officers were aware of or worked to the goals and objectives stated by the chief constable. In the same force the majority of superintendents canvassed described the system as: 'a worthwhile exercise requiring a lot of work before it becomes truly effective' (OPR, 1990, Ch. 2, p. 13).

Regrettably the work needed is not made explicit; however the difficulties of PBO have been suggested above, and may be summarized as its apparent failure to be related into the behavioural patterns of operational police personnel, its time consuming and bureaucratic nature, and difficulty in providing acceptable measurements for the objectives and action plans pursued, much of which rests upon measures of police activity rather than the results of that activity. To be truly effective, the systems of PBO would have to become a part of the patterns of thinking and planning of the majority of police personnel, carried out almost automatically and seen by all personnel as a proper means of both planning and evaluating police work. As yet there are arguments that the evaluation it claims to provide is firstly limited and secondly unnecessary, providing little that could not have been suggested without the time spent in conducting evaluation. PBO has not yet captured the hearts or minds of many police officers, and with police time constantly being drawn away from planned activity to provide response to unforeseen events, such as the Strangeways Prison incident and its follow up in other prisons, it appears unlikely to do so. It is further argued that by concentrating upon the easily measurable quantitative aspects of policing, measurement being essential to the pursuit of more resources, the police are ignoring their true function, which is to convey by their presence on the streets in uniform the authority of the State, and provide reassurance (Waddington, 1986)—an argument that supports his thesis that it is behaviour in public and of a minor 'yobbish' nature that the police appear not to control, and it is this that has induced the fear of crime that most damages public confidence in the police. This argument discusses the other main issue with PBO. It measures only 25 per cent of the activities of police, providing little evidence of the effectiveness or efficiency with which police carry out their service roles, which are far larger than is generally realized, service calls being over 50 per cent of calls for police attendance. Perhaps the continuing public demand for 'more bobbies on the beat' supplies some small support for this line of reasoning.

Given the criticisms, PBO has provided measures of police performance and clear evidence of priority setting according to proper analysis rather than a belief founded upon experience or claims to better insight than that possessed by others. It provides managers with some, albeit limited, proven evidence of demands and changing demands, and of their success or otherwise in seeking to meet demands. It allows managers to present to their staff and consultative groups discussion founded on analysis and seek their help from solid foundations rather than the shifting sands of beliefs and 'professional' judgement. It has also produced evidence that police rosters and working patterns are not necessarily matched to demands, and has provided managers with the information necessary to support their arguments for changes to work patterns. By challenging assumptions long held as to what constitutes good management and leadership, the process has arguably improved management and provided police managers with a better understanding of their role. Its future may rest in the success of other initiatives now discussed and the possibility that the present regulations regarding duty rosters may become more flexible. It also rests in the willingness of senior police policy makers to devolve that power, an initiative now discussed.

11.8   Decentralization

It has been suggested that one of the problems of PBO and Scarman's local consultative groups was the inability of local managers rapidly to alter work patterns, funding arrangements or policy. In consequence, their ability to influence issues was diminished and seen to be so. It may be that realization of this and a more general trend towards moving downwards responsibility and accountability, in the non-political sense, are the progenitors of the moves towards decentralization that have been a feature of many forces during the past decade. Again, there may be contrary views: during the early 1980s the works of Peters and Waterman (1982), *In Search of Excellence*, appeared to be required reading among senior police personnel, and many internal documents on management quoted extensively from it. The argument for a decentralized humanist approach to management may have struck a chord in the internal analyses taking place after the disorders of 1980/81. There are other arguments in favour of this approach in the police service.

Decentralization has many different origins; politically it may be seen as a realization that a central State and centralized control cannot provide flexible and speedy responses to sudden changes even at the level of local government and police force headquarters; it also admits to the arrival of 'differentiated consumers' (Hoggett, 1988), not necessarily white or able-bodied or heterosexual. It may also be seen apolitically as a desire to improve service delivery, though its necessary redistribution of power must have political implications if only internally within decentralizing organizations. Above all, it appears to be related to a more customer-orientated service, whatever the underlying rationale. Within the police service there is no overtly political rationale for the process as there has been, for instance, in the borough of Islington, London, which, in the late 1980s, appeared to be seeking to empower local citizens. However, the thoughts of Sir Peter Imbert noted earlier can suggest an empowering of the public.

Decentralization in the police appears to have come in concert with developing theories as to the proper way to run an organization. The police have always delegated certain authorities, for instance the power to initiate prosecutions on behalf of the chief constable could be held at chief inspector rank and powers to enter authorized firearms dealers at inspector rank. What is altered is the power or responsibility for initiating action in concert with the local public without prior reference to force headquarters, and the right to use finance. This gives local police managers discretion to make local policy, providing they act within the constraints of overall force policy, a power previously considered to be lacking. For the police service, government calls for greater efficiency and effectiveness, and public disquiet with police's ability to deliver the customer-orientated service they now require, appear to be the main factors behind this change. Alongside these concerns the hierarchic and overpopulated management structure of police organizations came under scrutiny. Analysis of the organizational structures of the police service demonstrated that at the superintending levels two ranks appeared to be carrying out the same function, or a function closely related. In traditional structures chief superintendents are divisional commanders and superintendents are subdivisional commanders; in addition, another superintendent's post is held as the deputy to the divisional commander. Many job descriptions describe the subdivisional commander as 'the representative of the chief superintendent on the subdivision'. Such a description shows with some clarity the limitations of the role of subdivisional commanders. The system induced chief superintendents to seek to maintain almost total awareness of all happenings in their commands and limited the role of superintendents to carrying out the policies and strategies of chief superintendents. Apart from stifling the development of superintendents, the system appeared to be founded upon analysis of past incidents and post-incident debate as to the correctness of actions taken, involving chief superintendents in too much detail, much of which was trivial, to the detriment of a role in developing organizational capabilities and inspection of systems, strategies and objectives set by local commanders. Such a perception of the command role is founded upon the consequences of not knowing of an incident, no matter how trivial, that a more senior officer has discovered. PBO and local consultation demonstrated some of the deficiencies of the prevailing structure. The impetus to alter the role of the chief superintendent to one more managerially based and supportive of subdivisions—while freeing the subdivisional superintendent to take the initiative with the community—grew and provided to some forces the opportunity to rationalize management structures. According to the Police Superintendents Association, the past decade has seen the number of chief superintendents in the police service decrease by 9 per cent.

Decentralization presents some difficult issues to resolve. Given that chief superintendents would need to adopt a new role, what would the role be? How many chief superintendents would be necessary? What would be the relationship between force headquarters and subdivisions, and between chief superintendents, force headquarters and subdivisions? Without command responsibility the argument suggests that chief superintendents could effectively 'manage' and 'monitor' greater numbers of officers and larger geographic areas: Kent Constabulary has already decreased its divisions from 11 to 5 and has plans for fewer yet; 17 other forces are following this path. The arguments in favour of decentralization would seem to be compelling. The placing of both authority and responsibility with subdivisional commanders permits them to approach their public and officers as the one local voice of policing and take the lead in discussing policing issues and responding to them. The duplication and allegedly inhibiting oversight having been removed, superintendents are able to initiate activities and longer term plans without constant recourse to permission from superiors less aware of their local needs than they, and more likely to prefer maintenance of the status quo. Responsibility and accountability is placed at the correct level, that of the local community and its police representative. In addition, chief superintendents are now able to assume a role previously lacking in police organizations, working in what Jones (1989) describes as the triangle between police policy makers, police operators and the police consumer. The role may be seen as that of an organizational analyst, testing policing in action at various levels and sounding out public, police operator and police policy maker as to the effectiveness and efficiency of chosen methods of operation and activities. The role also incorporates auditing the health of the organization and seeking to find remedies for poor or non-performance of both operational and supportive functions. Essentially managerial and forward looking, the role requires different abilities to those presently necessary.

Some forces, having adopted this philosophy, have followed it by placing responsibility for financial budgets with subdivisions also. The Kent Constabulary initiative with devolved budgeting is that most reported upon. As yet no studies have been presented to show whether or not the scheme has achieved its declared purposes. The argument for devolving budgeting responsibility is that it is not believed to be reasonable to expect subdivisions to accept responsibility for devolved decision-making unless they have control of the budget, and thus the ability to implement any changes in operations or support systems seen as necessary. Personnel, police and civilian, make up 85 per cent of police budgets. Therefore, given that subdivisions cannot choose to do without police officers in order to use the money elsewhere, savings accrue from proper analysis of demand and deployment according to demand as well as critical analysis of costs of maintenance and support structures. Budget-holders are permitted to vire monies, up to agreed amounts, from one budget head to another and to use monies saved, again up to a given amount for purposes agreed locally. Initially in the Kent initiative monies saved were spent on improving the working areas and rest areas of police stations, which brought an increase in motivation. While this initiative is some three years in being, there are no authoritative reports as to its success or otherwise. Its application in the police service fits in with the decentralist policies of those local authorities that have introduced it into their police force. It appears to be a developing trend and has support among those police subdivisional commanders who are managing local budgets.

It may be argued that devolving budgets poses difficulties. What, for instance, would happen if a budget-holder overspent? So far that does not appear to have occurred, and with the monitoring systems in force is not likely to. An overspender may find the following year's budget 'capped', an event that would be difficult to explain. Other fears are that the budget would take precedence in the planning of policing; the contrary view, which informs the Kent position, is that the proper management of the budget would improve operational arrangements and that a police manager who failed to provide sufficient police purely for budgetary reasons would be in error. The Kent Constabulary reports mentioned above suggest that decisions are better informed and that, at operational levels, a better understanding of the demands of finance and acceptance of decisions has followed. Devolved budgets also force local police commanders to concentrate upon this area of their responsibility; in doing so they are obliged to pass further down the organizational tree responsibility for matters that previously would have been held by them. Thus decentralization and its supportive strategies are acting to push responsibility and accountability down to levels closer to the front line. In doing so, front-line police officers and their operational supervisors are being invited to confront the financial reality of courses of action they wish to adopt and use cost as a factor in choosing between options. The benefit to the public will result from better and more informed analysis, leading to better choice of strategy.

Policing by objectives, decentralization and devolved budgeting appear to be congruent strategies. Alongside them civilianization programmes have brought the introduction of almost totally civilian staffed administrative support units and the use of civilian personnel in other areas previously kept for police personnel. Civilianization, led in part by Audit Commission papers—the most recent being upon Police Communication Rooms (Audit Commission Police Papers, No. 5), which criticizes the lack of performance measures for police control rooms and the lack of flexibility in deployment of personnel, and recommends the increasing use of civilian staff in control rooms—is annually challenged as having gone too far by police representative associations (OPR, 1990). Other Audit Commission papers have critiqued police training arrangements and the management of police vehicle fleets. The papers may have produced some unintended effects; the incidence of police officers retiring with ill-health pensions has increased radically in the past few years, that of Avon and Somerset being 66 officers retiring in 1989 against a predicted and budgeted 13 (Chief Constable's Annual Report for 1989), though special factors, including a desire to speed up the process of ill-health retirement, have also affected the figures. It would appear that increased civilianization restricts the non-operational jobs that ill or ageing police officers can fill. The alternatives are continuing on operational duty, which many on doctor's advice cannot do, or retirement. Civilianization has, however, not just affected the lower levels of the police force. The Audit Commission have recommended that one force replace an existing chief officer post with a civilian, while other forces have given up superintending and other senior posts to employ highly qualified civilian personnel to manage specialist areas on behalf of the force. Examples include the appointment as force administrative officer of a qualified accountant, whose role emphasized the financial imperatives to develop efficiency measures and increase monetary inflow, and the appointment of trained vehicle fleet managers to replace police officers. This development has potential for cost savings, the residual costs of police officers being higher than civilians. It also opens the possibility of police authorities or the Home Office questioning the need for senior police officers in non-operational posts. Police forces have Association of Chief Police Officers (ACPOs) and chief superintendents/superintendents in posts which arguably are suitable for further civilianization—for instance, could not an Institute of Personnel Managers' qualified person fill the most senior personnel post in a police force? Superficially the answer is in the affirmative. However, a non-police post-holder at that level and post would suffer a credibility problem, particularly in a post heavily involved in the promotion and specialist training arrangements of a police force. Even so, as with lower ranks the measure of the need for senior posts may be that of operational need, it not being beyond those seeking efficiency measures to produce an equation by which a force's need for operational senior officers could be assessed. At the operational level the most fundamental change in the administration of working arrangements is also being pursued. Rostering personnel for duty, a process savaged by *The Economist*, as noted earlier, is undergoing radical examination and more flexible arrangements are being sought. This issue is also not without some difficulty in presentation.

11.9   Flexible rostering
Flexible rostering, in use in the prison service, is called Fresh Start. Whether it is a successful scheme is a matter of some debate between the Home Office and

the Prison Officers Association (POA). It has had wider consequences than the reordering of duties; no overtime is now paid to prison officers obliged to work extra duties—a saving that the Home Office may also find irresistible in the police service. The previous stranglehold that the POA is claimed to have had on arranging duties is gone, and their power to influence events is diminished. Responsibility for management has allegedly been returned to prison governors (Grange, 1988). The police service is examining alternative flexible shift systems, and one is on test in the Hampshire Constabulary. Introduction across the 43 forces may be problematic. The existence of a subculture at the operational levels, which is not in sympathy with police management, has been discussed. Research conducted by the author in a large police force on the subject of flexible rostering produced evidence of a set of values anathematic to management, which supports in part the evidence documented by Smith (1983) and Ianni (1983). The views of a substantial minority of respondents on their management was both harsh and clear:

> I don't have confidence in management. I don't think that management would show any sensitivity in implementing flexible rostering.

> There are no possible safeguards that the Force would not abuse against the relief officer.

Other respondents giving similar reasons had so little service that questions could be raised about the speed with which they assimilate these views and other attitudes from their more senior operational colleagues. Responses from others pointed up perhaps a less intractable issue. Their views suggested that to them the police shift system was more than mere working arrangements. It is a social construct within which they conduct their working, social and cultural lives, and as such was a major binding element that enhances their lives as police officers. It also provided for safety; their friends would help and protect them.

> Please do not take away the only thing left that is important to us, the good working, friendship and happiness found on a relief.

> No group identity—less motivation, therefore less work.

These views are held by officers in a large city; they would not necessarily be supported by rural beat officers. However, they do suggest that any plans to change present systems would need to include in the implementation programme a hearts and minds campaign to reassure officers as to their safety and to prevent the suggested loss of motivation that would follow. The police service may have little choice in this area. *The Economist* report quoted above suggests that government may have changes in mind in the near future, and the present arrangements, which are a blockage to improving police responsiveness efficiently in financial terms, will come under increasing external scrutiny as other organizations lose their restrictive practices. The Hampshire experiment appears to provide benefits for managers and operational officers and may provide the basis for a solution, though the Police Federation may be expected to seek some form of compensatory arrangements.

11.10   Next steps?

The developing changes discussed above appear to have at their core the theme of decentralization and a more consumer-orientated model of policing. This change is not unique to the police service. Commentators have noted similar trends through private industry and the public services in the United Kingdom, Europe and the USA (Hoggett and Hambleton, 1988). The rationale for the choices made vary from the political (a belief in democratization of services by bringing them and therefore power to influence them closer to the community) to the consumerist approach, more linked to improving efficiency and effectiveness through a more localized and responsive service. Within the latter there need be no moves towards a more democratic and accountable organization. For the present it is this form of decentralization and consumerism that the police service appears to be adopting. Though decentralization provides for more direct contact between the local consumer and local police, what critics claim to be missing is the ability radically to influence how the police operate or select their priorities. While the police appear to have followed much of the prescriptions for excellence of Peters and Waterman (1982), critics argue that they fail to 'listen intently and regularly to the customer'. It is that charge that decentralization should seek to answer and, in many forces, it seems to be doing so. For the police, decentralization means devolving power and responsibility for creating local policy and strategy nearer to the service levels of policing. Alongside delegated responsibility for administrative matters, managers will have the discretion to act on their own initiative. To enable this change these managers need information and local advice. The increasing use of customer satisfaction surveys (Bristol, London and the West Midlands in the past 12 months) is one example, as is the police consultative group, which is the forum in which local consumers or customers are able to articulate their fears and requirements of policing.

Police consultative groups can change police priorities and produce evidence of unsatisfactory strategy and behaviour. The difficulty with consultative groups, crime prevention panels and other community-based groups lies in the evidence adduced by Scraton (1985) that these limited steps in consumerism do not include the poor or inarticulate and otherwise disenfranchised upon whom police activity most bears. There are other difficulties.

The police response to many demands is proscribed by the requirements of law. Abandoned vehicles, youth congregating, noisy parties and other claimed nuisances, which some customers of policing want removed or stopped, are not matters where the police can completely satisfy; they are not the responsible authority in one case and could be exceeding their rights in others. However, in other areas of concern police can and should act; in the vast majority they do. Police are also limited in the advocatory role some other public services appear to view as part of a customer-centred organization. While the police can provide a view upon the benefits or otherwise of traffic schemes, safety in new building developments and other issues of public concern, it is debatable that they should seek to speak on behalf of a customer group.

The lack of clarity or consistency in signals police receive from consumers presents further difficulty, though regular research among consumers, particularly persons who have sought the police service, may provide a more clear and consistent signal. There is also the issue of the police as prosecutors; should the wishes of local communities decide upon prosecution policy or play a part in it? The other bodies in the prosecution and judicial process may have a strong view on such a development. Finally, the question of consumer or customer complaints is fraught with problems; police officers investigate complaints against their colleagues, and there is an independent body that oversees the process. The process is designed more to discover whether disciplinary offences have been committed by the police officer rather than to satisfy complainants, and it can be a long process from initial complaint to conclusion. Discussion upon changing the system is beyond the parameters of this chapter but some form of alternative procedure—one exists for the most minor of complaints—may be necessary to increase public confidence.

The police are limited in developing a consumer orientation; identifying the consumer is difficult, the articulate is usually the one who gets heard; consumer choice is difficult to arrange, as yet there is only one police service. However, the creation of an ethic in which service attains dominance over force should be the next stage of police development. Some attempts to produce a more friendly public face are found in revamped and more user friendly front office and interview areas and similar building refurbishments, though whether this will improve the public face of the police officer and police force remains to be proved. The real question may be how that change will be brought about. Perhaps the process has begun with the inception of 'mission' statements and the presentation to police and public of policing philosophies, objectives and strategies that are clear, effective and supported by plans to achieve them. Within some elements of the private sector customer orientation is defined as quality—quality meaning the recognition of a customer's needs and expectations and the concomitant recognition that needs and expectations have to be seen from the customer's viewpoint. For police this message appears to suggest that police efforts should be designed better to understand what it is that the public as a group and as individuals require of the police service, and then to seek to provide it. Doing so means some loss of independence and self-developed professional status. Other caring professions are facing a similar issue; parent governors at schools may be one example. Decentralization provides one means of fostering a quality service ethic as police officers linked more closely to their communities should react by providing a better quality of service for them; however, such an outcome rests in the success of police managers in inculcating the service ethic among their staff.

The creation of a service ethic, which many police officers may claim already exists, is subject to the ability of police leaders and managers not just to will but to bring about the necessary changes in emphasis and cultures. For police managers that process may have begun with decentralization, local responsibility and authority and control of budgets. The next steps will involve the realignment of police organizations to produce, at high levels, officers whose main task is building quality into all aspects of policing endeavour and support systems. In private industry it is suggested that building quality into, accepting and increasing upon customer expectations assures success; in the public services retention of customer support and improvements in effectiveness may be expected to come from a management and operational level that seeks to provide a quality service. It is the examination of public (customer) aspirations and expectations and police systems, practices and behaviour that will provide a focal point for inculcating change in both internal systems and external behaviours from which should flow more efficiency and effectiveness in policing, and a more responsive customer-orientated service provision. The creation of quality assurance managers, which in essence is the new function of territorial chief superintendents, is the most interesting development of the past few years and is totally supportive of the other changes that have taken place.

11.11 Police managers of the next decade

The decentralist theme discussed above is a predictor of the types of manager the police service will be developing in the 1990s. The roles and responsibilities of chief police officers are unlikely radically to alter. Subject to major changes in the numbers of and sizes of police forces, little change can take place; should the national structure change there may be fewer ACPO posts. The roles of operational level supervisors—sergeants and inspectors—are in part set by legislation such as the PACE Act. Their role in managing and leading the activities of patrol and investigatory officers will become more important and more possible as administrative functions are increasingly undertaken by civilian personnel and other support staff. The Fayolian prescription of classical supervision and management will remain with the additional and more important responsibility of providing leadership as to the behavioural and moral standards expected of police officers. It is already the case that the Police Complaints Authority expect comment upon supervision in investigations supervised by their members.

At the superintending levels, the changes have been immense already. The next decade will see subdivisional superintendents assuming a role partly command, partly management and partly Hodgkinson's administrator (1983). Responsible for local consultation and liaison, local policy and strategy and local operations, they will be managing in the value laden area where decisions are less based on known and proven fact than on beliefs as to needs and expectations, on assumptions made as to the consequences of acts and upon the desire for a consensus among public and possibly police as to the correctness of chosen strategies and actions. Should the national infrastructure of policing alter towards regional or national organization, which is most unlikely in the near future, their focal role and importance will increase as they become the local voice upon policing issues. Should present trends continue they will have control of local police budgets and access to or control of the majority of supporting operational units, such as Traffic Department officers. Along with these changes will come responsibility for assessing priorities and resource allocation and accountability for decisions made. In the present and anticipated financial environment, resource allocations will not meet growing demand and they may be forced to seek means of rationing police responses or persuading the public to use alternative means of resolving issues previously left to the police.

Within their organizations they will be leading and managing the process of change. The past decade has been one of constant change and that may be expected to continue. Superintendents will be a focal point for future change as police organizations decentralize and seek more output from fewer resources. Increasing customer orientation has to be balanced against increasing expectations from within and operant cultures that may find openness and access complex to assimilate. They will need to understand how to address change; a process that the Police Staff Colleges now includes as a core element in its training of police superintendents. Superintendents may also play a larger role in the liaison processes with other public services locally. The national school curriculum and its police input and the present sensitive relationship between the police and the Crown Prosecution Service are examples of this need, though the demands of Locke (1990) for greater local collaboration by all involved in the judicial process may also be met.

For chief superintendents the changes may be even more complex. The loss of daily command, though they may still be called upon to command major incidents, has been a sadness to many. The developing role is that of quality assurance, and this role will increase in importance as greater pressures are placed upon police to identify good practice and disseminate it and to remove poor policy and practice. Managerial responsibility for large numbers of police personnel—in Kent, over 1000 personnel in the near future—includes a responsibility in ensuring that career development expectations are met, finding and developing talents, ensuring that each subdivision has a full range of expertise and uses it properly, and acting as arbiter between force headquarters and subdivisions competing for resources and attention. This managerial function will coexist with a responsibility for examination of practices, systems, strategies, equipment and personnel to ensure that a quality service is provided. The concept of thematic inspection is used in the police service. Its true meaning is the analysis of data provided by performance-measuring instruments, crime and other records, and surveys of the public as users of the police service to produce statements as to the present health of the organization in specific areas together with suggestions as to how its health can be improved.

Some may play a role in policy creation; all will play a positive role in the improvement of police support services and the understanding by police organizations of public perceptions of the service provided and the behaviour of police officers. The future role as organizational analyst and counsellor/ mentor to superintendents will be taxing and rewarding and, despite criticism that it is not a proper role, will be more in line with the needs of the police service than the present role. In organizations where uncertainty has become a daily reality, and in which competition for resources is likely to become intense, the management of risk and its tensions will become a regular feature of managerial life, they will provide the support and experience operational managers will need and the wide-ranging examination of systems and practices that will enable superintendents to plan and carry through change. From their role in inspecting and testing the health of various parts of the police organization, they may also be expected to be able to devise performance standards against which managers and operational police officers may be judged, and organizational and personal improvement fostered.

11.12   New domains for police managers?

The changes discussed above provide local police managers, superintendents, the opportunity to take command of the operations of local policing and local debate upon it. It provides chief superintendents with an enhanced managerial role and the possibility of a diminished operational role. The use of exception reporting systems will ensure that senior personnel should know only that which is important to the performance of their roles. Three levels, three domains will be reinforced by this process. At the highest levels the policy domain for the force will remain within the sway of the chief officer and his assistants. At the service level, intent upon local service delivery will be the subdivisional commander and the front-line resources. Between the two and operating alongside both, monitoring operational performance, the effects of force policy upon the policing output and the views of the consumers of policing will be the management domain. This domain will have as its primary responsibility the search for best practice, greater efficiency and effectiveness. It will also have a role in the inspection of the administrative tasks of a subdivision and the audit of its financial and other statutory roles—for instance, how property handed in to police is dealt with. Measures for success for each level will be markedly different, and their scales of reference different also. Subdivisional commanders may be expected to be somewhat parochial, their measure of success being public tranquillity and satisfaction in their area. For the new managerial strata the challenge will be to find and disseminate best practice and eliminate duplication, poor practice and poor policy. They will also assist in deciding who should receive resources from the policy level. The roles almost fit the domains of Kouzes and Mico like a glove, and the areas for tension and conflict as to priorities and the correct measures of success appear legion. The test of the new managerial roles may well be how chief superintendents, formerly able to command change, will now counsel and support change by others. Once over the initial difficulties of fitting personnel to these new roles, the tensions and potential for conflict may be seen as beneficial in that they encourage the expression of opinion and open debate upon systems, performance measures and personal performance, issues which previously were not deeply explored in the police.

However these changes occur, it is possible that some things will not change. There has always been a tension between the needs of the service deliverers of policing at the front line and the support units and headquarters departments. At its most basic, the one sees complaints as a consequence of doing the job while the other sees them as evidence of inattentiveness or incorrect attitudes. The roles of managers at these separate levels will differ, the one seeking resources and leading the police effort and the other monitoring the use of resources to ensure that they are deployed wisely. Between functional specialisms and general patrols similar tensions may be expected. Irrespective of the organizational change, the potential for inherent conflict and misunderstanding will remain and the management of it will form a focal role for managers in the police.

11.13   Conclusions

The chapter sought to suggest that the police have experienced the pressures that have created change in all the other public services and induced changes in their structures and attitudes towards the customer and the measurement of their performance. Those factors that have induced changes—central government concern for efficiency, public criticism and financial stringency—are familiar among the public sector organizations. The police, like others, have adopted what were seen as radical options to meet changing circumstances, seeking a closer orientation to the consumer of the police service to discover what it is that the consumer wants from policing and how the consumer actually views the police product both as an organization and in terms of the effect individual police officers have on the public. The major theme throughout the public sector has been that of decentralization, together with the creation of local cost centres and localized responsibility for budgets and the setting of local policy and priorities. The police service has mirrored that change, following the line of consumerism rather than the democratization of service provision chosen by some local authorities.

With these changes have come greater responsibility and accountability for the local managers of service provisions; in the case of police, the subdivisional superintendents are becoming the focal point between the police organization and its many consumers. The introduction of local financial management, and the enhanced and more public role in setting the local policing agenda in consultation with the public, is radically altering this role and that of those senior managers who hitherto had almost total control of policing operations. Governmental demands for greater and more measurable efficiency and effectiveness have introduced a form of management by objectives and the creation of measurable objectives and activities. To support this process, management information systems and information technology have been rapidly brought into use, creating what many see as a treadmill of action and measurement of a small part of the police input to society.

There have been costs in the creation of the support systems necessary to these changes, both financially and in human terms. As yet the changes have not taken root and for many they are merely fads that will lose credibility as quickly as having other management fads. Most recently it is being argued that the concentration upon management has damaged the service and that it is leadership that is needed, this being defined as the creation of a vision or a sense of direction as to the purposes of policing and the moral values needed to support a better quality police service. I would contend that the changes of the past decade are creating the circumstances in which those who can most influence the police product—local police commanders—are being given the tools, freedom and authority to do so. The creation of an organization incorporating three levels, those of policy, operations and monitoring of both, will create the distance necessary to policy makers to permit them to examine the future of their forces and concentrate upon preparing for the future while allowing their operational commanders to concentrate upon the present and near future.

In the space of a decade the police service, like other social agencies, has sought to alter its view of the world and its relationship with that world. From the most rigid of bureaucracies, boasting a hierarchic chain that held all authority and power at the centre, it is becoming a decentralized and more naturally responsive organization placing responsibility as close to the customer as is possible. In creating such a change there is an element of risk; it has been argued that some police management is not capable of adjusting to this new environment and that local police commanders are likely to make decisions that impose extra stresses upon other parts of the organization without consideration of their capacity to cope. Two centuries of ever-growing directives and instructions are being replaced by leaner and more guidance-styled manuals.

The most radical and far-reaching of the changes that have taken place has been decentralization. Police superintendents have become the focal point for all local policing in those forces that have decentralized. Their role is now more linked to mainstream management in the private sector than to administration in the public services. With the authority and finance to adjust their operations they are not only more able to alter plans but they are more accountable both within the police organization and outside it. The consumerist model of a police force fits more easily with decentralization than with the previous monoliths of central control. Locally planned and discussed policing is likely to be more in tune with public aspirations. The creation of small local police organizations containing under one command all the functions necessary to provide an effective service should make comparisons between managers and units easier and more acceptable. The future may see the steady decline and loss of the chief superintendent post if functions carried out at this level are civilianized, though an argument for retention of some operational command capability will be made. Should another projected change occur and regional or national police structures be created, the effect will be to create a further distance between local police units and the central policy makers. This could result in local police units becoming almost self-sufficient with their local public and politicians, and the creation of some form of informal district police unit. It would be an irony if the police service was to move from hundreds of small forces to 10 regional forces while at the same time creating a host of informal borough forces.

Decentralization will link police subdivisions more closely to local community and political entities. Some form of corporate organization between all the local social agencies may result—a consequence that would please Trevor Locke. What will result, subject to the ability and willingness of police, is a more open and responsive local police service. For police managers this will be the most complex of the challenges they can expect to face. An open and responsive service will demand skills in managing under pressure from critics and from staff who feel the criticism and find difficulty in accepting an altered relationship with a demanding and critical consumer. The continuing development of those skills and how they effect the manager's concept of how police organizations should be constructed, led and managed, will be one of the most interesting internal changes in the police service of the coming decade.

References

Bradley, D., Walker, N. and Wilkie, R. (1986) *Managing the Police*. Harvester, Brighton.
Brogden, M., Jefferson, T. and Walklate, S. (1988) *Introducing Policework*. Unwin Hyman, London.
Brooks, S. (1989) 'Report on a survey of police consumers in Kingswood, Bristol' (unpublished).
Burrows, T. and Lewis, H. (1988) *Directing Patrol Work: A Study of Uniformed Policing*. Home Office Research Papers No. 99.
Clarke, R. V. and Hough, M. (1984) *Crime and Police Effectiveness*. HMSO, London.

Drucker, P. F. (1955) *The Practice of Management*. Harper & Row, New York.

Graef, R. (1989) *Talking Blues, the Police in their Own Words*. Collins, London.

Grange, T. (1988) 'The deployment of police manpower: flexible rostering in the Metropolitan Police' (unpublished degree thesis).

Hodgkinson, C. (1983) *The Philosophy of Leadership*. Blackwell, Oxford.

Hoggett, P. and Hambleton, R. (eds) (1988) *Decentralisation and Democracy*. School of Advanced Urban Studies, Bristol.

Ianni, E. and Janni, F. (1983) *Two Cultures of Policing*. Transaction Inc., New Jersey.

Jefferson, T. and Grimshaw, R. (1984) *Controlling the Constable: Police Accountability in England and Wales*. Cobden Trust, London.

Jones, J. M. (1989) 'The new Chief Superintendent', *Policing*, 1989.

Kelling, G. L., Wasserman, R. and Williams, H. (1988) 'Police accountability and community policing', *Perspectives on Policing, No. 7*. US National Institute of Justice.

Kouzes, J. M. and Mico, P. R. (1979) 'Domain theory, an introduction to organisational behaviour in human service organisations', *Journal of Applied Behavioural Science*, 15 (4) 449–69.

Locke, T. (1990) *New Approaches to Crime in the 1990s*. Longman, London.

Lubans, V. and Edgar, J. M. (1979) *Policing by Objectives: A Handbook for Improving Police Management*. SDC, Connecticut.

Lustgarten, L. (1986) *The Governance of Police*. Sweet and Maxwell, London.

Males, S. (1983) *Police Management on Divisions*. Police Requirements Support Unit.

McGregor, K. I. (1990) 'Strategic Thinking. A Study of the Thames Valley Police', *Operational Policing Review*, Joint Consultative Committee of the Police Federation.

McKenzie, I. K. and Gallagher, G. P. (1989) *Behind the Uniform: Policing in Britain and America*. Wheatsheaf, Hemel Hempstead.

Morgan, R. (1987) 'Police accountability, the implications of local consultative committees'. Paper given at the Socio-Legal Group Conference, University of Sheffield.

Newman, Sir K. (1983) *Report of the Commissioner of the Metropolitan Police 1983*.

OPR (1990) *Operational Policing Review*. Joint Consultative Committee of the Police Federation.

Peters, T. and Waterman, R. (1982) *In Search of Excellence: Lessons from America's Best-Run Companies*. Harper & Row, New York.

Plumridge, M. D. (1983) *A Study of Police Management and Command Roles: Dilemmas of Police Management*. Sphere, London.

Plumridge, M. D. (1989) 'Management and organisation development in the police service: the role of Bramshill', in Southgate, P. (ed.), *New Directions in Police Training*. Home Office Research and Planning Unit.

Reiner, R. (1985) *The Politics of the Police*. Wheatsheaf, Brighton.

Reuss-Ianni, E. and Ianni, I. F. (1983) *The Two Cultures of Policing*. Transaction, New Jersey.

Scarman, Lord. (1982) *The Scarman Report: The Brixton Disorders 10–12 April 1981*. Penguin, London.

Scraton, P. (1985) *The State of the Police*. Pluto, London

Simey, M. (1988) *Democracy Rediscovered: A Study in Police Accountability*. Pluto, London.

Smith, D. J. and Grey, J. (1983) *The Police in Action. Police and People in London*. Policy Studies Institute, London.

The Economist (1990) 'An old force on a new beat', 10 February.

The Guardian (1989) 'An opening at the Met' and 'An astonishing shift of power'. Interviews with Sir Peter Imbert (8 November).

Waddington, P. J. (1986) 'Defining objectives: a response to Tony Butler', *Policing*, 2 (1).

Waddington, P. J. (1990) 'Safer on foot', *Police Review*, 1400–1 (13 July).

Weatheritt, M. (1986) *Innovations in Policing*. Police Foundation, London.

Weatheritt, M. (1989) *Police Research, Some Future Prospects*. Gower, Aldershot.

Weigh, B. (1980) 'Bristol: the Chief Constable's Report', *Police Review*, 9 May.

Wilson, O. W. (1950) *Police Administration*. McGraw-Hill, London.

Conclusion

Through the issues and cases thus far examined, the theme of the rediscovery of public services management has been pursued. This has been done explicitly by focusing attention on the nature of the publicly directed managerial tasks, where that of achieving counterpoise between competing demands is uppermost; and implicitly by emphasis on the especial complexity of public services managers' work, where independent action is variously constrained or energized by the extent and number of relevant inter-organizational relationships. A concept of 'rediscovery' is thus one that seeks recognition—among politicians, managers in private sectors, and citizens—of the value of public services management careers. It is one where there is regular celebration of public services management successes and good performances; and critically, where that good performance is not defined solely by comparison to a—believed—private sector counterpart. With public services management being identified as distinctive sets of managerial activities, a revaluing of public services work would follow, with managerial tasks moving beyond a 'can do' implementation model, which excludes the opportunity, and the right, to 'advise and warn'.

During the period of work for this study, political party leadership shifts and areas of public policy reorientation have begun to suggest that what has been called (whether from laudatory or rejecting perspectives) 'the new managerialism' in public services is now no longer 'new' and is increasingly recognizable for potentially inhibiting public services management development, through its overemphasis on and almost certain misinterpretation of a number of aspects of private sector management content and style. While managerialism implies an organizational predominance for one particular type of post-holder, the critical service element in public services means the existence in those organizations of professional/service delivery and policy-making domains; where inter-domain disagreement will mirror the conflicting concerns of the variety of interested 'publics'; and where that disagreement will need to be managed positively rather than eliminated by generalist managers with no allegiances at all to other domains. It is inherent in the nature of public services that managers have a strong grasp on organizational capabilities and priorities when they have a 'player' background, or are, at middle managerial levels, player-managers. This will continue to be important, even if the contractualizing trend in public services delivery continues. At its worst, part of the new managerialism may be seen as having set up inter-domain in-fighting in public services, which the player-manager model may be uniquely placed to handle.

It is not possible to write oneself out on the subject of public services management. Events and policies have moved and look like continuing to move too fast for this to happen. Certainly this book has had no such intention, and instead has focused very much on an exploration of the theory, content, outcomes and possible approaches in public services management since 1979 and into the 1990s. In pursuance of the rediscovery theme, a continuing research and policy agenda for public services management can be advanced, not least to provide opportunities for continuing management development among public sevices managers, by casting them, as well as others, in the researcher role. While no rejection of the critical reforming concept of 'value for money' is sought or implied, much of the contents of this study has indicated the extent to which the focus on the 'money' element in public services has lessened that on the nature of 'value'; and it is in assessing and deciding upon the latter that part of the rediscovery process may be undertaken.

ORGANIZATIONAL LEARNING

Central to this agenda are issues surrounding the degree, extent and direction of organizational learning in public services; and how personal managerial learning may be enmeshed into that wider organizational learning context. The preceding chapters, examining particular service areas, have demonstrated the extent to which imposed apparent innovations have resulted in what has been described as hard, curtailed forms of organizational learning. In the longer term these may come to be seen as an inefficient use of organizational resources. Private sector organizational learning models would seem to have limited applicability, even where they relate to service organizations (because, for example, of the common need for some public services to 'de-market'). Thus organizational learning concepts are called for that commence from an understanding of the roles of counterpoise and demand-balance that are the essence of public services management.

In reviewing research opportunities, a major comparative theoretical question concerns the ways in which public services and private sector organizations 'learn'; and how the personal learning styles of managers can be linked with the organizations in which they work. Commonsense notions of learning link that activity with the opportunity for and encouragement to experiment—an experience constrained within public services management as initiatives have speedily reached innovation status. A strong case may be made, therefore, in the cause of public services management improvement, for a research programme that evaluates the learning opportunities promoted—and taken—by managerial experimentation, as against widespread imposition of managerial prescription. Case study work on examples—actual or possible— of private sector managers' learning from public services managers' practice would further extend knowledge of the nature of managerial learning and raise the issue of transferability of management 'know-how' from a different perspective. Fruitful areas might include examinations of the managerial implications of concepts of 'service' as they affect major architectural practices or law firms; or of handling the consumers of a firm's products, in a sense far wider than that of the customer (for example, neighbours of a chemical factory).

ROLES AND TASKS

An increasing emphasis on public services distinctiveness may in itself encourage the organizational learning routes to divert from private sector models and solutions. The extent to which this could ultimately encourage the substantive learning model for the public services manager—tasked to query as appropriate the content and implementation of public policy, thus taking on a public servant role in the widest sense—is more debatable. It is possible that the 'can do' orientation has severely restricted public services managers' abilities and willingness to raise wider concerns about policy direction, implications and impact—a likelihood increased by the prevailing model of 'manager as problem solver' rather than 'manager as problem poser'. In the longer term, therefore, this implies a reassessment of the tasks that public services managers perform, with a critical review of the value and impact of the problem-posing function. Such a reassessment might appropriately be associated with a study of the apparent move of some public services management structures to more control-oriented and less collegial management structures; for it is in the latter that the substantive learning mode for the manager may most easily be adopted and deployed. In the medium term, it may be argued that the public services managers' central role in appraisal of policy and managerial options—that is, genuine and not cursory—should be enhanced and further explored. The contribution of the 'player-managers' here could be seen to be particularly relevant.

That said, the field of public services management practice provides extensive opportunities for empirical research. Such research could review not only the impact over time of importation of private sector techniques and approaches into public services organizations (and the resulting managerial behaviours), but also the practicalities of adaptation and usage in such situations, and thus the degree of portability likely between sectors. A specific example, from earlier discussion, would be the introduction of financial management mechanisms into public services, with the question posed as to the degree of sophistication required with these techniques to make them applicable for public services activity.

Research rooted in domain theory would link here, usefully going beyond corroborating domain existence, and identifying appropriate managerial strategies for making positive use of inter-domain disagreement, managing rather than eliminating the tensions. At the same time, the possibility of the existence of separate domains within private sector organizations, with equivalent or different implications for managing inter-organizational disagreement, deserves attention.

CUSTOMERS AND CONSUMERISM

The nature of public services and private sector 'customers', their differences and similarities, needs to be pursued. As one example, the procedures for and consequences of ignoring the customer for managers in public and private settings might be compared and contrasted, considering whether, as the ultimate indirect or direct customer sanction, company take-over or collapse may be equated with electoral defeat. Again, given that the customer may not always be 'right' in public services settings, how and where has this maxim operated within the private sector, and to what effect? And wherever private sector organizations take over public services activities, what, from public services experience, can they learn about their new customers and how they need be dealt with?

STRUCTURE AND ENTREPRENEURIALISM

Two major interlinked areas for research questioning present themselves here. Firstly, are some types of management structure more appropriate than others for public services organizations experiencing managerial change? Secondly, how may entrepreneurs be nurtured within public services organizations without enforcing an entrepreneurial culture, and so making it unreal? In relation to the question of management structures, research should have a part to play in showing whether it is important—rather than simply ironic—that many public services structures are becoming more control-oriented (managers 'able to manage', clear hierarchies of command), when some areas of the private sector are moving towards less hierarchical and more collegial management structures. At present it appears that such public services patterns may be appropriate for a transition phase, to speed delivery and ensure participants' compliance, but that these transitional patterns are in danger of being retained.

CULTURE IN PUBLIC SERVICES ORGANIZATIONS

A related issue is the need for defining and identifying the organizational culture(s) which best encourage public services effectiveness; and reviewing the means whereby such cultures can, if necessary, be created. Here again the public/private contrasts deserve attention. While in some private sector areas, culture type and quality of product are demonstrably linked, such patterns may not necessarily be appropriate or obvious for public services where the 'product' is neither unified nor easily identifiable. A culture review may also generate policy proposals; for example, it has been frequently unclear how reward systems, promotion ladders, recruitment and selection methods, the conduct of industrial relations, management development and change in public services have related to developing, rather than hindering, the organizational cultures supportive of managerial tasks and behaviours espoused by 1980s–1990s management initiatives.

RISK AND INNOVATION

Preceding chapters have documented the variety of risks to which public services have been exposed from the speedy elevation of initiatives to innovation status and a uniformity of introduction without a working through of the full results of the policy; or how an emphasis on entrepreneurialism in public services may have dysfunctional as well as functional consequences, leading to inter-organizational opportunism and consumer exploitation. Even the embracing of consumerist concepts in public services needs to be associated with risk-taking. On a wide scale of activity, a consumerist stance raises question of the need for equity within public services provision; and on a narrower day-to-day scale, it may need to be recognized and accepted that consumer responsiveness may also be managerially and organizationally inefficient. Against a background of public concern that seems to be seeking a risk-free environment, the notion of public services as risk taker and manager needs to be extended and, importantly, discussed publicly.

The period under review, during which many public services management practices were decried or even left unrecognized as management at all, produced potentially a further area of risk in the long term, as public services managers see their tasks redefined, and move within or outside public services. It can be a matter of conjecture only that the problems posed by 'organizational forgetting'—i.e. as expertise is lost, or even withheld; as personal managerial experience is under-valued until departure; and as direct service delivery is replaced by the purchaser/provider models—have been especially damaging to public services over this period of rapid change. Managerial research into the ways and means of combating organizational forgetting—the recording, storing, utilizing and valuing of the accumulated knowledge of organization members and managers—is urgently needed, so that dissemination of practice may be maintained.

A further line of research might be whether there are models of management other than the entrepreneurial which are central to public services management. The association of entrepreneurialism with apparently aggressive individualism might also be researched in a public services context, if only to discover 'reluctant entrepreneurs' willing to experiment but unwilling to cultivate allegedly entrepreneurial-style aggression. Given the rate of small business failure, further relevant research questions could include:

1 On what criteria are public services management entrepreneurial successes and failures to be identified?
2 What degree of failure in different areas of the public services may be risked? and, returning to the 'learning' theme,

3 What managerial lessons may be traced and learned from public services entrepreneurial failure as well as success?

In linking evidence of entrepreneurial activity and the identification of management initiatives that should or should not receive innovatory status, the value of developing further theoretical perspectives, to inform practice, is again apparent. A major example is the need for a means of

- classifying the range of management initiatives and innovations discussed above
- distinguishing between their testing and accepted status
- identifying the managerial values that underpin them

thus providing the bases for further understanding of the elements in them that encourage trialability, diffusion and acceptance or rejection.

DISTINCTIVENESS AND INTERDEPENDENCY

Accelerating external changes—in public funding, in demographic and employment patterns, and in legislative requirements—mean that public services managers will not only continue to be managing in a climate of uncertainty, but that the changes they face will be occurring with increasing rapidity. This implies that universalistic prescriptions for public organizations' managerial practice will be of increasingly limited value. While universalistic prescriptions—organizational cures—have merit in encouraging the growth of new competencies and new ways of viewing the organization products, ironically they may have encouraged an overly reactive managerial style. A recognition in the 1990s of the important distinctiveness not only of public services management overall, but of the distinctiveness within different areas of public services management concern, could help shift the focus away from externally imposed and 'common' prescriptions to those internally derived from organization members' experience and know-how. This could encourage experimentation, with the implied necessary organizational support for failure as well as success.

There would seem to be a role for future studies in examining the direction of public services management; but, arguably, studies rooted in managerial experiences and practices, and by public services managers themselves, and not founded solely on externally based views. Those chapters that have examined particular areas of public services have nevertheless emphasized strongly the extent to which managing in these areas must relate to the managerial decision-making occurring in other public services with which they are intimately related, though differentiated in the public eye. Of the range of managerial challenges for public services managers in periods of very fast change, that of managing organizations that are in practice interdependent in the ultimate delivery and impact of their services would seem to be the most critical. The extent to which there is interdependency between public services agencies from a user perspective is a highly familiar element in public and social policy analysis—

between health and housing services, between prison and employment services, and so on. A further element in the 1990s is the existing and growing interdependency between private and public service agencies. That such interdependencies impact critically on public services managers' decision-making and strategy choices needs to be stressed; and it is in the managing of that interdependency, to public benefit and to debated and agreed levels of service quality, that public services managers will be most stretched. Not surprisingly, management of organizational interdependence is a particular public services characteristic— which is a further argument why the value of the public services managers' skills of organizational and policy counterpoise should be rediscovered.

Index